Schreiber / Pommerening / Schoel

New Data Act

New Data Act

A Practitioner's Guide

by

Kristina Schreiber
Patrick Pommerening
Philipp Schoel

2026

BECK • HART • NOMOS

Published by
Nomos Verlagsgesellschaft mbH & Co. KG, Waldseestraße 3-5, 76530 Baden-Baden, Germany,
email: service@nomos.de

Co-published by
Verlag C.H.Beck oHG, Wilhelmstraße 9, 80801 München, Germany,
email: bestellung@beck.de

and

Hart Publishing, Kemp House, Chawley Park, Cumnor Hill, Oxford, OX2 9PH, United Kingdom,
online at: www.hartpub.co.uk

Published in North America by Hart Publishing,
An Imprint of Bloomsbury Publishing 1385 Broadway, New York, NY 10018, USA
email: mail@hartpub.co.uk

ISBN 978 3 7560 0991 6 (NOMOS Print)
ISBN 978 3 7489 4949 7 (NOMOS ePDF)
ISBN 978 3 406 83136 2 (C.H.BECK)
ISBN 978 1 5099 8494 7 (HART)

First Edition 2026

Preface

The EU's Digital Strategy gathered pace. In recent years, a large number of new 'Digital Acts', generally EU regulations, have been submitted in draft form or have already been adopted. As a central pillar of the Data Strategy, which is part of the EU's digital agenda, the Data Act (DA) has been published in the Official Journal of the EU and marks a new chapter for the European data economy. Most of its rights and obligations have become applicable on 12.9.2025.

A radical change has been under discussion since November 2025 at the latest: The Digital Omnibus on digital acquis, the Commission's proposal for a new regulation that will change several digital acts, is intended to streamline and reduce bureaucracy. However, the Commission's proposal envisages even a significant strengthening of the Data Act: It will remain at the centre of data economy regulation and is even to be expanded to incorporate several other legal acts in the future. This clearly demonstrates the central role that this legal act will continue to play in the EU's digital regulation.

From the EU's perspective, the Data Act contains key instruments to strengthen access to and use of data across the internal market, aiming to enable fairer allocation of value and broader innovation opportunities. The focus is notably on data generated by connected products, on enhancing data accessibility for users, on clarifying data usage rights, and on facilitating data sharing between business actors and public authorities in cases of exceptional need as well as cloud switching to avoid lock-in effects and open up the market. All these elements are accompanied by efforts to foster a robust data ecosystem that underpins the EU's digital transformation. The EU Commission expects the Data Act to boost the data economy, leading to significant growth in gross domestic product.

To achieve this, the Data Act brings with it a bundle of new rights and obligations for companies, private individuals, and the public sector. It aims to nurture new business models and new forms of cooperation within its regulatory framework. Businesses, public sector bodies, and other data actors are called upon to align with the far-reaching requirements and possibilities introduced by this new EU regulation.

But will the Data Act truly fulfil its ambitious objectives? Will it actually encourage broader data access and use by individuals and businesses, foster innovation, boost the data economy and lay the foundation for a competitive and fairer EU data economy? Critical voices have emerged ever since the first drafts were made public and persist even after the adoption of the final legal text. Some concerns are valid: For example, the relationship between the Data Act and existing data protection rules – including the General Data Protection Regulation – remains only partially resolved, with both frameworks often applying in parallel. The protection of trade secrets is also inadequately regulated and could thus have the opposite effect to the goal of promoting innovation. Those subject to this law must therefore rise to the challenge of adapting to a constantly evolving and sometimes overlapping legal system and rethinking risks for their product and business model development.

We are nevertheless convinced that the Data Act can make a significant contribution to improved, fair, and competitive data usage as well as opening up cloud services and boosting interoperability. A decisive factor for success will be a sound understanding of the rights and obligations laid down in the Act. Only those who are aware of which rights they enjoy, the requirements the Data Act places on new business models, and what duties now apply to all market participants, will be able to confidently implement and benefit from these new instruments. Only those who are prepared for the new set of obligations can avoid administrative proceedings with possible fines and civil proceedings, thereby protecting their company from damage.

We have thus approached the project of an introductory volume to the Data Act with considerable commitment and pleasure. The present explanations are the result of many hours of analysis, discussion, and practical experience with data-driven projects and legal advice for data-driven companies. We are especially pleased to publish this work in English, enabling our reflections on the practical application of the Data Act to be received and discussed across the EU. We are convinced that the potential of the Data Act can only be realised if there is a broad, fundamental understanding of this new framework, and if we manage to discuss the critical points broadly and thus optimise them in future amendments to the regulation. It is our hope that this introductory volume provides an accessible starting point and valuable compass.

Against this backdrop, we were delighted to realise this project with the outstanding editorial team at Nomos Verlag, especially Dr. Marco Ganzhorn and Mr. Christoph Krampe. This Practitioner's Guide is part of a highly relevant, comprehensive and valued series of volumes, handbooks and commentaries on the various new legal acts arising from the EU Digital Strategy, published in partnership with Verlag C.H.Beck and Hart Publishing.

You now hold in your hands a concise introduction to the Data Act, available shortly after its key obligations have become applicable in all EU Member States on 12.9.2025, and even before the remaining obligations come into full effect on 12.9.2026. We hope this guide forms a solid foundation for establishing a first understanding of and access to this new act. This Practitioner's Guide not only addresses the articles of the Data Act itself, but also examines the surrounding challenges that may arise in the application of its instruments – including legal protection against decisions based on the Data Act. Instead of a detailed article-by-article commentary, we present its subject areas in context and in terms of their practical significance.

This volume seeks to provide guidance not only to companies seeking to unlock the Data Act for new business models, but also to companies, public authorities and other stakeholders wishing to review or develop their own data strategies in light of new competences or obligations under the Act. The same applies to all those called to shape and supervise the European data landscape going forward. Where implementation in national law still bears relevance – despite the direct applicability of EU regulations – we use Germany as an illustrative example.

We wish to thank the publishers for their unwavering support, in particular Dr. Marco Ganzhorn and Mr. Christoph Krampe. Their dedication made it possible to complete this introductory work with such quality and at an impressive pace.

Our gratitude also goes to those who assisted in organising and, above all, proofreading this volume, and without whose efforts the manuscript could not have advanced so swiftly. Special thanks go to our assistants Katharina Oschwald and Natascha Knechtel, as well as our research associates Pauline Brinke, Michèle Nickel and Benjamin Fischbach, for their precise and patient support!

We look forward to supplementing this Practitioner's Guide in due course with emerging developments – including the full realisation of the EU Data Strategy. While the Data Act centres on commercial and user-generated data, its interplay with other frameworks will be an exciting field of further analysis. Until then, it is our hope that this work provides helpful guidance and inspiration for all those affected by, or entitled under, the Data Act's instruments. We welcome comments, discussions and pointers to sections warranting improvement – please feel free to contact us.

Cologne, January 2026

Kristina Schreiber *Patrick Pommerening* *Philipp Schoel*

Contents

Preface V
Authors XV
Abbreviations XVII
General bibliography XXIII

CHAPTER 1
THE EU DATA AND DIGITAL STRATEGY

A. EU Data Strategy 1
B. EU Digital Strategy 4
C. The EU's Omnibus Initiative with the Digital Package on Simplification 7

CHAPTER 2
OVERVIEW AND SCOPE OF THE DATA ACT

A. Goals 9
B. History of the Regulation 10
C. Scope of application 11
  I. Subject matter 11
  II. Data covered 12
  III. Addressees 12
  IV. Marketplace principle 13
D. Relationship to other regulations and contract design 13
  I. Data protection and trade secret protection 14
  II. Freedom of contract 15
E. Entry into force and implementation period 15
  I. Validity from September 2025 16
  II. Product design obligations: applicable only from September 2026 16
F. Symmetrical vs. asymmetrical regulation of the data economy 17

CHAPTER 3
DATA ACCESS AND MAKING DATA AVAILABLE

A. Regulation system 21
  I. Structure 21
  II. Exemptions for SMEs 22
B. Actors 23
C. Subject matter of the data access 26
  I. Connected products 26
  II. Related services 27
  III. Usage data and no content data 29
  IV. Virtual assistants 30

D. Data access rights 31
I. Factual data access claim: access by design 31
1. Obligated party 31
2. Material organisation 31
3. Generated data 32
4. User account 33
5. Legal consequences of non-compliance 33
6. Deviating agreements 34
II. Making data available by the data holder 35
III. Sharing data with third-party data recipients 36
IV. Duty to provide information 37
V. Data protection law and data access 39
VI. Restrictions on data access outside of data protection law 41
1. Security requirements 41
2. Restriction of competition pursuant to Art. 4(10), Art. 6(2)(e) DA 41
3. Relationship to trade secrets law 43
a) Data as a trade secret 43
b) Protection mechanisms in case of a data access request by the user 44
aa) Appropriate confidentiality measures as a prerequisite for access 44
bb) Withholding of data sharing in the event of a lack of secrecy 46
cc) Refusal of access in the event of serious economic damage .. 47
c) Protection mechanisms in case of a data access request in favour of third parties pursuant to Art. 5 DA 48
d) Technical protective measures in accordance with Art. 11(1) DA 49
e) Requirements for demonstrating the existence of a trade secret 50
4. No restrictions from database law 50
5. Restrictions arising from competition law 52
VII. Limitations on the use and disclosure of data by the data holder 52
1. Limited data use 53
2. Prohibition of data sharing 53
E. Making data available 53
I. Requirements for making data available 54
1. Area of application 55
a) Business-to-business relations 55
b) Obligation to make data available 56
c) Time of application 56
2. Making data available on FRAND terms 56
a) Fair, reasonable and not discriminatory 57
b) Procedure for determining FRAND 58
3. Transparency requirement 59
4. Ineffectiveness of unfair contract terms 60
5. Prohibition of discrimination 61
6. Protection of the user's data sovereignty 61
II. Compensation for making data available 62

III. Dispute settlement 63
1. Area of application 63
2. Requirements for certification 64
3. Costs 65
4. Relationship with courts and other bodies 65
5. Effect of the decision 65

CHAPTER 4
UNFAIR CONTRACTUAL TERMS

A. Introduction 66
B. Scope of application 66
I. Personal scope 67
II. Material scope 67
III. Temporal scope of application 68
C. Relationship to the Unfair Contract Terms Directive 68
D. Unilateral imposition 69
E. Unfair terms control 70
I. Black clauses (Art. 13(4) DA) 70
II. Grey clauses (Art. 13(5) DA) 70
III. General clause (Art. 13(3) DA) 72
IV. Legal consequences 73

CHAPTER 5
SWITCHING BETWEEN DATA PROCESSING SERVICES: CLOUD SWITCHING

A. Overview 74
B. Addressees and services covered 76
I. Data processing services 76
1. Cloud computing services 77
2. Hosting in the narrower sense 79
3. Edge computing services 79
II. Privileging of on-premise services 80
III. Original and acquiring providers 80
IV. No privileges for SMEs 80
V. Beneficiary customers 81
VI. Application exceptions 81
1. Customised data processing services 81
2. Data processing services for testing and evaluation purposes 82
VII. Switching to similar services, ICT infrastructure or simultaneous use of several providers 82
C. Requirements for data processing services 83
I. Technical aspects of the change 83
1. Infrastructure provider – IaaS 83
2. Providers of data processing services in other respects 84
3. Limitations 84

II. Switching charges 85
III. Duty of loyalty 85
IV. Contract and information 85
1. Publication obligation on the website 86
2. Customer information 86
3. Contract drafting and standard contractual clauses 86

CHAPTER 6
INTEROPERABILITY AND SMART CONTRACTS

A. Overview 90
B. Interoperability for data spaces and data sharing 91
C. Interoperability of data processing services 91
D. Interoperability for smart contracts 92

CHAPTER 7
EXCEPTIONAL NEED TO USE DATA

A. Introduction 94
B. Legal requirements 95
I. Entitled entities 96
1. Public sector bodies 96
2. Union bodies 96
3. Exclusion of application 96
II. Obligated parties 97
III. Legal requirements 97
1. Data request 97
a) Formal requirements 98
b) Material requirements 100
2. Exceptional needs 100
a) Responding to a public emergency 100
b) Fulfilment of specific tasks in the public interest 101
IV. Fulfilment and rejection of data requests 102
V. Relationship to other obligations to provide data 104
C. Scope of use 105
I. No further use under DGA and Open Data Directive 105
II. Obligations of the authorised bodies 105
III. Forwarding of the data obtained to other public bodies 106
D. Compensation for making the data available 108
E. Assistance and cross-border cooperation 109
F. Legal protection 109

CHAPTER 8
SUPERVISION AND ENFORCEMENT

A. Supervisory authorities 112
I. National design options 112

II. Independence 114
III. Data coordinator 115
IV. Responsibility and appointment of representatives 115
B. Penalties 116
C. Right of complaint and legal remedies 117
I. Right of complaint 117
II. Protective letter 118
III. Legal remedies 118
D. Civil court enforcement 120

CHAPTER 9
INTERNATIONAL DATA TRANSFER IN ACCORDANCE WITH THE DATA ACT

A. Introduction 121
B. Norm addressees 121
C. Third country transfer 122
I. International transfer 123
II. State access 124
III. Permissible compliance with official and court decisions 124
D. Protective measures 127

CHAPTER 10
THE EUROPEAN DATA INNOVATION BOARD

A. Introduction 128
B. Staffing 129
I. Task of the Commission 129
II. Members of the EDIB 130
III. Organisation 131
C. Tasks 132
I. Development of standardised practices 132
II. Development of standardised guidelines 133
III. Standardisation activities 133
1. Use and development of cross-sector standards 134
2. Data economy in the internal market 134
IV. Guidelines on 'Common European Data Spaces' 135
V. Facilitating cooperation 136
VI. Other tasks 137

Annex: Data Act 139

Index 231

Authors

Dr. Kristina Schreiber

Dr. Kristina Schreiber is an attorney and partner at Loschelder law firm. She is a specialised lawyer for administrative law and CIPP/E. She specialises in advising on regulatory issues, data protection, data usage, cybersecurity and artificial intelligence. With extensive experience advising corporations and public institutions, she focuses on the legal challenges arising from digital transformation and data-driven business models. Dr. Schreiber regularly publishes and speaks on topics relating to regulatory compliance, privacy and digital law. She is a lecturer at the University of Cologne and the FernUniversität in Hagen.

Dr. Patrick Pommerening

Dr. Patrick Pommerening is an attorney and partner at Loschelder law firm. He is a specialist in and advises on all issues relating to intellectual property law. His work focuses on all legal issues related to the acquisition, transfer and licensing of intellectual property, software and data, as well as the protection of trade secrets and know-how. Dr. Pommerening has many years of experience in drafting and negotiating IP contracts of all kinds, in particular license agreements, research and development agreements as well as software and IT contracts.

Philipp Schoel

Philipp Schoel was a lawyer at Loschelder law firm and specialised in data protection and IT law. He advised on the new European digital legislation and is co-author of the Practitioner's Guide on the Data Governance Act. His legal practice focused on data protection-compliant business models and the related contract drafting.

Abbreviations

AEUV	Vertrag über die Arbeitsweise der Europäischen Union (Treaty on the Functioning of the European Union)
AI	Artificial Intelligence
AktG	Aktiengesetz (German Stock Corporation Act)
alt.	alternative
API	Application Programming Interface
Art.	Article(s)
B2B	Business-to-Business
B2C	Business-to-Consumer
B2G	Business-to-Government
BB	Betriebs-Berater (journal)
BDSG	Bundesdatenschutzgesetz (German Federal Data Protection Act)
BfDI	Bundesbeauftragte fur den Datenschutz und die Informationssicherheit (German Federal Commissioner for Data Protection and Freedom of Information)
BGB	Bürgerliches Gesetzbuch (German Civil Code)
BGH	Bundesgerichtshof (German Federal Supreme Court)
BVerfG	Bundesverfassungsgericht (German Federal Constitutional Court)
BVerfGE	Entscheidungen des Bundesverfassungsgerichts (collection of decisions of the German Federal Constitutional Court)
cf.	compare
Ch.	Chapter
CJEU	Court of Justice of the European Union
CLOUD Act	Clarifying Lawful Overseas Use of Data Act
CR	Computer und Recht (journal)
DA	Data Act – Regulation (EU) 2023/2854 of the European Parliament and of the Council of 13 December 2023 on harmonised rules on fair access to and use of data and amending Regulation (EU) 2017/2394 and Directive (EU) 2020/1828 (Data Act) (OJ L, 2023/2854)
DA Proposal	Proposal for a Regulation of the European Parliament and of the Council on harmonised rules on fair access to and use of data (Data Act), COM(2022) 68 final

DB	Der Betrieb (journal)
DG	Directorate General (of the European Commission)
DGA	Data Governance Act – Regulation (EU) 2022/868 of the European Parliament and of the Council of 30 May 2022 on European data governance and amending Regulation (EU) 2018/1724 (Data Governance Act) (OJ 2022 L 152, 1)
DMA	Digital Markets Act – Regulation (EU) 2022/1925 of the European Parliament and of the Council of 14 September 2022 on contestable and fair markets in the digital sector and amending Directives (EU) 2019/1937 and (EU) 2020/1828 (Digital Markets Act) (OJ 2022 L 265, 1)
DSA	Digital Services Act – Regulation (EU) 2022/2065 of the European Parliament and of the Council of 19 October 2022 on a Single Market for Digital Services and amending Directive 2000/31/EC (Digital Services Act) (OJ 2022 L 277, 1)
DS-GVO	Datenschutz-Grundverordnung – Regulation (EU) 2016/679 of the European Parliament and of the Council of 27 April 2016 on the protection of natural persons with regard to the processing of personal data and on the free movement of such data, and repealing Directive 95/46/EC (General Data Protection Regulation) (OJ 2016 L 119, 1)
e.g.	for example
EC	European Community
ECB	European Central Bank
ECJ	European Court of Justice
ECLI	European Case Law Identifier
ed(s)	editor(s)
EDIB	European Data Innovation Board
edn	edition
EDPB	European Data Protection Board
EDPS	European Data Protection Supervisor
EEA	European Economic Area
EHDS	European Health Data Space
EIC	European Innovation Council
ENISA	European Union Agency for Cybersecurity
EnWG	Energiewirtschaftsgesetz (German Energy Industry Act)

ERegG	Eisenbahnregulierungsgesetz (German Railway Regulation Act)
et al.	and others
et seq./et seqq.	following
etc.	and so forth
EU	European Union
EuDIR	Zeitschrift für Europäisches Daten- und Informationsrecht (journal)
EUEB	EU Ecolabelling Board
EUR	Euro
EuR	Europarecht (journal)
EUV	Vertrag über die Europäische Union (Treaty on European Union)
EuZW	Europäische Zeitschrift für Wirtschaftsrecht (journal)
fig.	figure
FRAND	Fair, Reasonable and Non-Discriminatory
G2G	Government-to-Government
GBER	General Block Exemption Regulation – Commission Regulation (EU) No 651/2014 of 17 June 2014 declaring certain categories of aid compatible with the internal market in application of Articles 107 and 108 of the Treaty (OJ 2014 L 187, 1)
GDP	Gross Domestic Product
GDPR	General Data Protection Regulation – Regulation (EU) 2016/679 of the European Parliament and of the Council of 27 April 2016 on the protection of natural persons with regard to the processing of personal data and on the free movement of such data, and repealing Directive 95/46/EC (General Data Protection Regulation) (OJ 2016 L 119, 1)
GeschGehG	Geschäftsgeheimnisgesetz (German Act on the Protection of Trade Secrets)
GmbH	Gesellschaft mit beschränkter Haftung (German limited liability company)
GRUR	Gewerblicher Rechtsschutz und Urheberrecht (journal)
HdB	Handbuch (handbook)
HVD	High-Value Datasets
i.e.	that is

IaaS	Infrastructure-as-a-Service
IIC	International Review of Intellectual Property and Competition Law
IoT	Internet of Things
ITS	Intelligent Transport System
JuS	Juristische Schulung (journal)
K&R	Kommunikation und Recht (journal)
LG	Landgericht (German Regional Court)
LkSG	Lieferkettensorgfaltspflichtengesetz (German Supply Chain Due Diligence Act)
MCTs	Model Contractual Terms
MMR	Multimedia und Recht (journal)
mn.	margin number(s)
NIS	Network and Information Security
NJW	Neue Juristische Wochenschrift (journal)
no.	number(s)
OJ	Official Journal
OWiG	Gesetz über Ordnungswidrigkeiten (German Act on Regulatory Offences)
p.	page(s)
PaaS	Platform-as-a-Service
para.	paragraph(s)
PinG	Privacy in Germany (journal)
RBAC	Role-Based Access Control
RDi	Recht Digital (journal)
rec.	recital(s)
SaaS	Software-as-a-Service
SCCs	Standard Contractual Clauses
sent.	sentence(s)
SGB	Sozialgesetzbuch (German Social Security Code)
SME	Small and Medium-sized Enterprise
StGB	Strafgesetzbuch (German Criminal Code)
StPO	Strafprozessordnung (German Code of Criminal Procedure)
subpara.	subparagraph(s)

SWD	Staff Working Document
TDDDG	Telekommunikation-Digitale-Dienste-Datenschutz-Gesetz (German Telecommunications Digital Services Data Protection Act)
TFEU	Treaty on the Functioning of the European Union
TKG	Telekommunikationsgesetz (German Telecommunications Act)
TOMs	Technical and Organisational Measures
TTDSG	Telekommunikation-Telemedien-Datenschutz-Gesetz (German Telecommunications Telemedia Data Protection Act)
URL	Uniform Resource Locator
US	United States
UWG	Gesetz gegen den unlauteren Wettbewerb (German Act against Unfair Competition)
VwGO	Verwaltungsgerichtsordnung (German Code of Administrative Court Procedure)
VwVfG	Verwaltungsverfahrensgesetz (German Administrative Procedures Act)
WiVerw	Wirtschaft und Verwaltung (journal)
WRP	Wettbewerb in Recht und Praxis (journal)
ZD	Zeitschrift für Datenschutz (journal)
ZEuP	Zeitschrift für Europäisches Privatrecht (journal)
ZfBR	Zeitschrift für deutsches und internationales Bau- und Vergaberecht (journal)
ZfPC	Zeitschrift für Product Compliance (journal)
ZGE	Zeitschrift für Geistiges Eigentum/Intellectual Property Journal
ZGI	Zeitschrift für das gesamte Informationsrecht (journal)
ZPO	Zivilprozessordnung (German Code of Civil Procedure)

General bibliography

Auer-Reinsdorff/Conrad IT- und DatenschutzR-HdB	Auer-Reinsdorff/Conrad (eds), Handbuch IT- und Datenschutzrecht, 3rd edn, Munich 2019
BeckFormB IT-R	Weitnauer/Mueller-Stöfen (eds), Beck'sches Formularbuch IT-Recht, 6th edn, Munich 2025
BeckOGK	Gsell et al. (eds), beck-online.Grosskommentar, Munich 2025
BeckOK BGB	Hau/Poseck (eds), Beck'scher Online-Kommentar Bürgerliches Gesetzbuch (BGB), 76th edn, Munich 2025
BeckOK DatenschutzR	Wolff/Brink/v. Ungern-Sternberg (eds), Beck'scher Online-Kommentar Datenschutzrecht, 54th edn, Munich 2025
BeckOK OWiG	Graf (ed), Beck'scher Online-Kommentar Gesetz über Ordnungswidrigkeiten (OWiG), 48th edn, Munich 2025
BeckOK VwGO	Posser/Wolff/Decker (eds), Beck'scher Online-Kommentar Verwaltungsgerichtsordnung (VwGO), 75th edn, Munich 2025
Calliess/Ruffert	Calliess/Ruffert (eds), Vertrag über die Europäische Union (EUV)/Vertrag über die Arbeitsweise der Europäischen Union (AEUV) – Das Verfassungsrecht der Europäischen Union mit Europäischer Grundrechtecharta, 6th edn, Munich 2022
Emmerich/Habersack	Emmerich/Habersack, Aktien- und GmbH-Konzernrecht, 10th edn, Munich 2022
FormB-MietR	Schach/Riecke (eds), Mietrecht, Formularbuch, 4th edn, Baden-Baden 2019
Geppert/Schütz	Geppert/Schütz (eds), Beck'scher Kommentar zum Telekommunikationsgesetz (TKG), 5th edn, Munich 2023
Grabitz/Hilf/Nettesheim	Grabitz/Hilf/Nettesheim (eds), Das Recht der Europäischen Union, 86th edn, Munich 2025
Hennemann/Ebner/Karsten/Lienemann/Wienroeder Data Act	Hennemann/Ebner/Karsten/Lienemann/Wienroeder, Data Act (DA), Baden-Baden 2024
HK-BGB	Schulze et al., Bürgerliches Gesetzbuch (BGB), 12th edn, Baden-Baden 2024

HK-DatenR	Specht/Hennemann (eds), Data Act (DA)/ Data Governance Act (DGA), 2nd edn, Baden-Baden 2025
HK-DGA	Specht/Hennemann, Data Governance Act (DGA), Baden-Baden 2023
HK-DMA	Podszun (ed), Digital Markets Act (DMA), Baden-Baden 2023
HK-DS-GVO/BDSG	Sydow/Marsch (eds), Europäische Datenschutzgrundverordnung (DS-GVO)/Bundesdatenschutzgesetz (BDSG), 3rd edn, Baden-Baden 2022
HK-TTDSG	Assion (ed), Telekommunikation-Digitale-Dienste-Datenschutz-Gesetz (TTDSG), Baden-Baden 2022
Hoeren/Münker	Hoeren/Münker (eds), Gesetz zum Schutz von Geschäftsgeheimnissen (GeschGehG), Berlin 2021
Immenga/Mestmäcker	Immenga/Mestmäcker (eds), Wettbewerbsrecht, 6th edn, Munich 2021
jurisPK-InternetR	Heckmann/Paschke (eds), juris PraxisKommentar Internetrecht, 8th edn, Saarbrücken 2024
Keller/Schönknecht/Glinke	Keller/Schönknecht/Glinke, Gesetz zum Schutz von Geschäftsgeheimnissen (GeschGehG), Munich 2021
Köhler/Feddersen	Köhler/Feddersen, Gesetz gegen den unlauteren Wettbewerb (UWG), 43rd edn, Munich 2025
Kühling/Buchner	Kühling/Buchner (eds), Datenschutzgrundverordnung (DS-GVO)/Bundesdatenschutzgesetz (BDSG), 4th edn, Munich 2024
Lindner-Figura/Oprée/Stellmann Geschäftsraummiete-HdB	Lindner-Figura/Oprée/Stellmann (eds), Handbuch Geschäftsraummiete, 5th edn, Munich 2023
Mestmäcker/Schweitzer EuWettbR	Mestmäcker/Schweitzer, Europäisches Wettbewerbsrecht, 3rd edn, Munich 2014
Moos Datenschutz	Moos (ed), Datenschutz und Datennutzung, 4th edn, Cologne 2024
MüKoBGB	Säcker/Rixecker/Oetker/Limperg/Schubert (eds), Münchener Kommentar zum Bürgerlichen Gesetzbuch (BGB), 10th edn, Munich 2025

MüKoStGB	Erb/Schäfer (eds), Münchener Kommentar zum Strafgesetzbuch (StGB), 5th edn, Munich 2025
MüKoUWG	Heermann/Schlinghoff (eds), Münchener Kommentar zum Lauterkeitsrecht, 3rd edn, Munich 2020
MüKoWettbR	Säcker (ed), Münchener Kommentar zum Wettbewerbsrecht, 4th edn, Munich 2022
NK-DatenschutzR	Simitis/Hornung/Spiecker gen. Döhmann (eds), Datenschutzrecht, 2nd edn, Baden-Baden 2025
Paal/Pauly	Paal/Pauly (eds), Datenschutzgrundverordnung (DS-GVO)/Bundesdatenschutzgesetz (BDSG), 3rd edn, Munich 2021
Redeker IT-Verträge-HdB	Redeker (ed), Handbuch der IT-Verträge, 57th edn, Cologne 2025
Schoch/Schneider	Schoch/Schneider (eds), Verwaltungsgerichtsordnung (VwGO), 48th edn, Munich 2022
Schreiber/Pommerening/Schoel New DGA	Schreiber/Pommerening/Schoel, New Data Governance Act (DGA), Practitioner's Guide, Baden-Baden 2023
Schwarze	Schwarze/Becker/Hatje/Schoo (eds), EU-Kommentar, 4th edn, Baden-Baden 2019
Staudinger	Staudinger, Kommentar zum Bürgerlichen Gesetzbuch (BGB) mit Einführungsgesetz und Nebengesetzen, Berlin 2018 et seqq.
Stein	Stein, Kommentar zur Zivilprozessordnung (ZPO), 24th edn, Tübingen 2024
Stelkens/Bonk/Sachs	Stelkens/Bonk/Sachs (eds), Verwaltungsverfahrensgesetz (VwVfG), 10th edn, Munich 2023
von der Groeben/Schwarze/Hatje	von der Groeben/Schwarze/Hatje (eds), Europäisches Unionsrecht, 8th edn, Baden-Baden 2026

CHAPTER 1
THE EU DATA AND DIGITAL STRATEGY

Bibliography: Schmitz, 'Digitale-Gesetze-Strategie – Agilität oder „Act"ionismus?', ZD 2022, 189; Schreiber/Brinke, Datenschutz im EU-Gesundheitsdatenraum, PinG 2024, 251; Schreiber/Pommerening/Schoel, New Data Governance Act, A Practitioner's Guide, 2023.

A. EU Data Strategy 4

B. EU Digital Strategy 15

C. The EU's Omnibus Initiative with the Digital Package on Simplification 26

1 The **EU Digital Strategy** aims to position the European Union at the forefront of the development of the digital economy in a unified single market without borders by fostering a competitive, secure, and inclusive digital surrounding. It focuses on building a **digital single market** that benefits citizens, businesses, and governments, promoting innovation, and ensuring that digital technologies contribute to a sustainable and fair society. The public and private sectors are both involved. The EU expects the digital offensive to lead to a noticeable increase in the gross domestic products of the EU Member States and more prosperity for the society.

2 Complementing this, the **EU Data Strategy** as part of the EU Digital Strategy seeks to create a single European data space where data can flow freely and be accessed and utilised efficiently, securely and interoperably. This strategy envisions a data-driven economy that leverages the vast amounts of data generated within the EU to drive growth, innovation, and societal progress, as well as more trust in data intermediaries and altruistic data organisations.[1]

3 With the Data Governance Act (DGA) and the Data Act (DA), the EU has adopted two key measures on the way to an EU-wide data economy:

- The **Data Governance Act** was published as Regulation (EU) 2022/868 in the Official Journal of the EU on 3.6.2022 (OJ 2022 L 152, 1). It is officially referred to as the 'Regulation on European data governance and amending Regulation (EU) 2018/1724 (Data Governance Act)'.
- The **Data Act**, also an EU Regulation, whose official title is 'Regulation on harmonised rules for fair access to and use of data and amending Regulation (EU) 2017/2394 and Directive (EU) 2020/1828 (Data Act)', was published as Regulation (EU) 2023/2854 in the Official Journal of the EU (OJ L, 2023/2854) on 22.12.2023.

Together, these two legal acts form the backbone of the EU Data Strategy. In November 2025, a simplification of the Data Governance Act and Data Act is planned, initiated with the draft of a Digital Package on Simplification by the EU Commission (→ mn. 26 et seqq.).

A. EU Data Strategy

4 As components of the EU Commission's **Data Strategy**, the DA and DGA are embedded in Brussels' comprehensive Digital Strategy. In its Communication of

[1] Details cf. Schreiber/Pommerening/Schoel, New Data Governance Act. A Practitioner's Guide, Baden-Baden 2023, Ch. 3, Ch. 4.

19.2.2020 on a European Data Strategy,[2] the Commission outlines policies and investments to help build an efficient, innovative data economy, in line with European values, fundamental rights and rules.[3] According to the Commission, it is important to harness the potential of the growing amount of existing data for social and economic well-being by improving **access to data** and **promoting responsible data use**.[4]

5 The Commission's vision is a **single European Data Space**, i.e. an internal market for data where both personal and non-personal data is securely handled, where companies can easily access the data they need and (re)use it in compliance with applicable laws (across industries) – regardless of where it is stored in the EU.[5] In addition, the EU aims to ensure free and secure data flows with **third countries**, meaning that the European data space should be accessible to data from all over the world.[6]

6 The DGA and the DA aim to create suitable framework conditions for a **data-agile European economy**.[7] Both Regulations are cross-sectoral measures for data access and use.[8]

7 Based on identified problematic areas in the European data economy, the policy measures and financial support planned in the Data Strategy are divided into **four pillars**:

8 1. The first objective is to establish a cross-sectoral governance framework for **data access and data use** that avoids inconsistent approaches in the various sectors and Member States in the internal market.[9] The DA, with its data access requirements, and the DGA are the main instruments for achieving this objective. As horizontal measures, the DA and DGA address various players in the data economy across sectors.[10] The relationships between the stakeholders, in particular their rights and obligations, are to be standardised across the EU in order to promote the shared use of data, distribute the added value of data more fairly and increase the overall availability of data.[11]

9 A further component is the Implementing Regulation (EU) 2023/138 establishing certain high-value datasets (HVD) and the modalities of their publication and re-use, which supplements the Open Data Directive (EU) 2019/1024. The high-value datasets classified as such by the EU Commission and the Committee on Open Data and the Re-Use of Public Sector Information (see Art. 16(1) Open Data Directive) and included in the list must fulfil the conditions of Art. 14(1) subpara. 2 Open Data Directive after adoption of the implementing

---

[2] European Commission, 'Communication from the Commission to the European Parliament, the Council, the European Economic and Social Committee and the Committee of the Regions: A European strategy for data' (19.2.2020), COM(2020) 66 final.

[3] COM(2020) 66 final, 1 et seq.

[4] COM(2020) 66 final, 4 et seq.

[5] COM(2020) 66 final, 4 et seq.; rec. 2 sent. 1 DGA.

[6] COM(2020) 66 final, 4 et seq.; rec. 2 sent. 1 DGA.

[7] COM(2020) 66 final, 12.

[8] COM(2020) 66 final, 12.

[9] COM(2020) 66 final, 12.

[10] COM(2020) 66 final, 12.

[11] COM(2020) 66 final, 13 et seq.; European Commission, 'Proposal for a Regulation of the European Parliament and of the Council on harmonised rules on fair access to and use of data (Data Act)' (23.2.2022), COM(2022) 68 final, 2 et seq.

act. They must therefore be available free of charge, in machine-readable formats, via APIs and, where relevant, as a bulk download. With a view to the work in the committee, the German Federal Ministry for Economic Affairs and Climate Action had a study prepared on high-quality datasets in Germany, which was published on 10.2.2021.[12]

2. The second pillar of the Data Strategy aims to support **innovative, data-based business models** (especially financially) and to create the necessary infrastructural conditions for the vision of a single European Data Space.[13] After all, realising the potential of the European data economy requires data, cloud infrastructures and corresponding services that enable secure, sustainable, interoperable and scalable data storage and processing.[14] **10**

A first practical example of such a data space is the **European Health Data Space (EHDS)**: With its Regulation on the European Health Data Space (Regulation (EU) 2025/327 – 'EHDS Regulation'), the EU legislator has taken the first step towards creating a sector-specific common data space. The EHDS Regulation entered into force on 26.3.2025 and will be applicable from 26.3.2027 onwards. The EHDS is intended to establish a kind of platform – a decentralised data space – on and in which natural persons can post their health data and control further processing (primary data use). The EHDS Regulation is in its structure and idea based on the Data Governance Act.[15] **11**

The **EHDS Regulation** is intended to create provisions for common standards and procedures, infrastructures and a governance framework within which health data can be used for primary and secondary purposes.[16] The Regulation is based on the right of patients to access their electronic health data in a secure environment, where they can make sovereign decisions about making this data available for further processing. This will be based on a central platform for health services – **MyHealth@EU** – set up by the Commission, and a canon of obligations for systems for electronic patient records and so-called wellness applications, which, among other things, prescribes certain technical requirements and compliance with common specifications (primary use). Research and innovation stakeholders and political decision-makers should then be able to utilise this data in a trustworthy and secure manner (secondary use).[17] This regulation of secondary data use will also be highly relevant in the context of the training data required for AI applications and research. This is particularly true in light of the fact that the EHDS Regulation will also regulate the use of data under data protection law and create a corresponding basis for authorisation. This is a significant difference and advantage compared to the DA and DGA, which merely leave the GDPR 'untouched' and thus do not solve the data protection challenges. **12**

---

[12] See <https://www.bmwk.de/Redaktion/DE/Publikationen/Studien/studie-hochwertige-datensaetze-in-deutschland.html> (last accessed: 7.1.2026).

[13] COM(2020) 66 final, 15 et seqq.

[14] COM(2020) 66 final, 20 et seq.

[15] COM(2022) 197 final, 4 et seq.

[16] Comprehensive overview by Schreiber/Brinke PinG 2024, 251 et seq.; Ruff/Schreiber EuDIR 2025, 318.

[17] Cf. COM(2022) 197 final, 1.

13 3. The Commission also believes that the EU needs more qualified workers, data experts and overall **data literacy** throughout the population.[18] To achieve this, financial resources should be channelled into training and recruiting talent, women should be more involved and companies should receive targeted advice and support in order to develop and efficiently use data-based business models.[19] The Commission also plans to further empower individuals with regard to their data. There are discussions about strengthening the right to data portability under Art. 20 GDPR, giving individuals more control over who can access and use machine-generated data.[20]

14 4. In addition to the above, the European Commission has announced the development of **common European Data Spaces in strategic sectors and areas of public interest**.[21] Data spaces are initially to be established in nine different sectors (manufacturing, 'Green Deal', mobility, health, finance, energy, agriculture, public administration, skills).[22] More detailed descriptions of these sectors and sector-specific measures can be found in the annex to the Data Strategy.[23]

B. EU Digital Strategy

15 The Data Strategy forms part of the EU Commission's broader Digital Strategy. The Digital Strategy is a comprehensive policy document published together with the Data Strategy on 19.2.2020. In its Communication **'Shaping Europe's digital future'**,[24] the EU Commission presented more than 50 specific key measures,[25] which together form the Digital Strategy. With the Digital Strategy, the EU Commission meets the 'twin challenge of green and digital transformation' and announces a 'substantial societal transformation' to achieve a 'better digital future for everyone'.[26] The aim is to shape the digital transformation – based on European values – in a way that benefits everyone, puts people at the centre and creates new opportunities for the economy.[27]

16 The Digital Strategy is based on **three key objectives**:

- First, to develop and deploy trustworthy **technology that works for people**, transforming their daily lives while respecting European values.
- Second, to promote a **fair and competitive economy** in the single market, where all businesses have the opportunity to increase their productivity and global competitiveness by developing, marketing and using digital technologies,

---

[18] COM(2020) 66 final, 10 et seq.

[19] COM(2020) 66 final, 20 et seq.

[20] COM(2020) 66 final, 20 et seq.

[21] COM(2020) 66 final, 21 et seq.

[22] COM(2020) 66 final, 22 et seq.

[23] COM(2020) 66 final, 26 et seqq.

[24] European Commission, 'Communication from the Commission to the European Parliament, the Council, the European Economic and Social Committee and the Committee of the Regions: Shaping Europe's digital future' (19.2.2020), COM(2020) 67 final.

[25] Critically and instructively Schmitz ZD 2022, 189.

[26] COM(2020) 67 final, 1.

[27] COM(2020) 67 final, 1 et seq.; European Commission, see <https://digital-strategy.ec.europa.eu/en/policies/europes-digital-decade> (last accessed: 7.1.2026).

products and services, and where consumers can be confident that their rights are respected.
- And third, digital technologies should contribute to an **open, democratic and sustainable society**.[28]

The Commission describes how it intends to shape Europe's digital future and achieve its goals in three sections, which are subordinated to the key objectives. The respective **key measures** are listed at the end of each section and, in some cases, provided with a timeframe for implementation. As one of these key measures, the European Data Strategy falls under the second aspect – promoting a fair and competitive economy. 17

Key aspects of the agenda include accelerating the expansion of **digital infrastructures** and networks, creating the necessary **trust in the security** of digital applications and products, both with regard to cyber threats and the technology itself (especially artificial intelligence-based technology), and investing in digital **skills for all Europeans**. In addition, **fair access** to data should be ensured, data sharing should be encouraged and the market power of large digital corporations and companies should be limited.[29] 18

Core elements of the Digital Strategy have now been implemented and came into force. Following the GDPR in 2018, other Regulations and Directives that must be observed for digital offerings and the handling of (personal and non-personal) data have been in force for several years now, in particular the Platform-to-Business Regulation (Regulation (EU) 2019/1150), the Regulation on the Free Movement of Data (Regulation (EU) 2018/1807) and finally the Directive on Digital Content and Services (Directive (EU) 2019/770) as well as the Directive on certain contractual aspects of the sale of goods (Directive (EU) 2019/771 – Sales of Goods Directive), which also covers goods with digital elements. 19

In the lead-up to the 2024 European Parliament elections, additional legislative components of the Digital Strategy were adopted and entered into force. In addition to the Data Strategy, the most important regulatory areas of the more recent legislative procedures relate to the regulation of digital gatekeepers, information security and the regulation of artificial intelligence: 20

- **Digital gatekeepers**: Two central measures of the Digital Strategy, the Digital Services Act (Regulation (EU) 2022/2065) and the Digital Markets Act (Regulation (EU) 2022/1925), particularly affect online platforms and digital players with market power. The Digital Services Act (DSA) introduces a revised legal framework that defines the responsibilities and obligations of intermediary services such as online platforms. The Digital Markets Act (DMA) complements competition law and limits the power of large platforms with significant network effects that act as gatekeepers. The EU Commission has designated several gatekeepers, including Alphabet (Google), Apple, Amazon, ByteDance, Meta and Microsoft.[30] Both Regulations entered into force in November 2022. 21

---

[28] COM(2020) 67 final, 2 et seq.

[29] See the overview at: <https://digital-strategy.ec.europa.eu/en/policies/europes-digital-decade> (last accessed: 7.1.2026).

[30] See <https://digital-markets-act.ec.europa.eu/gatekeepers_en> (last accessed: 7.1.2026).

22 – **Artificial intelligence (AI)**: The EU aims to establish a legal framework for trustworthy AI that enhances public confidence in AI-based solutions while encouraging innovation and investment.[31] In April 2021, the EU Commission presented its AI package, including a proposal for a Regulation with harmonised rules for artificial intelligence.[32] The original objective of taking an early pioneering role in the risk regulation of AI applications through rapid adoption was only partially achieved. After intensive negotiations, a political agreement on the AI Regulation was reached in spring 2024. The AI Act was published in the Official Journal of the European Union on 12.7.2024 (Regulation (EU) 2024/1689). The AI Act introduces a risk-based approach that prohibits the use of AI for forbidden practices with an unacceptable risk and intensively regulates AI systems with a high risk. Transparency obligations are imposed on specific AI models, systems and outputs (esp. deepfakes). Finally, there is, among other things, an obligation to develop AI literacy, special regulations for GPAI models, and various requirements for market surveillance and enforcement.

23 – **Cybersecurity**: Especially for digital solutions, cybersecurity is a key factor for confidentiality, availability and integrity. The experience of numerous cyberattacks in recent months and years has emphasised the importance of this issue to the general public. In order to increase the confidence of people and companies in the security of their applications and products, the Digital Strategy also provides for a wide range of measures to strengthen resilience to cyber threats.[33] At its heart is the EU Cybersecurity Strategy for the Digital Decade,[34] which sets out the direction of EU cybersecurity policy. In implementing the Security Strategy, the NIS2 Directive (EU) 2022/2555 and the CER Directive (EU) 2022/2554 on critical infrastructure was announced for the turn of 2023. The Cyber Resilience Act, a Regulation that addresses the security of digital products (Regulation 2024/2847), was published in November 2024. Under the Cyber Resilience Act, security updates will become a clear obligation for the life cycle or five years for digital products, whichever is longer.

24 The various legal acts of the Digital Strategy affect all digital services and products, as well as the handling of data. They have different but overlapping objectives. A major and justified **criticism** of the new legal acts is that they are not harmonised in detail: Most of them provide that other legal acts, in particular the GDPR, are not affected. This leaves considerable legal uncertainty, which in the worst-case scenario could have a negative impact on innovation and Europe as a place to do business. This issue is addressed by the Digital Package on Simplification described in → mn. 26 et seqq.

25 This can be clearly seen, for example, in the **definition of data**: While the GDPR defines data as 'information' about a natural person (digital, analogue in any form; Art. 4(1) no. 1 GDPR), DA (Art. 2 no. 1), DGA (Art. 2 no. 1) and DMA (Art. 2 no. 24) describe data as a digital representation of acts, facts or information, including the form of sound, visual or audiovisual recordings. However, these laws refer to

[31] COM(2020) 67 final, 5.

[32] AI Regulation proposal: COM(2021) 206 final.

[33] COM(2020) 67 final, 5.

[34] European Commission, 'Joint communication to the European Parliament and the Council: The EU's cybersecurity strategy for the digital decade' (16.12.2020), JOIN(2020) 18 final.

Art. 4 no. 1 GDPR for the definition of personal data. This leads to an unclear understanding of what constitutes 'data', especially as the GDPR is supposed to prevail in case of a conflict. The differences in the definition of processing are less serious, but the GDPR is also open to analogue forms; the definition in the DA refers only to digital data.

C. The EU's Omnibus Initiative with the Digital Package on Simplification

In November 2025, the European Commission published a **proposal** for a regulation aimed at revising and simplifying digital legislation: The Proposal for a Regulation of the European Parliament and of the Council amending Regulations (EU) 2016/679, (EU) 2018/1724, (EU) 2018/1725, (EU) 2023/2854 and Directives 2002/58/EC, (EU) 2022/2555 and (EU) 2022/2557 as regards the simplification of the digital legislative framework, and repealing Regulations (EU) 2018/1807, (EU) 2019/1150, (EU) 2022/868, and Directive (EU) 2019/1024.[35] It is abbreviated as 'Digital Omnibus on digital acquis'. The planned legal act will also affect the Data Strategy, Data Governance Act, and Data Act. 26

This proposal is part of the European Union's **'Omnibus Initiative'**, which arises from the recognition that the increasing complexity of digital legislation poses significant challenges to legal certainty and regulatory coherence. The rationale behind the Omnibus approach is to streamline and modernise existing frameworks by introducing coordinated amendments to multiple interconnected legal instruments simultaneously. This strategy aligns directly with the objectives of the Draghi Programme, which prioritises legislative simplification as a means to foster a more dynamic, efficient, and innovation-friendly EU internal market. 27

The choice to focus on **simplification** in the digital sector is particularly pertinent. Digital regulation in the EU has expanded rapidly over the past decade, often not fully coordinated and harmonised with each other in the individual digital acts. The rapid and overlapping drafting of various legal acts led to overlaps, contradictory definitions, and fragmented legislative amendments, which shall be resolved by the Omnibus legislation. 28

With the upcoming 'Digital Package on Simplification', the European Commission intends to **simplify** the digital regulation specifically targeting adjustments across the main digital legislative acts. The proposed regulation touches several legal acts, e.g. the GDPR, but also the Data Act. Regarding the Data Act, this package will refine certain definitions (for instance, those relating to data intermediaries and gatekeepers), standardise enforcement provisions and streamline reporting obligations. The initiative also responds to feedback from national authorities and businesses calling for greater coherence and predictability in the EU's digital acquis. The Data Governance Act is to be repealed and incorporated into the Data Act in relevant parts. Those amendments to the Data Act are summarised in Art. 1 of the proposed Regulation.[36] 29

First, the proposal will consolidate and streamline several rules in the Data Act as the future core Regulation for the data economy: The revised Data Act 30

[35] COM(2025) 837 final.
[36] COM(2025) 837 final, 20.

shall absorb and replace the Free Flow of Non-Personal Data Regulation (EU) 2018/1807, the Data Governance Act (Regulation (EU) 2022/868), and the Open Data Directive (EU) 2019/1024, consolidating previously fragmented regimes into a **single legal framework**.[37]

31 Second, the Data Act itself is to be further developed in some details. Art. 4(8) of the proposed revised Data Act shall include a right for data holders to refuse to disclose **trade secrets** if there is a high risk of unlawful access, particularly to third-country recipients in jurisdictions with weak or non-equivalent protections. This ground builds on objective factors such as confidentiality levels and enforceability of protection and requires timely written notification to users and authorities.[38] However, the conditions for such a refusal will remain strict, and the possibilities for resorting to it are limited to a few cases. The public sector data sharing (business-to-government, B2G) shall be narrowed to cover only **'public emergencies'** (as newly defined in Art. 2(29)).[39] Further some more **exemptions for SMEs** are planned. Art. 36 dealing with smart contracts shall be deleted due to market immaturity and risk of legal uncertainty.

32 From the Free Flow of Non-Personal Data Regulation especially the prohibition of any non-personal data localisation requirements is reaffirmed and transferred to the Data Act, with a reporting and notification obligation to the Commission by Member States. A **'Single Information Point'** shall provide a searchable register of data assets and simplified information channels (especially for SMEs, SMCs, researchers) to facilitate transparency and re-use across the EU.

33 Although it is not yet clear what form this proposal will take as it goes through the legislative procedure, this Omnibus package will in any case play a decisive role in shaping the framework of future conditions for digital players in the EU. The approach reflects a general shift towards agile regulatory governance and continuous legal harmonisation.

[37] COM(2025) 837 final, 5.
[38] Art. 1(3) COM(2025) 837 final, 24.
[39] COM(2025) 837 final, 35 et seq.

CHAPTER 2
OVERVIEW AND SCOPE OF THE DATA ACT

Bibliography: Bomhard, 'Der Anwendungsbereich des Data Act', MMR 2024, 71; Hennemann/Steinrötter, 'Der Data Act. Neue Instrumente, alte Friktionen, strukturelle Weichenstellungen', NJW 2024, 1; Kumkar, 'Zu den Vorschlägen der EU-Kommission für eine Europäische Datenstrategie', in Baumgärtel/Kiparski (eds), DGRI Jahrbuch 2021/2022, Cologne 2023, p. 51; Pauly/Wichert/Baumann, 'Schutz von Geschäftsgeheimnissen nach dem Data Act', MMR 2024, 211; Steinrötter, 'Verhältnis von Data Act und DS-GVO', GRUR 2023, 216; Wiebe, 'Der Data Act – Innovation oder Illusion?', GRUR 2023, 1569.

A. Goals ... 1

B. History of the Regulation ... 7

C. Scope of application ... 8
I. Subject matter ... 9
II. Data covered ... 11
III. Addressees ... 13
IV. Marketplace principle ... 14

D. Relationship to other regulations and contract design ... 16
I. Data protection and trade secret protection ... 19
II. Freedom of contract ... 22

E. Entry into force and implementation period ... 24
I. Validity from September 2025 ... 25
II. Product design obligations: applicable only from September 2026 ... 27

F. Symmetrical vs. asymmetrical regulation of the data economy ... 36

A. Goals

The purpose of the Data Act, which itself consists of 50 Articles, is to facilitate access, use and disclosure of data generated by the use of connected products or related services (rec. 5 DA). This refers to products that are often referred to as 'smart' – meaning that they are connected to the internet and generate data during their use (the so-called Internet of Things, or IoT for short). The DA goes even further: An internet connection is not necessary. It is sufficient that the products generate data during their use, which can at least be accessed via an interface in the product. 1

The DA aims to ensure a **fair distribution of the value of data** among stakeholders in the data economy and to promote access to and use of data.[1] It aims to remove barriers to data sharing in order to realise the full potential of data and data-driven innovation.[2] The DA should also enable the public sector to use private data in order to better serve the public interest (business-to-government data sharing).[3] The background to this is that IoT products in particular generate vast amounts of valuable data (rec. 1 DA). However, the EU Commission assumes that 80 % of such industrial data simply remains unused.[4] 2

[1] COM(2022) 68 final, 2.
[2] COM(2022) 68 final, 1.
[3] Kumkar in Baumgärtel/Kiparski, p. 51 (64 mn. 24).
[4] European Commission, 'Data Law: Commission proposes measures for a fair and innovative data economy' (press release, 23.2.2022) <https://ec.europa.eu/commission/presscorner/detail/de/ip_22_1113> (last accessed: 7.1.2026).

3 As part of the **EU Data Strategy** (→ Ch. 1 mn. 1),[5] the DA aims to create a true single market for data and give Europe a leading role in the global data economy.[6] It is designed to help ensure the innovation and competitiveness of EU businesses, increase the empowerment of individuals with regard to their data and enable businesses and public authorities to better respond to public emergencies and exceptional situations.[7] In addition to fair data use and fair data access, it also focuses on easier switching between data processing services and data interoperability.

4 As a horizontal measure, the DA addresses different **actors in the data economy** across sectors.[8] It aims to standardise the relationships between stakeholders, in particular their rights and obligations, across the EU in order to promote the sharing of data, to distribute the added value from data more fairly and to increase the overall availability of data.[9] The DA is intended to provide a harmonised legal framework setting out the conditions for the use of IoT data (rec. 4 DA).

5 The Commission expects significant **economic growth** as a result of the Data Act. In its impact assessment report, the Commission formulates a significant increase in the GDP of the EU Member States (by 1.98 percentage points by 2028), the expectation of 2.2 million additional jobs and a turnover of almost 200 billion EUR per year by 2028 from data access claims alone.[10]

6 The **main points** of the Regulation are

- the transfer of data between companies and from companies to consumers (access to and supply of data),
- obligations of data holders who are obliged to disclose data under Union law,
- protection against unfair contractual terms in relation to data access and use between companies,
- making data available to public sector bodies and Union institutions, bodies, offices and agencies on grounds of exceptional need,
- switching between data processing services,
- lawfulness of international government access and international transfers of non-personal data,
- interoperability requirements, including for smart contracts.

B. History of the Regulation

7 The Commission introduced the DA through its proposal for a Regulation laying down harmonised rules on fair access to and use of data of 23.2.2022.[11] The DA falls under the first pillar of the EU Data Strategy.[12] As part of the ordinary legislative procedure, the Economic and Social Committee, the European Committee of the

[5] COM(2020) 66 final.

[6] COM(2022) 68 final, 1.

[7] COM(2022) 68 final, 2 et seq.

[8] COM(2020) 66 final, 12.

[9] COM(2020) 66 final, 13 et seq.; COM(2022) 68 final, 2 et seq.

[10] European Commission, 'Commission Staff Working Document: Executive summary of the impact assessment report accompanying the document Proposal for a Regulation of the European Parliament and of the Council on harmonised rules on fair access to and use of data (Data Act)' (23.2.2022), SWD(2022) 35 final, 2.

[11] COM(2022) 68 final.

[12] COM(2020) 66 final.

Regions and the European Central Bank have issued opinions on the first draft of the Regulation. In its first reading, the European Parliament adopted several amendments and submitted the amended draft DA to the Council on 14.3.2023. This was unanimously adopted by the Council on 27.11.2023 and thus adopted. The Regulation was then published in the Official Journal of the EU on 22.12.2023. The DA entered into force 20 days after its publication and, with a few exceptions, will apply in all EU Member States from 12.9.2025 (Art. 50 DA).

C. Scope of application

Art. 1 DA describes the subject matter and scope of the DA. The provision dis- 8
tinguishes between the main areas of regulation, the data covered and the addressees. However, the Regulation does not contain a clearly defined scope of application that applies to all provisions of the DA in terms of subject matter, territory, subjectivity and time.[13]

I. Subject matter

Art. 1(1) of the DA contains a general summary of the regulations made by the 9
DA. Accordingly, the DA contains **harmonised rules on**, among other things,

- the making available of product data and related service data to the user of the connected product or related service (point (a)),
- the making available of data by data holders to data recipients (point (b)),
- the making available of data by data holders to public sector bodies, the Commission, the European Central Bank and Union bodies where there is an exceptional need for those data for the performance of a specific task carried out in the public interest (point (c)),
- the facilitation of switching between data processing services (point (d)),
- the introduction of safeguards against unlawful access by third parties to non-personal data (point (e)) and
- the development of interoperability standards for data to be accessed, transferred and used (point (f)).

It remains unclear whether this is merely an overview of the subsequent regu- 10
lation or whether Art. 1(1) DA has its own regulatory content.[14] The provision makes it clear at the beginning that the DA contains 'harmonised rules', which would otherwise only result in a fragmentary manner from the DA and could constitute its own regulatory content. This could also be an indication of full harmonisation, in which neither stricter nor more lenient regulations are allowed for Member States. However, this is not so clearly stipulated and, on closer inspection, 'harmonised' means neither 'full' nor 'partial'. The list of regulatory content in Art. 1(1) DA is not complete either, as the Chapters on unfair contract terms and on the application and enforcement of the Regulation are missing. If the provision had an independent regulatory content, it would remain unclear what should apply with re-

[13] See also Hennemann/Steinrötter NJW 2024, 1 (2); cf. on the open questions Bomhard MMR 2024, 71.
[14] Bomhard MMR 2024, 71.

gard to the provisions not listed.[15] Ultimately, it is probably only an **overview extract** at the beginning of the regulatory part.

II. Data covered

11 According to Art. 1(2) DA, the Regulation covers both personal and non-personal data. In the context of the DA, 'data' means any digital representation of acts, facts or information as well as compilations of such acts, facts or information, including in the form of sound, visual or audiovisual recordings (Art. 2 no. 1 DA). A distinction is made between different **categories of data** according to the individual Chapters of the Data Regulation:

- Chapter II DA applies to data relating to the performance, use and environment of connected products and related services (point (a)).
- Chapter III DA (point (b)) applies to all private sector data that is subject to legal obligations with regard to data transfer.
- In contrast, Chapter IV DA covers private sector data accessed and used on the basis of contractual agreements between businesses (point (c)).
- Chapter V DA (point (d)) applies to all private sector data focussing on non-personal data.
- Chapter VI DA applies to data and services processed by providers of data processing services (point (e)).
- Finally, Chapter VII DA applies to all non-personal data held in the EU by providers of data processing services (point (f)).

12 It is also not clear from Art. 1(2) DA whether this list has its own regulatory content or is merely intended to provide an overview. For example, the phrase **'private sector data'** could contain regulatory content in the sense that such data must be clearly distinguished from public sector data within the meaning of the DA. However, even this is not clearly regulated. What exactly is meant by the term is also not clear from the DA. There is no legal definition and nowhere outside of Art. 1(2) DA is any mention of 'private sector data'. Ultimately, Bomhard has already argued that this is probably just a declaratory formulation that creates (further) **ambiguity** for the user of the law.[16]

III. Addressees

13 Art. 1(3) DA specifies the addressees of the DA. Accordingly, the DA applies to

- **manufacturers** of IoT products placed on the EU market and **providers** of related services, regardless of where these manufacturers and providers are established (point (a)),
- the **users in the EU** of the products and services referred to in point (a) (point (b)),
- **data holders**, irrespective of their place of establishment, that make data available to data recipients in the EU (point (c)),

[15] Bomhard MMR 2024, 71.

[16] Bomhard MMR 2024, 71 (72).

- these same **data recipients** to whom data is made available (point (d)),
- **public sector bodies**, the EU Commission, the European Central Bank and EU bodies requesting data holders to provide data in the event of an exceptional need to use data for the performance of a specific task in the public interest, and the data holders making the data available (point (e)),
- **providers of data processing services**, irrespective of their place of establishment, who offer their services to customers in the EU (point (f)) and
- **participants in data spaces** and vendors of applications using **smart contracts** and persons whose trade, business or profession involves the use and deployment of smart contracts for others in the context of execution of an agreement (point (g)).

IV. Marketplace principle

With regard to the addressees of the DA, Art. 1 of the DA specifies the marketplace principle as decisive for the DA: A **specific reference to the EU** is required in order to be addressed by the Regulation. The DA should apply to all products, services and data offered in the EU. However, this requirement cannot be found verbatim in Art. 1(3)(e) and (g) DA. It remains to be seen whether this is due to a drafting error: In any case, the DA only applies in areas covered by European Union law.[17] 14

Ultimately, what matters is whether a product is placed on the market in the EU, a user is based in the EU, or a data processing service is offered to customers in the EU as intended. The establishment of the addressees of the Regulation is not decisive. 15

D. Relationship to other regulations and contract design

According to Art. 1(5), (6) subpara. 2 DA, the Regulation does not affect a number of existing EU legal acts. What exactly the **'without prejudice'** clause means for the respective normative relationship can only be determined on a case-by-case basis. In general, there is no clear definition of the relationship with the non-affected regulations. In case of doubt, both regulations apply and the conflict leads to practical challenges. 16

According to Art. 1(5) DA, the DA applies 'without prejudice' to the **GDPR**, the ePrivacy Directive 2002/58/EC and Regulation (EU) 2018/1725 on the protection of personal data. These regulations should **take precedence** in the event of an objection. 17

Art. 1(6) DA refers in subpara. 1 to the remaining **private autonomy**. Subpara. 2 stipulates that other legal acts are not to be affected by the DA: This applies to various legal acts on **criminal prosecution**, the maintenance of public order and the like, as well as to international cooperation in these areas. 18

[17] Bomhard MMR 2024, 71 (72).

I. Data protection and trade secret protection

19 Among other provisions, the DA contains rules governing the access to, use of, and sharing of personal data – activities which must always comply with data protection law. The relationship between the **GDPR** and the DA is addressed in Art. 1(5) DA. According to this, the DA 'is without prejudice to Union and national law on the protection of personal data, privacy, confidentiality of communications and integrity of terminal equipment', in particular the GDPR and the ePrivacy Directive.[18] The provisions of Chapter II DA (data transfer from companies to consumers and between companies) expressly supplement the right of access under Art. 15 GDPR and the right to data portability under Art. 20 GDPR, insofar as users are data subjects (on GDPR and Chapter II DA → Ch. 3 mn. 22).

20 In the event of a conflict between the provisions of the DA and the national provisions on data protection or the protection of privacy under Union law or adopted on the basis of Union law, the **data protection law shall prevail** (Art. 1(5) DA). The DA should not be interpreted and applied in such a way as to undermine data protection rights or the right to privacy and confidentiality of communications (rec. 7 DA). The Explanatory Memorandum to the draft already stated that the DA should be consistent with the GDPR and complement existing provisions.[19] However, a clear explanation of the relationship between the two Regulations is hardly found in the explanations given, which is a major point of criticism of the DA.[20] What is certain is that the DA does not constitute a legal basis for the processing of personal data within the meaning of Art. 6 GDPR.[21] This alone leads to **enormous legal uncertainty**.

21 If the data that is to be disclosed under the DA also contains **trade secrets**, the legislator's intention to facilitate data disclosure under the DA may conflict with the provisions on the protection of trade secrets. The main criticism is that the DA would limit the protection of trade secrets too much in favour of easier access to data. In particular, trade secrets are not excluded from the scope of the regulation, as is the case in the Open Data Directive.[22] Instead, possible objections in the event that trade secrets are affected have been regulated at individual points in the DA (see, for example, Art. 19(3), Art. 21(5), Art. 30(6) DA). However, these are difficult to apply and may not be fully thought through. The restrictions in the DA are restrictive and reflect the legislator's decision to **prioritise data access** over the protection of trade secrets.[23] This leads to a number of consequential challenges if innovation is to be strengthened at the same time.

[18] Directive 2002/58/EC of the European Parliament and of the Council of 12 July 2002 concerning the processing of personal data and the protection of privacy in the electronic communications sector (Directive on privacy and electronic communications), last updated by the Cookie Directive 2009/136/EC, OJ 2009 L 337, 11.

[19] COM(2022) 68 final, 3 et seq.; Steinrötter GRUR 2023, 216.

[20] Steinrötter GRUR 2023, 216 (217); Wiebe GRUR 2023, 1569 (1574); Hennemann/Steinrötter NJW 2024, 1 (5 et seq.).

[21] Wiebe GRUR 2023, 1569 (1574).

[22] Pauly/Wichert/Baumann MMR 2024, 211.

[23] Pauly/Wichert/Baumann MMR 2024, 211 (215).

II. Freedom of contract

In principle, the principle of freedom of contract also applies in the context of the DA. However, when considering the various provisions of the DA which also affect the drafting of contracts, this is not entirely the case: The provisions of the DA must be observed when drafting contracts in the future and will regulate them.[24] Accordingly with Art. 1(6) subpara. 1, (10) DA, this is also recognised by the DA and the DA does not prevent voluntary, lawful data sharing contracts, provided that they comply with the requirements of the Regulation. Whether this leads to a **restriction of contractual design**[25] depends on the perspective – the regulations will have a restrictive effect on those actors in the data economy who are bound by the DA and must, for example, grant data access in a certain way.[26] 22

The **model contractual terms** to be published by the Commission pursuant to Art. 41 DA will also be of great importance: Even if these are non-binding and therefore not legally binding, they have the potential to have a de facto effect depending on the negotiating position. They can serve as a benchmark in negotiations, as well as an indication of what might be reasonable and balanced in a subsequent judicial (or official) review. On 19.11.2025 the Commissions draft of the model contractual terms was approved and published.[27] The model contractual terms have been designed for a variety of use cases. The terms in Annex II of the Communication have been designed for contracts between a data holder and a user of a connected product or related service, where the data holder wishes to use data generated using the product or service. In Annex III there are terms designed for contracts between a user of a connected product or related service and a third-party data recipient under Art. 5 DA. Terms in Annex IV have been designed for contracts between a data holder and a third-party data recipient who is a business, where a data holder is obliged (under Art. 6 DA) to make data available to a recipient when requested to do so by a user of the product. The terms may also be used with appropriate amendments where a data holder is obliged to make data available to a third-party data recipient under other Union law or national legislation adopted under Union law. And lastly the terms in Annex V have been designed for contracts between a data sharer and a data recipient where the data sharer wishes to make data available to a data recipient voluntarily and independent of any request by a user or similar party. Parties can now identify their own situation and use the therefore applicable model contractual terms if they wish to. 23

E. Entry into force and implementation period

Art. 50 DA regulates its entry into force and the date of application. The DA came into force on the twentieth day after its publication, i.e. on 2.1.2024, but most of its provisions will only be directly applicable from 12.9.2025. 24

---

[24] Moos/Arning in Moos Datenschutz A. mn. 15.10a et seq. speak of 'specifications' for the drafting of the contract.

[25] Thus Bomhard/Siglmüller in Redeker IT-Verträge-HdB 9.6 Datenlizenzvertrag mn. 12.

[26] This is discussed in detail in the following sections, in particular with regard to data access claims and abuse control.

[27] C(2025) 7750 final.

I. Validity from September 2025

25 Specifically, the **obligation to make data available** in Chapter III DA applies to all obligations under EU law from 12.9.2025. Where data provision is required under national law, the provisions of Chapter III DA only apply if the national legislation enters into force after 12.9.2025. Therefore, there is no obligation to adapt the DA requirements to existing regulations; Member States are free to adopt them on a voluntary basis.

26 The **contract design** obligations from Chapter IV DA apply to contracts concluded after 12.9.2025. The requirements will only apply to old contracts from 12.9.2027 if the contracts run indefinitely or are due to end on or after 11.1.2034. This ensures that long-term adjustments can be made.

II. Product design obligations: applicable only from September 2026

27 An exception to the date of application in 2025 is the obligation under Art. 3(1) DA to design and manufacture connected products or to design and provide related services in such a way that the data is directly accessible to the user. This **product design obligation** only applies to connected products that are put on the market after 12.9.2026.

28 Caution is advised in that the data access requirements will also apply from 2025, as will all other requirements of the DA. For example, information on available data according to Art. 3(2) and (3) DA must be provided from 12.9.2025; data holders must be granted access to existing data from 12.9.2025. Only the implementation period for the obligation to consider the product design itself is longer.

29 It is questionable to which products this applies, in particular what is meant by the moment of **'placing on the market'**: Does it refer to the placing on the market of a specific product type, e.g. a 2026 car model, or to the conclusion of each individual supply contract for a specific product? It is also questionable whether it depends on the time of the first conclusion of the contract for a connected product or on the time of the first actual making available of the product. According to Art. 2 no. 22 DA, placing on the market means 'the first making available of a connected product on the Union market'. This indicates that it is the actual making available of a specific product version in the EU that is relevant and not the time of the first conclusion of the contract or the individual distribution. This means that contracts can also be concluded at an earlier stage without the validity of the DA being circumvented if the products are only available later.

30 The postponement of the date of application to 2026 has been made because the product concept – the product design – involves **considerable effort**. Manufacturers need the time between the Regulation's entry into force in January 2024 and its application date in September 2026 to have any chance of implementing the requirements with reasonable effort and in compliance with the Charter of Fundamental Rights.

31 In fact, the implementation period only runs until September 2026 if the date when the product is actually made available on the market is decisive, but the validity of the DA could not be postponed by concluding a contract earlier.

A more differentiated assessment is required as to whether the first placing on the market of a specific product version is also relevant or whether each individual placing on the market of an individual product has to be taken into account. 32

The assumption that it depends on the **product version or series** is supported by the fact that, otherwise, series developed earlier may no longer be marketed without adjustments after 12.9.2026. If a series starts before 12.9.2026, Art. 3(1) DA would otherwise have to be observed for this product if further distribution takes place after 12.9.2026. For example, if a car model from 2025 continues to be sold. The argument against this is that it would be almost impossible to set a uniform date and – also with regard to sustainability concerns – established series and versions could no longer be made available on the market without modifications. In addition, this would be the only way that the implementation period would actually run until 12.9.2026, since once a product version has been designed and manufactured, this process is complete, even if the series is distributed over a longer period of time. An argument against this – and in favour of focusing on the **distribution of each individual product** – is that otherwise the validity of the DA for individual products could be postponed indefinitely. 33

In product liability law, the ECJ confirms that a product is placed on the market 'when it leaves the production process operated by the producer and enters a marketing process in the form in which it is offered to the public in order to be used or consumed'.[28] Reference is made to a single product, which argues against the above consideration that products first marketed before 12.9.2026 may continue to be marketed in their series and version after 12.9.2026. The ECJ confirms a broad understanding of the term in product liability cases involving compensation for damage. The **unity of the legal system** also argues in favour of a transfer to the understanding of the term under the DA; the Commission's aim is to apply it as widely as possible in order to increase the data economy as much as possible. 34

Ultimately, however, a **narrower understanding of the term**, according to which it depends on the actual first provision of a connected product of a version or series, is convincing in view of the aspect of sustainability and the considerable intervention in the provision of used products for the DA. This strikes an appropriate **balance** between the various interests in the **widest** possible **application of the DA** on the one hand and the protection of manufacturers' **commercial interests** on the other. An unchanged transfer of ECJ case law is also not required from the point of view of the unity of the legal system, since the DA is concerned with economic promotion and not, as in product liability, with risks of damage. 35

F. Symmetrical vs. asymmetrical regulation of the data economy

As a symmetrical regulatory approach, the DA basically addresses all sectors in principle and does not differentiate between them. Sector-specific regulatory approaches to the data economy are already being developed. These will asymmetrically establish special regulations for the sectors addressed in each case. 36

Among the planned sectoral regulatory projects is the European Health Data Space (**EHDS**) published as Regulation (EU) 2025/327 in March 2025. This is the 37

[28] ECJ 9.2.2006 – case C-127/04, ECLI:EU:C:2006:93 para. 27.

first Regulation for a sector-specific common European data space, as proposed in the European Data Strategy.[29] The aim of the EHDS is to improve people's access to and control over their **health data** for the purposes of healthcare, research, innovation and other secondary uses.[30] Other specific data spaces currently being planned are the **Mobility Data Space**,[31] a Common European Energy Data Space and data spaces for public administration.

38 In December 2023, the Committee of the Regions called on the Commission to 'put forward without delay a specific proposal on access to non-personal data – along the lines of the Data Act – also for the **automotive sector**, with a view to promoting the data economy and new business models'.[32] Such a proposal is currently being drafted in Brussels and it is to be expected that the regulations will not lag behind those of the DA.

---

[29] COM(2022) 197 final, 1.

[30] Overview in Ruff/Schreiber EuDIR 2025 (in print).

[31] European Commission, 'Communication from the Commission to the European Parliament, the Council, the European Economic and Social Committee and the Committee of the Regions: Creation of a common European mobility data space' (29.11.2023), COM(2023) 751 final.

[32] Committee of the Regions, 'Opinion' (22.12.2023) <https://eur-lex.europa.eu/eli/C/2023/1328/oj/eng> (last accessed: 7.1.2026), mn. 41.

CHAPTER 3
DATA ACCESS AND MAKING DATA AVAILABLE

Bibliography: Antoine, 'Datenzugangsrechte im finalen Data Act – Fortschritt, Rückschritt, neue Fragen? Schlüssel zur Förderung datengetriebener Geschäftsmodelle?', CR 2024, 1; Antoine, 'Datenzugang im Spannungsfeld zwischen DS-GVO, Geschäftsgeheimnisschutz und Datenbankherstellerrecht', CR 2024, 7; Assion/Willecke, 'Der EU Data Act. Die neuen Regelungen zu vernetzten Produkten und Diensten', MMR 2023, 805; Bomhard, 'Der Anwendungsbereich des Data Act. Offene Fragen rund um Art. 1 DA', MMR 2024, 71; Bomhard/Merkle, 'Der Entwurf eines EU Data Acts', RDi 2022, 168; Drexl et al., 'Position Statement of the Max Planck Institute for Innovation and Competition of 25 May 2022 on the Commission's Proposal of 23 February 2022 for a Regulation on harmonised rules on fair access to and use of data (Data Act)' (17.7.2022) <https://pure.mpg.de/rest/items/item_3388757_4/component/file_3395639/content> (last accessed: 7.1.2026; cited as: Drexl et al. Position Statement); Ducuing/Margoni/Schirru, 'White Paper on the Data Act Proposal' (CiTiP Working Paper, 26.10.2022) <https://openfuture.eu/wp-content/uploads/2022/10/CiTiP_WhitePaperDataAct.pdf> (last accessed: 7.1.2026; cited as: Ducuing/Margoni/Schirru White Paper on the Data Act Proposal); Ehlen/Sebulke, 'Der Data Act: Zwischen Markt- und Vertragsgestaltung. Auswirkungen auf die Ausgestaltung von Datenüberlassungsverträgen aus der Perspektive von Nutzern', CR 2024, 84; Etzkorn, '(Vertragliche) Datenzugangsansprüche nach dem Data Act', RDi 2024, 116; Grapentin, 'Datenzugangsansprüche und Geschäftsgeheimnisse der Hersteller im Lichte des Data Act', RDi 2023, 173; Habich, 'FRAND Access to Data: Perspectives from the FRAND Licensing of Standard-Essential Patents for the Data Act Proposal and the Digital Markets Act', IIC 2022, 1343; Heimgärtner, 'Handlungsvorschlag zum Vorgehen im Rahmen der Sachmängelhaftung bzgl. der von den Manipulationsvorwürfen betroffenen VW-Dieselfahrzeuge (Verbrauchsgüterkauf)', DAR 2015, 622; Heinzke/Herbers/Kraus, 'Datenzugangsansprüche nach dem Data Act', BB 2024, 649; Hennemann/Steinrötter, 'Der Data Act. Neue Instrumente, alte Friktionen, strukturelle Weichenstellungen', NJW 2024, 1; Kim, 'Der Datenbankschutz sui generis nach dem Data Act', MMR 2024, 87; Kirchhefer-Lauber, 'Verbraucherverträge über digitale Produkte', JuS 2021, 1125; Körber, 'Orange-Book-Standard Revisited. Zugleich Anmerkung zu EuGH, 16.7.2015 – C-170/13 – Huawei Technologies/ZTE u.a.', WRP 2015, 1167; Krüger/Wiencke/Koch, 'Der Datenpool als Geschäftsgeheimnis', GRUR 2020, 578; Lorenzen, 'Geschäftsgeheimnisschutz und Data Act', ZGE 2022, 250; Louven, 'Vorschriften im Data Act zur Ausgestaltung und Kompensation von Datenbereitstellungspflichten', MMR 2024, 82; Metzger/Schweitzer, 'Shaping Markets: A Critical Evaluation of the Draft Data Act', ZEuP 2023, 42; Pauly/Wichert/Baumann, 'Schutz von Geschäftsgeheimnissen nach dem Data Act', MMR 2024, 211; Podszun/Bongartz/Kirk, 'Digital Markets Act – Neue Regeln für Fairness in der Plattformökonomie', NJW 2022, 3249; Podszun/Offergeld, 'Zugang zu Daten nach dem europäischen Datengesetz (Data Act)', WiVerw 2023, 103; Podszun/Pfeifer, 'Datenzugang nach dem EU Data Act: Der Entwurf der Europäischen Kommission', GRUR 2022, 953; Radauer et al., 'Study on the legal protection of trade secrets in the context of the data economy – Final report' (Publications Office of the European Union, 2022) <https://data.europa.eu/doi/10.2826/021443> (last accessed: 7.1.2026; cited as: Radauer et al. Study on the legal protection of trade secrets); Rammos/Wilken, 'Der Data Act – Chancen und Risiken für Unternehmen durch das geplante europäische Datengesetz', DB 2022, 1241; Sattler/Zech, 'The Data Act: First Assessments', Trier 2024; Schmidt-Kessel, 'Heraus- und Weitergabe von IoT-Gerätedaten', MMR 2024, 75; Schreiber, 'Die Anforderungen an die Datenqualität: Regulatorische Umbrüche für Daten in der Produkt-Compliance', ZfPC 2025, 46; Specht-Riemenschneider, 'Der Entwurf des Data Act', MMR 2022, 809; Steege, 'Technische Schutzmaßnahmen des Dateninhabers im Data Act: Der Regelungsgehalt des Art. 11 Abs. 1 DA', MMR 2024, 91; Steinrötter, 'Verhältnis von Data Act und DS-GVO. Zugleich ein Beitrag zur Konkurrenzlehre im Rahmen der EU-Digitalgesetzgebung', GRUR 2023, 216; Weiß, 'Streitbeilegung nach Art. 10 Data Act', MMR 2024, 101; Wiebe, 'Schutz von Maschinendaten durch das sui-generis-Schutzrecht für Datenbanken', GRUR 2017, 338; Wiebe, 'Access rights at the Intersection with Database Rights and Trade Secret Protection', GRUR 2023, 227; Wiebe, 'Der Data Act – Innovation oder Illusion?', GRUR 2023, 1569; Wiedemann/Conrad/Salemi, 'Bereitstellung von Daten nach dem Data Act – offene Fragen und verbleibende Probleme', K&R 2024, 157.

A. Regulation system 1
I. Structure 2
II. Exemptions for SMEs 9

B. Actors 12

C. Subject matter of the data access 24
I. Connected products 25
II. Related services 29
III. Usage data and no content data 37

IV. Virtual assistants 43

D. Data access rights 45
I. Factual data access claim: access by design 46
1. Obligated party 47
2. Material organisation 48
3. Generated data 52
4. User account 54
5. Legal consequences of non-compliance 55
6. Deviating agreements 60
II. Making data available by the data holder 61
III. Sharing data with third-party data recipients 68
IV. Duty to provide information 75
V. Data protection law and data access 82
VI. Restrictions on data access outside of data protection law 89
1. Security requirements 90
2. Restriction of competition pursuant to Art. 4(10), Art. 6(2)(e) DA 92
3. Relationship to trade secrets law 96
a) Data as a trade secret 98
b) Protection mechanisms in case of a data access request by the user 100
aa) Appropriate confidentiality measures as a prerequisite for access 102
bb) Withholding of data sharing in the event of a lack of secrecy 107
cc) Refusal of access in the event of serious economic damage 111
c) Protection mechanisms in case of a data access request in favour of third parties pursuant to Art. 5 DA 114
d) Technical protective measures in accordance with Art. 11(1) DA 117
e) Requirements for demonstrating the existence of a trade secret 120
4. No restrictions from database law 122
5. Restrictions arising from competition law 126
VII. Limitations on the use and disclosure of data by the data holder 127
1. Limited data use 129
2. Prohibition of data sharing 131

E. Making data available 132
I. Requirements for making data available 136
1. Area of application 137
a) Business-to-business relations 137
b) Obligation to make data available 142
c) Time of application 143
2. Making data available on FRAND terms 144
a) Fair, reasonable and not discriminatory 147
b) Procedure for determining FRAND 149
3. Transparency requirement 153
4. Ineffectiveness of unfair contract terms 156
5. Prohibition of discrimination 158
6. Protection of the user's data sovereignty 159
II. Compensation for making data available 160
III. Dispute settlement 166
1. Area of application 167
2. Requirements for certification 171
3. Costs 175
4. Relationship with courts and other bodies 176
5. Effect of the decision 177

A. Regulation system

Chapter II DA regulates the 'business-to-consumer and business-to-business data sharing', and thus governs the **central element of the DA**[1] in Art. 3–7. This is followed in Chapter III DA entitled 'Obligations for data holders obliged to make data available pursuant to Union law'. Systematically, this Chapter III DA is consistent with the new and essential obligations to which the regulations apply, namely the data access and making data available obligations standardised in Chapter II DA. 1

I. Structure

The requirements of Chapter II DA are internally challenging. A clear system is only apparent at second glance and the prima facie coherent sequence is repeatedly disrupted when analysed in detail. 2

The **anchor provision is Art. 3(1) DA**, which contains a passively formulated **product design obligation** that applies from 12.9.2026 to products placed on the market after this date (on the concept of placing on the market → Ch. 2 mn. 27): 'Connected products shall be designed and manufactured, and related services shall be designed and provided, in such a way that the product data and related service data […] are by default […] directly accessible to the user.' This lays the foundation for data access requirements. The aim is comprehensive **'access by design'**. 3

In order to be able to use the access right, Art. 3 DA provides for comprehensive **information obligations** in para. 2 and 3, in which the entities providing the product or service inform the user comprehensively about which data is accessible and how. 4

If data access requires the cooperation of an actor other than the user, Art. 4 DA then obliges the data holder to comply with this and to actually provide the corresponding product and related service data (**obligation to make available**). The standard thus covers cases in which the product design obligation under Art. 3(1) DA – lawfully or unlawfully – is not implemented in such a way that access can take place without further ado; a purely factual prerequisite for the activation of the mechanism in Art. 4 DA is that the user cannot directly access the corresponding data. 5

To round things off, Art. 5 DA then provides for the **right of users to share data** with third parties; this primarily concerns the authorisation of the so-called data recipients, who may use the data for offers of follow-up and value-added services etc., and must comply with the obligations set out in Art. 6 DA. 6

In their basic structure, the data access and making available obligations of Chapter II DA build on each other or interlock as follows: 7

[1] Antoine CR 2024, 1, for example, refers to these regulations as the 'centrepiece'.

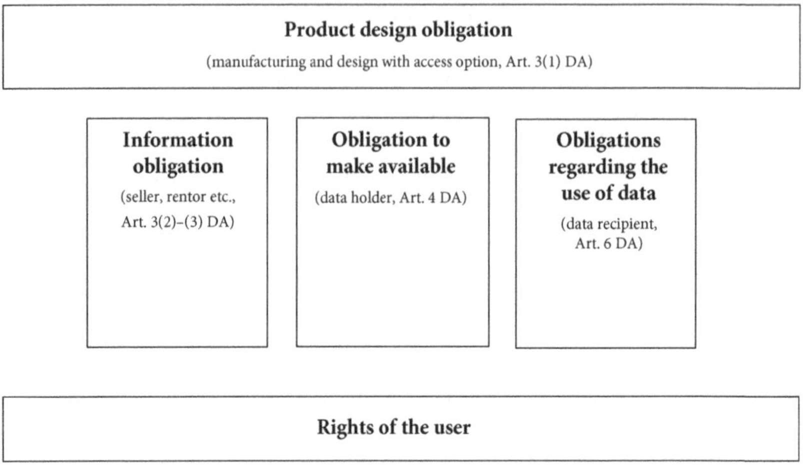

Fig. 1: Data access and making available obligations.

8 The **interplay** of the individual rights and obligations is **complex** in detail, especially as there remains room for interpretation as to which actors are obliged in detail and how these obligations can be enforced, both through direct claims or official proceedings and possibly through the assertion of product defects (see in detail → mn. 12 et seqq., 47 et seqq., 166 et seqq.).

II. Exemptions for SMEs

9 Pursuant to Art. 7(1) subpara. 1 DA, data generated during the use of connected products manufactured by a **micro- or small enterprise** are generally exempt from the obligations of Chapter II DA. Data of related services are also excluded if the related services are provided by a micro- or small enterprise. In EU law, micro- or small enterprises are usually defined as such in accordance with Commission Recommendation 2003/361/EC or Annex I to the GBER.[2] These are companies with less than 50 employees and an annual turnover or annual balance sheet of no more than 10 million EUR (small companies). Microenterprises end with ten employees and an annual turnover or annual balance sheet of max. 2 million EUR. According to both documents, when calculating the thresholds, not only the legal entity must be taken into account, but also partner companies – especially those with a controlling influence. It is therefore surprising that Art. 7(1) subpara. 1 DA, despite its reference to Recommendation 2003/361/EC, emphasises precisely this once again.

10 The exception does not apply, so that Art. 3 et seqq. DA apply, if the micro- or small enterprise has been **subcontracted** with the manufacture or design of the connected product or the provision of a related service. This avoids circumvention constellations, although it remains questionable whether the exception also applies if the client is also a micro- or small enterprise. The aim is to ensure that the excep-

[2] Commission Regulation (EU) No 651/2014 of 17 June 2014 declaring certain categories of aid compatible with the internal market in application of Articles 107 and 108 of the Treaty on the Functioning of the European Union, OJ 2014 L 187, 1.

tion does not apply if a medium-sized or large enterprise can exert decisive influence (and contribute corresponding financial resources) as the client.

11 A temporary privilege through an exception from Art. 3 et seqq. DA, Art. 7(1) subpara. 2 DA also provides for two types of exemption for **medium-sized enterprises:**[3] The exemption applies for one year in each case, namely (1) if the enterprise has just crossed the threshold to become a medium-sized enterprise or (2) for the first year after a medium-sized enterprise places a connected product on the market.

B. Actors

12 The provisions on data access rights under Chapter II DA recognise different actors, each with their own rights and obligations, in particular:

- manufacturers,
- data holders,
- contractual partner of the user (seller, rentor, lessor, service provider),
- users,
- third parties as recipients of data.

13 Among the various actors, two are fixed in every case: manufacturer and user (rec. 6 DA). All others can be identical to the manufacturer (data holder, contractual partner) and user (data recipient) or different persons.

14 The precise definitions of terms and roles in Chapter II DA can be structured as follows, although there is still room for interpretation:

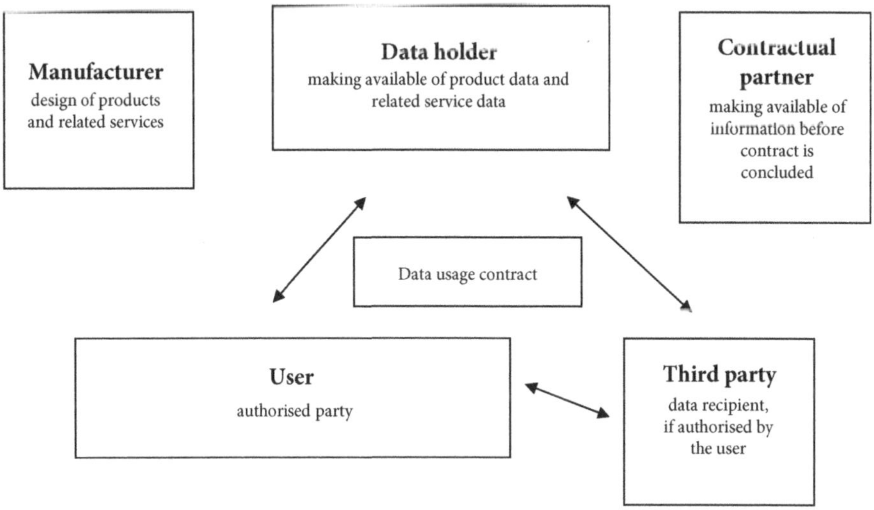

Fig. 2: Actors according to Chapter II DA.

[3] According to Art. 2 of Commission Recommendation 2003/361/EC, these are companies with fewer than 250 employees and either an annual turnover of no more than 50 million EUR or an annual balance sheet total of no more than 43 million EUR.

15 The **manufacturer** is not legally defined in the Data Act. The term can be found in the regulatory part, in particular in Art. 1(3)(a) DA, but without further indications for the interpretation of the term. The recitals provide an indication of the understanding of the term: For example, according to rec. 6 DA, there is the 'designer or manufacturer' of a connected product, who decides on the design according to rec. 14, 15 DA. Manufacturers have 'control of the technical design of the connected products or related services' (rec. 20 DA). There may also be several manufacturers (rec. 21 DA). The term will ultimately have to be **interpreted in a result-oriented manner**: The manufacturer, within the meaning of the Data Act, is the person who determines and controls the design of a connected product and who can actually and legally influence it. This is because the Data Act focuses on the product, without explicitly making the manufacturer liable: According to Art. 3(1) DA, products must be manufactured and designed in such a way that data access is possible.

16 In contrast, the **data holder** is legally defined in the Regulation and directly obligated. The data holder may be the manufacturer (rec. 21 DA), but another person (another legal entity) may also be the data holder. According to Art. 2 no. 13 DA, the data holder is 'a natural or legal person that has the right or obligation, in accordance with this Regulation, applicable Union law or national legislation adopted in accordance with Union law, to use and make available data, including, where contractually agreed, product data or related service data which it has retrieved or generated during the provision of a related service'. The definition is circular: Obliged *is* anyone who *has* the right or obligation under the DA (or other legal norms) to use and make data available retrieved or generated during the provision of a related service.

17 The primary concern is that the data holder has the right or obligation to use and make available the data concerned. This must be in compliance with the applicable law, but the obligation or authorisation as such does not have to arise therefrom ('in accordance with').

18 This understanding of the term is also in line with rec. 25 DA, according to which the DA does not grant the data holder a new right to use data, but is based on what already exists (rec. 25 DA). Taking into account the meaning and purpose with regard to the central obligation standard for data holders (Art. 4 DA), the data holder is anyone who lawfully holds control over the data to which the user is to have access in accordance with the provisions of Chapter II DA. Similarly, the data holder is also legally defined in Art. 2 no. 8 DGA as the person who is authorised to grant access to certain data or to share it. The requirement that the data holder also has actual control over the conception was abandoned in the course of the Regulation procedure;[4] only the **legal authorisation** is decisive.

19 As a rule, the data holder will therefore also be **the controller** within the meaning of Art. 4 no. 7 GDPR, as it exercises control over the data.[5] **Processors** within the meaning of Art. 4 no. 8 GDPR cannot be data holders. This issue remained unresolved during the legislative process,[6] but was clarified in the final version of the Regulation: 'Processors as defined in Article 4, point (8), of Regulation (EU) 2016/679 are not considered to act as data holders.'[7] This is convincing insofar as

[4] See Schmidt-Kessel MMR 2024, 75 (77).
[5] See also Steinrötter GRUR 2023, 216 (219).
[6] Steinrötter GRUR 2023, 216 (219 et seq.).
[7] Rec. 22 DA; see also rec. 29 DA.

the processor does not decide on the purpose and means of data processing and therefore has no legal authorisation to grant access to the data: It is subject to instructions and is only authorised to grant access if the controller instructs it to do so within the meaning of Art. 4 no. 7 GDPR.

In addition to the manufacturer and data holder, the obligated parties also include the **contractual partners** of the users, who are sellers, rentors or lessees of connected products or providers of related services. The seller, rentor or lessor may also be the manufacturer (rec. 24, Art. 3(2) DA), but may also be different parties. The decisive factor is who maintains direct legal contact with the user and is therefore in a position to fulfil the information obligations of Art. 3(2), (3) DA. 20

On the opposite side to the authorised parties is the **user**. The user is the linchpin of all data access claims, as he or she determines whether and how access is granted, including to the data recipients. According to Art. 2 no. 12 DA, a user is 'a natural or legal person that owns a connected product or to whom temporary rights to use the connected product have been contractually transferred, or that receives related services'. The decisive factor is who holds certain (permanent or temporary) rights to the product and the data generated by its use, as owner, renter or lessee (rec. 18 DA). There may also be several users, for example in the case of co-ownership or if the owner, renter and lessee share rights to access or use the data (rec. 18, 21 DA). The decisive factor is who is legally authorised to use the connected product and the related service. Rec. 5 DA summarises the objective of the DA: 'This Regulation ensures that users of a connected product or related service in the Union can access, in a timely manner, the data generated by the use of that connected product or related service and that those users can use the data, including by sharing them with third parties of their choice.' As the user bears the risks of using the connected products, he should also have the right of access (rec. 18 DA).[8] The Data Act establishes a system strictly orientated around the user as the central actor, a **'user-centric model'** that gives users the strongest position.[9] 21

Data subjects within the meaning of Art. 4 no. 1 GDPR are to be distinguished from the user:[10] Users and data subjects can, but do not have to be identical (rec. 7 DA).[11] If the user is not also a data subject, the user becomes the controller within the meaning of Art. 4 no. 7 GDPR through the right of access and the related data processing. Depending on the structure, there may be **joint controllership** within the meaning of Art. 26 GDPR with the data holder. In most cases, however, this is unlikely because the data holder and the user process the data for different purposes: the data holder to fulfil its legal obligations under the Data Act, the user for its own purposes that deviate from this. In this case, however, there is no common purpose characterising the joint responsibility. Such joint controllership is more likely to exist between the user and the third-party data recipient. This is because the user ultimately determines the purpose and can also choose a structure in which the data recipient and user jointly determine this within the meaning of Art. 26 GDPR. 22

The user may also request that the data be shared with a **third party**, who will then be considered a **data recipient**. According to Art. 2 no. 14 DA, the data recipient 'means a natural or legal person, acting for purposes which are related to that 23

[8] See also Hennemann/Steinrötter NJW 2024, 1 (2).
[9] Antoine CR 2024, 1 (2 mn. 3).
[10] On the relationship of access claims to data protection law → mn. 82 et seq.
[11] Steinrötter GRUR 2023, 216 (220).

person's trade, business, craft or profession, other than the user of a connected product or related service, to whom the data holder makes data available'. According to the further definition, data recipients are also ('including') third parties 'following a request by the user to the data holder or in accordance with a legal obligation under Union law or national legislation adopted in accordance with Union law'. The data recipient thus becomes the actor in the network of DA protagonists whose activities could generate the enormous increases in GDP and turnover that the Commission expects (→ mn. 68). The data recipient receives data directly from the data holder at the request of the user and uses it for value-added and support offers, but not for competitive offers (→ mn. 92 et seqq.). Excluded from the position of data recipient are the so-called **gatekeepers**, i.e. the digital players with a strong market position, which were qualified by the Commission as already strong players under the Digital Markets Act (Regulation (EU) 2022/1925) (Art. 5(3) DA). These should not become even stronger as a result of the Data Act. If a data recipient is involved, a (to be contractually regulated, → mn. 132 et seqq.) triangular relationship arises:

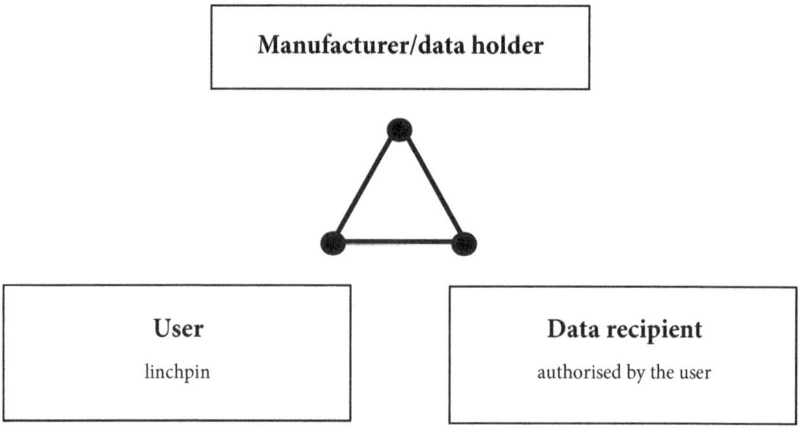

Fig. 3: Triangular relationship of manufacturer/data holder, user and data recipient.

C. Subject matter of the data access

24 Data access is granted to certain data from connected products and services related to them. This includes data generated during the use of **IoT products**, regardless of whether it is personal or non-personal. As clear as this initial access appears, however, it is challenging to define in detail which products, which services and which data are actually covered by the Data Act's data access claim.

I. Connected products

25 A connected product to whose data access is to be granted is legally defined in **Art. 2 no. 5 DA** as 'an item that obtains, generates or collects data concerning its use or environment and that is able to communicate product data via an electronic communications service, physical connection or on-device access, and whose pri-

mary function is not the storing, processing or transmission of data on behalf of any party other than the user'.

The following attributes define the term: 26

- **Item**: A real product is required, pure software offerings are not covered. Chapter II of the Data Act addresses **IoT products**.
- **Data** about the use or environment that is obtained, generated or collected and is to be distinguished from pure content data.
- **Communication capability**: The product must be able to make the product data accessible. The way in which this can be technically realised is irrelevant. It can be an electronic communication link via telecommunication networks or a purely physical interface.
- **Exception**: Products whose main function is to process data on behalf of a party other than the user are excluded; these are cloud and server infrastructures. **Prototypes** are also outside the scope of the Data Act (rec. 14 DA).

Such products are, for example, the initial ideas in the regulatory process for 27 **aircraft** that could be used in future to call on a company other than the manufacturer for maintenance services, large **wind farms** and **connected cars**. The Data Act is asymmetrical and does not relate to specific sectors: 'Connected products are found in all aspects of the economy and society, including in private, civil or commercial infrastructure, vehicles, health and lifestyle equipment, ships, aircraft, home equipment and consumer goods, medical and health devices or agricultural and industrial machinery' (rec. 14 DA).

Smartphones are also such a 'connected product': In the original Commission 28 draft, rec. 15 of the DA-proposal explicitly excluded smartphones: 'In contrast, certain products that are primarily designed to display or play content, or to record and transmit content, amongst others for the use by an online service should not be covered by this Regulation. Such products include, for example, personal computers, servers, tablets and smart phones [...].' The exception still contained in the final text of the Data Act is formulated much more narrowly. Products are only exempt if their 'primary function is the storing, processing or transmission of data on behalf of any party other than the user'. These are not smartphones because the user is regularly also the party for whom the smartphone works. Also, the main function of the smartphone is not the processing or transmission of data, but the facilitation of communication services, which are regularly labelled as such. In addition, there are the examples that are included for the exception in rec. 16 DA: It is about cloud server structures that a provider operates for its customers. In this case, the difficult-to-access wording within the scope of the exception that it concerns functions 'for parties, who are not the user' also makes sense.

II. Related services

The definition of related services is more challenging: According to Chapter II 29 DA, access must be granted to product data and related service data. The related services thus move to the centre of the access claims, while data generated by non-related services are not the subject matter of the access claims. This directly shows how **fundamental** the **distinction** between connected and non-related services is.

30 According to Art. 2 no. 6 DA, a related service is 'a digital service, other than an electronic communications service, including software, which is connected with the product at the time of the purchase, rent or lease in such a way that its absence would prevent the connected product from performing one or more of its functions, or which is subsequently connected to the product by the manufacturer or a third party to add to, update or adapt the functions of the connected product'. In view of the lack of significance of the time of the connection and the broad definition of 'service', the decisive factor for qualification as a related service is whether the connection between the service and the product is sufficiently close: The product must be unable to perform its **functions** without the service.

31 According to the DA, examples of such services are 'auxiliary consulting, analytics or financial services, or regular repair and maintenance' (rec. 17 DA). Such a close connection is probably closer to the **operating system** of a laptop, the **control software** of a robot or the **map software** on a navigation system.

32 Such a close connection is also required in the Sale of Goods Directive (EU) 2019/771 for the qualification of goods as **goods with a digital element**. According to Art. 2 no. 5(b), goods with digital elements are 'tangible movable items that incorporate or are inter-connected with digital content or a digital service in such a way that the absence of that digital content or digital service would prevent the goods from performing their functions'. The Sale of Goods Directive (EU) 2019/771 is implemented in Germany through the provisions on the sale of digital consumer goods regulated in §§ 474 et seqq. of the German Civil Code (BGB) and legally defined in § 327a(3) sent. 1 BGB as follows: 'Goods that incorporate or are inter-connected with digital products in such a way that the absence of those digital products would prevent the goods from performing their functions (goods with digital elements)'. The parallel to the definition of related services is obvious from a linguistic point of view.

33 The debate on the demarcation of goods with digital elements has progressed further. A 'closest connection' is required.[12] This is considered to be the case if there is a causality between the purpose of the item and the digital element as the means by which the purpose is to be achieved.[13] A product cannot fulfil its function without the digital element if it is no longer functional as a whole according to the public perception, i.e. if it loses more than just part of its functionality.[14] In the case of a smartphone, for example, the pre-installed operating system including standardised and pre-installed applications such as alarm and camera functions are to be 'digital elements' of the goods, whereas (even pre-installed) weather apps are not.[15]

34 In practice, an **overall assessment** will then have to be made, in the context of which **indications** may include whether the corresponding service is also offered individually, is not linked to the product in every offer or can be optionally purchased with the product as a bundle or not. It will also depend on the extent to which the product can be used without the service. The contract design is an indicator here; related services will regularly (have to) be offered with the connected product in a uniform contract, as otherwise the product cannot fulfil its functions.

---

[12] Fries in BeckOGK BGB § 327a mn. 13; Steinrötter in Staudinger BGB § 327a mn. 22.
[13] Kirchhefer-Lauber JuS 2021, 1125 (1226).
[14] Metzger in MüKoBGB § 327a mn. 12; Schulze in HK-BGB § 327a mn. 6.
[15] Rec. 21 DID Directive (EU) 2019/770; Fries in BeckOGK BGB § 327a mn. 17.

'Users could reasonably expect them to be provided taking into account the nature of the connected product and any public statement made [...] in previous links of the chain of transactions' (rec. 17 DA).

In any case, services 'which do not have an impact on the operation of the connected product and which do not involve the transmitting of data or commands to the connected product by the service provider' are **excluded** (rec. 17 DA). 35

It is significant that, according to rec. 17 DA, a related service is to be affirmed in the event of doubt. This is not consistent with the wording and the intensity of the interference of Chapter II DA, but is probably in line with the meaning and purpose of the most effective and far-reaching, effective data access claims. Whether an **'in dubio pro related service'** will actually prevail in practice, however, is more than questionable for dogmatic reasons alone: The obligations under Chapter II DA are far-reaching **encroachments** on the freedom to conduct a business of producers, data holders and providers, which are enshrined in the **Charter of Fundamental Rights**. Interference requires a clear legal basis, which is difficult to see in a 'doubt' sentence in the recitals. 36

III. Usage data and no content data

Access must be granted to and provided for the **usage data** from the connected products and related services, specifically the so-called product data and related service data. 37

'**Product data** means data generated by the use of a connected product that the manufacturer designed to be retrievable, via an electronic communications service, physical connection or on-device access, by a user, data holder or a third party, including, where relevant, the manufacturer'.[16] The decisive factor is that it is data that is **generated** through the **use of** the product. The definition of the term is not very helpful, as it can be found in the respective access and making data available obligations and is self-evident anyway, given that provisions cannot demand the impossible. The definition directly reflects a core idea of the DA: The user should have access to the data in accordance with Chapter II of the DA because it is the user himself who directly enables its generation and creation in the first place by using it. It is categorised as an **imbalance** and unfair that, in the opinion of the regulators, users have had little or insufficient access to this data to date, even though it would not exist without their involvement.[17] 38

Accordingly, **related service data** as defined in Art. 2 no. 16 DA is 'data representing the digitisation of user actions or of events related to the connected product, recorded intentionally by the user or generated as a by-product of the user's action during the provision of a related service by the provider'. Here, too, the focus is on data generated through use, through **user actions**, whether intentional or incidental. This data would also not exist without the actual use. Examples include 'data about the connected product's environment or interactions' (rec. 15 DA). It is not just about the information that a product has been used, but also about 'all data that the connected product generates as a result of such use, such as data generated 39

---

[16] Rec. 15, Art. 2 no. 15 DA.

[17] See also Antoine CR 2024, 1 (2).

automatically by sensors and data recorded by embedded applications, including applications indicating hardware status and malfunctions' (rec. 15 DA).

40 **Raw data** or data that has already been processed is included under the DA. For example, the DA refers to 'source or primary data which refer to data points [...] which have been pre-processed for the purpose of making them understandable and useable prior to subsequent processing and analysis' (rec. 15 DA). These are data recorded by sensors that indicate physical properties or changes, pressure, fluid level, acceleration, or speed.

41 The Data Act does not **impose** an **obligation to reprocess** (rec. 15 DA). The 'design choice' remains with the manufacturer.[18] However, if data is processed anyway in the course of use, it must also be made accessible.[19] In any case, the distinction between the data to which access must be granted, as it is data originally generated by use (raw or processed), and the next level of data, which is no longer covered by the right of access, is unclear and will still lead to some discussion in the application of the DA: Merged, derived data should no longer be covered, whereby their delimitation from processed data is challenging.[20] In theory, the boundary between 'data generated during use' and subsequent processing steps may seem clear, but in practice it is by no means obvious.

42 Excluded are **content data**[21] and corresponding data 'which is the outcome of additional investments into assigning values or insights from the data, in particular by means of proprietary, complex algorithms, including those that are a part of proprietary software' (rec. 15 DA).

IV. Virtual assistants

43 Virtual assistants are also subject to the obligations in Chapter II DA. Art. 1(4) DA stipulates: 'Where this Regulation refers to connected products or related services, such references are also understood to include virtual assistants insofar as they interact with a connected product or related service.' The data generated by the use of virtual assistants is therefore also covered if the assistance service as such is not a connected product or related service. According to **Art. 2 no. 31 DA**, virtual assistants are 'software that can process demands, tasks or questions including those based on audio, written input, gestures or motions, and that, based on those demands, tasks or questions, provides access to other services or controls the functions of connected products'. Where the line is drawn here is questionable, especially in view of the ever-increasing spread of bots and the like.[22]

44 All data resulting from the interaction should be recorded, especially in view of the **growing importance** of virtual assistants: 'Virtual assistants can act as a single gateway in, for example, a smart home environment and record significant amounts of relevant data on how users interact with products connected to the internet, including those manufactured by other parties, and can replace the use

[18] Antoine CR 2024, 1 (3 mn. 13).

[19] Subject to existing limits, → mn. 82 et seqq., 89 et seqq.

[20] See the review of the state of the discussion in Wiedemann/Conrad/Salemi K&R 2024, 157 (161).

[21] Art. 1(2)(a) DA: 'with the exception of content'.

[22] Podszun/Bongartz/Kirk NJW 2022, 3249 (3250) refer to Alexa and Siri as established 'classics' as examples of Art. 2 no. 31 DA; Bomhard MMR 2024, 71 (73) refers to the vagueness in the scope of the term.

of manufacturer-provided interfaces such as touch screens or smartphone apps' (rec. 23 DA).

D. Data access rights

45 Chapter II DA standardises the data access rights. A fundamental distinction must be made between the de facto right of access under Art. 3(1) DA (→ mn. 46 et seqq.) and making the data available by the data holder (→ mn. 61 et seqq.). In addition to the user's own access, the user can also request the sharing of data to a third-party data recipient, which is accompanied by special requirements (→ mn. 68 et seqq.). Finally, information must be provided about access (→ mn. 75 et seqq.) and it can be refused or restricted under certain strict conditions (→ mn. 82 et seqq.). Beyond this, Chapter II DA also contains some general restrictions on the use of the collected data to the detriment of the data holders (→ mn. 89 et seqq.).

I. Factual data access claim: access by design

46 Art. 3(1) DA stipulates in passive formulation: 'Connected products shall be designed and manufactured, and related services shall be designed and provided, in such a manner that product data and related service data, including the relevant metadata necessary to interpret and use those data, are, by default, easily, securely, free of charge, in a comprehensive, structured, commonly used and machine-readable format, and, where relevant and technically feasible, directly accessible to the user.' This standardises the principle of **'access by design'** or, more precisely, **'accessibility by design'**[23] or **'accessibility by default'**.[24]

1. Obligated party

47 The passive formulation raises the challenging question of whether the standard contains a specific obligation and whom it addresses. Steinrötter aptly sees this as a provision that (arguably) imposes an obligation on the manufacturer.[25] Since the **manufacturer** is the only actor who can implement the requirements of Art. 3(1) DA due to his actual, factual influence, it is obvious to regard him as **the obligated party of the provision** by way of interpretation. The drafting of the provision is not successful at this point. The lack of clarity in the provision is likely to reach its limits in practice, particularly when it comes to the imposition of fines.

2. Material organisation

48 Materially, it is crucial that connected products and related services are accessible to the user. Where 'relevant and technically feasible', this should be possible without the involvement of other parties, in particular the data holder. In a systematically coherent synopsis, Art. 4(1) DA also stipulates that the data holder must actively provide the data if and because the user cannot access it 'directly' by accessing the

[23] On this term Steinrötter GRUR 2023, 216 (220).
[24] Specht-Riemenschneider MMR 2022, 809 (812) on this term.
[25] Steinrötter GRUR 2023, 216 (220).

product and service. Access, provision ('making available') from the product itself and thus an **in situ right** is justified,[26] but not a right to data transmission in the sense of sending data to the user and probably not a right of access in the sense that the user can directly copy, transmit, store or otherwise transfer the data made available.[27]

49 Depending on the product and service, it must be decided in detail which requirements must be implemented in order to fulfil the requirements of Art. 3(1) DA. The following **requirements** are decisive for this:

- by default,
- easily,
- securely,
- free of charge,
- in a comprehensive, structured, commonly used and machine-readable format,
- directly accessible.

50 The requirements are not further specified. According to general usage, taking into account the meaning and purpose of the regulations, **'default'** should require access that is possible without any special individual features.[28] This is **easily** possible if there are no special hurdles to accessing the data. **Security** relates to data security: in many cases, opening an access option is likely to require the opening of an **interface**. Opening such a door may entail the risk of unauthorised use by third parties. Securing the technical aspects and guaranteeing security is therefore central to granting access. This is done **free of charge** if no additional fee is required, whereby the data recipient – not the user – can be required to pay such a fee in accordance with Art. 9 DA (see further → mn. 160 et seqq.). The data format must be selected in such a way that it is also technically accessible, i.e. **comprehensive, structured, commonly used and machine-readable**.

51 According to the wording, only the last requirement, **direct accessibility**, is subject to **relevance and technical feasibility**. All other requirements must therefore always be met. This is also consistent in conjunction with Art. 4(1) DA, as the data holder is dependent on the data being accessible in order to provide the data. If it is not possible to provide the data securely, this may constitute a reason for refusal (→ mn. 90 et seqq.). If the manufacturer were not obliged to enable secure accessibility, this could be used to circumvent the data access claim. Nevertheless, it would have been more convincing to at least make these and the other requirements subject to technical feasibility. Ultimately, however, this applies anyway: A legal provision cannot effectively oblige an impossible action. If, for example, a safe way of making data available is not possible under any circumstances, this must be ruled out. However, the manufacturer must do everything possible in the design and manufacture to allow data to be made available in a safe way.

3. Generated data

52 It is important to note that access must only be provided to the product data and related service data, including the relevant metadata that **is generated during**

---

[26] Specht-Riemenschneider MMR 2022, 809; see also Ehlen/Sebulke CR 2024, 84 (86 mn. 11).
[27] See Podszun/Pfeifer GRUR 2022, 953 (957).
[28] Heinzke/Herbers/Kraus BB 2024, 649 (651): 'regular, customary and expectable'.

use. This means that no (re)design must be carried out in such a way that new or different data is generated in the first place. The data that is already available, or can be generated according to the concept chosen by the manufacturer, must be made accessible. A door must be created; the interior architecture remains unchanged. The data that is already generated by the product and associated service when it is used is made accessible. This can be seen in the wording of rec. 15 DA, for example, which states that product data and related service data are generated through use and that the product and service must then be designed in such a way that this data is accessible. The Data Act itself does not impose an obligation to **store or delete data.**[29]

According to Art. 2 no. 2 DA, **metadata**, which must also be made accessible, is 53
'structured description of the contents or the use of data facilitating the discovery or use of that data'. This is therefore classic auxiliary information that facilitates the structured use of the data or even enables its use in the first place. This includes context data and time stamps, sorting functions and data points. 'Such data are potentially valuable to the user and support innovation and the development of digital and other services to protect the environment, health and the circular economy, including through facilitating the maintenance and repair of the connected products in question' (rec. 15 DA).

4. User account

It should be permissible to **require** a user account for the granting of access if it 54
is (only) secured in such a way that the user and not a third party is granted access.[30] In terms of data protection law, a parallel can be drawn here to the guest access required by the data protection supervisory authorities in a – legally non-binding – decision for online shops,[31] which speaks in favour of enabling access without a user account, provided this is feasible. However, the Regional Court of Hamburg recently did not confirm the obligation of guest access.[32] According to Art. 4(5) DA, for example, the data holder shall not require that person to provide any information 'beyond what is necessary' to ensure that the user is also the user. A user account is likely to be an **adequate means** in many cases.

5. Legal consequences of non-compliance

However, the standard is silent on the legal consequences of non-compliance 55
with Art. 3(1) DA: What follows from the fact that a manufacturer does not design a connected product and a related service in such a way that the requirements of Art. 3(1) DA are fulfilled is not clearly regulated.

In the first step, Art. 4(1) DA applies if there is no direct accessibility: The **data** 56
holder must make the data available.

At the secondary level, two questions arise in particular: Is a product and a relat- 57
ed service that was designed in deviation from Art. 3(1) DA defective, resulting in

[29] See also, in relation to data protection law, Steinrötter GRUR 2023, 216 (222).
[30] See also Steinrötter GRUR 2023, 216 (222) on the challenges under data protection law.
[31] German Data Protection Conference, Decision of 24.3.2022, Information from the DSK – Data protection-compliant online trading via guest access.
[32] LG Hamburg 22.2.2024 – 327 O 250/22, GRUR-RS 2024, 5321.

the corresponding **secondary contractual claims**? Can a breach of Art. 3(1) DA be **penalised** by the authorities to be designated in accordance with Art. 37 DA?

58 According to Art. 37(1) DA, the **competent authorities** are responsible for the **'application and enforcement'** of the DA, and therefore, according to the general wording, also for the enforcement of the obligations under Art. 3(1) DA. Sanctions must be possible against violations of the DA, which must be specified in accordance with national law.[33] With regard to the violation of Art. 3(1) DA, the challenge here is whether, despite the passive formulation, it is clear enough who can be the obligated party and thus also the perpetrator of a violation.

59 The DA does not regulate whether the non-design and conception in accordance with the requirements of Art. 3(1) DA constitutes a **product defect** or **material defect** of the connected product and related service. This must therefore be assessed in accordance with general civil law. Insofar as there are no express provisions, the Data Act leaves contract law unaffected (rec. 9 DA). Digital consumer contract law, which was enshrined in the German Civil Code (BGB) in the implementation of the Digital Content Directive (EU) 2019/770 and the Sale of Goods Directive (EU) 2019/771, stipulates that a material defect exists for digital products and for the purchase of goods with digital elements – ultimately, the connected products and related services are likely to fall into one of the categories – if, among other things, the thing is not suitable for normal use and does not have the quality that is usual for things of the same type (§§ 327e, 434 BGB). Can a user expect and does it correspond to the 'usual' quality that products have been manufactured in accordance with the law? There are good reasons for this: A customer can expect that a product made available on the market complies with legal requirements. A defect in a rental object can also be caused by the lessor's breach of the main contractual obligations.[34] In sales law, it has been argued, particularly in the VW emissions scandal, that a breach of the law directly constitutes a material defect.[35] The argument against this is that the liability for material defects may be extended and the relevant legal provisions do not speak of legal conformity. Ultimately, it will probably have to be examined (empirically) in individual cases and in light of the general development after Art. 3(1) DA comes into force on 12.9.2026 whether the compliance with 'accessibility by design' requirements of connected products and related services will be an objective expectation for this type of product.[36]

6. Deviating agreements

60 In any case, it could be possible to contractually agree that no design is owed in accordance with Art. 3(1) DA. **Contractual clauses** that deviate from the provisions of Chapter II DA to the detriment of the user are **not binding** under Art. 7(2) DA and are therefore **ineffective** in the usual contractual doctrine. It is questionable whether this can actually exclude an individual contractual deviating agreement, i.e. whether it should replace **private autonomy** so comprehensively. This would then go further than the consumer protection law of the Digital Content Directive (EU)

[33] Art. 40 DA; also generally → § 8 mn. 18, 76.

[34] Burbulla/Schäfer in FormB-MietR § 5 mn. 183; Hübner in Lindner-Figura/Oprée/Stellmann Geschäftsraummiete-HdB § 14 mn. 290.

[35] Heimgärtner DAR 2015, 622 with further evidence.

[36] Schmidt-Kessel MMR 2024, 122 (127 et seq.) also characterises this as a challenge.

2019/770 and the Sale of Goods Directive (EU) 2019/771, which allow deviating agreements to the detriment of the consumer in digital contract law if these are expressly and separately agreed (see §§ 327h, 476 BGB). Schmidt-Kessel therefore argues that Art. 7(2) DA is to be understood as a semi-compulsory provision of user rights and excludes 'contractual restrictions or exclusions in general'.[37]

II. Making data available by the data holder

61 If there is no direct accessibility in accordance with Art. 3(1) DA, Art. 4(1) sent. 1 DA states that the **data holder** must provide the user with 'readily available data, as well as the relevant metadata necessary to interpret and use those data, accessible to the user without undue delay, of the same quality as is available to the data holder, easily, securely, free of charge, in a comprehensive, structured, commonly used and machine-readable format and, where relevant and technically feasible, continuously and in real-time'. According to sentence 2 of the provision, a 'simple request' is sufficient and the data must be made available 'through electronic means' where technically feasible.

62 Unlike in the case of Art. 3(1) DA, an action by the data holder is necessary here in order to enable the user to access the data. Art. 4(1) DA therefore actively speaks of **making available**.

63 However, this is a **statutory right of access**. In the basic version of making data available to the user, a contract between the user and data holder is not required to implement the making data available in accordance with Art. 4(1) DA.[38]

64 Most of the criteria in Art. 4(1) DA correspond to Art. 3(1) DA (without undue delay, easy, secure, free of charge, in a comprehensive, structured, commonly used and machine-readable format). However, it does not – logically – provide for direct accessibility, but instead requires that data be made available **continuously and in real-time**, which is regularly only possible via appropriate interfaces.

65 Only data that is **easily accessible** must be made available. The data holder – like the manufacturer – does not have to modify connected products and related services in such a way that new data is created in the first place.[39] The data holder does not have to redesign the product and the service in such a way that the data can be extracted in the first place (this obligation exists under Art. 3(1) DA and Art. 4(1) DA applies precisely when Art. 3(1) DA has not enabled access). According to Art. 2 no. 17 DA, '"readily available data" means product data and related service data that a data holder lawfully obtains or can lawfully obtain from the connected product or related service, without disproportionate effort going beyond a simple operation'.

66 The data holder only has to take action and provide data if the user **asserts** this, i.e. 'requests' it. In doing so, the data holder may ensure the identity of the user, but may not demand excessive information (Art. 4(4) DA). The obligation to ensure **identity** in accordance with Art. 4(5) DA, but without exaggerating this assurance and thus making claims more difficult, is known from Art. 12(2) sent. 2, (6) GDPR. Increasing casuistry is developing at authority level in this regard, the main features of which can also be applied under the Data Act. For example, a copy of an identity

[37] Schmidt-Kessel MMR 2024, 75 (77).
[38] Antoine CR 2024, 1 (5 mn. 23 with further evidence).
[39] See Assion/Willecke MMR 2023, 805 (807).

card may not be requested per se. However, the creation of a user account (→ mn. 54) with identity verification, e.g. by means of licence keys or email combinations, will generally be permissible.

67 In general, data must be made available effectively and must not be **unreasonably impeded** by accompanying circumstances (Art. 4(4) DA).

III. Sharing data with third-party data recipients

68 The user is not restricted to access and making data available in his favour. According to Art. 5 DA, the user is also entitled to request the making available of data to a **third party**. The third party thus becomes the **so-called data recipient**. In practice, this arrangement will become very important, as users will not usually be able to analyse and use the data themselves. The very idea of the Data Act is to enable third-party data recipients to generate follow-up services, support and value-added offers by receiving data from various users.

69 Art. 5(1) DA states: 'Upon request by a user, or by a party acting on behalf of a user, the data holder shall make available readily available data, as well as the relevant metadata necessary to interpret and use those data, to a third party without undue delay, of the same quality as is available to the data holder, easily, securely, free of charge to the user, in a comprehensive, structured, commonly used and machine-readable format and, where relevant and technically feasible, continuously and in real-time. The data shall be made available by the data holder to the third party in accordance with Articles 8 and 9.'

70 The **data holder** remains subject to the obligation to provide the data. The **data recipient** is entitled to receive the data upon the user's request. No data may be received by so-called **gatekeepers** (Art. 5(3) DA), which are strong players in the digital world that have been qualified accordingly by the EU Commission under the Digital Markets Act.

71 Once again, data is only made available **on request**. The data holder must therefore only take action when requested to do so. This request must always be traceable to the **user** who holds the power of disposal in accordance with Chapter II DA. However, the user does not have to make the request themselves. They can also authorise a third party to act on their behalf (**authorised representative**). This becomes a gateway for data recipients who can develop new business models and activate users to issue them with corresponding authorisations – under German law within the meaning of § 164 BGB. In the relationship between users and third-party data recipients, this could lead to an increasing commercialisation of data sharing.[40]

72 The right of the data recipient under Art. 5 DA does not go any further than the user's claim under Art. 4(1) DA. If, for example, data is not to be made available due to a lack of easy accessibility according to Art. 4(1) DA, it does not have to be provided according to Art. 5 DA either.

73 The right to share data with third parties is more limited than the right under Art. 4(1) DA. According to Art. 5(2) DA, **'readily available data'** is exempt if it concerns data in the context of new products. This exception, like that of prototypes, protects **innovation**.

[40] See also Etzkorn RDi 2024, 116 (120 et seq.).

74 If third parties receive data as data recipients under Art. 5 DA, they are subject to **specific obligations** set out in Art. 6 DA, which are typically enforced through contractual agreements with the data holder (→ mn. 135).

IV. Duty to provide information

75 According to Art. 3(2), (3) DA, the contractual partner is obliged to provide the user of connected products and related services with certain information before the contract is concluded. The information obligation is intended to ensure transparency so that access to the data is simplified as much as possible for the user (rec. 24 DA). This is immediately plausible: the user must know how to access which data in order to be able to exercise this right at all.

76 **The party obliged** to provide information in accordance with Art. 3(2) and (3) DA is the direct contractual partner of the user, i.e. the legal entity that provides the user with the right of use. For connected products, this is typically the **seller, rentor** or **lessor**, who are also explicitly named in Art. 3(2) DA. With regard to related services, this is the **provider of the service** in accordance with Art. 3(3) DA. Based on the telos and the regulatory system, the actor who contracts directly with the user is obliged. It is also possible for this party to provide information. The obligation of this actor is the most effective way of ensuring that the information is actually provided.

77 The **user** is the **authorised** actor. The information must be made available to the user before the contract is concluded. **Provision** within the meaning of the Regulation presupposes that the user can readily take note of the information. It must be made available and accessible to the user.[41] In data protection law, it has sometimes been discussed whether the provision of mandatory information in accordance with Art. 13, 14 GDPR is also sufficient if the data subjects can only take note of it after a media disruption. This discussion should carry less weight under the DA: The recitals expressly provide for the – practical – possibility of linking the relevant information, for example via a QR code or a URL that is not too complex (rec. 24 DA).

78 In terms of time, the information must be provided **before the contract is concluded** so that the user can take the availability of data into account when deciding whether to conclude the contract. In terms of time, this presupposes that the user can access the information before making a binding declaration with the intention to be legally bound to purchase the product or service – be it purchase, rental or similar. This is possible, for example, if the information is stored in the digital order process before clicking on 'Buy now for a fee' or, in the case of an analogue purchase in a retail store, can be called up on the networked device itself before passing through the checkout area by means of a printed QR code.

79 The information obligations include, in particular, details on the type and nature of the available data, the scope and timing and the access options. In detail, **providers of connected products** must provide the following information:

[41] See for example Wendland/Soritz in BeckOK BGB § 327b mn. 11 on this understanding of the German translation 'bereitstellen' from § 327b BGB in implementation of the DID Directive (EU) 2019/770.

- the type, format and estimated volume of product data that the connected product can generate;
- information on whether the connected product is able to generate data continuously and in real time;
- whether the connected product is capable of storing data on a device or a remote server, including the intended storage period, if applicable;
- information on how the user can access, retrieve or erase the data, including the technical means to do so, as well as the relevant terms of use and quality of service.

80 **Providers of related services** must provide detailed information on the following topics:

- the nature, estimated volume and collection frequency of product data that the prospective data holder is expected to obtain and, where relevant, the arrangements for the user to access or retrieve such data, including the prospective data holder's data storage arrangements and the duration of retention;
- the nature and estimated volume of related service data to be generated, as well as the arrangements for the user to access or retrieve such data, including the prospective data holder's data storage arrangements and the duration of retention;
- whether the prospective data holder expects to use readily available data itself and the purposes for which those data are to be used, and whether it intends to allow one or more third parties to use the data for purposes agreed upon with the user;
- the identity of the prospective data holder, such as its trading name and the geographical address at which it is established and, where applicable, of other data processing parties;
- the means of communication which make it possible to contact the prospective data holder quickly and communicate with that data holder efficiently;
- how the user can request that the data are shared with a third party and, where applicable, end the data sharing;
- the right of the user to lodge a complaint with the competent authority referred to in Art. 37 for a breach of one of the provisions of Chapter II DA;
- whether a prospective data holder is the holder of trade secrets contained in the data that is accessible from the connected product or generated during the provision of a related service, and, where the prospective data holder is not the trade secret holder, the identity of the trade secret holder;
- the duration of the contract between the user and the prospective data holder, as well as the arrangements for terminating such a contract.

81 The information must be provided in a **clear and comprehensible manner**. The data protection information pursuant to Art. 13, 14 GDPR, for example, must also be presented clearly (Art. 12(1) sent. 1 GDPR). Similar requirements are also known from general terms and conditions and consumer protection law. The decisive factor is that the average user can utilise and evaluate the information in such a way that they can assess it and its benefits for themselves. It must be taken into account that the user will often not be a natural person and that legal entities in commercial transactions may be required to carry out more extensive checks and pay more at-

tention than consumers. Ultimately, it depends on the specific design and the target group in each individual case.

V. Data protection law and data access

The DA and, in particular, its data access rights apply **'without prejudice'** to the GDPR and the ePrivacy Directive 2002/58/EC (Art. 1(5) sent. 1 DA). In the event of a conflict, the latter shall take precedence over the provisions of the DA. 82

Conflicts can arise in particular when users within the meaning of the DA and data subjects within the meaning of the GDPR differ. This can always be the case if, for example, the owner or tenant is the user and other people use the connected product: Employees operate a machine in business traffic or use a company vehicle for business trips. In this respect, the principle of **'accessibility by design'** enshrined in Art. 3(1) DA potentially comes into conflict with the principle of **'privacy by design'** laid down in Art. 25 GDPR.[42] This is because personal data generated in the connected product and related service is always accessible through consistent implementation of Art. 3(1) DA, without it having been clarified on the basis of the DA whether there is also a corresponding permission for this accessibility in accordance with the GDPR and whether the other data protection principles of the GDPR are complied with in the specific case. The responsibility for data protection-compliant handling then lies once again with the user, for whom the data is now accessible, which may not have been the case without Art. 3(1) DA in the implementation of strict 'privacy by design'. The fact that Art. 25 GDPR prohibits an accessible design within the meaning of Art. 3(1) DA and is generally decisive due to the priority provision in Art. 1(5) DA is likely to be relevant in practice in exceptional cases only. The reason for this is that Art. 25 GDPR does not impose many clear prohibitions, but rather regularly leaves room for manoeuvre. Such room for manoeuvre could then also lie in the fact that, in individual cases, an existing accessibility in accordance with Art. 3(1) DA is not used or only used under additional conditions. 83

Art. 4(12) DA stipulates that a user who is not the data subject within the meaning of the GDPR only receives **personal data** if this is covered by a corresponding **legal basis** (permission) in Art. 6, 9 GDPR or Art. 5(3) ePrivacy Directive 2002/58/EC. The DA does not provide such permission to process personal data by providing or granting access: 'Where the user is not the data subject, this Regulation does not create a legal basis for providing access to personal data or for making personal data available to a third party [...]' (rec. 7 DA). 84

This means that if there is a right to data access under the DA, this is only to be granted if the **data is non-personal data** or permission has been granted for the processing of personal data. In this case, however, access must also be granted. If no valid legal basis exists and the data is personal data, access must not be granted. Data access should 'in no way alter or interfere with the rights of data subjects who may be interacting with a connected product or a related service regarding personal 85

[42] See also Bomhard MMR 2024, 71 (74); differentiating Steinrötter GRUR 2023, 216 (220).

data generated by the connected product or during the provision of the related service'.[43]

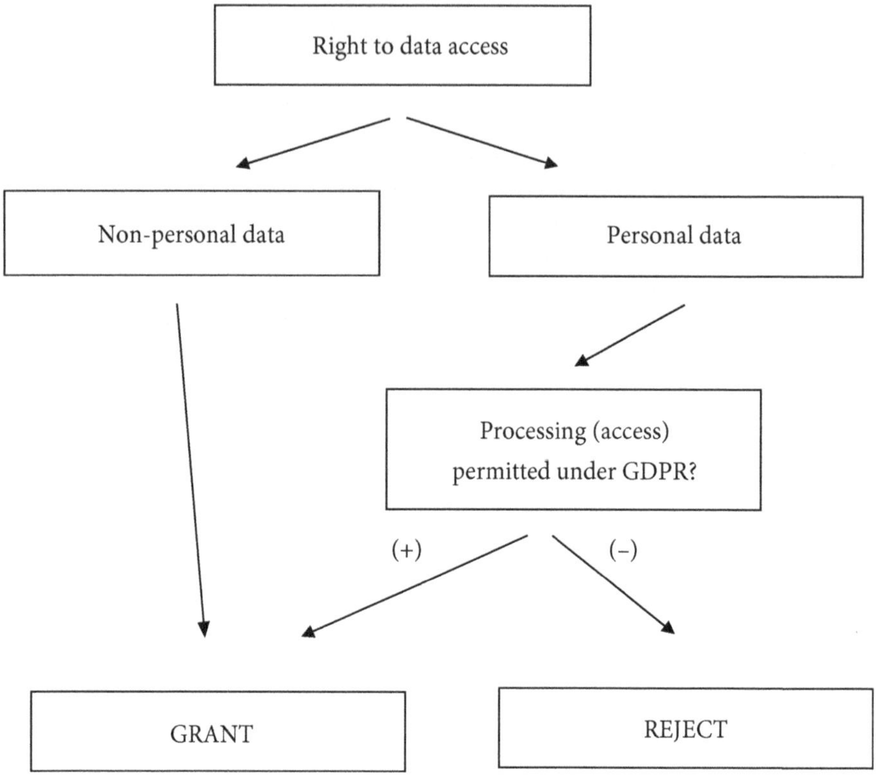

Fig. 4: Right to data access.

86 If there is no legal basis under the GDPR, access to the non-personal data must still be granted. Access may not generally be refused. It is highly questionable whether personal data must be additionally processed, i.e. **anonymised** or **pseudonymised**, in order to grant access. Rec. 7 DA may argue for such a position when it states in the last sentence: 'As this Regulation should not adversely affect the data protection rights of data subjects, the data holder can comply with requests in those cases, inter alia, by anonymising personal data or, where the readily available data contains personal data of several data subjects, transmitting only personal data relating to the user.' However, nowhere in the Data Act is there an obligation to process the data in such a way – through pseudonymisation or anonymisation – that it can then be made available in compliance with data protection regulations. On the contrary: Data access must be granted to the data generated by the product and service, and appropriate access must be designed, but the product or service does not have to be designed in such a way that certain data is generated in the first place (→ mn. 48 et seq.). According to the prevailing view, anonymisation also

[43] Rec. 18 DA; for the complex coordination as a whole, cf. also Lienemann/Wienroeder in Hennemann/Ebner/Karsten/Lienemann/Wienroeder Data Act, p. 94 et seq.

requires a separate legal basis under the GDPR,[44] which cannot be found in the Data Act.

This leads to the challenge of implementing and applying the data access requirements: 87

- clearly **qualifying** personal data as such and
- clearly **determining** whether or not there is a legal basis for processing in line with the GDPR.

This should not be underestimated in view of the enormous legal uncertainties 88 that continue to surround both issues.[45] The solution sometimes practised of not processing personal data if the legal basis is uncertain is inadmissible if there is a right to data access in accordance with Art. 3(1), Art. 4(1) DA: In this case, a 'yes or no' decision on authorisation must be made and acted upon accordingly. Because anyone who is too cautious in denying a legal basis under the GDPR, even though it actually exists, is in breach of the Data Act by refusing access to data.

VI. Restrictions on data access outside of data protection law

Chapter II and Chapter III DA grant users and third parties comprehensive 89 rights of access, use and further sharing with regard to the data generated when using connected products and related services. However, these rights are not unlimited. In order to balance the legitimate interests of data holders, there are certain **restrictions on access** and **use**.

1. Security requirements

A first barrier can be found in Art. 4(2) DA and relates to the legal security re- 90 quirements applicable to IoT products. According to this, users and data holders can **contractually restrict** access, use and further sharing of data if the processing could undermine statutory security requirements and thereby result in a serious adverse effect on the health, safety or security of natural persons.

The wording of Art. 4(2) sent. 1 DA initially suggests that the restriction of data 91 access requires a contractual agreement between the user and the data holder. Failing to agree on the restrictions necessary to ensure safety and security would jeopardise achieving the objective of the provision. According to Art. 4(2) sent. 3 DA, the data holder therefore has a **right to refuse to share data, subject to notification.**[46] If the data holder refuses access to the data, it must notify the competent authority in accordance with Art. 37 DA (→ mn. 58).

2. Restriction of competition pursuant to Art. 4(10), Art. 6(2)(e) DA

Restraints on the use of data after their receipt also result from the restrictions of 92 competition provided for in Art. 4(10) DA (regarding the relationship between the data holder and the user) and in Art. 6(2)(e) DA (regarding the relationship be-

[44] BfDI, Position paper on anonymisation under the GDPR with special consideration of the telecommunications industry (29.6.2020) <https://www.bfdi.bund.de/SharedDocs/Downloads/DE/Konsultationsverfahren/1_Anonymisierung/Positionspapier-Anonymisierung.pdf> (last accessed: 7.1.2026).

[45] See also Bomhard MMR 2024, 71 (74); see also Bomhard/Merkle RDi 2022, 168 mn. 27.

[46] Schmidt-Kessel MMR 2024, 75 (79).

tween the data holder and the data recipient). The user or data recipient may not use the data obtained to develop a **competing product** or to enable third parties to do so. While the European Parliament's negotiating position proposed limiting this prohibition to *directly* competing products, this restriction was not included in the final version of the Data Act – probably not least due to the practical difficulties of delimitation that would have arisen from such a restriction.[47] According to rec. 32 DA, the non-compete obligation is intended in particular to avoid undermining the investment incentives for innovation, which could otherwise result from unrestricted access to data.

93 The question of whether the IoT products concerned are in competition with each other can be based on the **principles of antitrust law** for **defining** the relevant product market.[48] According to these principles, products compete with each other if they are considered interchangeable or substitutable by users from the perspective of the buyer, in particular due to their characteristics, their price and their intended use (so-called **relevant market concept**).[49] However, according to rec. 32 DA, the relevant geographic market is not relevant for determining the competitive relationship. The recipient may therefore not use the data to become active with a competing product on another geographic market on which the data holder is not (currently) present with its product.[50]

94 By contrast, developing a service connected to the IoT device using the data obtained is not restricted. It is precisely the declared aim of the Data Act to promote the development of new, innovative connected products or related services and to drive **innovation** in the downstream markets – also and especially through access to and use of the data generated by the use of the connected products and related services (in the primary markets). Rec. 32 DA also clarifies that **reverse engineering**, i.e. the reconstruction of a device using the data obtained (e.g. for repair purposes, to extend the life of a connected product or to provide aftermarket services), may constitute a legitimate purpose for the use of the data and is therefore not covered by the restrictions.

95 Pursuant to Art. 4(10) alt. 2 DA and Art. 6(2)(e) DA, users or data recipients are prohibited from sharing the data with a third party or using it themselves in order to derive **insights** about the economic situation, assets and production methods of the manufacturer of the connected product or the data holder (Art. 4(10) alt. 2 DA). This aims to prevent the possibility of this data being used to 'spy' on the **economic situation** of the manufacturer or data holder,[51] e.g. with regard to their production methods. Accordingly, Art. 4(13) DA also limits the rights of the data holder itself, who may not use the data for such purpose even if it has obtained a right of use.[52]

[47] Heinzke/Herbers/Kraus BB 2024, 649 (654).

[48] Expressly rec. 32 DA.

[49] ECJ 21.2.1973 – case 6/72, ECLI:EU:C:1973:22 para. 32 – Europemballage & Continental Can v Commission; ECJ 14.2.1978 – case 27/76, ECLI:EU:C:1978:22 para. 11 et seq. – United Brands v Commission; ECJ 11.12.1980 – case 31/80, ECLI:EU:C:1980:289 para. 25 – L'Oréal; ECJ 9.11.1983 – case 322/81, ECLI:EU:C:1983:313 para. 37 – Michelin.

[50] Heinzke/Herbers/Kraus BB 2024, 649 (654).

[51] Assion/Willecke MMR 2023 805 (808).

[52] On the requirement of contractual authorisation by the user → mn. 129.

3. Relationship to trade secrets law

According to its concept, the Data Act should be interpreted in such a manner as to **'preserve the protection afforded to trade secrets'** in accordance with the Trade Secrets Directive (EU) 2016/943 (rec. 31 DA). Because of its clear commitment to the protection of trade secrets, the provisions of the Data Act are, at least on the face of it, capable of restricting the intended data flows. **96**

While the protection of trade secrets was only given sporadic consideration in the Commission's draft, it was strengthened during the legislative process. The final version of the Data Act now provides for a **tiered objection system** for the protection of trade secrets. Nevertheless, even if the information contained in the data concerned fulfils the requirements for legal protection as a trade secret within the meaning of Art. 2 no. 1 of the Trade Secrets Directive, the data holder cannot comprehensively refuse access to this data by invoking the necessary protection of trade secrets. Rather, data holders are also obliged to provide data to users and third parties named by the users 'even when such data qualify for protection as trade secrets'. To preserve the confidentiality of such information, **contractual safeguards** between the data holder and the user or the third party must be implemented. This mechanism seeks to create the necessary balance between two competing concerns: On the one hand the risk of excessive 'overclaiming' of trade secret protection; on the other hand, legitimate concerns over insufficient protection of trade secrets in mandatory data-sharing scenarios.[53] **97**

a) Data as a trade secret

The question of how requests for access under the Data Act interact with the protection of trade secrets presupposes that the data generated during the use of an associated product or service qualifies as a trade secret within the meaning of Art. 2(1) of the Trade Secrets Directive. This requires that data falls under the technologically neutral concept of information, has a commercial value, is secret and is subject to appropriate confidentiality measures.[54] **98**

Rec. 15 sent. 8 DA emphasises that the access rights relate solely to data that has not been substantially modified, meaning that primarily **raw data** falls within the scope of the Data Act. In this respect, some commentators dispute whether such raw data possesses the necessary semantic content to qualify as 'information' under trade secret law. For example, an expert opinion prepared on behalf of the Commission suggested that IoT machine data lacked semantic content.[55] However, according to widely held opinion, raw or pre-processed data[56] can indeed qualify as, or at least contain, trade secrets within the meaning of Art. 2 no. 1 of the Trade Secrets Directive.[57] The data sets and data collections often contain product-related data consisting of or resulting from multi-dimensional measurement series, may allow conclusions to be drawn – e.g. through aggregation or pattern recognition tech- **99**

---

[53] Antoine CR 2024 73 (76).

[54] Art. 2(1) of the Trade Secrets Directive.

[55] Radauer et al. Study on the legal protection of trade secrets, p. 89.

[56] This refers to raw data that is prepared for data analysis by cleansing, transforming and integrating it; see Wiebe GRUR 2023, 227 (229).

[57] Something else may apply with regard to individual, context-free data points (e.g. a temperature measurement point); in this case, the classification as a trade secret seems doubtful due to a lack of sufficient information content, see Krüger/Wiencke/Koch GRUR 2020, 578 (580).

niques – regarding the functioning of a connected product or service. This applies particularly in the context of **big data analyses**. In such cases, the insights derived may reveal commercially valuable information, such as conclusions from the data that originates from the use of a connected device or a related service and gain knowledge about how a device works.[58] Usually, this sensor-generated data is **secret** within the meaning of the Trade Secrets Directive, as the composition of the corresponding data sets is not generally known, and is protected by the manufacturer's security measures. Given the broad definition of 'commercial value', even raw data can be considered to have such a value, as it can form the basis of data-based business models or allow competitors to identify potential vulnerabilities.[59]

b) Protection mechanisms in case of a data access request by the user

100 If the data concerned is classified as a trade secret, the data holder does not have an absolute right of refusal. Also, unlike the balancing provision of Art. 20(4) GDPR regarding the right to portability of personal data, the right to data access under the Data Act generally does not require a balancing of the data holder's interests. This aims to prevent the risk of **'overclaiming'** a need for trade secret protection.[60]

101 Rather, the data access rights of the Data Act mean that the data concerned must be made available despite the trade secrets contained therein or information that allows conclusions to be drawn about information that is itself protected as a trade secret of the data holder. The user or data recipient can lawfully obtain this data within the meaning of trade secret law. The interests of the data holder or of the manufacturer or other holder of a trade secret shall be protected by allowing the data holder to make the granting of access subject to the prior agreement of the measures necessary for the adequate protection of the secrets (→ mn. 102 et seqq.). Only under certain narrow conditions may the data holder refuse access to the data for reasons of confidentiality (→ mn. 107 et seqq.).

aa) Appropriate confidentiality measures as a prerequisite for access

102 Specifically, the confidentiality of trade secrets should be protected by agreeing appropriate **technical and organisational measures (TOMs)**. To this end, the data holder or, if the data holder and the trade secret holder are different persons, the trade secret holder must first specify the data protected as a trade secret. It must be taken into account that in the context of complex connected products with a wide range of associated services, the ex-ante identification and designation of protected data as trade secrets presents a substantial challenge for data holders.[61] The large amount of the data generated significantly complicates any precise and complete classification. In particular, with regard to raw data and metadata, it is often not possible to reasonably estimate which insights may subsequently be derived from their analysis – especially by third parties. Consequently, establishing a prior classification that is both legally sound and practically feasible will prove challenging in practice. In a second step, the user should be obliged to comply with appropriate technical and organisational measures through agreements with the data holder

[58] Grapetin RDi 2023, 173 (175).
[59] Grapetin RDi 2023, 173 (175).
[60] Antoine CR 2024, 73 (76).
[61] Sattler in HK-DatenR DA Art. 4 mn. 93.

(Art. 4(6) DA). Such measures must be proportionate to the specific risk, technically and economically implementable and must not impose an unreasonable burden on the user. Art. 4(6) DA lists 'model contractual terms, confidentiality agreements, strict access protocols, technical standards and the application of codes of conduct' as examples of **necessary confidentiality measures**. It remains to be seen how far such confidentiality agreements may extend in individual cases, for example with regard to the law on general terms and conditions. The model contractual terms to be developed by the Commission in accordance with Art. 41 DA were expected to shed light on this. The Commission published and approved on 19.11.2025 model contractual terms (MCTs) on data access and standard contractual clauses (SCCs) for cloud computing contracts.[62] Although these non-binding MCTs and SCCs on data access and use as recommended provide draft wording for contractual agreements between the parties involved, these remain at a rather abstract level.

According to the Commission's model contractual terms, confidentiality agreements should be tailored to the nature and content of the respective trade secret, the risk of disclosure or re-identification (particularly through data aggregation or combination), the type of access provided (e.g. on-premise access, read-only, data export, one-time or continuous access), and the economic value of the trade secret to the holder. Technical safeguards – such as end-to-end encryption, access logging, or role-based access control (RBAC) – may be supplemented by organisational measures, including compliance training, clearly defined internal data release procedures and identity verification systems.[63] 103

However, the model contractual terms still provide very little guidance for the drafting of specific clauses in individual cases that protect the legitimate interests of trade secret holders on the one hand, but are, on the other, still appropriate with regard to the rights of users and data recipients and in line with the provisions of the Data Act. Consequently, in practice, the clauses still leave room for considerable discretion and require balancing of interests, which impose significant burdens on data holders. In addition, the risk of unintended disclosure – particularly in the case of raw data or metadata – remains difficult to assess ex ante. 104

After all, when drafting **confidentiality agreements** to ensure adequate protection of trade secrets under the regime of the Data Act, a challenge arises that at first glance seems to require squaring the circle. According to rec. 31 DA, data that falls under the protection of trade secrets must be disclosed, while the protection of trade secrets should be safeguarded in accordance with Directive (EU) 2016/943. Despite the clear commitment to the protection of trade secrets, this is problematic, as the Trade Secrets Directive does not form a self-contained statutory system for trade secret protection. To a large extent, the European Union law on trade secrets relies on contractual agreements between trade secret holders and third parties, particularly in cases where the owner of the secret makes the information protected as a trade secret accessible to a third party on its own initiative. In these cases, the Trade Secrets Directive does not specify what is permitted and prohibited when dealing with trade secrets, but instead delegates to the parties involved to determine the scope and limits of the lawful use of trade secrets. Art. 4(3)(c) of the Trade Secrets Directive merely states that the use or disclosure of a trade secret shall be con- 105

[62] C(2025) 7750 final, Annex p. 24; Schreiber ZfPC 2025, 46 (49).
[63] C(2025) 7750 final, p. 19 et seqq.

sidered unlawful whenever carried out, without the consent of the trade secret holder, by a person who is found to be in breach of a contractual or any other duty to limit the use of the trade secret.

106 If two or more parties decide to exchange sensitive information, it is therefore essential that they conclude a **confidentiality agreement** that appropriately regulates the handling of the information exchanged. The core of any such confidentiality agreement must therefore be the definition of a legitimate purpose for which the sensitive information may be used (as narrowly as possible from the perspective of the trade secret owner), followed by an unambiguous clause clearly stating that the use of that information for any other purpose is prohibited. It is doubtful how this customary procedure, which is necessary in view of the requirements of European Union trade secrets law, can be harmonised with the requirements of the Data Act. According to rec. 30 DA, the user should be free to use the data generated by its use of a connected product or a related service 'for any lawful purpose'. This also includes making data available or sharing data with a data recipient or other data-receiving third party. Art. 7(2) DA further stipulates that contractual clauses which, to the detriment of the user, exclude the application of the user's rights in relation to data access and making data available, derogate from them or vary the effect of these rights shall not be binding on the user. A purpose limitation that imposes a general ban on any onward sharing of the data to third parties is therefore very likely to be invalid. In this context, some authors argue that not all contractual provisions which exclude, deviate from, or modify the effect of user rights are necessarily invalid.[64] According to this view, Art. 7(2) DA does not apply to contractual terms which exclude, deviate from, or modify the effect of the users' rights, provided that such provisions are not to the detriment of the user. This is the case where the users receive adequate consideration in return – such as payment, a rendered service, or access to other data.[65] In light of such compensation, the agreement is no longer deemed to operate to the user's detriment. However, whether and to what extent such clauses are legally enforceable will likely only be determined with certainty through judicial interpretation.

bb) Withholding of data sharing in the event of a lack of secrecy

107 As long as the data or trade secret holder is negotiating with the user about the measures required to protect trade secrets, it does not yet have to share data concerned. If the negotiations fail or if agreed protective measures are not implemented by the user or not implemented as agreed, the data holder's right to withhold or suspend access to the data may become a right to **refuse access** in accordance with Art. 4(7) DA.

108 The data holder shall **substantiate** its decision to withhold or suspend the sharing of data and **inform** the user in writing without undue delay. The data holder must also notify and explain the decision to withhold or suspend to the competent authority (Art. 4(7) sent. 3 DA). This requirement also intends to ensure that data holders do not prematurely refuse access to data generated through the use of a

[64] Sattler/Zech, p. 59.
[65] Sattler in HK-DatenR DA Art. 7 mn. 24.

connected product or a related service. In particular, the **obligation to notify** the competent authority should create an additional threshold.[66]

If the data holder exercises its right to refuse, withhold or suspend access to the data, the user has options to seek redress and obtain legal protection. For example, the user can lodge a **complaint** with the competent authority (Art. 37(5)(b) DA) in accordance with Art. 4(9) DA (in addition to civil proceedings before the courts of the respective Member State) and, if the agreement with the data holder contains a provision on **dispute settlement**, the user may appeal to the dispute settlement body (Art. 10(1) DA; → mn. 166 et seqq.). 109

In contrast to Art. 7(8), Art. 7(7) DA does not distinguish between the data and the trade secret holder. The rule therefore will cause difficulties in situations where data holder and trade secret holder are not the same entity.[67] As a result, data holders may find themselves caught between conflicting obligations regarding the need to fulfil the access rights of users under Art. 4(1) DA and the protection of third-party trade secrets under Art. 7(7) DA. In this regard, it has been suggested that the data holder may be under an obligation to separate the data relating to the trade secret holder.[68] Implementing such a strategy may, however, reduce the legal risks arising from the data holder's dual obligations. 110

cc) Refusal of access in the event of serious economic damage

During the legislative process, a further means to protect trade secrets was added, which allows data holders to completely refuse a request for data access under certain circumstances on a case-by-case basis (Art. 4(8) DA). Art. 4(8) sent. 1 DA establishes a general clause, further substantiated by the examples listed in Art. 4(8) sent. 2 DA. This right to deny access covers cases in which the data holder is at risk of **serious economic damage** if the data is disclosed, despite the confidentiality measures that it may request in accordance with Art. 4(6) DA. While the user's own behaviour can influence whether the data holder is entitled to withhold or suspend access to the data under Art. 4(7) DA, the right of refusal under Art. 4(8) DA exists **irrespective of the user's behaviour**. 111

However, the **requirements** for refusing the user's request for data access are **very high**. The data holder must prove on the basis of 'objective elements' that it is 'highly likely' that it will suffer 'serious economic damage' as a result of the disclosure of trade secrets 'in exceptional circumstances' despite the technical and organisational measures to be taken by the user in accordance with Art. 4(6) DA. The provision is intended to remain limited to very special **exceptional cases** only. Such circumstances may arise, for example, due to the difficulty of enforcing the law in third countries, the nature and degree of confidentiality of the information concerned or the uniqueness and novelty of the product. According to rec. 31 sent. 13 DA, potential cybersecurity risks may also constitute grounds for establishing serious economic harm. The high requirements are intended to prevent the risk of data holders abusively invoking their right of refusal.[69] 112

[66] Hennemann/Steinrötter NJW 2024, 1 (4).
[67] Schmidt-Kessel MMR 2024, 75 (81).
[68] Schmidt-Kessel MMR 2024, 75 (81).
[69] Hennemann/Steinrötter NJW 2024, 1 (4).

113 If the data holder exercises its right of refusal, the user has the right to seek legal protection. In addition to civil proceedings before the courts of the respective Member State pursuant to Art. 4(9) DA, the user may lodge a complaint with the competent authority (Art. 37(5)(b) DA) and, if the agreement with the data holder contains a provision on dispute settlement, may also appeal to the dispute settlement body (Art. 10(1) DA; → mn. 166 et seqq.).

c) Protection mechanisms in case of a data access request in favour of third parties pursuant to Art. 5 DA

114 The **data access right of third parties** pursuant to Art. 5(9) DA may also extend to data that contains trade secrets or allows conclusions to be drawn about trade secrets of the data holder, the manufacturer or other holders of trade secrets. Although the mechanisms for the protection of trade secrets are systematically largely parallel to those in the case of a data access request by the user pursuant to Art. 4 DA (agreement on the technical and organisational measures necessary for the protection of trade secrets pursuant to Art. 5(9) DA, right to withhold or refuse data access pursuant to Art. 5(10) DA, right of refusal pursuant to Art. 5(11) DA), there are nevertheless **particularities** with regard to data access by third parties under Art. 5 DA and the associated risks.[70]

115 Sharing data with third parties entails the **risk** for the data holder of losing trade secrets to any third party. This is particularly risky for the data holder because the third parties receiving the data could be **direct competitors**.[71] Art. 5(9) DA therefore stipulates that the data holder must only make data that concerns trade secrets accessible to third parties to the extent that this is absolutely necessary to fulfil the purpose contractually agreed upon between the user and the third party. However, it is doubtful to what extent this requirement will contribute to limiting the risk for the data holder and to providing appropriate protection of the data holder's trade secrets.[72] What is particularly problematic is that the data holder has **no influence on the purposes** of the data access and the use of the data to be made accessible; these are agreed solely between the user and the third parties receiving the data. The purpose is determined 'over the data holder's head',[73] even though the user and third parties have completely different interests in the transfer than the data holder. Consequently, the third party will normally have an interest in defining the purpose as broadly as possible, which is contrary to effective trade secret protection.[74] In this context, the model contractual clauses approved by the European Commission (→ mn. 102) propose clear purpose limitations in the relationship with the data recipient – both between the data holder and the data recipient, and between the user and the data recipient. These limitations are also legally permissible, as the data recipient does not qualify as a 'user' within the meaning of Art. 7(2) DA and is therefore not subject to the prohibition on purpose limitation clauses. However, a key issue could lie in the lack of coherence between the respective purpose agreements in the

[70] This is particularly the case if the third party is a direct competitor of the data holder, see Pauly/Wichert/Baumann MMR 2024, 211 (213 et seq.).

[71] Pauly/Wichert/Baumann MMR 2024, 211 (214).

[72] See also Grapentin RDi 2023, 173 (177); Wiebe GRUR 2023, 227 (235); Metzger/Schweitzer ZEuP 2023, 42 (76).

[73] Wiebe GRUR 2023, 1569 (1572).

[74] Lorenzen ZGE 2022, 250 (261).

two contractual relationships: there is currently no mechanism for aligning the intended uses defined in the respective model clauses, which may result in contradictions and legal uncertainty. A possible solution could be the inclusion of a purpose-alignment clause. Such a clause could stipulate that the data recipient may only use the data for the purpose that is identically defined in both contractual relationships – that is, in the agreement with the data holder and in the agreement with the user. This clause would bind the data recipient to refrain from any unilateral extension of the intended use without the prior and explicit consent of both contracting parties.

A certain requirement to define the agreed purpose with some certainty can be **116** derived from the **absolute necessity** criterion. According to some, this should go so far as to exclude an obligation to grant access to data relating to trade secrets if the purposes for which the data may be used by the data recipient cannot be determined from the contractual agreement.[75]

d) Technical protective measures in accordance with Art. 11(1) DA

According to the concept of the Data Act, the protection of trade secrets is large- **117** ly left to contractual agreements. In addition, Art. 11(1) DA allows the data holder to take appropriate technical protection measures, including smart contracts as defined in Art. 2 no. 39 DA and encryption, in order to ensure compliance with Art. 4,[76] 5, 6, 8 and 9 DA.[77] **Limiting the purposes** for which technical protection measures may be used also limits the risk of the data holder applying prohibitively far-reaching technical measures. This is intended to prevent the data holder from creating or maintaining *de facto* data control through the use of technical protection measures.[78]

Conversely, Art. 11(1) sent. 3 DA provides for a general **prohibition of circum- 118** **vention**. Accordingly, users, third parties and data recipients may not alter or remove the data holder's technical protection measures without the data holder's consent.[79] In the relationship between the data holder and the user, the prohibition of circumvention is supplemented by Art. 4(11) DA, according to which the user may not use coercive means or exploit gaps in the data holder's existing technical infrastructure to protect the data in order to gain access to data.

Technical protection measures are also an important instrument for the data **119** holder with regard to its right to refuse access to data pursuant to Art. 4(7) or Art. 5(10) DA if the agreed measures for the protection of trade secrets are not implemented. They enable the data holder to **exercise de facto control**, which will be all the more important for the protection of trade secrets, as otherwise there is little possibility of monitoring the compliance of the user or third-party data recipient with their contractual obligations towards the data owner.[80] In addition to such control, Art. 11(2) and (3) DA provide for a number of **rights for the data holder** in the event that the data recipient or another third party receiving the data has ob-

[75] Pauly/Wichert/Baumann MMR 2024, 211 (214).

[76] The German version lacks the reference to Art. 4 DA contained in the English version.

[77] According to Art. 12(1) DA, Art. 11 DA only applies to business-to-business transactions. On the scope of application → mn. 137 et seq.

[78] Antoine CR 2024, 73 (77).

[79] According to the wording, this prohibition of circumvention also includes any unauthorised technical protective measures, see Steege MMR 2024, 91 (92 et seq.).

[80] Heinzke/Herbers/Kraus BB 2024, 649 (653).

tained data through unauthorised measures, has violated prohibitions of use or disclosure or has not complied with or has modified agreed protective measures. According to Art. 11(2)(a) DA, the infringed party can request the erasure of the data made available by the data holder and any copies. According to Art. 11(2)(b) DA, the data holder can demand that the data recipient or other third parties end the production, offering, placing on the market or use of goods, derivative data or services produced on the basis of knowledge obtained through such data, or the importation, export or storage of infringing goods for those purposes, and destroy any infringing goods. As an additional condition, however, there must be a serious risk that the unlawful use of those data will cause significant harm to the data holder, the trade secret holder or the user and that the measure is not disproportionate. According to Art. 11(2)(d) DA, the data holder or trade secret holder can also demand compensation for damages. The data holder or trade secret holder is entitled to the same rights against the user pursuant to Art. 11(4) DA if the user changes or cancels the agreed technical protection measures or does not comply with the measures agreed with the data holder or the owner of the trade secret for the protection of secrets.

e) Requirements for demonstrating the existence of a trade secret

120 According to the concept of the Data Act, it is the responsibility of the data holder or, where they are not the same entity, the trade secret holder to **'identify'** the data protected as a trade secret, including relevant metadata (Art. 4(6) sent. 2 and Art. 5(9) sent. 2 DA). However, the Data Act leaves open the extent to which the data holder must demonstrate and justify in a specific case that data subject to the right of access to data contains trade secrets. In this respect, the recitals merely state that a mere reference to any trade secrets worthy of protection is not sufficient, as such a reference would undermine the intended objective of the Data Act (rec. 31 sent. 8 DA).

121 On the other hand, excessive requirements would be questionable in view of the irreversible consequences of disclosure.[81] In this respect, a comparison with the requirements for applications for measures to preserve the confidentiality of trade secrets in the course of legal proceedings under Art. 9 of the **Trade Secrets Directive** may be appropriate.[82] To avoid overburdening the data or trade secret holder, it may be appropriate to follow the requirements of the Trade Secrets Directive, which do not require complete proof, but only a duly substantiated application.[83]

4. No restrictions from database law

122 While data holders may, under certain conditions, withhold, refuse or reject access to data relating to or containing trade secrets, they may not invoke any right as maker of a database in order to overcome the right of the user or third parties to access the data. The ***sui generis* right of** the **database maker** under Art. 7 of the Database Directive 96/9/EC cannot be held up as a barrier to the access rights under Art. 4 and 5 DA. Rather, Art. 43 DA stipulates that the database maker's right

---

[81] Rammos/Wilken DB 2022, 1241 (1244).

[82] See also Pauly/Wichert/Baumann MMR 2024, 211 (212).

[83] Hauck in Hoeren/Münker GeschGehG § 16 mn. 48; Schönknecht in Keller/Schönknecht/Glinke GeschGehG § 16 mn. 33.

does not apply if data is obtained from or generated by a connected product or related service falling within the scope of the Data Act.[84] Data holders are therefore **precluded from** invoking *sui generis* database protection in order to refuse to make data available to users or third parties under the conditions set out in Art. 4 and 5 DA.

The original idea was to limit the scope of the *sui generis* right in order to ensure legal certainty by excluding the application of the *sui generis* right to databases containing data obtained or generated during the use of a connected product or a related service. The Commission's proposal was based on the assumption that data generated by sensors do not meet the requirements for protection under database law. This assumption was based on CJEU case law according to which a distinction must be made between the obtaining and the mere generation of data with regard to the requirement of a **'substantial investment'** which is relevant for the existence of the right of the maker of a database (Art. 7(1) Database Directive).[85] According to CJEU case law, the database maker's right depends on the rightholder having made a substantial investment in obtaining, verification or presentation of the contents of the database. This is intended to encourage the creation of databases using existing information or data, but not to encourage the creation of new data organised in a so-called 'sole source' database, where the database content is available only to the database maker as a result of the 'invention' or 'creation' of the database maker concerned, thus creating the risk of an exclusive position in the data itself.[86] Contrary to the Commission's draft, the final version of Art. 43 DA only provides that the database maker's right does not apply if the data is obtained or created by means of a connected product or related service falling within the scope of the Data Act. In practice, however, both wordings are likely to lead to the same result, as the broad scope of application of the Data Act to all IoT products means that the vast majority of sensor-generated data is covered.[87] 123

However, it is unclear how the exclusion under Art. 43 DA affects **mixed databases** that do not consist exclusively of data generated through the use of a connected product or a related service. According to rec. 112 DA, the database maker's right remains fully applicable to data that does not fall within the scope of the Data Act. Pursuant to one view, mixed databases should be approached in a nuanced manner: If a database contains both protectable and excluded elements, *sui generis* protection should still apply to the former – provided that the requirements of substantial investment under Art. 7 of Directive 96/9/EG are fulfilled.[88] According to a broader opinion, however, rec. 112 DA does not affect the handling of mixed databases. Considering the main objective of the Data Act to promote the creation and development of data-based secondary markets, an extension of Art. 43 124

[84] For criticism with regard to the conceptual inconsistency of the provision, see also Kim MMR 2024, 87 (88 et seq.).

[85] ECJ 9.11.2004 – case C-203/02, CR 2005, 10 para. 30 et seqq. – BHB v Hill; see also Wiebe GRUR 2017, 338 (341). It is unclear whether the specific investment in measurement infrastructure is to be regarded as an 'obtaining' of the database content that can be taken into account; affirmative BGH 25.3.2010 – I ZR 47/08, CR 2011, 43 mn. 13 et seqq. – Autobahnmaut.

[86] For more details, see Kim MMR 2024, 87 (88).

[87] Antoine CR 2024, 73 (78).

[88] Brenzen in HK-DatenR DA Art. 43 mn. 19; BeckOK DatenschutzR/Richter DA Art. 43 mn. 29.

DA to mixed databases would be appropriate. Otherwise, the effectiveness of the exclusion of protection could be undermined in practice.[89]

125 It is also questionable whether Art. 43 DA also covers databases that consist of further processed, aggregated data. According to rec. 15 DA, processed data is not covered by the scope of the Data Act if the data is substantially modified and the data processing requires a substantial investment. Assuming that the **compilation of aggregated data** in databases requires significant investment, protection of such databases remains possible under Art. 7 Database Directive.[90] In this situation, there is no risk of the undesired creation of sole-source databases: The raw data remains accessible to users and third parties, so that they are able to compile corresponding data collections consisting of aggregated data with comparable effort. Corresponding database maker rights can therefore exist for such data collections without conflicting with the objectives of the Data Act, provided that the creation of such a database constitutes a substantial investment in the 'obtaining' of data that can be taken into account within the meaning of CJEU case law.

5. Restrictions arising from competition law

126 A primary legal barrier, which takes precedence over secondary data access rights under the Data Act, is the prohibition of anti-competitive agreements under Art. 101 TFEU. The provision prohibits the exchange of competitively sensitive data,[91] as extensive data exchange always harbours the risk of transferring competitively sensitive data, such as price information, sales figures or information on customer relationships.[92] This can become relevant in constellations in which competitors **grant each other access rights** via the Data Act and can thus draw conclusions with regard to the specific competitive behaviour of the competition.[93] In this case, a restriction of competition may arise from coordinated behaviour in breach of Art. 101(1) TFEU.[94] Rec. 116 DA clarifies in this regard that the Data Act does not justify any anti-competitive agreements. Insofar as there is a risk of a breach of Art. 101 TFEU, access to data must therefore be refused.

VII. Limitations on the use and disclosure of data by the data holder

127 Beyond data access rights, Chapter II DA also introduces fundamental innovations in another dimension: Data holders are largely regulated in their right to use and dispose of the collected product and service usage data themselves. In practice, data holders, who are regularly identical to the manufacturers, are currently largely free to use the data in a variety of cases. This is consistent with the principle that there is no data ownership. The Data Act intervenes here and shifts the balance of power **in favour of the user**.

---

[89] Antoine CR 2024, 73 (78).
[90] Antoine CR 2024, 73 (78).
[91] Wagner-von Papp MüKoWettbR AEUV Art. 101 mn. 350 et seq.
[92] Hennemann/Steinrötter NJW 2024, 1 (6).
[93] Podszun/Offergeld WiVerw 2023, 103 (108).
[94] European Commission, 'Guidelines on the applicability of Article 101 of the Treaty on the Functioning of the European Union to horizontal co-operation agreements', 2023/C 259/01, mn. 377.

Under the Data Act, Chapter II now stipulates various restrictions that must be observed by the data holder and taken into account when **drafting** future **contracts**. The latter applies in particular against the background of the restrictions under Art. 7(2) DA, according to which deviations from Chapter II DA to the detriment of the user are not binding (→ mn. 60). 128

1. Limited data use

According to Art. 4(13) sent. 1 DA, the data holder may only use **non-personal data** on the basis of a contract with the user. Such a general legal restriction has not previously existed for non-personal data. For **personal data**, it also follows from the prohibition with reservation of authorisation enshrined in the GDPR: Personal data may only be processed if permission has been granted in accordance with Art. 6 GDPR, depending on the data category in conjunction with Art. 9 GDPR. 129

If data holders wish to continue to use this data for their own purposes after the Regulation has come into force on 12.9.2025, they need a contractual arrangement. According to Art. 4(13) sent. 2 DA, the use of the data to 'derive insights about the economic situation, assets and production methods of, or the use by, the user in any other manner that could undermine the commercial position of that user on the markets in which the user is active' is excluded. 130

2. Prohibition of data sharing

According to Art. 4(14) DA, the making available of **non-personal data** by data holders to third parties for purposes other than the fulfilment of a contract with the user is also prohibited. The transfer of **personal data** is regulated in the GDPR, which remains unaffected by the Data Act and takes precedence over it. The right to share data therefore ultimately lies solely with the user.[95] 131

E. Making data available

According to Art. 4(1) DA, data holders are obliged to **make accessible** readily available data to users within the meaning of Art. 2 no. 17 DA (including the metadata necessary to interpret and use those data), unless the user can access the data directly from the connected product or related service (→ mn. 48 et seqq.). According to Art. 5(1) DA, data holders must make available readily available data and the relevant metadata to a third party designated by the user at the request of a user or a party acting on behalf of a user (→ mn. 68 et seqq.). The Data Act only specifies in general terms how this data is to be made available ('of the same quality as is available to the data holder, easily, securely, free of charge to the user, in a comprehensive, structured, commonly used and machine-readable format and, where relevant and technically feasible, continuously and in real-time', Art. 4(1), Art. 5(1) DA). The user may request the making available of data without having to comply with any particular formal requirements or deadlines. Users may exercise their rights to data being made available by **simply notifying** the data holder and naming the third party (→ mn. 71). 132

[95] See in particular Art. 5(1) and Art. 8(4) DA, → mn. 69, 159.

133 It is the responsibility of the parties involved, i.e. the data holder and the **third party** to whom the data must be made available at the user's request, to organise their relationship and to specify the conditions under which the data must be made available. Chapter III (Art. 8–12 DA) only regulates – at least for commercial transactions between data holders and data recipients – the general conditions under which data holders must make data available. The provisions of Chapter III DA do not apply to the making available of data to the user.

134 The Data Act leaves it to the contractual agreements between the data holder and the third party receiving the data to organise the specific conditions of making data available (Art. 8(1) DA). Art. 12(2) DA refers to these contracts as **'data sharing agreements'**. Chapter III and Chapter IV DA merely set out the legal framework within which the data sharing agreements may operate. In particular, data must be shared on fair, reasonable and non-discriminatory terms (**'FRAND'**) and in **a transparent manner** (Art. 8(1) DA; → mn. 144 et seqq.). The data holder may demand **reasonable compensation** for making the data available to the third party (Art. 9(1) DA; → mn. 160 et seqq.). Furthermore, the data holder may require compliance with technical protection measures that prevent unauthorised access to data and the associated metadata and ensure compliance with the applicable framework conditions (Art. 11(1) DA; → mn. 117 et seqq.). However, these protective measures must not go so far as to restrict the rights of users or third parties under the Data Act. In certain cases of misuse or violation of an agreed limitation of use, the data holder has the right to cancellation and other claims against third parties (Art. 11(2)–(5) DA; → mn. 119).

135 In order to ensure that data holders who are obliged to make data available do not abuse the freedom granted in principle to determine the conditions for making data available, the provisions on **unfair contractual terms** in Chapter IV DA (Art. 13) must also be observed pursuant to Art. 8(1) DA (→ Ch. 4 mn. 13 et seqq.). A further restriction on the data holder's freedom to negotiate and dispose of the data results from Art. 6(1) DA. The data holder cannot and may not influence the purpose of the making available of data to or use of data by the third party; such purpose is to be agreed solely between the user and the third party. In the event that disputes arise in connection with the rights and obligations of the parties involved, the Data Act provides for the possibility of out-of-court dispute settlement before independent dispute settlement bodies (Art. 10 DA; → mn. 166 et seqq.). This provision plays a key role in advancing the objectives of the Data Act by counteracting the de facto data exclusivity traditionally enjoyed by the data holder and the corresponding structural competitive advantage it entails.[96]

I. Requirements for making data available

136 According to Art. 8(1) DA, the data holder must make data available to the data recipient on the basis of an agreement on 'fair, reasonable and non-discriminatory terms and conditions' (**FRAND terms**). In addition, Art. 8 DA sets out further conditions that data holders must observe when making data available to data recipients.

[96] Steinrötter in HK-DatenR DA Art. 8 mn. 10.

1. Area of application

a) Business-to-business relations

The obligation of the data holder to provide data on FRAND terms does not apply to every making available of data to a third party. According to the wording of Art. 8(1) DA, the scope of application is limited to cases in which a data holder is obliged to make data available to a data recipient **'in business-to-business relations'**. The same wording is used in Art. 12(1) DA, according to which Chapter III (only) applies if a data holder is obliged to do so 'in business-to-business relations'. 137

The wording is linguistically unclear, as it leaves open the circumstances under which a 'business-to-business relation' can be said to exist, and the nature of such a B2B relationship. The ambiguities arise from the fact that the obligation of the data holder to make data available to third parties is **user-accessory**, i.e. the obligation of the data holder to make data available to a third party only exists at the request of the user (→ mn. 114). The obligation to make data available to a third party therefore requires a business relation between the data holder and the user; such a relationship does not necessarily have to exist between the data holder and the (designated) data recipient prior to the user's request to make data available. 138

In many cases, the relationship between data holder and user required to establish an obligation to provide data to a third party will be a **relationship between a business and a consumer**. Neither the provisions nor the recitals of the Data Act provide any indication that the provisions of Chapter III DA and the obligations to make data available on the basis of an agreement on FRAND terms should only apply to making data available based on a request by a user arising from a business-to-business relation. Rather, this is likely to mean that the obligation to conclude agreements on FRAND terms and the other provisions of Chapter III DA always apply if the relation between the data holder and the data recipient – which may be established by the user's request to make data available in the first place – is a business-to-business relation. 139

On the part of the data recipient, this further restriction would not have been necessary. According to Art. 2 no. 14 DA, a 'data recipient' is a natural or legal person only if they are acting 'for purposes relating to their trade, business, craft or profession' (→ mn. 23). **Data recipients** within the meaning of the definition differ from other data-receiving third parties precisely in their **business status**. 'Data holder' within the meaning of Art. 2 no. 13 DA, on the other hand, is any natural or legal person who is authorised or obliged under the relevant legal provisions to use and provide data that they have retrieved or generated during the provision of a related service (→ mn. 16). These will generally, but not necessarily, be businesses. Even if the Data Act focuses almost exclusively on consumers as users or data-receiving third parties, Art. 2 no. 13 DA does not exclude **consumers** from the role of data holder. 140

The obligation of the data holder to provide data on the basis of a contractual agreement therefore always exists if a **data holder** operating as a business is obliged to provide data to a **data recipient** (by definition operating as a business) at the request of a user (regardless of whether they are a consumer or a business). However, the requirements do not apply to making data available by the data holder to the user or to a third party receiving data that is not a business. They also do not apply to the (probably rather theoretical) case that the data holder is a consumer within 141 the meaning of Art. 2 no. 23 DA. Agreements between such a data holder and the data recipient must comply with the requirements of EU consumer protection law in the same way as agreements between a business data holder and a consumer as a data-receiving third party do (Art. 1(9), rec. 9 sent. 2 DA).

b) Obligation to make data available

142 Substantively, Art. 8(1) DA primarily covers the obligation of the data holder to make data available to a data recipient pursuant to Art. 5(1) DA, but is not limited thereto. Art. 8(1) DA also applies with regard to obligations of a data holder to make data available to a data recipient under other applicable European Union law or under national law enacted in accordance with European Union law. The Data Act thus opens the door to further obligations to make data available **outside the Data Act**, which are expected in supplementary, sector-specific regulations.[97] This could apply, for example, to the Intelligent Transport Systems (ITS) Directive (EU) 2010/40, which mandates equal access to mobility data to ensure fair competition in downstream digital transport services.[98]

c) Time of application

143 The requirements of Chapter III DA, including the obligation to make data available on the basis of an agreement on FRAND terms, apply from **12.9.2025** (Art. 50(2) DA). With regard to obligations to make data available other than those under Art. 5(1) DA, which exist under European Union law or under national law adopted in accordance with European Union law, Chapter III DA only applies in accordance with Art. 50(4) DA if these obligations enter into force after the date of application of the Regulation, i.e. from 13.9.2025. With regard to existing obligations that have come into force by 12.9.2025, Chapter III DA will therefore not apply from 12.9.2025.[99]

2. Making data available on FRAND terms

144 According to Art. 8(1) DA, data must be made available on fair, reasonable and non-discriminatory terms ('FRAND'). FRAND conditions are primarily known from **patent and competition law**.[100] In patent law, they typically play a role when the (allegedly infringing) patent user invokes the compulsory licence defence under antitrust law against an infringement claim raised by the patent holder. This defence applies if enforcing the patent holder's injunction claims would inevitably result in an abuse of a dominant market position within the meaning of competition law. The objection therefore plays a role in particular in connection with so-called standard-essential patents (i.e. patents that are essential for a standard set by a standardisation organisation in the sense that the technical teaching embodied therein must be used in order to manufacture standard-compliant products); however, the dominant position of the patent proprietor can also arise from other circumstances. In order to avoid being accused of abusing a dominant market position, the patent

---

[97] In this regard, Louven MMR 2024, 82 (83).
[98] Steinrötter in HK-DatenR DA Art. 8 mn. 26.
[99] See also Louven MMR 2024, 82 (83).
[100] See in particular ECJ 16.7.2015 – case C-170/13, GRUR 2015, 764 – Huawei.

holder must offer third parties licences to the patent on the basis of a licence agreement on FRAND terms.[101]

145 Agreements on FRAND terms are also becoming increasingly important in European **digital legislation.**[102] For example, Art. 6(12) DMA stipulates that the general access conditions of gatekeepers to centralised platform services must be **'fair, reasonable and non-discriminatory'** in relation to the user. Similarly, although differing in detail, providers of data intermediation services in the EU must ensure that the procedure for access to their service is fair, transparent and non-discriminatory for data subjects, data holders and data users, including with regard to prices and terms and conditions, in accordance with Art. 12(f) DGA.

146 In the Data Act, the legislator has decided not to regulate the conditions under which data must be provided and the potential conflicts that may arise between data holders and data recipients, but merely to specify the **general conditions** for the necessary **agreement between the parties** by obliging them to conclude agreements on FRAND terms. The obligation to agree terms on the basis of fairness, appropriateness and non-discrimination therefore establishes a fundamental principle for data law. Contractual agreements on FRAND terms are an essential element of the Data Act in order to achieve the central objective of promoting competition through data access rights.[103]

a) Fair, reasonable and not discriminatory

147 According to Art. 8(1) DA, the conditions for making data available must be fair, reasonable and non-discriminatory. The provision does not contain a concrete definition of what FRAND means in this context. Rec. 5 DA provides some guidance, according to which the provision is intended to prevent the data holder or data recipient from exploiting contractual imbalances in their favour. The three elements of the FRAND test cannot be clearly distinguished from each other in this context and are therefore read as a **common requirement**:[104]

- The concept of **fairness** is a **key concept** in the context of the Data Act.[105] According to rec. 5 DA, fair data access and fair data use are defined in particular by the **prevention of contractual imbalances.**[106] Fairness is an expression of reasonable regard for the legitimate interests of others.[107] With regard to the conditions of making data available, it can be concluded that no disproportionate obligations may be imposed on the data recipient in the relationship with the data holder. An imbalance between the rights and obligations of the parties should be avoided.
- **Reasonableness** is the result of a balancing of interests.[108] Accordingly, a condition is reasonable if it can reasonably be demanded by the other party without

[101] In detail Körber WRP 2015, 1167; on the obligations of patent proprietor and patent user BGH 5.5.2020 – KZR 36/17, GRUR 2020, 961 – FRAND-Einwand.
[102] Schwab in HK-DMA Art. 6 mn. 297.
[103] Wiebe GRUR 2023, 1569 (1572); with further information on the problems with implementation in detail. Ducuing/Margoni/Schirru White Paper on the Data Act Proposal, p. 35.
[104] Schwab in HK-DMA Art. 6 mn. 304.
[105] The title already refers to regulations for 'fair data access and fair data use'.
[106] See the identical provision in the DMA: Schwab in HK-DMA Art. 6 mn. 305 et seq.
[107] Schubert in MüKoBGB § 242 mn. 8.
[108] Schwab in HK-DMA Art. 6 mn. 306.

disturbing the balance of interests between the parties pursued by the Data Act.[109] By contrast, a condition is unreasonable if the obligations imposed on the data recipient restrict them excessively – economically or legally; for example, if the data holder demands conditions that are not technically or financially feasible for the data recipient.

- A condition is applied **in a non-discriminatory manner** if it applies equally to all similar data recipients.[110] This results in the obligation to objectively justify unequal treatment of data recipients by the data holder and prohibits the data holder from applying different contractual terms arbitrarily.

148 The concrete interpretation of these principles will depend in particular on the **specific purpose of the provision** from which the obligation to make data available arises in the individual case.[111] As a result, very different contractual arrangements may be considered fair and reasonable under the respective circumstances, as the mutual rights and obligations may differ in terms of structure and scope depending on the purpose pursued with making the data available and require tailored agreements. For example, some obligations may require the real-time provision of data with extensive access rights, while in other cases a one-off final transfer would suffice.[112]

b) Procedure for determining FRAND

149 It is not easy to specifically determine which conditions fulfil the FRAND criteria under the respective circumstances.[113] In patent law, **procedural solutions** have been established in dealing with FRAND in order to determine what is fair, reasonable and non-discriminatory in individual cases.[114] Both parties must cooperate in reaching an agreement on fair and reasonable terms, whereby any difference in treatment between the licence seeker and other licensees must be objectively justified.[115] The extent to which these principles must be applied to data access claims is left open by Art. 8(1) DA; the recitals do not provide any indications in this respect either. However, certain aspects of previous FRAND practice, in particular the **procedural obligations** of the parties involved, can be transferred to the negotiation of data sharing agreements on FRAND terms.

150 It remains to be seen how the obligation to agree FRAND terms will affect the **balance of power** between the data holder and the data recipient. In this respect, there is a structural difference compared to the situation in patent law:[116] There, the stakes are generally high for both parties, because a failure to reach agreement on FRAND terms may result either in the patent holder exploiting a dominant market position in a way that violates competition law, or in the patent user infringing the patent (unless the patent user refrains from the intended use). In the relationship between the data holder and the data recipient, the situation is different insofar

[109] Schwab in HK-DMA Art. 6 mn. 306.
[110] Habich IIC 2022, 1343 (1353).
[111] Louven MMR 2023, 82 (84).
[112] Louven MMR 2023, 82 (84).
[113] Louven MMR 2023, 82 (84).
[114] Schwab in HK-DMA Art. 6 mn. 306.
[115] The principles from the ECJ decision 16.7.2015 – case C-170/13, GRUR 2015, 764 para. 59 et seq. – Huawei, summarised by Körber WRP 2015, 1167 (1169 et seq.).
[116] For a detailed comparison, see also Habich IIC 2022, 1343 (1361 et seqq.).

as the **data holder** is **under unilateral pressure to receive sanctions**. If data holders reject the data recipients' offers to conclude a data sharing agreement on terms that meet the FRAND criteria, they violate their obligations under the Data Act. This breach can be sanctioned in accordance with the Data Act (→ Ch. 8 mn. 29 et seqq.). The data recipients are not threatened with a comparable legal sanction if they refuse a corresponding offer from the data holders; the refusal would remain without sanction for the data recipients. In this case, the data recipients may initially not be able to use the data that they request to be made available. However, they could still enforce their rights to data access if they believe that the data holders' offers did not fulfil the FRAND criteria.

Difficulties are likely to continue to arise in particular when determining what constitutes fair and reasonable terms with regard to the **substance of the data sharing agreement**. In patent law, the parties can draw on a wealth of experience from decades of dealing with patent licence agreements. In data law, there is no comparable source; rather, the status quo in the data economy is to be broken up by the new legal acts. 151

According to Art. 9 DA, the Data Act lays down at least some substantive requirements for the **amount of remuneration**, which is limited by the Regulation (→ mn. 163).[117] Further guidance and indications as to the circumstances under which data sharing agreements are fair and reasonable is provided by the non-binding **model contractual terms (MCTs)** that the Commission published and approved in accordance with Art. 41 DA on 19.11.2025 (→ mn. 102). The model contractual terms provide an indication of how contractual data-sharing frameworks under the Data Act could be structured in practice. The clauses give concrete shape to this general principle by imposing contractual safeguards and procedural mechanisms that ensure transparency and equal treatment in data access arrangements. The fairness aspect is underpinned by mandatory disclosure obligations concerning the scope, format, and permitted uses of the data, as well as procedural protections such as designated points of contact and mechanisms for alternative dispute resolution. With regard to non-discrimination, the model clauses contain specific provisions aimed at preventing discriminatory treatment of data recipients.[118] Under these provisions, data holders are obliged to grant comparable terms to equivalent data recipients, particularly with respect to pricing, access modalities, and technical conditions. Fairness is further reflected in the requirement of proportionality between the value of the data, the scope of usage rights granted, and the remuneration requested. This includes provisions on compensation,[119] contract duration, and termination clauses,[120] all of which must be structured in a way that avoids unjustified burdens or lock-in effects for the data recipient. 152

3. Transparency requirement

In addition to the obligation of the data holder to provide data to data recipients on FRAND terms, Art. 8(1) DA contains a transparency requirement that is specifi- 153

[117] See also Drexl et al. Position Statement, mn. 102.
[118] C(2025) 7750 final, p. 85.
[119] C(2025) 7750 final, p. 78 et seq.
[120] C(2025) 7750 final, p. 81 et seq.

cally emphasised.[121] According to this, the data holder must provide the data **'in a transparent manner'**. However, the content and meaning of this transparency requirement remain unclear.

154 According to the wording, the transparency requirement does not refer to the data sharing agreement, but to the **making data available** as such. This is surprising insofar as the language of the transparency requirement is directly related to the requirements for the conditions of data sharing agreements. It would therefore be logical to infer from Art. 8(1) DA a requirement for transparency in the contractual terms and conditions. In particular, contractual terms that are so expansive, complicated or scattered that the bundle of rights and obligations is no longer comprehensible for the data recipient would be prohibited.

155 According to rec. 38 DA, the Data Act is intended to strengthen the autonomy, decision-making ability and freedom of choice of users of connected products and related services and to prevent the use of design techniques that serve to deceive users or induce them to make decisions that have negative consequences for them (**'dark patterns'**). To this end, Art. 4(4) DA prohibits data holders from unreasonably impeding the exercise of choices or rights by the user, for example by undermining or impairing the user's autonomy, freedom of decision or freedom of choice through the structure, design, function or operation of a digital user interface. There is no comparable regulation for the relationship between data holder and data recipient, but the transparency requirement in relation to the way data is made available can also be understood as a prohibition of 'dark patterns' in this relationship. Here too, the MCTs (→ mn. 102) developed by the Commission's Group can provide a starting point: The MCTs require, in the contractual relationship between data holder and data recipient, a specific description of the relevant data categories (e.g. sensor data, usage data, maintenance logs), their technical format, and the access modalities (e.g. API interface or one-time export).[122] Moreover, the MCTs stipulate that the origin and method of generation of the data must be clearly indicated (i.e. whether the data were generated by machines or input by users). This is complemented by requirements concerning technical protection measures, as well as information on data availability, integrity, and potential processing by third parties. It is, for instance, recommended to include an annex to the contract in which each relevant data category is documented together with its data structure and any usage restrictions.[123]

4. Ineffectiveness of unfair contract terms

156 Art. 8(2) DA restricts the contractual freedom of the data holder and the data recipient when concluding data sharing agreements. In particular, contractual **restrictions of the user rights** provided for in Chapter II DA are ineffective. Art. 8(2) DA stipulates that a contractual term is not binding if it excludes, derogates from or varies the effect of the exercise of the user's rights under Chapter II DA to the detriment of the user. In addition, Art. 8(2) DA refers to the provisions on unfair contractual terms pursuant to Art. 13 DA (→ Ch. 4 mn. 13 et seqq.). A contractual

[121] This is not the case with Art. 6(12) DMA, where the transparency requirement is not specifically mentioned, see also Schwab in HK-DMA Art. 6 mn. 306.
[122] C(2025) 7750 final, p. 67 et seqq.
[123] C(2025) 7750 final, p. 66 et seq.

term relating to data access and use or liability and remedies for breach or termination of data-related obligations is also not binding if it constitutes an**unfair term** within the meaning of Art. 13.

It is unclear whether the reference to Art. 13 DA is a legal reference to the unfairness test as a whole or 'only' the substantive standards, in particular para. 3–5, are referred to.[124] In the first case, the unfairness test would only apply if the term were imposed unilaterally within the meaning of Art. 13(6) DA, while in the latter case the unfairness test would also apply to data sharing agreements that were negotiated individually.[125] Since the data holder is in any case obliged under Art. 8(1) DA to conclude data sharing agreements on FRAND terms and in accordance with Chapter IV DA (Art. 13), there are good reasons to believe that the legislator wanted to set limits to the contractual freedom of the data holder and data recipient also in **individual agreements** in business transactions. Without the provision in Art. 8(1) DA, it would be left to the national law of each individual Member State to decide whether unfair terms in an individual agreement in commercial transactions would be effective within the meaning of Art. 13(3)–(5) DA. In addition, there was no need for a (further) legal reference to Art. 13 DA in Art. 8(2) DA. For unilaterally imposed terms in data sharing agreements between the data holder and the data recipient, Art. 13 DA applies anyway; the invalidity consequence in this case (also) results from Art. 13(1) DA. 157

5. Prohibition of discrimination

Art. 8(3) DA complements the obligation to conclude data sharing agreements on non-discriminatory terms, which already arises from Art. 8(1) DA (→ mn. 147). The provision contains a **sector-specific prohibition of discrimination**, according to which the data holder may not discriminate between comparable categories of data recipients regarding the conditions of making data available. In particular, the data holder may not treat partner enterprises or linked enterprises more favourably than other data recipients. If a data recipient considers the conditions under which data is made available to be discriminatory, the data holder must provide information without undue delay in response to a reasoned request in order to prove that there is no discrimination. In case of doubt, the data holder must therefore be able to **justify** the conditions under which the data is made available.[126] 158

6. Protection of the user's data sovereignty

Art. 8(4) DA guarantees the user's data sovereignty with regard to the data generated by their use of a connected product or a related service. The user alone should decide to whom the data is made available. Accordingly, Art. 8(4) DA stipulates that the data holder may only make data available to a data recipient if the user requests this in accordance with the provisions of Chapter II DA (→ mn. 71). The user request under Chapter II DA is a prerequisite for the data to be lawfully made available; making data available without a user request is **unlawful**. 159

[124] Drexl et al. Position Statement, mn. 128; Metzger/Schweitzer ZEuP 2023, 42 (70 et seq.).

[125] See also Wiebe GRUR 2023, 1569 (1572 et seq.).

[126] Louven MMR 2023, 82 (84).

II. Compensation for making data available

160 According to Art. 9 DA, the data holder may agree a **compensation** with the data recipient for making data available in business-to-business relations. The compensation must be **non-discriminatory** and **reasonable** and may include a **margin**. The aim behind this is to incentivise the data holder to continue investing in the generation of valuable data and the relevant technical tools.[127] The data holder may not demand any consideration from the user, regardless of whether the data holder provides the data to the user (Art. 4(1) DA) or, at the user's request, to the data recipient (Art. 5(1) DA).

161 The model contractual terms published and approved by the Commission (→ mn. 102) specify the requirements for a fair, reasonable, and non-discriminatory (FRAND) compensation in the context of data provision. According to these terms, data holders are permitted to request remuneration, provided that the data recipient is not a privileged entity such as an SME or a non-profit organisation (→ mn. 164). The remuneration must be proportionate to the economic value of the data, the scope of the usage rights granted, and the intended purpose of use.[128] In addition to monetary compensation, the MCTs also recognise alternative forms of consideration. To ensure transparency, the MCTs require clear information on pricing structures, applicable discounts, licence durations, and payment terms – preferably documented in a dedicated annex to the contract.

162 With regard to the question of when a compensation including a margin is appropriate, the provisions contained in Art. 9(2) and (3) DA must be taken into account:

- According to **Art. 9(2)(a) DA**, the **costs** incurred in making data available must be included in the calculation of a reasonable compensation. In particular, the costs for formatting the data, dissemination by electronic means and storage may be included. Factors such as the frequency and duration of making data available must be taken into account when calculating the compensation (rec. 47 DA).
- According to **Art. 9(2)(b) DA, investments** in the collection or production of data should also be taken into account.
- According to **Art. 9(3) DA**, the compensation may also depend on the **size**, **format** or **nature** of the data.

163 The **amount of the compensation** may therefore **vary** depending on the factors mentioned. For example, the data holder's margin may be higher if high investments had to be made to collect the data. Furthermore, according to rec. 47 DA, a limitation or even an exclusion of the acceptable margin is possible in cases 'where the use of the data by the data recipient does not affect the data holder's own activities'. According to Art. 9(5) DA, the Commission is to issue additional **guidelines** for the calculation of an appropriate compensation, taking into account the recommendation of the European Data Innovation Board (EDIB).

164 Stricter rules apply under Art. 9(4) DA regarding the calculation of compensation for making data available if the data recipient is an **SME** (within the meaning

---

[127] Podszun/Pfeifer GRUR 2022, 953 (957).

[128] C(2025) 7760 final, p. 78 et seq.

of Art. 2 of the Annex to Commission Recommendation 2003/361/EC, cf. rec. 3 DA) or a **non-profit research organisation**. In these cases, Art. 9(4) DA stipulates that the compensation may not exceed the costs for making data available listed in Art. 9(2)(a) DA. The data holder may not demand a margin in these cases. This is intended in particular to protect SMEs from high economic burdens that would make it excessively difficult for them to develop innovative business models.

According to Art. 9(7) DA, the data holder is also obliged to provide the data re- 165 cipient with a substantiated explanation of the calculation basis and the information required therefor. According to rec. 51 DA, this requirement aims at creating **transparency** and is intended to enable the data recipient to check the appropriateness of the compensation, including the margin (rec. 51 DA). If there is a breach of Art. 9(1) DA, there is no basis for compensation.

III. Dispute settlement

The Data Act follows the **recent trend** in EU digital legislation and provides for 166 the possibility of out-of-court dispute settlement through **impartial** and **independent dispute settlement bodies to be established.**[129] According to Art. 10(1) DA, users, data holders and data recipients should have access to a certified dispute settlement body for the settlement of certain disputes in connection with making data available in accordance with Chapter III and Chapter IV DA. The Commission realised that making data available under the Data Act has the potential to give rise to numerous disputes between the parties involved.[130] Art. 10 DA attempts to address these issues through a dedicated dispute settlement mechanism.

1. Area of application

According to Art. 10(1) DA, users, data holders and data recipients must have ac- 167 cess to dispute settlement bodies to resolve disputes relating to Art. 4(3) and (9) and Art. 5(12) DA, as well as disputes relating to the fair, reasonable and non-discriminatory conditions for making data available, and the transparent manner in which data is made available in accordance with Chapter III and Chapter IV DA. The dispute settlement mechanism is thus intended to cover **in particular** disputes arising from the **making available of data** by data holders to data recipients.

In contrast to the Commission draft, the access to dispute settlement under 168 Art. 10(1) DA is available not only to data holders and data recipients,[131] but also to **users** and other third parties who are not data recipients. Users can go to a certified dispute settlement body in **two scenarios**: Firstly, in the event of a dispute with the data holder in relation to a dispute about contractual restrictions pursuant to Art. 4(2) DA (→ mn. 90; Art. 4(3)(b) DA), and secondly, to challenge a data holder's decision to refuse, withhold or suspend the sharing of data in order to protect its trade secrets contained in the data pursuant to Art. 4(7), (8) DA (→ mn. 107 et seqq.; Art. 4(9)(b) DA). Third parties other than data recipients may appeal to a dispute settlement body if the data holder decides to refuse, withhold or suspend making data available to the third party in order to protect its trade secrets.

---

[129] For example, in Art. 6(12) subpara. 2 DMA.
[130] Weiß MMR 2024, 101 (101).
[131] See COM(2022) 68 final: Art. 10.

169 In the **relationship between the data holder and the data recipient**, there are no corresponding restrictions on specific disputes. Data holders and data recipients may refer any dispute relating to the fair, reasonable and non-discriminatory conditions for making data available and the transparent manner in which data is made available in accordance with Chapter III and Chapter IV DA to a dispute settlement body. Proceedings before a certified dispute settlement body aim to provide data holders and data recipients a simple, fast and cost-effective way of resolving disputes, especially if they cannot agree on fair, reasonable and non-discriminatory conditions for making data available.

170 The dispute settlement procedure provided for under the Data Act is a **voluntary procedure** that users, data holders, data recipients and other third parties receiving data can, but do not have to, agree to use (rec. 52 DA). The parties involved are free to contact a **dispute settlement body of their choice**. This may also be established in a Member State other than that of the parties (rec. 53 DA).

2. Requirements for certification

171 Dispute settlement by a dispute settlement body within the meaning of Art. 10 DA requires that the body has been authorised by the Member State in which it is established. An application from the dispute settlement body is required for **certification**.

172 To be certified, the dispute settlement bodies must fulfil the cumulative **requirements** set out in **Art. 10(5) DA**, namely:

- it is impartial and independent, and issues its decisions in accordance with clear, non-discriminatory and fair rules of procedure (Art. 10 (5)(a) DA);
- it has the necessary expertise, in particular in relation to fair, reasonable and non-discriminatory terms and conditions, including compensation, and on making data available in a transparent manner, allowing the body to effectively determine those terms and conditions (Art. 10(5)(b) DA);
- it is easily accessible through electronic communication technology (Art. 10(5)(c) DA); and
- it is capable of adopting its decisions in a swift, efficient and cost-effective manner in at least one official language of the Union (Art. 10(5)(d) DA).

173 Unlike the original Commission draft,[132] the final version of Art. 10 DA does not provide for the Member States themselves to set up public dispute settlement bodies. As a result, dispute settlement bodies are to be set up as **private entities.**[133] However, the Member States can influence the constitution of the dispute settlement bodies via the certification procedure pursuant to Art. 10(5) DA. As the Data Act leaves open and does not specify which requirements the dispute settlement bodies must fulfil (e.g. with regard to the necessary expertise or the clarity and fairness of the procedural rules), there remains a certain scope of **discretion**, which the Member States can use.

174 According to Art. 10(6) DA, the Member States must notify the Commission of the dispute settlement bodies authorised under Art. 10(5) DA. The Commission is

[132] See COM(2022) 68 final: Art. 10.
[133] White MMR 2024, 101 (102).

obliged to maintain a **list** of the bodies on a website set up specifically for this purpose and to keep it up to date.

3. Costs

Art. 10(2), (3) DA contains provisions regarding the fees for the use of the dispute settlement body. According to Art. 10(2) DA, the dispute settlement bodies must inform the parties concerned of the fees or the methods used to determine the fees before they request a decision. The obligation to provide **transparency** before proceedings are initiated ensures that the parties can calculate the fees associated with the procedure and promote cost-effective dispute resolution.[134] 175

4. Relationship with courts and other bodies

Art. 10(7) DA regulates the relationship between the dispute settlement bodies and the national courts. The dispute settlement body shall decline to deal with a request for dispute settlement that has already been brought before another dispute settlement body or a court of any Member State. This is intended to **avoid conflicting decisions** on the same dispute. The dispute settlement body shall be prevented from dealing with a dispute if proceedings are already pending before the court of any Member State in respect of that dispute, irrespective of whether it is the Member State in which the dispute settlement body is established.[135] 176

5. Effect of the decision

The decision of a dispute settlement body is only binding for the parties in accordance with Art. 10(12) DA if they have **expressly consented** to the **binding effect** before the dispute settlement procedure begins. 177

Under no circumstances should participation in a dispute settlement procedure before a certified dispute settlement body prevent a party from 'exercising their fundamental rights to an effective remedy and a fair trial' (rec. 56 DA). Art. 10(13) DA therefore stipulates that the right of the parties to bring an effective **'remedy'** before a court of a Member State is not affected. However, how the procedure before the dispute settlement bodies fits into **state jurisdiction** is not explicitly regulated and remains unclear. The wording of Art. 10(13) DA suggests that the decision of a dispute settlement body can subsequently be reviewed by state courts.[136] However, in conjunction with Art. 10(7) DA, the provision can also be understood to mean that the proceedings before the dispute settlement body only constitute a temporary bar to parallel proceedings before the ordinary courts for the duration of the dispute settlement proceedings.[137] 178

---

[134] White MMR 2024, 101 (102).
[135] White MMR 2024, 101 (102).
[136] For more details see Weiß MMR 2024, 101 (102).
[137] Weiß MMR 2024, 101 (102).

CHAPTER 4
UNFAIR CONTRACTUAL TERMS

Bibliography: Beinke/Daute, 'Der Fairnesstest des Data Acts', RDi 2024, 69; Bomhard/Merkle, 'Der Entwurf eines EU Data Acts', RDi 2022, 168; Czychowski, 'Shaping the Data Economy: Ausgestaltung von Datenüberlassungsverträgen aus Herstellerperspektive', CR 2024, 80; Drexl et al., 'Position Statement of the Max Planck Institute for Innovation and Competition of 25 May 2022 on the Commission's Proposal of 23 February 2022 for a Regulation on harmonised rules on fair access to and use of data (Data Act)' (17.7.2022) <https://pure.mpg.de/rest/items/item_3388757_4/component/file_3395639/content> (last accessed: 7.1.2026; cited as: Drexl et al. Position Statement); Graf von Westphalen, 'Der neue Data Act – Eine Kaskade AGB-rechtlicher Verbote im unternehmerischen Verkehr', BB 2024, 515; Schwamberger, 'Die Klauselkontrolle in Art. 13 Data Act', MMR 2024, 96; Staudenmayer, 'Der Verordnungsvorschlag der Europäischen Kommission zum Datengesetz', EuZW 2022, 596; Wiebe, 'Der Data Act als vertragsrechtlicher Rahmen für Datennutzungsverträge', CR 2023, 777; Wiebe, 'Der Data Act – Innovation oder Illusion?', GRUR 2023, 1569.

A. Introduction 1

B. Scope of application 2
I. Personal scope 3
II. Material scope 4
III. Temporal scope of application 7

C. Relationship to the Unfair Contract Terms Directive 8

D. Unilateral imposition 10

E. Unfair terms control 13
I. Black clauses (Art. 13(4) DA) 14
II. Grey clauses (Art. 13(5) DA) 17
III. General clause (Art. 13(3) DA) 20
IV. Legal consequences 24

A. Introduction

1 The Data Act aims to address the risks that arise when one party has a stronger bargaining position when negotiating access to data and could exploit this position to the detriment of the other contracting party (rec. 58 DA). Such **contractual imbalances** to the detriment of companies that are not in a position to negotiate the conditions for access to data must be prevented. Chapter IV DA, which consists of a single Article, subjects certain data-related contractual clauses to a **fairness test**. According to Art. 13(1) DA, 'a contractual term concerning access to and the use of data or liability and remedies for the breach or the termination of data related obligations, which has been unilaterally imposed by an enterprise on another enterprise shall not be binding on the latter enterprise if it is unfair'. Art. 13 DA constitutes mandatory law and may not be derogated from by agreement where applicable.[1]

B. Scope of application

2 The scope of Art. 13 DA is broad and includes contractual terms concerning the use of and access to data, liability, rights and claims for breach or the termination of data-related obligations in contracts between enterprises.

[1] Raue in BeckOK DatenschutzR DA Art. 13 mn. 84.

I. Personal scope

In terms of personal scope, the fairness test under Art. 13 DA applies to all **business-to-business transactions**. Although the Commission's draft[2] only intended to protect SMEs, a corresponding restriction of the personal scope of application did not find its way into the final version of the Regulation. 3

II. Material scope

In fact, Art. 13(1) DA presupposes that the respective contractual term **relates to data**. There are no further restrictions to certain types of contracts or contract types. Therefore, both data sharing agreements within the scope of Art. 4 and 5 DA as well as data sharing or data use agreements fall within the scope of the fairness test under Art. 13 DA. 4

However, the exact scope of application of the provision remains unclear. In particular, it is not explicitly determined which types of contracts or groups of clauses fall within the ambit of Art. 13 DA. Terms used such as 'data access' and 'data use' are not defined in the Regulation and the definition of 'data' in Art 2(1) DA is exceptionally broad. This has led to varying interpretative approaches in the legal literature: While a narrower interpretation seeks to confine Art. 13 DA to contractual exchange relationships within the scope of Art. 4 et seq. DA,[3] a broader approach argues for extending its applicability to all data-related contracts between undertakings, provided that access to or use of data plays an autonomous contractual role.[4] Accordingly, the decisive criterion for determining applicability is not the type of contract as such, but rather the functional significance of the clause in question with regard to the processing, use, or provision of data. On the one hand, this includes contractual terms that regulate access to and use of data. On the other hand, the fairness test also covers contractual terms that regulate liability and measures in the event of a breach or termination of data-related obligations. In contrast, the fairness test does not apply to contractual terms that are not related to data. According to rec. 60 DA, this may lead to a **split review of the** same contract, distinguishing between data-related and other provisions. As not all Member States have extended unfair terms control to B2B contracts, the distinction between data-related and non-data-related contractual terms will be of varying importance in the different Member States. However, even for those Member States that do not subject B2B contracts to an unfair terms control, the distinction is important with regard to the reversal of the burden of proof under Art. 13(6) sent. 2 DA. 5

Contractual terms that define the **major obligations** of the contracting parties are also **excluded** from the review. Art. 13 DA expressly does not apply to contractual clauses determining the main subject matter of the contract or to the adequacy of the price in relation to the data supplied in exchange (Art. 13(8) DA). This corresponds in principle to the provisions of Art. 4(2) of the Unfair Contract Terms Directive.[5] The main difference, however, is that terms on major obligations are sub- 6

[2] COM(2022) 68 final.
[3] Determann/Hennemann in HK-DatenR DA Art. 13 mn. 40.
[4] See Wiebe CR 2023, 777 (785); Beinke/Daute RDi 2024, 69 (70).
[5] Council Directive 93/13/EEC of 5 April 1993 on unfair terms in consumer contracts, OJ 1993 L 95, 29.

ject to review under the Unfair Contract Terms Directive if they are not drafted in a clear and comprehensible manner.[6] The determination of what constitutes a major obligation can be challenging in the context of the different contractual arrangements of data-related contracts. Contractually defined requirements regarding data quality and quantity, as well as provisions governing access to and use of the data, may constitute core obligations, thereby excluding them from the scope of control under Art. 13(8) DA. The MCTs and SCCs published and approved by the Commission (→ Ch. 3 mn. 102), for example, propose defining specific data quality parameters in a separate annex (e.g. update intervals, technical formats).[7] These provisions form part of the individualised principal performance obligation and are therefore, in principle, not subject to review under unfairness control. At the same time, such clauses must be clearly distinguished from ancillary provisions that are subject to review – such as terms granting unilateral modification rights or imposing restrictions on data use. This distinction becomes particularly relevant with regard to Article 13(5)(c) DA, which aims to protect the economic usage rights of the data-providing party without challenging the principal obligations of the contract.[8]

III. Temporal scope of application

7 With regard to the temporal scope of application, the question arises as to whether the provision also applies to contracts concluded before the entry into force or before the date of application of the Regulation. In this respect, Art. 50(5) DA provides that the provisions of Chapter IV DA apply to contracts concluded after 12.9.2025. For contracts concluded on or before this date, the provisions of Chapter IV DA shall apply as of 12.9.2027, provided that such contracts are either of indefinite duration (Art. 50(6)(a) DA) or due to expire at least 10 years after 11.1.2024 (Art. 50(6)(b) DA).

C. Relationship to the Unfair Contract Terms Directive

8 The fairness test under Art. 13 DA is limited to business-to-business contracts. Art. 1(9) DA states that European Union law which aims to promote the interests of consumers and to ensure a high level of consumer protection and to protect their health, safety and economic interests **shall not be prejudiced**; the Directive on Unfair Contract Terms is expressly mentioned as an example.

9 In contracts between companies and consumers, data-related contractual clauses are therefore also subject to the Unfair Contract Terms Directive. Some have criticised that the unfair terms control in **B2C contracts** likewise requires adaptation to the realities of a modern data economy for contracts and that specific provisions on data should be incorporated accordingly. However, regardless of whether this criticism is justified, its practical impact is mitigated by the fact that the standards established in Art. 13(4) and (5) DA are likely to influence the interpretation and ap-

[6] Schwamberger MMR 2024, 96 (98).

[7] C(2025) 7750 final, p. 17.

[8] Determann/Hennemann in HK-DatenR DA Art. 13 mn. 50 et seqq.

plication of the unfair terms control under the Unfair Contract Terms Directive and may at least be taken into account indirectly.[9]

D. Unilateral imposition

Only those contractual terms which are 'unilaterally imposed' by one company on another, within the meaning of Art. 13(6) sent. 1 DA, are subject to a fairness test pursuant to Art. 13 DA. Terms are deemed to be unilaterally imposed if they are introduced by one contracting party without the other party being able to **influence** their content, despite having made a genuine but unsuccessful attempt to negotiate them. According to rec. 59 DA, a term is not deemed to be unilaterally imposed if the other party accepted it without having attempted to negotiate it in vain. The same applies to terms that have been modified during the course of negotiations. 10

It follows that terms which have been **accepted without objection** are not subject to a fairness test under Art. 13 DA. In this respect, there is a significant difference to the control of terms under the Unfair Contract Terms Directive and the applicable national law on general terms and conditions.[10] This has prompted criticism that such a requirement overly restricts the scope of application of the fairness test and, in practice, creates incentives for the drafting party to circumvent the fairness test. For example, the mere offer of an 'accept' button and its confirmation by the other party may suffice to exclude the applicability of Art. 13 DA.[11] However, rec. 59 DA suggests that this is the intended consequence and that in business transactions only the party who has made a genuine but unsuccessful attempt to negotiate should benefit from the fairness test. This raises the question of when an attempt to negotiate is sufficient and whether the negotiating party must explicitly communicate that negotiations are taking place.[12] 11

It remains doubtful to what extent inconsistencies arising from this provision can be offset by the **burden of proof rule** in Art. 13(6) sent. 2 DA.[13] According to this provision, the burden of proof that a contractual term was not unilaterally imposed lies with the party introducing the contractual term.[14] The user can fulfil its burden of proof by demonstrating that the clause in question was amended during the course of contract negotiations. Alternatively, it may argue that the other contracting party made no attempt to negotiate the term, meaning it does not qualify as unilaterally imposed within the meaning of Art. 13(6) sent. 1 DA. Due to the difficulty of proving negative facts, the other party would arguably bear a secondary burden of proof. In this respect, it is foreseeable that potential contractual partners will, in practice, make a **'strategic attempt at negotiation'**,[15] which they should well document, even in cases where meaningful negotiation appears unlikely. 12

---

[9] Drexl et al. Position Statement, mn. 129; Bomhard/Merkle RDi 2022, 168 (173) more cautious.

[10] Negotiation in accordance with § 305(1) sent. 3 BGB requires that the user is prepared to seriously negotiate the content of a contractual term.

[11] Czychowski CR 2024, 80 (83).

[12] Hennemann/Ebner/Karsten/Lienemann/Wienroeder Data Act, p. 143.

[13] Schwamberger MMR 2024, 96 (97 et seq.) tends to be optimistic.

[14] See also Wiebe CR 2023, 777 (779).

[15] Schwamberger MMR 2024, 96 (98).

E. Unfair terms control

13 The structure of the provisions in Art. 13 DA mirrors the structure of the Unfair Contract Terms Directive. Unfair terms control pursuant to Art. 13 DA similarly follows a **three-step approach**: Art. 13(3) DA sets out a general clause, which is further specified by a list of terms deemed unfair without the need for further assessment ('black clauses') in Art. 13(4) DA, and by a list of terms that are considered unfair only upon an assessment of the specific circumstances ('grey clauses') in Art. 13(5) DA.

I. Black clauses (Art. 13(4) DA)

14 According to the catalogue of unfair terms in Art. 13(4) DA, a contractual term is considered unfair in particular if its object or effect is to

- exclude or limit the liability of the party that unilaterally imposed the term for **intentional acts or gross negligence** (point (a));
- exclude the remedies available to the party upon whom the term has been unilaterally imposed in the case of **non-performance of contractual obligations**, or the liability of the party that unilaterally imposed the term in the case of a breach of those obligations (point (b)); or
- give the party that unilaterally imposed the term the exclusive right to determine whether the **data** supplied are **in conformity with the contract** or to interpret any contractual term (point (c)).

15 Neither Art. 13(4)(a) nor (b) DA are specifically tailored to data sharing agreements or data use agreements. Similar restrictions are also found in the Unfair Contract Terms Directive with respect to business-to-consumer transactions. In contrast, Art. 13(4)(c) DA constitutes a data-specific provision addressing the issue of **data quality**. In particular, this provision may call into question the effectiveness of so-called **'as is' clauses** that seek to limit responsibility for the quality of the data provided.[16] As the contractual terms defining the major obligations are not subject to the fairness test, it is advisable for the user of the term to define the data quality explicitly and make it the subject of a service description (→ mn. 6).[17]

16 Rec. 62 DA clarifies that terms directed against the individual elements of this Regulation are 'always considered unfair' and are therefore **'not binding'** within the meaning of Art. 13(1) DA.[18] Such terms are not subject to any further assessment.

II. Grey clauses (Art. 13(5) DA)

17 Art. 13(5) DA lists clauses that may be deemed unfair depending on an **assessment of the circumstances** in which they are used. The party imposing the contract term in question has the opportunity to disprove its unfairness.[19] Contract terms are considered unfair if they have the following purpose or effect:

---

[16] Wiebe GRUR 2023, 1569 (1575).
[17] Wiebe GRUR 2023, 1569 (1575).
[18] Graf von Westphalen BB 2024, 515 (516).
[19] Raue in BeckOK DatenschutzR DA Art. 13 mn. 53.

- inappropriately limit remedies in the case of **non-performance of contractual obligations** or liability in the case of a breach of those obligations, or an extension of the liability of the enterprise upon whom the term has been unilaterally imposed (point (a));
- allow the party that unilaterally imposed the term to **access and use** the data of the other contracting party in a manner that is significantly detrimental to the legitimate interests of the other contracting party, in particular when such data contain commercially sensitive data or are protected by trade secrets or by intellectual property rights (point (b));
- prevent the party upon whom the term has been unilaterally imposed from **using** the data provided or generated by that party during the period of the contract, or to limit the use of such data to the extent that that party is not entitled to use, capture, access or control such data or exploit the value of such data in an adequate manner (point (c));
- prevent the party upon whom the term has been unilaterally imposed from **terminating** the agreement within a reasonable period (point (d));
- prevent the party upon whom the term has been unilaterally imposed from obtaining a **copy of the data** provided or generated by that party during the period of the contract or within a reasonable period after the termination thereof (point (e));
- enable the party that unilaterally imposed the term to terminate the contract at **unreasonably short notice**, taking into consideration any reasonable possibility of the other contracting party to switch to an alternative and comparable service and the financial detriment caused by such termination, except where there are serious grounds for doing so (point (f));
- enable the party that unilaterally imposed the term to **substantially change** the price specified in the contract or any other **substantive condition** related to the nature, format, quality or quantity of the data to be shared, where no valid reason and no right of the other party to terminate the contract in the case of such a change is specified in the contract (point (g)).

The prohibitions under Art. 13(5) DA are formulated **more openly** and, in this respect, stand between the categorical prohibitions in Art. 13(4) DA and the general clause according to Art. 13(3) DA.[20] As in the blacklist pursuant to Art. 13(4), Art. 13(5) DA also contains general terms that are **not data-related**. These include, for example, the inappropriate limitation of contractual liability and legal remedies in Art. 13(5)(a) DA and the prevention of termination at short notice in Art. 13(5)(f) DA.[21] 18

In contrast, the other elements of (b), (c) and (d) contain **data-specific rules**. These are related to Art. 3 et seq. and Art. 6 DA. On the one hand, the contracting party should be protected against unjustified access to and use of its own data by the other party. On the other hand, the other party should not be excessively restricted in the use of the data. 19

[20] Wiebe CR 2023, 777 (781).
[21] Wiebe CR 2023, 777 (781).

III. General clause (Art. 13(3) DA)

20 The general clause in Art. 13(3) DA contains **two elements** reminiscent of Art. 3(1) Unfair Contract Terms Directive. It states that contractual terms are unfair if (i) their use grossly deviates from good commercial practice in data access and use, (ii) contrary to good faith and fair dealing.

21 The **relationship between the two criteria** remains unclear. The German language version combines them by using the conjunction 'or', thereby suggesting the assumption of an alternative relationship between the two elements.[22] As a result, a contractual term would already be considered unfair if either of the two elements was fulfilled. In contrast, the English version omits the 'or', thus implying a cumulative relationship that requires both conditions to be met.[23] The French language version also seems to assume **cumulative** requirements. This discrepancy suggests that the deviation in the German version is due to a drafting error.

22 With regard to the concept of **good commercial practice**, it is questionable whether such a standard currently exists, given the lack of binding legal provisions or model contract terms on data access and use. However, the recitals can at least serve as a point of reference. Rec. 58 DA refers in particular to the abuse of a stronger negotiating position. Rec. 61 DA explicitly emphasises that the economic advantage of one party falls within the scope of the contractual freedom and that a gross deviation from commercial practices exists only if the ability of the contracting party to protect its legitimate economic interests in relation to the data is objectively impaired. The threshold of intervention under Art. 13(3) DA therefore appears to be higher than under the Unfair Contract Terms Directive.[24]

23 The notion of **good faith**, as referenced in Art. 13(3) DA, also forms part of Art. 3(1) of the Unfair Contract Terms Directive. Taking into account the previous CJEU's case law, it is likely to be interpreted as requiring an assessment of whether the user of the term could reasonably have expected the other contracting party to accept the clause after individual negotiations on the basis of loyal and fair behaviour.[25] The model contract terms, which the Commission will recommend before 12.9.2025, should provide further guidance on the application of the general clause. The MCTs and SCCs published and approved by the Commission do not explicitly refer to the general clause in Art. 13(3) DA. Nevertheless, several elements within the model clauses implicitly reflect the fairness standards embedded in that provision. For instance, in the context of data provision, it is noted that the data sharer should at least ensure intelligibility of the data by providing appropriate metadata – a requirement described as a 'bare consequence of good faith in the conclusion of the Contract'.[26] This directly invokes the benchmark of 'good faith and fair dealing' as codified in Art. 13(3) DA. More broadly, the MCTs often pursue a balanced contractual structure intended to prevent unilateral exploitation of structural power asymmetries, e.g. through mutual termination rights, reciprocal liability clauses, and clearly defined access limitations. These elements align functionally with the objective of Art. 13 DA as clarified in rec. 58 DA. However, the

[22] Graf von Westphalen BB 2024, 515 (517).
[23] See also Wiebe CR 2023, 777 (782).
[24] See also Staudenmayer EuZW 2022, 596 (599).
[25] ECJ 14.3.2013 – case C-415/11, ECLI:EU:C:20143:164 = EuZW 2013, 464 para. 69 – Aziz.
[26] C(2025) 7750 final, p. 97.

reference to the general clause remains purely implicit. In this respect, the model terms fall short of addressing the uncertainties regarding the scope and application of the general clause. A more practice-oriented elaboration with specific criteria or guidance on how to determine whether a 'gross deviation from commercial practice' exists would be helpful in light of the current lack of binding norms or recognised standards for data access and use.

IV. Legal consequences

According to Art. 13(1) DA, unfair terms are **not binding**. However, according to Art. 13(7) DA, the rest of the contract shall remain in force, provided that the unfair term is **severable** from the contract. The law thus intends to preserve the contract in order to ensure the contracting party's access to data. A validity-preserving reduction (blue-pencilling) does not apply. 24

CHAPTER 5
SWITCHING BETWEEN DATA PROCESSING SERVICES: CLOUD SWITCHING

Bibliography: Bomhard, 'Auswirkungen des Data Act auf die Geschäftsmodelle von Cloud-Anbietern, Abbau von Wechselbarrieren', MMR 2024, 109; Bomhard/Merkle, 'Der Entwurf eines EU Data Acts. Neue Spielregeln für die Data Economy', RDi 2022, 168; Chebyshev/Cauchy, 'Edge Computing: Architectures, Challenges and Opportunities, Scitech Conferences', DOI:10.13140/RG.2.2.21021.52968 (cited as: Chebyshev/Cauchy Edge Computing); Falkhofen, 'Infrastrukturrecht des digitalen Raums – Data Governance Act, Data Act und Gaia-X', EuZW 2021, 787; Lagoni, 'Cloud Switching gemäß Data Act: Die Abschaffung von Switching Charges. Was ist ein Wechselentgelt und welche Wechsel sind betroffen?', CR 2024, 91; Mell/Grance, 'The NIST Definition of Cloud Computing' (2011) <https://nvlpubs.nist.gov/nistpubs/legacy/sp/nistspecialpublication800-145.pdf> (last accessed: 7.1.2026; cited as: Mell/Grance NIST Definition); Piltz/Zwerschke, 'Cloud Switching nach dem Data Act aus der Beratungsperspektive: Zentrale Herausforderungen für die vertragliche Ausgestaltung hindernisfreier Wechsel zwischen Datenverarbeitungsdiensten', CR 2024, 153; Pommerening/Nickel, 'Wechsel zwischen Datenverarbeitungsdiensten nach dem Data Act', RDi 2024, 289; Sattler, 'Anbieterwechsel nach dem Data Act – Standardvertragsklauseln für Verträge über Cloud-Computing', CR 2024, 213.

A. Overview 1

B. Addressees and services covered 9
I. Data processing services 10
1. Cloud computing services 19
2. Hosting in the narrower sense 27
3. Edge computing services 28
II. Privileging of on-premise services 33
III. Original and acquiring providers 34
IV. No privileges for SMEs 37
V. Beneficiary customers 39
VI. Application exceptions 42
1. Customised data processing services 43
2. Data processing services for testing and evaluation purposes 46
VII. Switching to similar services, ICT infrastructure or simultaneous use of several providers 47

C. Requirements for data processing services 52
I. Technical aspects of the change 53
1. Infrastructure provider – IaaS 54
2. Providers of data processing services in other respects 58
3. Limitations 62
II. Switching charges 64
III. Duty of loyalty 68
IV. Contract and information 69
1. Publication obligation on the website 70
2. Customer information 72
3. Contract drafting and standard contractual clauses 76

A. Overview

1 Chapter VI of the Data Act with its Art. 23–31 provides regulations for switching between data processing services, also known as **'cloud switching'**. The providers of such services are obliged to take measures and remove obstacles to enable effective switching. According to the provisions of the Data Act, this requires not only technical feasibility with continuous service provision but also the gradual reduction of switching fees.

2 The **aim** of these rules is to 'facilitate switching between data processing services [...] for a customer to terminate a contract for a data processing service, to

conclude one or more new contracts with different providers of data processing services, to port its exportable data and digital assets and, where applicable, benefit from functional equivalence' (rec. 84 DA). According to the regulators, this is a 'key condition for a more competitive market with lower entry barriers for new providers of data processing services, and for ensuring further resilience of the users of these services' (rec. 78 DA). Competition is to be strengthened through corresponding minimum obligations[1] for a smooth transition. This **promotion of competition** is at the forefront of the objectives of Chapter VI DA; customer protection follows.[2]

Three different constellations are covered by the scope of Art. 23 DA and therefore will be analysed in this Chapter: 3

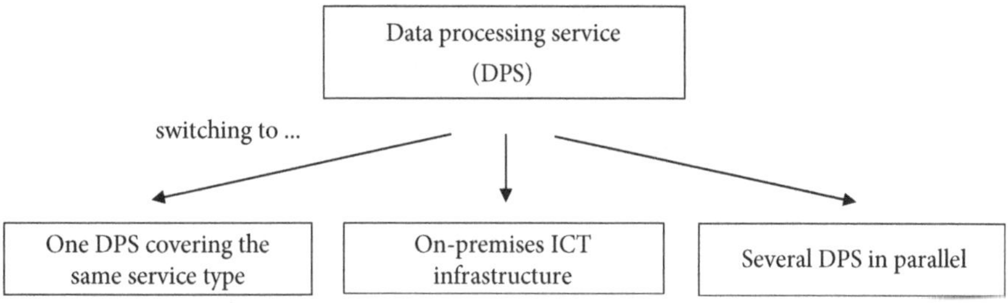

Fig. 1: Cloud switching constellations.

While the first constellation on the left is at the centre of the discussion, options 2 and 3 sometimes seem to be overlooked. This should not happen, as option 3 in particular can lead to considerable challenges in practice if parallel operation must be possible permanently and continuously, as this may also require corresponding interoperability and interfaces. Irrespective of the switching, Art. 34 DA provides for specific interoperability requirements in operations in the case of **data processing services used in parallel** and supplements this with a right to remuneration if this regulatory obligation leads to corresponding costs. 4

During the regulatory procedure, it was disputed whether such regulations were necessary: This presupposed that there would actually be **lock-in effects** in the market that would burden users and competitors and that switching between data processing services would not occur to the extent possible because technical and commercial obstacles would prevent this. The regulators have affirmed this: Insufficient technical interoperability standards and a lack of, or obstructive specifications on, switching fees and schedules hindered switching.[3] 5

Chapter VI DA is systematically divided into **Art. 23 DA** as the **starting standard**, which provides for the basic obligation of providers of data processing services to implement the measures provided for in the following Articles in order to enable customers to switch providers. These measures are requirements for: 6

- contract design and information obligations (Art. 25, 26, 28 DA),
- duties of conduct (good faith, Art. 27 DA),

[1] Piltz/Zwerschke CR 2024, 153 (155 mn. 7).
[2] See also Sattler CR 2024, 213 (214 mn. 2).
[3] Cf. on the background Falkhofen EuZW 2021, 787 (791).

- remuneration structure (Art. 29 DA),
- functional equivalence (technical measures, Art. 30 DA).

7 In addition, the interoperability requirements of Chapter VIII DA (→ Ch. 6 mn. 1 et seq.) and safeguards for third-country transfers in accordance with Chapter VII DA (→ Ch. 9 mn. 1 et seq.) apply.

8 According to Art. 41 DA, the Commission will present **standard contractual clauses** for cloud computing contracts by 12.9.2025, which implement the requirements of Art. 23 et seq. DA.[4] However, the final standard contractual clauses have only been published in November 2025 (→ mn. 82).[5] These are **not intended to be binding**. Nevertheless, they will (could) effectively represent a market standard that facilitates contract negotiations and could become a benchmark for other contractual arrangements. This is because the implementation of Art. 23 et seq. DA is mandatory. With the standard contractual clauses, the Commission shows a way in which it believes implementation can succeed. If there is a deviation from this, this is legally permissible, but requires justification as to why the deviating design fulfils the requirements of Art. 23 et seq. DA.

B. Addressees and services covered

9 The scope of application of Art. 23–31 DA extends to so-called data processing services and obliges the **providers** of such services.

I. Data processing services

10 According to **Art. 2 no. 8 DA**, a data processing service is 'a digital service that is provided to a customer that enables ubiquitous and on-demand network access to a shared pool of configurable, scalable and elastic computing resources of a centralised, distributed or highly distributed nature that can be rapidly provisioned and released with minimal management effort or service provider interaction'. It is then not clear whether the various criteria – in particular 'shared pool', 'elasticity' and 'scalability' – must all be technically present at the service provider or whether it is sufficient for one criterion to be present only at a **sub-service provider**.[6] Since Art. 23 et seq. DA apply to the offering of data processing services, there is some evidence that the offering as such must fulfil the criteria, regardless of the technical parameters at the level of the sub-service provider. If the provider limits the services of the sub-service provider to the effect that the technical possibilities, e.g. of scalability, elasticity or configurability, are not used for the provider's own customers and are therefore not (technically) part of the services in terms of design and contract, there is no data processing service within the meaning of the provisions of the Data Act.

11 The individual defining components of the 'data processing service' according to Art. 2 no. 8 DA are to be understood as follows:

---

[4] Sattler CR 2024, 213 for more details.
[5] C(2025) 7750 final, p. 116 et. seqq.
[6] Bomhard MMR 2024, 109 (110); Schmidt-Wudy in BeckOK DatenschutzR DA Art. 23 mn. 31.

- The first requirement of the definition in Art. 2 no. 8 DA is nationwide and on-demand network access. In the recitals of the DA, network access is described as **ubiquitous** and **on-demand** (rec. 80 DA). The provision of computing capacity should therefore be via the 'network and accessed through mechanisms promoting the use of heterogeneous thin or thick client platforms (from web browsers to mobile devices and workstations)' (rec. 80 DA). Put simply, this means the data processing service can be accessed at any time and from anywhere via a network (usually the internet). 12

- **Minimal management effort** and **minimal interaction** should mean that customers of data processing services can allocate computing capacities such as server time or network storage space themselves and without interaction with the provider of data processing services (rec. 80 DA). 13

- In addition, in order to be a data processing service, the data processing service must provide access to a 'shared pool of configurable, scalable and elastic computing resources of a centralised, distributed or highly distributed nature' in accordance with Art. 2 no. 8 DA. 14

  'Shared pool' means computing resources that are made available to multiple users. These users access the service via a shared access, with processing being performed separately for each user, even though the service is provided on the same electronic equipment (rec. 80 DA). 15

  These computing resources include networks, servers, virtual or physical infrastructures and software. They also include development tools for software, storage, applications and services (rec. 80 DA). These computing resources are **'scalable'** if they can be flexibly allocated by the provider of data processing services, regardless of their geographical location, in order to compensate for fluctuations in demand. **'Elastic'** describes computing resources that can be provided and released according to demand. This means that resources can be quickly expanded or reduced depending on the workload (rec. 80 DA). 16

  Computing resources are **distributed** if they are available on different networked computers or devices and can communicate and coordinate with each other by exchanging messages. 'Highly distributed' describes data processing services in which data is processed closer to where it is generated or collected, e.g. in a networked data processing device. Such highly distributed data processing services include, for example, edge services (rec. 80 DA). 17

This leads to a qualification of the following services as data processing services: 18

1. Cloud computing services

The terms cloud computing, cloud services or simply the 'cloud' are widely used, but are often vaguely defined. The term 'cloud' is often used to describe a situation in which data is not stored locally on the user's own device – but on an **external data centre** – and is made available via network access. This is basically correct, but in order to be able to legally categorise and differentiate it from other IT provision models, the terms need to be **defined more precisely**. Even with a pure hosting service in the narrow sense, the resources utilised are not located on the customer's own server. In this case, customers are allocated specific, limited and clearly defined 19 server resources in a specific data centre. It is questionable whether these pure hosting services are also covered by data processing services within the meaning of Art. 2 no. 8 DA.

20 The definition of cloud computing by the US standardisation body **NIST** describes cloud computing as a model 'for enabling ubiquitous, convenient, on-demand network access to a shared pool of configurable computing resources (e.g. networks, servers, storage, applications, and services) that can be rapidly provisioned and released with minimal management effort or service provider interaction'.[7]

21 According to this definition, cloud computing is characterised by **five properties**:

- broad network access (network access via interfaces),
- resource pooling (pooling of resources),
- rapid elasticity (scalability and elasticity),
- on-demand self-service (self-service and on-demand availability),
- measured service (usage-dependent and measurable service provision).

22 The European Union Agency for Cybersecurity (**ENISA**) also defines cloud computing as an 'on-demand service model for IT provision, often based on virtualisation and distributed computing technologies'.

23 In contrast to pure hosting in the narrower sense, these cloud computing services do not process the services on a specific computer. Instead, they are transferred and moved back and forth **between various servers** as required (or optimised by the provider). This allows resources to be offered and scaled flexibly in the shortest possible time.[8]

24 The term 'cloud' is defined in other laws, taking these differentiations into account, although a generally applicable definition has not yet been established. The Digital Markets Act (Art. 2 no. 13 DMA) and the NIS-2-Directive (rec. 17 DA) define cloud computing services as a 'digital service that enables access to a scalable and elastic pool of shareable computing resources'. § 384 sent. 1 no. 5 of Book Five of the German Social Security Code (SGB V) defines the cloud computing service as a digital service 'that enables on-demand management and comprehensive remote access to a scalable and elastic pool of shareable computing resources, even if these resources are distributed across multiple locations'.

25 This means that the definitions describing cloud computing services are almost identical to the definition of **data processing services** in Art. 2 no. 8 DA. Cloud computing services therefore fall under the provisions of Art. 23 et seqq. DA.

26 As typical examples of services covered, rec. 80 DA mentions the classic forms of cloud computing as Infrastructure-as-a-Service (IaaS), Platform-as-a-Service (PaaS) and Software-as-a-Service (SaaS). Storage-as-a-Service and Database-as-a-Service are also mentioned. In the market, however, these designations are not used according to strictly technical characteristics. The result depends on whether the definitions according to Art. 2 no. 8 DA are fulfilled.

---

[7] Mell/Grance NIST Definition, p. 2.
[8] Missling in BeckFormB IT-R H. 7, p. 663.

2. Hosting in the narrower sense

Pure hosting services in the narrower sense are **not** likely to be **covered** by the definition of data processing services. It is true that in the case of hosting, the service is usually accessed or provided via an interface, usually the internet. However, with pure hosting in the narrower sense, a **specific storage space**, a specific server or similar is always rented so that the user always knows on which physical computer the application is running. The elasticity and scalability required for a data processing service within the meaning of Art. 2 no. 8 DA is then lacking. 27

3. Edge computing services

According to rec. 80 DA, edge computing services also constitute a data processing service pursuant to Art. 2 no. 8 DA. **Edge services** are a form of this highly distributed data processing, which could generate new business models that should be open and interoperable from the outset (rec. 80 DA). 28

Edge services are services that are based on edge computing infrastructures. With edge computing, data is processed **close to its source of generation,** such as with IoT devices, instead of sending the data to remote data centres and processing it there in order to then send the processed data back again, as is usually the case with hosting services or cloud computing services.[9] Edge services are based on edge computing infrastructures, which represent a type of cloud computing architecture or a cloud service or can have a connection to these, but are not necessarily dependent on them, as the processing for edge services can either take place locally on the edge device itself or in a nearby edge infrastructure. Edge services use this localised processing to process data in real time, minimise latency and save bandwidth. These services can support a wide range of applications. 29

While some edge services may be integrated into **cloud services** in order to utilise additional computing power, storage or data analysis, others are completely autonomous and perform all necessary calculations and actions locally at the edge, without a (constant) connection to a cloud. It is therefore questionable to what extent edge services fall under data processing services pursuant to Art. 2 no. 8 DA or are excluded as hosting in the narrower sense. Similar to cloud services, edge services can be dynamic and flexible. In many cases, these services can also be accessed via a network. 30

In most cases, however, edge services do not utilise a shared pool of computing resources. Instead, edge services usually use **localised computing resources** that are closer to the end users or the data sources they serve. In some cases, however, multiple edge services may access shared resources, especially if these services are deployed on a shared edge platform or edge computing cluster, in order to optimise resources such as computing power or storage and make them more efficient. 31

These characteristics will ultimately always depend on the respective architecture and implementation of the specific edge services. Whether edge services therefore fall under the definition of Art. 2 no. 8 DA and thus under the obligations of Art. 23 et seqq. DA depends on the respective edge service and its architecture. Even if these are mentioned as an example in rec. 80 DA, only those edge services 32

[9] Chebyshev/Cauchy Edge Computing, p. 2.

that fulfil all the requirements mentioned there are to be qualified as data processing services within the meaning of Art. 2 no. 8 DA.

II. Privileging of on-premise services

33 Traditional on-premise services will regularly not fulfil the criteria of data processing services pursuant to Art. 2 no. 8 DA due to a lack of scalability and elasticity or a 'shared pool'. In addition, Art. 2 no. 34 DA only defines a switching of provider as the transition between cloud providers or from a cloud provider to an on-prem provider. 'Switching of data processing services' according to Art. 2 no. 34 DA therefore does not include the change between on-prem providers or an on-prem provider to a cloud provider.[10] In other provisions of the Data Act, too, a switch between data processing services is only ever understood to mean a switch between cloud providers or from a cloud provider to an on-prem provider (cf. Art. 23, Art. 25(1), (3)(b) DA).

III. Original and acquiring providers

34 According to Art. 24 DA, the responsibility of providers of data processing services pursuant to Art. 23, 25, 29, 30 and 34 DA only applies to the services, contracts or business practices offered by the original provider (**'source provider'**) of the data processing services. This is to be distinguished from the **'destination provider'**.

35 There is no explicit definition of the terms in the Data Act. However, it is clear from the context that the source provider is to be understood as the existing provider with whom the customer previously had a contractual relationship. The provider to which the customer wishes to switch is the destination provider.[11]

36 Such an understanding is consistent, as the obligations to facilitate continuous switching must primarily affect the **source provider**, whose economic interests could lie in retaining the customer via the lock-in effect and by **making switching more difficult**. Even without regulatory requirements, the destination provider will have an interest in taking over the new customer with as few obstacles as possible, as this promises economic advantages and is essential for customer acquisition.

IV. No privileges for SMEs

37 Small and medium-sized enterprises are not privileged. If they offer data processing services, they are obliged by Art. 23 et seqq. DA in the same way as large undertakings.

38 In principle, SMEs should benefit from the provisions of the Data Act.[12] However, this does not mean that they are not also subject to obligations. It was discussed whether the inclusion of SMEs in Chapter VI DA would place an unreasonable burden on them, whereby the overall weighing up of the burdens and benefits

---

[10] Cf. similar argumentation of Schmidt-Wudy in BeckOK DatenschutzR DA Art. 23 mn. 31.
[11] See also Bomhard MMR 2024, 109 (110).
[12] Cf. e.g. rec. 3, 19 DA.

led to the legislative decisions in favour of an obligation.[13] Whether the provisions of the Data Act actually strengthen the **innovative capacity** of SMEs is to be re-assessed by the Commission's review by 2028 (see Art. 49(1)(m) DA). Depending on the outcome, the provisions for SMEs will then be revised (Art. 49(2), (4) DA).

V. Beneficiary customers

Customers are the beneficiaries. According to Art. 2 no. 30 DA, a customer 39
means a natural or legal person 'that has entered into a contractual relationship with a provider of data processing services with the object of using one or more data processing services'. This includes both **traders** within the meaning of § 14 of the German Civil Code (BGB) and **consumers** within the meaning of § 13 BGB or the EU definition of consumer.

The Commission's draft discussed whether only **business customers** should be 40
favoured by the provisions of Chapter VI DA. The starting point was the fact that the Commission expressly referred to favouring business customers in its explanations.[14] However, this limitation was not found in the regulatory part of the first draft and is not implemented in the final provisions either.

In order to enable effective switching between data processing services, the group 41
of beneficiaries also includes **non-commercial customers** of a data processing service. The ability of customers to switch between services is a 'key condition for a more competitive market with lower entry barriers for new providers of data processing services, and for ensuring further resilience of users of these services' (rec. 78 DA). The competitive conditions for providers are independent of whether customers use the services commercially or privately.

VI. Application exceptions

Art. 31 DA exempts certain data processing services from the obligations of 42
Art. 23 et seqq. DA or restricts them. According to Art. 31(3) DA, the customer must be informed of any restrictions before the contract is concluded.

1. Customised data processing services

Art. 31(1) DA exempts such data processing services from the obligations to es- 43
tablish functional equivalence pursuant to Art. 23(d) DA, the gradual abolition of switching fees pursuant to Art. 29 DA and certain technical switching aspects pursuant to Art. 30(1)–(3) DA where 'the majority of main features has been custom-built to accommodate the specific needs of an individual customer or where all components have been developed for the purposes of an individual customer'. This requires more than just **customising** standardised applications. As a rule, individual developments[15] or at least extensive customising will be required.

The DA does not specify when **'most'** of the central functions were developed 44
individually. The wording requires a scope of more than 50 % in any case. In some

[13] Cf. e.g. rec. 49, 51, 100 DA.
[14] COM(2022) 68 final, 14.
[15] Sattler CR 2024, 213 (216 mn. 16) is restrictive in this respect.

cases, a higher proportion of at least 75 % is even required.[16] At best, there are reasons for this in the sense and purpose of the regulations to enable competition as far as possible. However, the fact that 'mostly' only requires more than half speaks against such an increased requirement.

45 Furthermore, the service may not be offered on a large commercial scale 'via the catalogue of provider of data processing services'. This is the case if the corresponding service is also offered to other customers to a significant extent **by default**.

2. Data processing services for testing and evaluation purposes

46 If data processing services are not provided as a full version, but only for test and evaluation purposes and only for a limited period of time, they are excluded from the scope of Art. 23 et seqq. DA as a whole (Art. 31(2) DA).

VII. Switching to similar services, ICT infrastructure or simultaneous use of several providers

47 Art. 23(1) DA limits the obligations to switching to a data processing service 'covering the same service type, which is provided by a different provider of data processing services or to on-premises ICT infrastructure, or, where relevant, [enable customers] to use several providers of processing services at the same time'.

48 A change to the **same type of service** requires that the change is to be made to a data processing service with the same primary objective, the same service model and the same main functionalities (Art. 2 no. 9 DA). When exactly a 'same' service exists still needs to be clarified in individual cases. Based on the telos, it must be an **interchangeable service in competition**, as only then can the feared lock-in effects arise. In this case, reference points for the interpretation could also be taken from competition law, which has developed an empirical approach to the identification of interchangeable services for the market definition via the SSNIP test ('Small but Significant Non-transitory Increase in Price').[17]

49 The switch to the customer's own server structures, which is referred to in the wording of the provision as **'on-premises ICT infrastructure'**, is also privileged. According to Art. 2 no. 33 DA, these are 'ICT infrastructures and computing resources owned, rented or leased by the customer, located in the data centre of the customer itself and operated by the customer or a third party'.

50 In addition, the envisaged measures should enable the customer of data processing services to utilise **several providers** of such services **at the same time**, if necessary. This should enable customers to combine different services in their own interest and for their own purposes.[18]

51 In all of this, a **switch** pursuant to Art. 2 no. 34 DA occurs when a process is initiated in which 'a source provider of data processing services, a customer of a data processing service and, where relevant, a destination provider of data processing services, whereby the customer of a data processing service changes from using a data processing service to using another data processing service of the same service

[16] Schmidt-Wudy in BeckOK DatenschutzR DA Art. 31 mn. 14.

[17] See Commission, Notice on the definition of the relevant market for the purposes of Community competition law, OJ 1997 C 372, 5.

[18] Schmidt-Wudy in BeckOK DatenschutzR DA Art. 23 mn. 36.

type or other service, offered by a different provider of data processing services, or to an on-premises ICT infrastructure, including through extracting, transforming and uploading the data'. The switch therefore does not require the **termination** of the old contract and certainly not the effectiveness of such a termination. If desired, a customer can also switch to a new similar service without changing the existing contract.

C. Requirements for data processing services

If data processing services are addressed by the provisions of Art. 23 et seqq. DA, there are **four main areas of obligation**, namely technical (→ mn. 53), commercial (→ mn. 64), with regard to behaviour (→ mn. 68) and finally for the design of contractual documents and information (→ mn. 69). 52

I. Technical aspects of the change

Art. 30 DA addresses 'Technical aspects of the switching'. Depending on the scope of services, the providers of data processing services have different obligations. 53

1. Infrastructure provider – IaaS

Data processing services that are limited to the provision of infrastructure – regularly so-called **Infrastructure-as-a-Service** offerings, or IaaS for short – are only subject to limited technical requirements in accordance with Art. 30(1) DA. 54

The limited obligations of para. 1 apply to providers of services that are 'limited to infrastructural elements such as **servers**, **networks** and the **virtual resources** necessary for operating the infrastructure'. These services do not include access to software or other applications; rather, only the infrastructure or infrastructure elements are provided. 55

Providers of such services limited to the infrastructure level must take exclusively available, appropriate measures to implement the technical requirements in accordance with Art. 30(1) DA to enable **functional equivalence** in the use of the receiving data processing service. The original provider of data processing services facilitates the change in accordance with Art. 30(1) sent. 2 DA 'by providing capabilities, adequate information, documentation, technical support and, where appropriate, the necessary tools'. 56

According to rec. 86 DA, functional equivalence means that after the switch 'a minimum level of functionality in the environment of new data processing service of the same service type after switching, where the destination data processing service delivers a materially comparable outcome in response to the same input for shared features supplied to the customer under the contract'. The concept of functional equivalence thus remains extremely vague.[19] When a **'minimum level of functionality'** is achieved is not specified in more detail. The decisive factor will be whether a switch is successful or whether the infrastructure of the transferring service provider prevents this. 57

---

[19] See also Sattler CR 2024, 218.

2. Providers of data processing services in other respects

58 All providers of data processing services that are covered by the cloud switching requirements, but are not limited to the provision of infrastructure elements, must comply with the technical requirements of Art. 30(2)–(5) DA.

59 **Open interfaces** for switching must be provided by these standard addressees. These interfaces must be sufficient to develop software for communication when switching, in particular the corresponding interface information must be available (Art. 30(2) DA).

60 In addition, **compatibility** with common specifications based on open interoperability specifications or harmonised interoperability standards must be ensured in accordance with Art. 30(3) DA. The implementation period for this is individually twelve months after publication. Corresponding measures must be documented in the online register in accordance with Art. 26(b) DA. If there are no such specifications or standards, the data must be exported in a structured, commonly used and machine-readable format in accordance with Art. 30(5) DA.

61 The open **interoperability specifications** or **harmonised standards for interoperability** are regulated in more detail in Art. 35 DA in the Chapter on interoperability (→ Ch. 6 mn. 8). In particular, it lists the content and objectives they cover and pursue, as well as the conditions and procedure under which they are adopted. The Commission plays a central role here through the delegated acts within its remit (see also → mn. 8, 38).

3. Limitations

62 The addressed providers are not obliged 'to develop new technologies or services, or to disclose or transfer digital assets that are protected by intellectual property rights or that constitute a trade secret, to a customer or a different provider of data processing services or compromise the customer's security and integrity of service' (Art. 30(6) DA). This sets out exceptions to the obligation to technically enable and facilitate the change, focussing on three elements:

- no **obligation to innovate**,
- no disclosure of **trade secrets** and copyright protection,
- no impairment of **IT security**, including integrity.

63 When these exceptions apply must be assessed on a case-by-case basis and examined by the norm addressee and, in the event of a dispute, presented and proven. A risk for IT security can occur in the switching process in particular regarding the data processing itself (including the transfer and retrieval), identity management, access control, and data integrity and availability.

II. Switching charges

Art. 29 DA provides for the **gradual withdrawal** of switching charges: 64

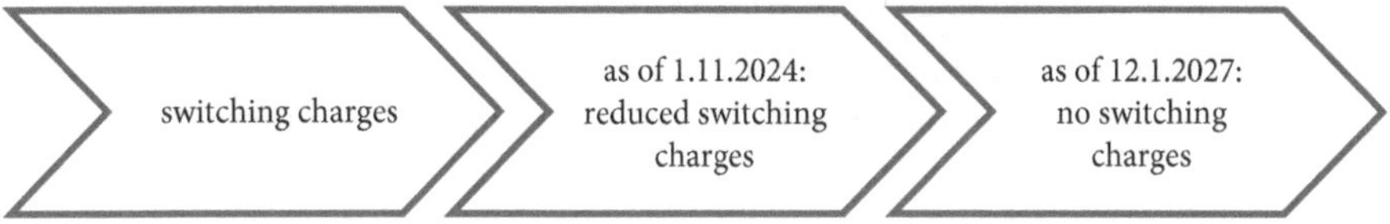

Fig. 2: Gradual withdrawal of switching charges.

According to Art. 29(3) DA, reduced switching charges may not exceed the costs 65 incurred in connection with the switching in question. A cap on the amount of the **actual costs** caused by a specific service – in this case switching – is familiar from the regulation of charges in the network industries, for example. In particular, this covers **data extraction costs.**[20] The costs must be calculated in detail and disclosed in the event of a review. According to the wording, they are limited here to the variable costs incurred by an individual bill; **overheads** should not be allocated to this due to the close connection to the relevant bill ('directly linked'). A reasonable **return on equity** is included as a cost item, as are **debt costs**.

Customers must be **informed** of the respective switching fees prior to the conclu- 66 sion of the contract as soon as the Data Act comes into force (Art. 29(4) DA). The information should be provided via the website or otherwise easily accessible (Art. 29(6) DA).

The question of how effective this regulation actually is remains open, as the 67 costs incurred for switching are now likely to be priced in elsewhere. It is relevant insofar as it prevents **prohibitive pricing** to avoid switching.

III. Duty of loyalty

Art. 27 DA obliges all parties involved in a switching to be mutually loyal in or- 68 der to actually enable and always support the goal of a successful switching. Whether this standard has an enforceable, actionable regulatory content is questionable. In particular, it will become the basis for the concretisation of specific **secondary obligations** via the standard of **good faith** and will play an important role in the **interpretation of contracts**.

IV. Contract and information

The basis and foundation for enabling simple switching between data processing 69 services is the corresponding information and the definition of the associated contractual regulations. Art. 25, 26, 28 DA contain correspondingly extensive provisions.

[20] Cf. Lagoni CR 2024, 91 (92).

1. Publication obligation on the website

70 Providers of data processing services whose services are not limited to the EU must provide specific information on their websites about the data processing services they offer in accordance with Art. 28 DA:

- **jurisdiction** (para. 1 point (a)) and
- general description of the **technical, organisational and contractual measures** to prevent unauthorised international governmental access to or unlawful transfer of non-personal data stored in the EU (para. 1 point (b)).

71 Reference must be made to the website in the respective contract documents. Information on **switching fees** must also be provided online in accordance with Art. 29(6) DA (→ mn. 64).

2. Customer information

72 In addition, providers of data processing services must provide their (potential) customers with certain information prior to the conclusion of the contract in accordance with Art. 26 DA. This is unilateral information that **does not** have to become **part of the contract**. Providers are well advised not to make this part of the contract, if only to obtain simpler modification options.

73 Specifically, this involves information about

- the **switching procedure** (available switching and porting methods and formats as well as restrictions and technical limitations) and
- the details of the **data structures** and data formats and on the relevant standards and open interoperability specifications in which the exportable data are available.

74 The purpose of the obligation to provide information is to ensure the **easy availability** of **information** that is particularly important for a change and that may also be relevant for the acquiring service.

75 In this respect, Art. 26(b) DA refers to an **online register** in which the current specifications and standards are to be stored in a retrievable format. It remains unclear whether this is a format to be created by each individual provider or whether a centralised online register will be set up by a public sector body. As long as such a register does not exist, the individual providers will have no choice but to systematically store the relevant information online themselves in order to fulfil their obligations and provide information about it accordingly.

3. Contract drafting and standard contractual clauses

76 The rights of the customer and the obligations of the provider of a data processing service in relation to a possible change must be set out in a **written contract** in accordance with Art. 25(1) sent. 1 DA. According to sent. 2 of the provision, this contract must be made available to the customer in a storable and reproducible form **prior to signing**. Sent. 2 already suggests that the written form requirement according to sent. 1 cannot mean a paper copy with a handwritten signature on paper, which in view of the market environment would also run counter to the established processes of electronic drawing without justifying such an intensive warning function. However, under German law, the requirement could lead to the strict legal

form of § 126 BGB, so that only the qualified electronic signature pursuant to § 126a BGB could take the place of the paper copy. However, this ignores the fact that the term is used in the Data Act and is therefore to be interpreted as a term under EU law and not under German civil law. From the perspective of EU law, there are strong arguments in favour of 'written' merely serving to distinguish it from 'orally' and encompassing any representation consisting of words and/or numbers that can be read, reproduced and communicated, regardless of whether on paper or electronically.[21] This corresponds to the requirements of Art. 25(1) sent. 2 DA.

According to the new regulations, contracts for a data processing service within the meaning of Art. 2 no. 8 DA must also contain a number of **minimum provisions** in which the provider agrees to provide switching support. 77

Specifically, the contract must at least contain provisions on the following aspects, all of which are listed in detail in Art. 25(2) DA: 78

- clauses **enabling** the customer to **switch** to a data processing service offered by another data processing service provider upon request or to port all exportable data and digital assets to an on-premises ICT infrastructure without undue delay and in no event later than the end of the mandatory transition period of 30 calendar days from the end of the maximum notice period;
- the obligation of the provider of data processing services to **support** the customer's **exit strategy** relevant to the contracted services, including by providing all relevant information;
- a clause specifying that the contract shall be considered **terminated** and the customer shall be notified of the termination if the switch is successful or if the customer wishes to delete their data;
- a **maximum notice period** for initiating the change, which shall not exceed two months;
- an exhaustive specification of all **categories of data** and digital assets that can be **ported** during the switching process;
- an exhaustive specification of categories specific to the internal functioning of the provider's data processing service that are to be exempted from the exportable data (**trade secrets**);
- a **minimum period for data retrieval** of at least 30 calendar days after a transition period;
- a clause guaranteeing that all exportable data and digital assets generated directly by the customer or relating directly to the customer will be completely **erased** at the end of the retrieval period;
- **switching charges**.

The requirements for contract design are comprehensive. In some places, there are concerns that these obligations will require providers of data processing services to disclose expertise and data architectures, thereby limiting their **competitiveness**. However, unlike in the context of data access rights, there should be no obligation to disclose trade secrets here, not even with a confidentiality agreement. This is 79

---

[21] See for example ECJ 7.12.2023 – case C-441/22, ECLI:EU:C:2023:970 = ZfBR 2024, 62 (69 para. 58) – Obshtina Razgrad.

shown by the limitation provided for in the listing to be able to refrain from a transfer in the event of risks to trade secrets.

80 The specification of a **maximum termination period** of two months to conclude the switching is noteworthy. Without the wording being clear, this is probably intended to reduce the overall contract term and exclude minimum terms of longer duration.[22] One argument in favour of such an interpretation is that lock-in effects are to be avoided, which could also be promoted by long-term contracts. In addition, there are various other provisions that rule out the possibility of the notice period being extended again by circumvention, in particular in Art. 23(a) DA or in Art. 25(3) DA. There is currently a debate as to whether it is possible to deviate from this, either through individual contracts or with the express consent and confirmation of the customer. One argument in favour of this is that customers often have an interest in longer-term commitments due to the complex implementation processes involved in new applications. Whether commercial advantages may be taken into account here is debatable in view of the prohibition of switching fees in the DA. One argument in favour of this is that in the case of a longer contract term, it is not only the switching fees that are a commercial aspect, but also, for example, the requirements for the implementation of new customers, training, and management processes. It should also be noted that, according to a narrow interpretation of the standard, a corresponding short-term right of termination only applies to the corresponding switch, but not if the customer wishes to switch to a different type of service or terminate use altogether.

81 This and the various support obligations also make it clear that the requirements for contract design are not just about creating suitable terms of use, but about far-reaching **obligations** to act and product design as well as commercial considerations.

82 According to Art. 41 DA, the Commission is to publish **standard contractual clauses** (SCCs), also known as **model contractual terms**, before 12.9.2025. The Commission did not publish the SCCs in time. The final model contractual terms and standard contractual clauses have been published in November 2025.[23] The SCCs are not intended to be binding, but will nevertheless provide significant guidance for the drafting of contracts, as they set out how the Commission would interpret and apply the provisions of the DA. Even though Art. 41 DA only refers to cloud computing and not to cloud switching, the provisions there only make sense if the Commission publishes standard contractual clauses specifically for cloud switching and for the implementation of Art. 25 DA.[24] The Commission consulted initial drafts of its SCCs with stakeholders in winter 2024 as well as in the first half of 2025 and obtained comments in extensive discussions. The final SCCs have been published in November 2025.[25] As planned there are six blocks with the following core content:

[22] Thus with convincing criticism Bomhard/Merkle RDi 2022, 168 (175 mn. 56); Bomhard MMR 2024, 109 (111).

[23] C(2025) 7750 final.

[24] Cf. comprehensively Sattler CR 2024, 213 (221).

[25] C(2025) 7750 final, p.116 et. seqq.

- **Non-Dispersion**: The provider undertakes that all contractual arrangements will be easily, readily and continuously findable, available and accessible for the customer.
- **Non-Amendment**: Unilateral amendments and supplements are largely excluded, with only a few exceptions explicitly listed.
- **Liability**: The provider is fully liable, customer data is fully protected. Limitations of liability are planned, for example, for custom-build solutions.
- **Security and Business Continuity**: The provider undertakes 'the most appropriate technical and organisational measures to ensure the level of security and resilience appropriate to the risks presented by the services and their intended and reasonably foreseeable use'.
- **Termination**: The provider specifies when exactly the contract is considered to be terminated and formulates various options for how the contract period and the right of termination can be formulated.
- **Switching and Exit**: The provider specifies what has to be switched (exportable data, digital assets) and recommends a switching and exit plan as Annex. In particular, the exportable data categories and digital assets should be fully listed and risks to continuity mentioned.

The Commission's proposals are extensive and do not stop at a regulation with a **83**
single paragraph for each issue. There are even 14 paragraphs just for security and business continuity.

CHAPTER 6
INTEROPERABILITY AND SMART CONTRACTS

A. Overview ... 1
B. Interoperability for data spaces and data sharing ... 5
C. Interoperability of data processing services ... 8
D. Interoperability for smart contracts ... 14

A. Overview

1 Chapter VIII DA lays down specific interoperability requirements in its Art. 33–36. According to Art. 2 no. 40 DA, interoperability refers to 'the ability of two or more data spaces or communication networks, systems, connected products, applications, data processing services or components to exchange and use data in order to perform their functions'. The interoperability requirements in the Data Act are intended to define the basic requirements for **extensive and simplified exchange of data**. The aim is to remove barriers to the sharing of data across common data spaces and between different products. From the Commission's perspective, this is an essential prerequisite for open innovation in the European data economy.[1] As the Commission believes that market-driven processes are not capable of defining technical standards or norms, the Data Act is intended to promote standardisation.

2 Structurally, the standards differ depending on the target group:

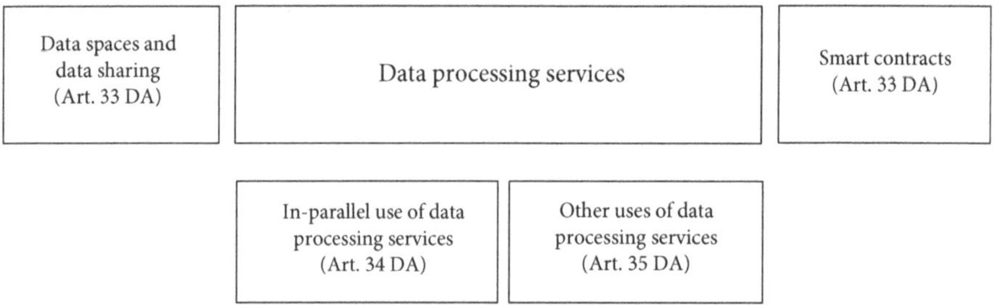

Fig. 1: Interoperability requirements.

3 Interoperability has taken on a special significance in the EU's new digital law. It is becoming increasingly important. Accordingly, the Commission has also stated: 'Data interoperability and quality [...] are key for the exploitation of the data value, [...]'.[2]

4 The interoperability requirements of the Data Act are **minimum requirements**. They are an introduction to interchangeable services across the three product segments addressed. The requirements remain abstract at the outset in order to extend the scope of application to as many technical and contractual constellations as possible and to keep it **open to development**. The delegated acts, specifications and standards to be issued under the regulations will have a decisive influence on the material arrangements.

[1] COM(2020) 66 final, 12.
[2] COM(2020) 66 final, 8.

B. Interoperability for data spaces and data sharing

Art. 33 DA addresses operators of data spaces, i.e. centralised actors with access to a wide range of data collections. One example of such a data space is currently being promoted in the healthcare sector at the EU level with the European Health Data Space (**EHDS** for short). The EHDS is established by Regulation (EU) 2025/327 on the European Health Data Space (EHDS). The regulation entered into force on 26.3.2025. Further data spaces for various sectors are to follow.[3] Art. 33 DA sets out a sector-neutral, high-level interoperability framework for data spaces.[4] **5**

To ensure interoperability within the data spaces, the DA emphasises **transparency** in the first pillar. Data space operators must provide a range of defined information and details so that data recipients and users can use them to establish the interoperability of data and data utilisation mechanisms: **6**

- The **content of a dataset**, use restrictions, licences, data collection methods and data quality must be defined so that the data recipient can easily find, access and use the data.
- This also applies to the description of **data structures**, data formats, vocabulary, classification schemes, taxonomies and code lists to be provided in a publicly accessible and consistent manner.
- The **technical means for data access** (e.g. programming interfaces and their terms of use) must be clearly described to allow for automatic access and automatic transmission of data between the parties continuously in a machine-readable format.

The Commission can also develop specific harmonised requirements through **delegated acts**. This forms the second key element of effective interoperability:[5] in addition to the first pillar of information, the second pillar also shapes the material and content of interoperability through **standardisation**. **7**

C. Interoperability of data processing services

Art. 34 and 35 DA regulate the interoperability of data processing services and thus supplement the provisions of Art. 23 et seqq. DA on cloud switching (→ Ch. 5 mn. 1 et seqq.), whereby a distinction is made between data processing services for parallel use (Art. 34 DA) and other data processing services (Art. 35 DA). **8**

For **data processing services used in parallel**, Art. 34 DA declares certain requirements, which otherwise only apply to technical switching via Art. 30 DA, to be generally applicable. This enables switching between data processing services that are used concurrently during operations and thus to use them in an interoperable and compatible manner. The associated obligations regarding the security of the services are a cause for concern. **9**

Art. 34(2) DA authorises **charges**: When a data processing service is used in parallel with another data processing service, the providers of data processing services **10**

---

[3] See the overview at <https://digital-strategy.ec.europa.eu/en/policies/data-spaces> (last accessed: 7.1.2026).

[4] Lienemann in Hennemann/Ebner/Karsten/Lienemann/Wienroeder Data Act, p. 223.

[5] Schmidt in BeckOK DatenschutzR DA Art. 33 mn. 7 also refers to the 'two pillars' of Art. 33 DA.

may **impose data egress charges,**[6] but solely to pass on the actual extraction costs incurred without exceeding them. The limitation to the variable **actual costs** based on actual causation mirrors the calculation of reduced switching fees (→ Ch. 5 mn. 64 et seqq.) in accordance with Art. 29 DA. As a result, no **overheads** may be allocated, and causation must be precisely explained and verified. A profit must be taken into account as part of the appropriate return on equity.

11 Art. 35 DA then regulates the objectives and content of interoperability for **data processing services**. The specifications and standards to be adopted by the Commission should meet the following criteria:

- technically achieve interoperability between different data processing services of the same service type,
- enhance the transferability of digital assets,
- facilitate functional equivalence,
- avoid any compromise of the security and integrity of the data processing services and
- be designed to be open to development.

12 In terms of regulatory content, Art. 35(2) DA lists

- **transport interoperability**, syntactic interoperability, semantic data interoperability, behavioural interoperability and policy interoperability;
- syntactic **data portability**, semantic data portability and the portability of data rules;
- the syntactic **portability of applications**, the portability of application commands, the portability of application metadata, the portability of application behaviour and the portability of application rules.

13 Reference is then made to the traditional requirements for standardisation and the procedure for **delegated acts**, which provides a sound framework for the preparation.

D. Interoperability for smart contracts

14 Providers of applications in which **smart contracts** are used are addressees of the interoperability obligations of Art. 36 DA. Art. 2 no. 39 DA defines 'smart contract' as 'a computer program used for the automated execution of an agreement or part thereof, using a sequence of electronic data records and ensuring their integrity and the accuracy of their chronological ordering'.

15 The interoperability obligations are intended to improve the **marketability** of smart contracts. To this end, requirements are defined that providers of applications with smart contracts or those who provide them commercially for third parties must fulfil:

- **robustness** to prevent malfunctions and manipulation by third parties,
- ensure **safe termination** or interruption of transactions to prevent or reverse (unintended) executions,

[6] For the term, see Lagoni CR 2024, 91 (92).

- **data archiving and continuity** to record transaction data and programming and make it verifiable, and
- strict **access controls** over operational elements.

In addition, the definition of **harmonised standards and norms** for specific interoperability requirements is also planned here. 16

CHAPTER 7
EXCEPTIONAL NEED TO USE DATA

Bibliography: Bomhard, 'Der Anwendungsbereich des Data Act', MMR 2024, 71; Hennemann et al., 'The Data Act Proposal – Literature Review and Critical Analysis, Part II; Version 1.0' (January 2023) <https://www.jura.uni-passau.de/fileadmin/dokumente/fakultaeten/jura/institute/irdg/Research_Paper_Series/23_02.pdf> (last accessed: 7.1.2026; cited as: Hennemann et al. The Data Act Proposal); Höne/Knapp, 'Von Daten- und Diskurssilos – Überlegungen zum B2G-Datentzugang nach dem Data-Act-Entwurf', ZGI 2023, 168; Leistner/Antoine, 'IPR and the use of open data and data sharing initiatives by public and private actors', PE 732.266 (Mai 2022) <https://www.europarl.europa.eu/RegData/etudes/STUD/2022/732266/IPOL_STU(2022)732266_EN.pdf> (last accessed: 7.1.2026; cited as: Leistner/Antoine PE 732.266); Remke, 'Rechtsdurchsetzung unter dem Data Act – Beschwerderecht, Rechtsbehelfe und Sanktionen', MMR 2024, 117; Schaller/Zurawski, 'Staatlicher Kompetenzenaufwuchs im Data-Act-Entwurf', ZD-Aktuell 2022, 01169; Schröder, 'Bereitstellung von Daten wegen außergewöhnlicher Notwendigkeit', MMR 2024, 104; Specht-Riemenschneider, 'Der Entwurf des Data Act – Eine Analyse der vorgesehenen Datenzugangsansprüche im Verhältnis B2B, B2C und B2G', MMR 2022, 809.

A. Introduction ... 1

B. Legal requirements ... 4
I. Entitled entities ... 5
1. Public sector bodies ... 6
2. Union bodies ... 7
3. Exclusion of application ... 9
II. Obligated parties ... 10
III. Legal requirements ... 13
1. Data request ... 14
a) Formal requirements ... 17
b) Material requirements ... 20
2. Exceptional needs ... 22
a) Responding to a public emergency ... 24
b) Fulfilment of specific tasks in the public interest ... 28
IV. Fulfilment and rejection of data requests ... 32
V. Relationship to other obligations to provide data ... 42

C. Scope of use ... 47
I. No further use under DGA and Open Data Directive ... 48
II. Obligations of the authorised bodies ... 49
III. Forwarding of the data obtained to other public bodies ... 53

D. Compensation for making the data available ... 60

E. Assistance and cross-border cooperation ... 68

F. Legal protection ... 72

A. Introduction

1 Access to data held by public bodies has been the subject of regulatory measures for some time now as a result of open data legislation and the DGA. The discussion about transparency obligations of the public sector goes back even further into the past. Chapter V of the DA now deals with the opposite situation: Art. 14–22 DA contain regulations on the situations in which, and the purposes for which, the public sector bodies themselves may request data to be made available by private companies. This is intended to provide public sector bodies with an instrument for accessing and subsequently using company data in situations of exceptional need.[1] The regulations thus enable government access to data from private actors, i.e. a

[1] Leistner/Antoine PE 732.266, p. 109.

forced **business-to-government (B2G)** data flow.[2] In contrast to the in-house production of data or the use of market mechanisms to meet demand, the state entitlement provided for in the DA is only possible in certain exceptional situations and only as **a last resort** due to the intensity of the governmental intervention associated with it.[3] The request for data by public authorities held by private actors is therefore only standardised in specific areas; in particular, it is known in Germany from telecommunications and telemedia law in §§ 172 et seqq. of the Telecommunications Act (TKG),[4] §§ 21et seqq. TDDDG[5] and the corresponding provisions in the German Code of Criminal Procedure (StPO), for example.

The obligation to provide data to public authorities is justified by the fact that 2
public emergencies and other exceptional situations require the mandatory sharing of data between companies and public authorities.[6] In such exceptional cases, the public interest in using the data should outweigh the interest of companies in being able to freely dispose of the data they hold (rec. 64 DA). The DA thus creates an opportunity for the **state to fulfil its data requirements**. However, the obligation to make data available to public authorities only exists if there is an exceptional need to use this data to fulfil a specific task of public interest (Art. 1(1)(c) DA). The provisions of Chapter V DA apply to both personal data and non-personal data from the private sector, with the focus being on non-personal data.[7]

It is clear that the Commission had measures to combat the **COVID-19 pan-** 3
demic in mind when drafting the regulations in Chapter V DA. In spring 2020, for example, Deutsche Telekom provided anonymised mobile phone data to the Robert Koch-Institute in order to be able to carry out contact tracing and thus track and combat the spread of COVID-19.[8] A legal framework is now to be created for comparable data access with the regulations on making data available due to exceptional needs. Conceivable application examples would be access to weather data to combat severe weather disasters or access to traffic data to monitor and control refugee movements.[9]

B. Legal requirements

Chapter V DA sets out in detail the conditions under which public bodies may 4
assert the right to data access against companies and the specific requirements for assertion.

[2] Schröder MMR 2024, 104 (105).

[3] Höne/Kapp ZGI 2023, 168 (169).

[4] For example, Eckhardt in Geppert/Schütz TKG §§ 172 et seqq.

[5] For example, Schreiber in Geppert/Schütz TDDDG §§ 21 et seqq.; Basar/Santagatti-Bergmann in HK-TTDSG §§ 21 et seqq.

[6] COM(2022) 68 final, 3 et seq.

[7] Art. 1(2)(d) DA; see also → Ch. 2 mn. 8 et seqq.; on the (non-)regulatory content, see also Bomhard MMR 2024, 71 (72).

[8] See <https://www.telekom.com/de/konzern/details/corona-vorhersage-telekom-unterstuetzt-rki-596772> (last accessed: 7.1.2026).

[9] Schaller/Zurawski ZD-Aktuell 2022, 01169.

I. Entitled entities

5 Art. 14 DA lists the entities that can claim access to company data: public sector bodies, the Commission, the European Central Bank (ECB) or Union bodies are entitled to access company data.

1. Public sector bodies

6 Public sector bodies are defined in Art. 2 no. 28 DA as the national, regional and local authorities of the Member States, bodies governed by public law of the Member States or associations formed of one or more of these authorities. In contrast to the definition of 'public authorities' in Art. 2 no. 17 DGA, the definition of the DA names the **'authorities'** instead of the 'state' as the entitled entities. Under German administrative law, an 'authority' is any body that performs public administrative tasks (§ 1(4) VwVfG). Public authorities are entities incorporated into the state administration that are appointed to act under public authority to achieve the purposes of the state or purposes promoted by the state.[10] Otherwise, the definitions of public sector bodies in the DA and DGA are identical in content. Rec. 63 DA mentions **research-performing and research-funding organisations** as examples of eligible public sector bodies or bodies governed by public law. Whether Art. 14 et seqq. DA also grant mixed-economy companies a right to data access is assessed differently.[11]

2. Union bodies

7 According to Art. 2 no. 27 DA, the Union bodies are bodies, offices and agencies of the Union set up by, or pursuant to, acts adopted on the basis of the Treaty on European Union, the TFEU, or the Treaty establishing the European Atomic Energy Community. These are **bodies created by secondary legislation**, i.e. the 'classical EU executive'.[12]

8 In the Commission's DA Proposal, in addition to a public sector body, Union institutions, agencies, or bodies were also envisaged as eligible (Art. 14 DA Proposal). This has been deleted in the final version. This **restriction** is based on a suggestion by the EU Council.[13] Union institutions such as the European Parliament, the Council and the ECJ are therefore not eligible.

3. Exclusion of application

9 Excluded from the scope of Chapter V DA are bodies and institutions that carry out activities for the prevention, investigation, detection or prosecution of **criminal offences** or the execution of criminal penalties, or for **customs and taxation purposes** (Art. 16(2) sent. 1 DA). The DA already does not apply to these areas according to its Art. 1(6) subpara. 2, so that this exclusion of application in Chapter V DA merely has a clarifying, repetitive function.[14]

---

[10] Cf. the definition in BVerfG 14.7.1959 – 2 BvF 1/58, BVerfGE 10, 20.

[11] Schaller/Zurawski ZD-Aktuell 2022, 01169; Schröder MMR 2024, 104 (105) negates this.

[12] Schröder MMR 2024, 104 (105).

[13] Council document 13342/22, 50.

[14] Barczak in BeckOK DatenschutzR DA Art. 16 mn. 5.

II. Obligated parties

Data holders within the meaning of Art. 2 no. 13 DA (→ Ch. 3 mn. 16) are obliged to provide data. Only data holders that are **legal persons** other than public bodies are obliged to do so (Art. 14 DA). The right to data access cannot therefore be directed at natural persons. The provisions concern **data from the private sector.**[15] There is no entitlement to data from other public bodies, meaning that no **government-to-government (G2G)** data flow is regulated.[16] Public sector bodies are therefore generally not covered by the concept of obligated data holders under Chapter V DA; however, public undertakings are included in the concept of obligated 'data holder' (rec. 63 DA). 10

In the draft version, **small and microenterprises** within the meaning of Art. 2 of Commission Recommendation 2003/361/EC were excluded from the scope of the obligation to provide data (Art. 14(2) DA Proposal). In the final version of the DA, this exemption now only applies to cases where the exceptional need is not a public emergency (Art. 15(2) DA). Small and microenterprises, i.e. companies with fewer than 50 employees and an annual turnover or an annual balance sheet total of no more than 10 million EUR, are therefore only covered by the obligation to provide data if this is necessary to respond to a **public emergency** in accordance with Art. 15(1)(a) DA (→ mn. 22 et seq.). 11

On the other hand, the Legal Affairs Committee also considered cancelling the privileged status of small and microenterprises altogether during the legislative process.[17] The final compromise version is based on a suggestion by the Council Presidency.[18] 12

III. Legal requirements

The assertion of the right to data access by the authorised bodies has various formal and material requirements; it is always embodied in a formal data request. 13

1. Data request

In order to assert their right to access and use data, the authorised bodies must submit a data request to the data holder in accordance with the requirements of Art. 17 DA. Under German administrative law, such a data request will generally qualify as an **administrative act** within the meaning of § 35 sent. 1 VwVfG; however, the requirements set out in Art. 17 DA for the data request go far beyond those of § 35 sent. 1 VwVfG.[19] 14

An **informal request** for data without regulatory effect and therefore as a non-administrative act would also be conceivable. However, this would not utilise the power to regulate in a compulsorily enforceable manner, as Chapter V DA now enables the requesting authorities to do. Data holders would not have to respond to 15

[15] Cf. Art. 1(2)(d) DA; on the unclear terminology see Bomhard MMR 2024, 71 (72).
[16] Schröder MMR 2024, 104 (105).
[17] Parliament Doc. PE736.696v01-00, 40.
[18] Hennemann et al. The Data Act Proposal, p. 2.
[19] Schröder MMR 2024, 104 (106).

an informal request. This would therefore be outside the requirements of Chapter V DA.

16 Compliance with these requirements is intended to ensure that the usage of data holders is specific, transparent and proportionate. On the one hand, the requesting body should be given appropriate **flexibility** in the performance of its tasks in the public interest and, on the other hand, the **burden** on data holders should be **minimised** (rec. 69 DA). To ensure transparency, the ECB and the Union bodies – but not the public sector bodies under Art. 2 no. 28 DA – must inform the Commission of their data requests (Art. 17(2) subpara. 2 DA).

a) Formal requirements

17 Art. 17(1) and (2) DA mainly contain **formal requirements** for the data request. According to Art. 17(1) DA, the request must

- specify **which data**, including the relevant metadata necessary to interpret and use this data, is required (point (a));
- demonstrate that the conditions of **exceptional need** pursuant to Art. 15 DA (→ mn. 22 et seqq.) are met (point (b));
- explain the **purpose of** the request, the intended use of the requested data – including by third parties, if applicable – the duration of the use and, where relevant, the manner in which the processing of personal data is to address the exceptional need (point (c));
- where possible, indicate the expected **date of erasure** by all parties who have access to the data (point (d));
- justify the **choice** of the requested data holder (point (e));
- specify all other entitled bodies and third parties pursuant to Art. 14 DA with whom the requested data is expected to be **shared** (point (f));
- if personal data is processed, specify all technical and organisational measures that are necessary and proportionate to implement the **data protection principles**, such as pseudonymisation, and whether the data holder can carry out anonymisation before making the data available (point (g));
- state the **legal provision** under which the requesting entity is entrusted with the specific task carried out in the public interest that is relevant to the data request (point (h));
- specify the **deadline by** which the data must be provided and the period within which the request may be refused or its amendment requested pursuant to Art. 18(2) DA (→ mn. 35) (point (i));
- make its best efforts to avoid that the fulfilment of the data request leads to **liability of the data holder** for infringements of Union or national law (point (j)).

18 Art. 17(2) subpara. 1 DA contains further requirements for the data request. Beyond the requirements of Art. 17(1) DA the data request must

- be made in **writing** and expressed in clear, concise and plain language understandable to the data holder (point (a));
- be specific regarding the **type of data requested** and correspond to the data that the data holder has control over at the time of the request (point (b));

- be proportionate to the exceptional need and **duly justified** regarding the granularity and volume of the data requested and the frequency of access to the requested data (point (c));
  These requirements of points (a)–(c) correspond to the generally applicable principles of certainty and proportionality of administrative acts in German administrative law, compliance with which is a matter of course, at least from a German perspective.[20]
- respect the **legitimate aims of the data holder** while ensuring the protection of trade secrets in accordance with Art. 19(3) DA (→ mn. 50 et seqq.) and taking into account the costs and effort required to make the data available (point (d));
- concern **non-personal data**, unless this is not sufficient to respond to the exceptional need to use data in accordance with Art. 15(1)(a) DA (→ mn. 22), in which case the data must be requested in pseudonymised form and the technical and organisational measures taken to protect the data must be specified (point (e));
  From the outset, this requirement from point (e) can only refer to data requests in situations of public emergency, since in all other cases only non-personal data may be requested anyway.[21]
- inform the data holder of the **penalties** that will be imposed by the competent authority designated pursuant to Art. 37 DA in accordance with Art. 40 DA if the data holder fails to comply with the request (point (f));
- if the request is made by a public sector body, be transmitted to the competent **data coordinator** designated pursuant to Art. 37 DA (→ mn. 41, 72) in order to enable the publication of the data request, unless the data coordinator considers the publication to be a risk to public security (point (g));
- if the request is made by the Commission, ECB or a Union body, be made **available online** without undue delay (point (h));
- in the event that personal data is requested, be reported to the competent **data protection authority** (point (i)).

By fulfilling these numerous requirements, the data holder should be able to check the data request and fulfil it precisely.[22] In addition, by fulfilling this extensive catalogue, the requesting body should be forced to deal with the content of certain topics of the data request.[23] However, it can be difficult for the entitled bodies to fulfil the requirements of the data request and, in particular, to specify the data, as there is often no precise knowledge of the specific data held by the data holder. Since data holders may refuse a data request due to non-availability (→ Ch. 3 mn. 61 et seqq.), there is a risk that an information imbalance could jeopardise the effectiveness of the right to data access.[24] In this respect, it should be considered whether an **information request** is included in the authorisation standard as a minus. 19

[20] Schröder MMR 2024, 104 (106).
[21] Barczak in BeckOK DatenschutzR DA Art. 17 mn. 6.
[22] Hennemann et al. The Data Act Proposal, p. 9.
[23] Barczak in BeckOK DatenschutzR DA Art. 17 mn. 4.
[24] Hennemann et al. The Data Act Proposal, p. 9.

b) Material requirements

20 The only **material requirement** of the catalogue from Art. 17(1) DA is the obligation of the entitled bodies to exclude infringements by the data holder as far as possible when fulfilling the data request (point (j)). This obligation raises questions about the relationship between the obligation to provide data under the DA and other obligations.[25] This provision is intended to counter the risk that the data holder may violate other legal requirements – e.g. under the GDPR – by fulfilling the data request. However, it remains unclear how this is to be ensured in practice. In some cases, it is inferred from the provision that the fulfilment of data requests should be given priority over other obligations and that liability or sanctioning of the data holder should be accepted.[26] A more obvious solution would be to **limit the data holders' inspection obligations**, as is the case in Germany with §§ 172 et seqq. TKG, §§ 22 et seqq. TDDDG is convincingly advocated (see also → mn. 72 et seqq.). Art. 17(2) subpara. 1 DA also contains additional material requirements, such as proportionality and the exceptional need.

21 In order to facilitate compliance with all requirements under Art. 17(1), (2) subpara. 1 DA, the Commission will develop a **model template for data requests** (Art. 17(6) DA). This appears to make sense in the interest of standardised data requests, although the template will have to leave room for manoeuvre for the specifics of the individual case against the background of the large number of material and formal requirements for the data request.[27]

2. Exceptional needs

22 The core provision of Chapter V of the DA is Art. 15, which sets out the material requirements for an exceptional need for the use of certain data. Art. 15 DA distinguishes between two circumstances in which an exceptional necessity exists:[28]

- The data is required to respond to a **public emergency** (para. 1 point (a)).
- If there is no public emergency within the meaning of para. 1 point (a), access to non-personal data can only be requested if this is necessary for the **fulfilment of legally defined tasks in the public interest** (para. 1 point (b)).

23 If one of these circumstances exists, the requirements for a temporary and limited exceptional need for data use by the requesting authorities are met. The **burden of proof** for this circumstance lies with the requesting body.

a) Responding to a public emergency

24 Art. 2 no. 29 DA contains the definition of a public emergency, which exists under the following **cumulative conditions**:

- A temporary **exceptional situation** (e.g. public health emergencies or as a result of natural disasters and major human-induced disasters, including major cyber security incidents),

[25] Schröder MMR 2024, 104 (106).
[26] Schröder MMR 2024, 104 (109); Barczak in BeckOK DatenschutzR DA Art. 17 mn. 5.
[27] Barczak in BeckOK DatenschutzR DA Art. 17 mn. 12.
[28] Cf. Wienroeder in Hennemann/Ebner/Karsten/Lienemann/Wienroeder Data Act, p. 154 et seq.

- which has a **negative impact on the population** of the Union or of a Member State or a part thereof,
- involves a **risk of serious and lasting repercussions** for **living conditions**, **economic or financial stability** or a risk of significant and direct damage to **economic assets** in the Union or in the Member State concerned, and
- is **determined or officially declared** in accordance with the relevant procedures of Union or national law.

The right to data access exists only for the response to a public emergency, i.e. not for the **prevention** of or recovery from such an emergency.[29] 25

It is necessary that the data **cannot** be obtained in a timely and effective **manner** under equivalent conditions – unlike in Art. 15(1)(b) DA, however, it is not necessary in the context of a public emergency that the authorised body has exhausted all other available means to obtain the data. In particular, the public sector bodies do not have to resort to market solutions to obtain the data. In cases of public emergency, the state will also not be able to conclude contracts with relevant private parties in advance for access to data sets in purely practical terms.[30] 26

The existence of a state of public emergency can be determined or declared by procedures under Union law, the law of the Member States and by relevant international organisations (rec. 64 DA). This can lead to legal uncertainty in this regard due to **different procedures** for determining a state of public emergency in the Member States. A harmonised European procedure would therefore lead to greater legal certainty with regard to the obligation to provide data in the event of exceptional needs.[31] 27

b) *Fulfilment of specific tasks in the public interest*

If there is no public emergency within the meaning of Art. 15(1)(a) DA, the right to data access pursuant to Art. 15(1)(b) DA exists if **cumulatively** 28

- the entitled body is acting pursuant to Union or national law and has identified specific data, the lack of which prevents it from performing a specific **task in the public interest** explicitly provided for by law, such as the production of official statistics or the mitigation of or recovery from a public emergency, and
- the entitled body has **exhausted** all other means available to it to obtain such data (last resort). Exhaustion of all the available means expressly includes the acquisition of non-personal data on the market by offering market tariffs or relying on existing obligations to provide data. The possibility of adopting new legislative measures which could ensure the timely availability of the data must be exhausted as a requirement for the data access.

This right to data access for the fulfilment of legally defined tasks in the public interest only exists in relation to **non-personal data** and, according to Art. 15(2) DA, only in relation to companies with more than 50 employees and an annual turnover or annual balance sheet of more than 10 million EUR, i.e. not in relation to small and microenterprises (→ mn. 11). 29

---

[29] Schröder MMR 2024, 104 (105).
[30] Höne/Kapp ZGI 2023, 168 (170).
[31] Hennemann et al. The Data Act Proposal, p. 4.

30 The authorised entity may only make a data request if it could not obtain the data in a timely and effective manner and under equivalent conditions by other means. The primary means to be utilised are, in particular, the procurement of data via voluntary agreements or recourse to existing obligations to provide data. If **data is acquired on the market**, the respective market price should be offered (rec. 65 DA). The right to data access outside the management of a public emergency is therefore subsidiary to market solutions.[32] Together with the reservation to enact special legislation if necessary, the scope of application of this right is likely to be limited in practice.[33]

31 Finally, the entitled bodies are also obliged to demonstrate within the data request that the conditions of an exceptional need are met (Art. 17(1)(b) DA). However, public authorities are not obliged to demonstrate that the non-personal data could not be obtained on the market if access to the data is requested for the production of official statistics and the acquisition is not allowed under national law (Art. 15(3) DA).

IV. Fulfilment and rejection of data requests

32 If a data holder is confronted with a data request from the entitled bodies, it must make the requested data available without undue delay, taking into account the technical, organisational and legal measures necessary for making the data available (Art. 18(1) DA). The last half-sentence is intended to minimise the effort involved in providing the data.[34] The entitlement also includes access to the metadata required for the interpretation and use of the requested data.

33 The fulfilment of the data request does not include an obligation to transmit the data to the authorised body, but merely an **obligation to make the data available in situ**.[35]

34 The data holder is also obliged to **disclose trade secrets** in order to fulfil the data request, insofar as this is essential for achieving the purpose of the request (Art. 19(3) sent. 1 DA; → mn. 50 et seqq.).

35 In the following three cases, the data holder may **decline** the data request pursuant to Art. 18(2) DA or seek its **modification**:

- The data holder has **no control** over the requested data (point (a)).
- A **similar data request** has already been made for the same purpose by one of the authorised entities and the data holder has not yet been informed of the deletion pursuant to Art. 19(1)(c) DA (point (b)). In this case, the data holder must identify the authorised entity that previously requested the data for the same purpose (Art. 18(3) DA).
- The data request **does not meet the conditions** of Art. 17(1) and (2) DA (point (c)).

36 Data holders are therefore not obliged to fulfil the data request if it does not meet the **requirements of Art. 17(1) and (2) DA**. Due to the scope of the requirements

[32] Höne/Kapp ZGI 2023, 168 (170).
[33] Schröder MMR 2024, 104 (105).
[34] Barczak in BeckOK DatenschutzR DA Art. 18 mn. 1.
[35] Schröder MMR 2024, 104 (106); Specht-Riemenschneider MMR 2022, 809 (826).

for the data request set out in Art. 17 DA, this is likely to be the most significant reason for refusal in practice, but also the most conflict-prone due to the ambiguous requirements.[36] It is therefore incumbent on the data holder to check the data request for compliance with the requirements for the data request if it intends to refuse the data request (the data holder could also be obligated to check the data request, as otherwise liability risks may arise, for example from data protection, if it possibly transmits unauthorised third-party data to the requesting body). This examination relates solely to the formal requirements for the data request; the data holders do not have to examine the material requirements of exceptional need under Art. 15 DA (→ mn. 13 et seqq.).

Compliance with legal requirements prior to the fulfilment of government requests for information is also known from other areas of law: The requests for information from various state authorities to providers of telemedia services regulated in the German §§ 21 et seqq. TDDDG also contain differentiated formal requirements for the request for information, in particular with regard to the prerequisites for a request for information from the authorised authorities named in detail. Here too, the obligated providers of telemedia services must review the request for information for compliance with its formal requirements (see § 21(6) sent. 2, § 23(4) sent. 2 TDDDG). The fulfilment of such a request for information may only take place in the event of a positive test result.[37] 37

This examination of the data request for compliance with the requirements of Art. 17 DA harbours **risks** for the data holders: If they fulfil the data request even though the differentiated requirements of Art. 17 DA are not met, there is a risk of violating national or EU law (in particular the GDPR, but also copyright or confidentiality agreements) with the disclosure (the authorisation basis 'legal obligation' from Art. 6(1) subpara. 1(c) GDPR, for example, is then not fulfilled, as the transfer could have been refused under Art. 18(2)(c) DA). If, on the other hand, the data holder wrongly considers the data request not to meet the requirements of Art. 17 DA and therefore refuses to fulfil it, this constitutes a breach of the obligation to provide the data per se, which can be prosecuted by the supervisory authority (→ mn. 72 et seqq.). The legislator has recognised this potential conflict and placed the obligation on the entitled body to ensure that the data holder does not violate national or Union law by fulfilling the data request (Art. 17(1)(j) DA). However, it remains to be seen how this is to be implemented in practice. It may become particularly important for the assessment of the fault of the data holder and possible contributory negligence on the part of the requesting body if the data holder is held liable for an infringement. 38

If the data holder wishes to decline the data request or seek its modification, this must be done **immediately**, in the event of a public emergency within five working days at the latest and in all other cases of exceptional need within 30 days of receipt of the data request. 39

If personal data is affected by the data request, the data holder must **anonymise** it properly. This alone poses considerable challenges, as effective anonymisation is technically difficult or even impossible and, moreover, it remains unclear whether absolute anonymisation or anonymisation within the meaning of rec. 26 GDPR and 40

[36] Barczak in BeckOK DatenschutzR DA Art. 18 mn. 5.
[37] See Basar/Santagattti-Bergmann in HK-TTDSG § 23 mn. 31.

ECJ case law, i.e. taking into account the relative approach in which the proportionality of the means of re-identification must be examined, is required. According to current ECJ case law, anonymity must be assessed from the perspective of the individual processor. Data that is pseudonymous for one controller may be anonymous for a third party.[38] Something else only applies if the disclosure of personal data is necessary to fulfil the data request (Art. 18(4) DA).

41 If the authorised entity challenges the data holder's declination of the data request or if the data holder wishes to challenge the data request and the matter cannot be resolved by an appropriate modification of the data request, the matter shall be referred to the **competent authority** of the Member State in which the data holder is established, **designated** in accordance with Art. 37 DA (Art. 18(5) DA; see also → mn. 74).

V. Relationship to other obligations to provide data

42 The provisions on making data available due to exceptional needs do not apply to the obligations laid down in national or Union law with regard to reporting, complying with requests for access to information or demonstrating or verifying compliance with legal obligations (Art. 16(1) DA). This **exception** is intended to exclude from the scope of Chapter V DA data access requests by the authorised entities to verify compliance with applicable regulations. This also applies to cases in which public sector bodies delegate the task of verifying compliance with applicable regulations to bodies other than public sector bodies (rec. 66 DA).

43 The exclusion of application from Art. 16(1) DA is intended to clarify that, insofar as public authorities or persons authorised by them can also request access to data in order to monitor compliance with certain legal provisions, the requirements of Chapter V DA do not have to be met. Such **reporting obligations** to or control powers of public bodies are regulated in numerous economic sectors. Examples in German law include the comprehensive information rights of the competent authorities in the sector-specific regulated network industries, such as under § 69 of the German Energy Industry Act (EnWG), or the obligation of certain companies to report to the competent authorities in accordance with the German Supply Chain Supervision Obligations Act (§ 12(1) LkSG).

44 The DA supplements Union and national law governing access to data for **statistical purposes** and their use for statistical purposes, such as the EU Statistics Regulation (EC) No 223/2009 and the national legal acts relating to official statistics (rec. 67 DA). In this respect, the public sector's right to data access under Chapter V DA has a subsidiary fall-back function for cases in which the authorised bodies cannot already request data access under other legal acts.[39]

45 The applicable provisions of Union and national law on the protection of personal data also remain unaffected in accordance with Art. 16(2) 2 DA regarding

[38] ECJ 4.9.2025 – case C-413/23 P, ECLI:EU:C:2025:645 – SBR.

[39] Barczak in BeckOK DatenschutzR DA Art. 16 mn. 3.

- prevention, investigation, detection or prosecution of **criminal or administrative offences**,
- execution of criminal or administrative penalties and
- customs or tax administration.

These restrictions on the scope of application show that Chapter V DA is intended to regulate only **'ad hoc' data access.**[40] In the areas mentioned, the authorised bodies should rely on their powers granted by Union or national law (rec. 68 DA). The exclusion covers in particular the Regulation on addressing the dissemination of terrorist content online (Regulation (EU) 2021/784), the Digital Services Act (Regulation (EU) 2022/2065), the e-Evidence Preservation Regulation (Regulation (EU) 2023/1543) and the e-Evidence Service Provider Legal Assistance Directive (Directive (EU) 2023/1544). The exclusion also covers international cooperation in these areas.[41] **46**

C. Scope of use

The Data Act contains specific provisions on the extent to which the authorised bodies may use the data obtained and what obligations they must comply with. **47**

I. No further use under DGA and Open Data Directive

The DGA and the Open Data Directive do not apply to data obtained through a data request from a public authority. In particular, the data obtained through the data request may **not** be made available to third parties **for reuse** within the meaning of Art. 2 no. 2 DGA or Art. 2 no. 11 of the Open Data Directive (Art. 17(3) DA). However, this exclusion of use should only apply to the data itself obtained through the data request. The Open Data Directive should remain applicable to official statistics based on data obtained in accordance with the Data Act. In addition, the possibility of sharing the data for **research purposes** or for the development, production and dissemination of official statistics should remain unaffected, provided that the conditions laid down in the DA are met (rec. 70 DA). **48**

II. Obligations of the authorised bodies

Pursuant to Art. 19 DA, the authorised bodies are subject to extensive obligations with regard to the data obtained through a data request. Art. 19(1) DA sets out general requirements for the **handling** of the data obtained: The authorised body **49**

- shall not use the data in a manner that is incompatible with the **purpose** of the data request (point (a));
- shall have taken **technical and organisational measures** that preserve the confidentiality and integrity of the requested data and the security of data transfers – especially in the case of personal data – and to safeguard the rights and freedoms of the data subject (point (b));

---

[40] Hennemann et al. The Data Act Proposal, p. 8.
[41] Barczak in BeckOK DatenschutzR DA Art. 16 mn. 6.

- shall **erase** the data as soon as they are no longer required for the stated purpose and inform the data holder and the data recipients of the erasure without delay in accordance with Art. 21(1) DA, unless the archiving of the data is required under Union or national law on public access to documents in context with transparency obligations (point (c)).

50 Art. 19(2) and (3) DA contain more specific provisions on the **protection of trade secrets** of the data. According to these provisions, the authorised entities are not entitled to use the data received or knowledge about the economic situation, assets and production or operating methods of the data in order to develop or enhance connected products or related services that compete with those of the data (Art. 19(2)(a) DA), or to share the data with another third party for these purposes (Art. 19(2)(b) DA). This **non-compete clause** corresponds to the non-compete clause directed at users of connected products and related services (Art. 4(10) DA), which also applies to third parties to whom users provide the data (Art. 6(2)(e) DA).

51 The disclosure of trade secrets to the requesting body is only deemed necessary to the extent that this is strictly required to achieve the purpose of a request in the event of exceptional needs in accordance with Art. 15 DA (Art. 19(3) sent. 1 DA). If trade secrets are affected by the data request, the data holder or, in the event of a difference in person, the holder of the trade secret must identify the data concerned, including relevant metadata (Art. 19(3) sent. 2 DA). Before disclosing trade secrets, the entitled entity shall take all necessary, appropriate technical and organisational measures to preserve the **confidentiality of the trade secrets**, including, where appropriate, the use of model contractual terms, technical standards and the application of codes of conduct (Art. 19(3) sent. 3 DA). For the technical and organisational measures, a rough orientation to Art. 25 GDPR – in the case of non-personal data in corresponding application – seems obvious.[42]

52 Finally, it is clarified that the authorised entity is responsible for the **security** of the data received (Art. 19(4) DA).

III. Forwarding of the data obtained to other public bodies

53 If the conditions of exceptional needs pursuant to Art. 15 DA are met, the authorised bodies may also **exchange** the data obtained on the basis of a data request with each other (Art. 17(4) sent. 1 DA). The prospective transfer of data to other authorised bodies must be indicated in the data request (Art. 17(1)(f) DA).

54 In addition, the authorised bodies may also provide the data **to a third party** if they have delegated technical inspections or other tasks to this third party within the framework of a publicly available agreement. The obligations of public bodies to preserve the confidentiality of business secrets under Art. 19 DA also apply to this third party (Art. 17(4) sent. 2 DA). The authorised entity that transmits or makes data available to another authorised entity or a third party must inform the data holder of this without undue delay (Art. 17(4) sent. 3 DA).

55 In addition, the authorised body is entitled to share the data received through a data request in accordance with Art. 21(1) DA

[42] Specht-Riemenschneider MMR 2022, 809 (825).

- with individuals or organisations with a view to carrying out **scientific research activities or analyses** compatible with the purpose of the data request (point (a)), and
- with national statistical institutes or the statistical office of the EU (Eurostat)[43] for the **production of official statistics.**

In connection with the obligation to use the data only for purposes compatible with the data request (**purpose limitation**), the question arises as to whether the disclosure for research purposes must be research that serves to deal with the specific emergency or whether only incompatible research is excluded.[44] Art. 5(1)(b) GDPR standardises a presumption of compatibility of purposes under the GDPR if data is to be further used for research purposes. Such a provision is missing in the DA. 56

Furthermore, disclosure to the bodies listed in Art. 21(1) DA is only permitted if they are acting on a not-for-profit basis or in the context of a **task of public interest** recognised under Union or national law (Art. 21(2) sent. 1 DA). Disclosure to organisations that are subject to significant influence by commercial undertakings, which could give them preferential access to the research results, is excluded (Art. 21(2) sent. 2 DA). Significant influence is deemed to exist if the commercial undertakings are able to exercise control due to the structural circumstances (rec. 76 DA). Based on other areas of law, it can be assumed that the requirements for the existence of a significant influence are less stringent than for the existence of a controlling influence within the meaning of Art. 3 Annex I GBER or §§ 15 et seqq. of the German Stock Corporation Act (AktG). 57

The individuals or organisations that receive the data from the entitled bodies under Art. 21(1) DA must comply with the same requirements as the latter under Art. 17(3) and Art. 19 DA (Art. 21(3) DA). The recipients may retain the data for a period of **up to six months** for the purposes of the data request after they have been erased by the disclosing body (Art. 21(4) DA). 58

If an authorised entity intends to disclose data in accordance with Art. 21(1) DA, it must immediately **notify** the data holder from whom the data was received and in doing so state 59

- the identity and contact details of the recipient,
- the purpose of the transmission or making available of the data,
- the period for which the data is to be used, and
- the protective measures and organisational measures taken

(Art. 21(5) sent. 1 DA). This also applies if personal data or trade secrets are involved. The data holder has the **right to lodge a complaint** with the competent authority of their Member State designated in accordance with Art. 37 DA if they do not agree with the disclosure of the data (Art. 21(5) sent. 2 DA; → mn. 72 et seqq.).

[43] See the website <https://ec.europa.eu/eurostat/de/> (last accessed: 7.1.2026).
[44] Schröder MMR 2024, 104 (107).

D. Compensation for making the data available

60 Art. 20 DA contains provisions on the **financial compensation of data holders** for making the data available. The provision of data to respond to a **public emergency** in accordance with Art. 15(1)(a) DA is only compensated for small and microenterprises. All other companies provide the data required to deal with a public emergency free of charge (Art. 20(1) sent. 1 DA). However, at the request of a data holder, the data-receiving bodies shall provide **public acknowledgement** to its contribution (Art. 20(1) sent. 2 DA).

61 Accordingly, only **small and microenterprises** with fewer than 50 employees and an annual turnover or annual balance sheet of up to 10 million EUR receive financial compensation for making data available in response to public emergencies. However, all companies can request public acknowledgement that they have made a contribution to overcoming a public emergency and thus claim a PR advantage for themselves.

62 For making data available **outside of a public emergency** – i.e. in accordance with Art. 15(1)(b) DA – the data holders can demand appropriate consideration in accordance with Art. 20(2) sent. 1 DA, which covers at least the following points (Art. 20(2) sent. 2 DA):

- costs for the technical and organisational fulfilment of the data request,
- costs of anonymisation, pseudonymisation, aggregation and technical adaptation, and
- a reasonable margin.

63 When calculating the compensation, the interests of the authorised entity must therefore be balanced with those of the data holder.[45] At the request of the authorised entity, the data holder shall provide **information on the basis of the cost calculation** and reasonable margin (Art. 20(2) sent. 2 DA). Small and microenterprises are entitled to information on the cost calculation accordingly and thus also in cases of public emergency (Art. 20(3) DA).

64 **Costs for anonymisation or pseudonymisation** can initially be requested from small and microenterprises, as only personal data can be anonymised or pseudonymised and personal data can only be requested to respond to a public emergency in accordance with Art. 15(1)(a) DA – all other cases only concern non-personal data (Art. 15(1)(b) DA). However, companies other than small and microenterprises must provide the data free of charge in the event of a public emergency (Art. 20(1) DA), so that the scope of application of the reimbursement of costs for pseudonymisation and anonymisation in this variant only applies to small and microenterprises.

65 For making data available in accordance with Art. 15(1)(b) DA, which only relates to **non-personal data**, it is questionable whether the costs of anonymisation are eligible for reimbursement. One argument in favour of this is that the required data is converted into a form that can be requested by the bodies, namely 'non-personal data'. An argument against this is that there is probably no entitlement to anonymisation in order to bring this data within the scope of Art. 15(1)(b) DA.

45 Leistner/Antoine PE 732.266, p. 111.

Finally, according to Art. 20(4) sent. 1 DA, the right to compensation does not exist if data is provided for the compilation of official statistics and the **purchase of data is not allowed by national law**. The Member States must inform the Commission if the purchase of data for the production of official statistics is not allowed under national law (Art. 20(4) sent. 2 DA). 66

If the authorised entity does not agree with the amount of the consideration requested by the data holder, it may lodge a **complaint** with the competent authority of the Member State designated in accordance with Art. 37 DA in which the data holder is established (Art. 20(5) DA; → mn. 73 et seqq.). 67

E. Assistance and cross-border cooperation

The public authorities, the Commission, the ECB and the institutions of the Union shall cooperate and assist each other to ensure the consistent implementation of Chapter V DA (Art. 22(1) DA). The data exchanged between the authorised bodies in this context may not be used in a way that is incompatible with the purpose of the data request (Art. 22(2) DA). 68

If a public sector body intends to address its data request to a data holder established in **another Member State**, it shall first notify the competent authority designated in accordance with Art. 37 DA (Art. 22(3) sent. 1 DA). This obligation to notify the competent authority applies in principle to the Commission, the ECB and Union bodies (Art. 22(3) sent. 2 DA). Insofar as personal data is requested, the competent data protection supervisory authority of the target state concerned should also be informed (rec. 77 DA). 69

The competent authority must examine the data request on the basis of the requirements set out in Art. 17 DA and then immediately take one of **two options** (Art. 22(4) subpara. 1 DA): 70

- It shall transmit the request to the data holder and, if applicable, advise the requesting authority to cooperate with the public authorities of the Member State in which the data holder is established in order to minimise the burden on the data holder (point (a)), or
- it rejects the data request on duly substantiated grounds in accordance with Chapter V DA (point (b)). A refusal will only be possible here on the grounds of Art. 18(3) DA.

Before taking further action, in particular resubmitting a data request, the requesting body must take into account the information provided by the competent authority and the reasons set out in subpara. 1 (Art. 22(4) subpara. 2 DA). 71

F. Legal protection

Chapter V DA provides for the primary legal protection option in connection with making data available due to exceptional necessity, in particular the **complaint** of the obliged data holder (Art. 38 DA) to the competent authority designated in accordance with Art. 37 DA. This can be considered in the following constellations: 72

- The data holder is of the opinion that his **rights** would be **violated** by the transmission or making available of data (Art. 17(5) DA).

- The data holder does not consent to the **transmission** of the data by the authorised body (Art. 21(5) sent. 2 DA).
- The authorised body does not agree with the **level of compensation** requested by the data holder pursuant to Art. 20 DA (Art. 20(5) DA).

73 The **complaint** is intended as a general legal remedy for natural and legal persons who believe that their rights under the DA have been violated. In Chapter V DA, it is specifically related to the instruments of making data available, but only for the data holder and not for third parties.

74 In addition, the authorised body can **challenge the refusal** of the data request by the data holder and the data holder has the option of challenging the data request, whereupon the matter is referred to the competent authority (Art. 18(5) DA).

75 Furthermore, under German administrative law, data holders always have the option of **bringing an action for annulment** pursuant to § 42(1) alt. 1 VwGO against a data request – if this qualifies as an administrative act pursuant to § 35 sent. 1 VwVfG (→ mn. 14). They have the right to an effective judicial remedy without prejudice to other administrative or extrajudicial remedies (Art. 39(1) DA). Accordingly, an annulment action can be brought directly against a data request without the need for a prior complaint or objection. According to Art. 37(8) DA, the competent authorities are not subject to any direct or indirect external influence or instructions from other authorities or private individuals when performing their tasks and exercising their powers, meaning that there is no need to conduct preliminary proceedings pursuant to § 68 VwGO due to the lack of a devolutive effect.[46]

76 Pursuant to Art. 40(4) DA, the supervisory authorities responsible for monitoring the application of the GDPR may ultimately impose **fines** in accordance with Art. 83 GDPR up to the amount specified in Art. 83(5) GDPR (→ Ch. 8 mn. 4) on the party in breach of the GDPR. The fine to be imposed under this provision is up to **20 million EUR or up to 4 % of the annual worldwide turnover of** the group of companies, whichever is higher.

77 This must be distinguished from the question of possible legal protection of **third parties** who feel that their rights have been violated by the data transfer, such as data subjects by data protection law or authors, owners of intellectual property rights or those who have concluded confidentiality agreements with the data holder. In practice, based on the experience gained from corresponding request processes in the telecommunications and telemedia sector, it will depend in particular on which requirements the transferring company has to check. This then determines whether and to what extent third parties can take action against the requesting body and/or the data providing company itself. According to Art. 17(1)(j) DA, the requesting body is authorised to keep liability risks away from the data. This places the requesting body under a special **obligation to assess**, although it remains highly questionable what impact this will ultimately have, especially as the requesting body only has to make 'best efforts': Does the data holder have a right of recourse against the requesting body in the event of an inadequate check? Or can the data holder refer third parties directly to the requesting organisation? Is the data holder not at fault if the requesting organisation does not adequately fulfil its obligations? All of this will have to be clarified on a case-by-case basis.

---

[46] Remke MMR 2024, 117 (120).

As it will generally not be possible for the company that is to transfer data to actually verify the content of the requirement of a public emergency or an exceptional necessity, the same will apply here as to §§ 22–24 TDDDG:[47] The responsibility for a **materially lawful data request** generally lies with the requesting public authority. Companies must check whether the formal requirements for the requests are met – if they fulfil this obligation to check, third-party claims for damages due to unlawful data transfers are likely to face major hurdles. 78

Third parties can take comprehensive action against the requesting authority in accordance with general German administrative law as long as their **subjective rights** have been violated. However, damages may not be compensated twice; in case of doubt, the requesting authority and the company become joint and several debtors. 79

[47] Schreiber in Geppert/Schütz TDDDG § 22 mn. 65.

CHAPTER 8
SUPERVISION AND ENFORCEMENT

Bibliography: Remke, 'Rechtsdurchsetzung unter dem Data Act, Beschwerderecht, Rechtsbehelfe und Sanktionen', MMR 2024, 117.

A. Supervisory authorities 2
I. National design options 2
II. Independence 11
III. Data coordinator 12
IV. Responsibility and appointment of representatives 14

B. Penalties 19

C. Right of complaint and legal remedies 25
I. Right of complaint 26
II. Protective letter 33
III. Legal remedies 34

D. Civil court enforcement 41

1 Chapter IX DA regulates the supervision of compliance with the Data Act and the effective enforcement of the rights and obligations arising from the Data Act. The Data Act follows the typical enforcement system for EU regulations, according to which the **Member States** are **primarily** entrusted with the enforcement of the binding legal act. In addition to provisions on enforcement by the supervisory authorities to be designated by the Member States in accordance with Art. 37(1) DA (→ mn. 2 et seqq., 19 et seqq.), Chapter IX also contains provisions on the right of appeal (→ mn. 26 et seqq.) and corresponding legal remedies (→ mn. 34 et seqq.). In addition, those affected also have the option of enforcing their rights in civil court outside of the supervisory authority proceedings (→ mn. 41 et seqq.).

A. Supervisory authorities

I. National design options

2 According to Art. 37(1) DA, each Member State shall designate one or more competent authorities that are responsible for the application and enforcement of the DA. Member States do not have full discretion in selecting **supervisory authorities**, as the designated body must have experience in the field of 'data and electronic communications services' with regard to the application and enforcement of the provisions on cloud switching (→ Ch. 5 mn. 1 et seqq.) and the interoperability of data processing services (→ Ch. 6 mn. 7 et seqq.) in accordance with Art. 37(4)(b) DA. In Germany, this could be the **Federal Network Agency** (Bundesnetzagentur), for example, with extensive experience in telecommunications regulation, or the **data protection supervisory authorities**. The final version of the DA no longer contains further requirements proposed in the regulatory procedure on experience in price regulation and dispute resolution for the application and enforcement of the requirements on data access conditions in Chapter III and the provision of data to public bodies under Chapter V.[1]

[1] Remke MMR 2024, 117.

At least for some areas, the DA provides further restrictions for the possible supervisory authorities: According to Art. 37 (3) DA, the **data protection supervisory authorities** are necessarily responsible for the protection of personal data in the context of the application of the DA. This could result in a fragmentation of responsibilities if Member States decide to transfer the supervision of compliance with the DA in relation to non-personal data to another body. 3

Even more complex is the interpretation of the requirement that Chapters VI and VII of the GDPR apply 'mutatis mutandis' to the competence of the data protection supervisory authorities under the DA. These are the provisions on independent supervisory authorities in Art. 51–59 GDPR and on cooperation and consistency in Art. 60–76 GDPR. There is debate in the literature as to whether the data protection supervisory authorities are being given **new tasks and powers** by the DA and, if so, how these interact with the GDPR tasks and powers.[2] There is some evidence in favour of the Member States having to regulate this specifically: If data protection supervisory authorities are to enforce the DA in relation to personal data and monitor its application, they must also be given the powers from the DA to do so in order to perform this task effectively, i.e. all authorisations, tasks and powers that other authorities also receive for their respective areas of responsibility under the DA. Otherwise, a data protection supervisory authority would not be able to enforce a request for access to personal data, for example, to which there is a right under the DA and which is also in line with the GDPR. This would lead to a fundamental enforcement deficit. As a result, a strict distinction must be made: Insofar as the GDPR is applied and enforced, tasks and powers also follow from it. This is the case, for example, if a request for data access is contrary to data protection law due to a lack of a legal basis according to Art. 6 GDPR. If, on the other hand, it is a matter of enforcing the DA, for example because a data access request is to be enforced in accordance with the GDPR, the tasks and powers must originate from the DA. This is also consistent with the fact that, according to Art. 40(4) DA, these authorities can resort to the framework of fines under Art. 83 GDPR in the event of infringements of data access requests, making data available obligations and conditions. The powers there are therefore also declared applicable for certain infringements of the DA. 4

According to Art. 37(4)(a) DA, **sectoral authorities** also remain competent in their respective areas. This raises similar questions regarding the delimitation of the areas of responsibility and powers of the data protection supervisory authorities. 5

The respective **supervisory authority(ies)** must be entrusted with at least the following **tasks and powers** (Art. 37(5) DA): 6

- supervision and enforcement: 7
  - **information requests** (requests for information) to users, data holders, data recipients and legal representatives in accordance with Art. 37(14) DA;
  - imposing effective, proportionate and dissuasive financial **penalties**, which may include periodic penalty payments and fines with retroactive effect, or initiating court proceedings to impose fines;
  - processing **complaints** about alleged infringements of the DA;

[2] Remke MMR 2024, 117.

- ensuring the **abolition of switching charges** in accordance with Art. 29 DA;
- examination of **data requests** in accordance with Chapter V DA.

8 – consultancy and monitoring:
- promoting **data literacy** and raising awareness among users and organisations that fall within the scope of the DA;
- conducting investigations on **issues relating to the application of** the DA;
- **monitoring** technological and relevant economic developments relevant to data sharing and usage.

9 – cooperation:
- **EU-wide cooperation** with the competent authorities of other Member States, the Commission or the European Data Innovation Board;[3]
- **national cooperation** with the relevant competent authorities responsible for the application of other Union or national legal acts, including with competent authorities in the field of data and electronic communications services, with the supervisory authority responsible for monitoring the application of the GDPR or with sectoral authorities, to ensure that the DA is enforced in accordance with other Union and national law;
- **cooperation** with the relevant competent authorities to ensure the **enforcement** of Art. 23–31, 34–35 DA;
- **administrative assistance** for justified requests in accordance with Art. 37(15) DA.

10 According to Art. 37(16) DA, the authorities are obliged to respect the **principle of confidentiality**, professional and business secrecy and the protection of personal data. Information exchanged in connection with a request for administrative assistance pursuant to Art. 37(15) DA may not be used for any other matters.

II. Independence

11 According to Art. 37(8) DA, the authorities must act **impartially** and free from any direct or indirect external influence, which also includes **independence from external influence**, both to other authorities and private parties. Similar independence is also required of the regulatory authorities established in sector-specific regulation. There, the ECJ has recently strengthened the position of the authorities in favour of the independence requirement: The authority must be able to act 'completely freely'.[4] This independence must also be made possible by appropriate **resources**. Art. 37(9) DA therefore obliges the Member States to ensure 'that the competent authorities are provided with sufficient human and technical resources and relevant expertise to effectively carry out their tasks in accordance with this Regulation'. The designated authorities must be notified to the Commission, which keeps a **public register** of them.

[3] On the EDIB → Ch. 10 mn. 1 et seq.
[4] ECJ 2.9.2021 – case C-718/18, ECLI:EU:C:2021:662 para. 108 – Kommission v Germany.

III. Data coordinator

12 If, as is likely, several authorities are designated, a **data coordinator** must be appointed from among the supervisory authorities in accordance with Art. 37(2) DA. According to rec. 107 DA, the data coordinator should act 'as a single point of contact for all issues related to the application of this Regulation'. Its area of responsibility is specified in Art. 37(6) DA. It includes:

- function as a **central contact point**,
- ensuring the **public availability** of data access requests made by public authorities in cases of exceptional needs in accordance with Chapter V DA,
- promotion of **voluntary data sharing agreements** between public authorities and data holders,
- **informing the Commission** of notified refusals of data access requests.

13 However, this raises the question of whether appointing a data coordinator alone is sufficient, if the supervision of compliance with the DA is assigned to **different bodies** for personal and non-personal data and in certain sectoral areas: Many IoT products or data processing services process both categories of data, so that the supervisory responsibility even varies with regard to a product or service.

IV. Responsibility and appointment of representatives

14 For legal entities obliged under the DA, the supervisory authority in the Member State in which the legal entity is established is responsible (Art. 37(10) sent. 1 DA). In the case of branches in several Member States, the **'one-stop shop system'** applies after the **main branch**. In cases of doubt, this refers to the branch from which 'the principal financial functions and operational control are exercised' (Art. 37(10) sent. 2 DA).

15 For addressees without an establishment in the EU, Art. 37(11) DA provides for the obligation to appoint a **representative in the EU**, as is also known from Art. 27 GDPR. The competent supervisory authority is then determined on the basis of the registered office of this representative (Art. 37(13) sent. 1 DA). According to Art. 37(13) sent. 3 DA, all Member State supervisory authorities are competent as long as no representative has been appointed.

16 All legal entities based in the EU that offer **networked products or services** that are covered by the data access rights in Chapter II DA must also appoint a **representative**. According to Art. 37(12) DA, this is to ensure that the DA is applied and enforced effectively. There must therefore be a **data access officer** in all obliged companies who has a less formalised role, but one that is similar in content to that of the data protection officer. Among other things, the representative must cooperate with the authorities.

17 In addition, the representative must be able to 'comprehensively demonstrate to the competent authorities, upon request, the actions taken and provisions put in place by the entity falling within the scope of this Regulation that makes connected products available or offers services in the Union to ensure compliance with this Regulation' (Art. 37(12) sent. 2 DA). This results in **an indirect accountability** that raises doubts about its effectiveness: the obligation does not apply to the company

itself as a legal entity, but only to its representatives – a person who typically holds far less decision-making power within the organisation.

18 If, according to Art. 37(13) sent. 2 DA, the appointment of a representative does not affect the **liability of the legal entity**, the question arises as to whether this also applies at all to the representatives pursuant to Art. 37(12) DA, since Art. 37(13) sent. 1 DA initially only refers to addressees without an establishment in the EU. On the other hand, this cannot lead to obligations directed at the representative applying to the legal entity by indirect means: The legal entity can and will only be liable for obligations that are also imposed on itself.

B. Penalties

19 Requests for information under Art. 37(14) DA are just as enforceable as all other obligations under the DA. According to Art. 40(1) DA, the Member States 'shall lay **down rules on penalties** applicable to infringements of this Regulation and shall take all measures necessary to ensure that they are implemented'. This transfer of enforcement to national law is common in EU law; the GDPR makes some exceptions to this. In Germany, for example, as in other regulated areas, it is possible to apply the German **Act on Regulatory Offences (OWiG)**, i.e. the German **law on administrative offences.**

20 All penalties provided for must be 'effective, proportionate and dissuasive' according to Art. 40(1) sent. 2 DA. German administrative offences law also follows these principles. When imposing penalties, the recommendations of the **European Data Innovation Board** (→ Ch. 10 mn. 48) must be taken into account. Furthermore, Art. 40(3) DA provides for the following criteria to be taken into account when assessing penalties; these are also known in a similar form from Art. 83 GDPR. The criteria are **not exhaustive,**[5] but are to be understood as standard examples:

- **nature, gravity, scale and duration** of the infringement,
- actions taken by the infringing party to **mitigate or remedy** the **damage** caused by the infringement,
- **previous infringements** committed by the infringing party,
- **financial benefits** obtained by the infringing party as a result of the infringement,
- **other** aggravating or mitigating **circumstances** of the respective case,
- **annual turnover** of the infringing party in the EU in the previous financial year.

21 While the first criteria are also known from the GDPR and can therefore be transferred in concrete terms, the last point is different: Annual turnover is not the basis for calculation, but only a factor to be taken into account. In addition, it only concerns the turnover of the specific company in the EU and not the global group turnover.

22 According to Art. 40(4) DA, the **data protection supervisory authorities** are authorised to apply the **powers to impose fines** under Art. 83 GDPR to infringements of the Data Act in certain cases (→ mn. 4).

[5] See also Remke MMR 2024, 117 (120).

According to Art. 40(2) DA, the Member States must **notify** the Commission of their **national rule on penalties** by 12.9.2025. Changes must also be communicated immediately. The Commission keeps an up-to-date public register of these. 23

A special provision can be found in Art. 40(5) DA: According to this provision, the **European Data Protection Supervisor** within the meaning of Art. 52 GDPR is authorised to impose fines in accordance with Art. 66 Regulation (EU) 2018/1725 in the event of violations of the provision of data to public sector bodies in accordance with Chapter V DA. In particular, EU institutions and bodies are penalised as potential actors in data requests under Chapter V DA.[6] 24

C. Right of complaint and legal remedies

Although supervisory authorities may act **ex officio**, it is likely that most cases initiated in response to a complaint – as is ultimately also the case in data protection law – are expected to account for the majority of official proceedings. In this respect, the DA contains both rights of complaint and – in particular for data access requests – provisions for (precautionary) defence similar to the system of **protective letters** and also regulates the judicial review of official proceedings initiated in response to such initiatives. 25

I. Right of complaint

Art. 38 DA regulates the right to lodge a complaint: According to para. 1 of the legal provision, natural and legal persons have 'the right to lodge a **complaint**, individually or, where relevant, collectively, with the relevant competent authority in the Member State of their habitual residence, place of work or establishment, if they consider that their rights under this Regulation have been infringed'. The right of appeal exists in parallel with other legal remedies and does not supersede them. It also does not take priority. Information on the right to lodge a complaint must be provided by the **data coordinator** (Art. 38(1) sent. 2 DA). 26

The Article also outlines basic procedural requirements: According to Art. 38(2) DA, the authority with which a complaint has been lodged shall **inform** the complainant of the status of the proceedings and the decision taken. The details are set out in national procedural law. If several areas are affected, authorities cooperate in the handling of complaints (Art. 38(3) DA). 27

Further requirements for the complaints procedure can be derived from other parts of the DA. For example, rec. 31 DA provides for an **immediate** decision. The proceedings must therefore be conducted and brought to a conclusion without undue delay. 28

Specific reference is made to the right to lodge a complaint, inter alia, in favour of the **user** in the case of the **right to data access** pursuant to Art. 3(3)(g) DA and Art. 4(3), (9)(a) DA. The right of **third parties (data recipients)** to lodge a complaint is also explicitly mentioned if a data holder refuses, withholds or suspends the sharing of data (Art. 5(12)(a) DA). The **data holder** may also lodge a complaint if it 29

---

[6] Remke MMR 2024, 117 (121), refers to the possible role of the EU institutions as data holders or users, which is only partially convincing due to the limitation of penalties for violations of Chapter V DA.

considers its rights to have been infringed, which may be the case in particular within the framework of the specific conditions of disclosure (Art. 17(5) DA).

30 **Public sector bodies** may also lodge a complaint if the data holder demands what they consider to be excessive compensation for the fulfilment of requests for making data available (Art. 20(5) DA). In this context, the **data holder** may have the right to lodge a complaint if it considers its trade secrets to be under threat (Art. 21(5) DA).

31 These explicit references to the right to lodge a complaint are **not exhaustive**. A complaint can always be lodged if an infringement of the DA or an infringement of one's own rights is seen through the application of the DA (Art. 38(1) sent. 1 DA). The above references to the right to lodge a complaint illustrate where the regulators have identified particular potential for disputes. They also make it clear that all stakeholders are entitled to lodge a complaint and not just the potential beneficiaries.

32 Complaints may be submitted **informally** and without adhering to specific deadlines.[7] There is no requirement to give reasons for the complaint or to submit an application. However, the reasons must be stated out of purely factual necessity so that the authority can process them effectively. Restrictions may arise under the general principle of **forfeiture** if the lodging of the complaint is no longer compatible with good faith vis-à-vis the burdened party due to a time and circumstance factor. The limit is wide and will only be reached in individual exceptional cases.

II. Protective letter

33 If a data holder refuses to make data available, it must not only justify this to the user, but also inform the authority in accordance with Art. 4(8), Art. 5(11) DA. This requires a kind of 'protective letter' from the addressees of the data access request who do not wish to grant it for specific reasons and are of the opinion that they have a right of refusal (→ Ch. 3 mn. 91 et seqq.). If the user subsequently complains, the authority already has the data holder's considerations; processing the complaint is then simplified. The authority can also intervene ex officio if, in its opinion, the refusal is not in accordance with the DA.

III. Legal remedies

34 Natural or legal persons affected by legally binding decisions of the supervisory authorities have recourse to the **courts**. This is provided for by Art. 39(1) DA and corresponds to the legal protection system in the EU.

35 For Germany, this will regularly mean that **actions for rescission or enforcement actions** pursuant to § 42(1) VwGO can be brought before the administrative courts, as the legally binding decisions of public authorities, as acts that have binding legal effect, will generally be **administrative acts** within the meaning of § 35 VwVfG. An administrative act is any sovereign decision made by a German administrative authority in the field of public law to regulate a specific individual case

[7] See also Remke MMR 2024, 117 (119).

with direct legal effect on the rights and duties of a person.[8] Such decisions will have to be made by the supervisory authorities, which affirm or deny violations of the DA, certify claims as given or deny them as unlawful.

36 As is usual in regulatory law, in many cases these administrative acts will be issued in a **triangular relationship** between the claimant, the potentially obligated party and the authority. In many cases, the administrative act will be addressed to the potentially obligated party, who already has a direct right of action for **subjective violation**. The potentially entitled party will also have a right of action in many cases, as the data access claims, or the rules on cloud switching or contract design will usually provide **third-party protection** in favour of the potential beneficiaries: Under German law, in **multipolar legal relationships**, all those who can establish a subjective violation of rights within the meaning of § 42(2) VwGO are authorised to sue. According to **the protective norm theory** under German law, this presupposes that the violation of a norm can be demonstrated that also serves the interests of third parties.[9] This must be examined in each case for the specific standard in question. This should be the case for the

- **users** requesting access in accordance with Chapters II and III DA,
- **inferior contracting parties** in the event of potentially unfair terms in accordance with Chapter IV DA,
- customers and users of data processing services in accordance with Chapter VI DA.

37 It is questionable whether the **data recipient** is already affected by a third party, as it does not enjoy an original right of access to data under the DA, but only a right of access derived from the user. This argues in favour of affirming third-party protection and thus the data recipient's right of action only and only to the extent that the user has already established the right in favour of a specific data recipient. If, in the second step, conditions pursuant to Chapters II and III DA are not met and official proceedings are conducted in this regard, the data recipient's subjective rights may also be affected. This is also reflected in the explicit mention of the right of complaint in Art. 5(12)(a) DA.

38 The third parties authorised to bring an action must also be involved in the administrative proceedings: Under German law as **parties** to be consulted, including with **rights to inspect files** in accordance with § 13 VwVfG in the administrative proceedings and in any case as simple **subpoena** within the meaning of § 65 VwGO.

39 The **action for failure to act** known from German administrative law is also regulated in the DA: if a supervisory authority fails to act in response to a complaint, Art. 39(2) DA states that 'any affected natural and legal person shall, in accordance with national law, either have the right to an effective judicial remedy or access to review by an impartial body with the appropriate expertise'. In German administrative procedural law, this leads to an action for failure to act in accordance with § 75 VwGO. Such an action generally requires that the authority has failed to decide on a case for more than three months without sufficient reason. The **complainant** is entitled to bring an action for failure to act.

---

[8] Cf. Stelkens in Stelkens/Bonk/Sachs VwVfG § 35 mn. 142.
[9] Fundamental Wahl/Schütz in Schoch/Schneider VwGO § 42(2) mn. 111 et seq.

40 The local courts have jurisdiction; Art. 39(3) DA clarifies that the authority of a Member State cannot be sued in the courts of another Member State. In this respect, the **substantive and local jurisdiction regulations** of the national legal systems apply in fulfilment of Art. 39(3) DA, in Germany for example §§ 45, 52 VwGO.

D. Civil court enforcement

41 The DA also allows for enforcement before civil courts outside of the supervisory authority proceedings: in particular, the **data access claims** under Chapter II DA, the **access conditions** of Chapter III DA, the requirements for **contract design** under Chapter IV DA and the requirements for **cloud switching** under Chapter VI DA establish direct rights and obligations in the relationship between the obligated parties and beneficiaries. Civil enforcement proceedings are neither a prerequisite for, nor subordinate to, supervisory authority appeals before the supervisory authorities; this is made clear not least by the wording of Art. 38(1) DA.

42 In particular, data access claims or the technically simple, continuous migration to other data processing services without excessive switching fees can also be brought before the **ordinary courts** as civil law claims by users, derived data recipients after original authorisation by the user and the customer by way of an action for performance. The same applies if contractual conditions are not complied with in breach of the DA, such as specific data access conditions or support obligations when switching data processing services.

43 It is also possible to seek **temporary injunctions** to enforce such claims if the relevant requirements are met. The wording of the DA opens up the entire repertoire of civil law enforcement.

CHAPTER 9
INTERNATIONAL DATA TRANSFER IN ACCORDANCE WITH THE DATA ACT

Bibliography: Gausling, 'Offenlegung von Daten auf Basis des CLOUD Act. CLOUD Act und DS-GVO im Spannungsverhältnis', MMR 2018, 578; Hessel, 'Der neue Angemessenheitsbeschluss für Datenübermittlungen in die USA', NJW 2023, 2969; Moos/Rothkegel, 'Anmerkung zum EuGH-Urteil vom 16.07.2020 – C-311/18 – Schrems II', ZD 2020, 511; Schwartmann/Burkhardt, '„Schrems II" als Sackgasse für die Datenwirtschaft? Verfahrensrechtliche Grenzen datenschutzrechtlicher Sanktionen', ZD 2021, 235; Spies, 'USA: Gesetzgeber billigt Datenzugriff außerhalb der USA (CLOUD ACT)', ZD-Aktuell 2018, 04291; Wiebe, 'Der Data Act – Innovation oder Illusion?', GRUR 2023, 1569.

A. Introduction ... 1
B. Norm addressees ... 2
C. Third country transfer ... 5
I. International transfer ... 8
II. State access ... 11
III. Permissible compliance with official and court decisions ... 13
D. Protective measures ... 22

A. Introduction

1 The DA stipulates – as the DGA does[1] – **protective measures and conditions** for preventing the unlawful transfer of non-personal data to third countries and for unlawful access to such data (Art. 32 DA and Art. 31 DGA). The protection of unlawful third country transfers of data is known from data protection law. The transfer of personal data to third countries is governed by Art. 44 et seqq. GDPR. In this regard, the – very similarly worded – Art. 32 DA and Art. 31 DGA do not contain any new provisions; rather, they supplement protection obligations for the transfer of non-personal data to third countries. According to rec. 101 DA, data transferred to third countries should be safeguarded to ensure that no third parties – in particular the governments of third countries – have access to these data under standards other than those recognised under EU law, in particular with regard to proportionality.

B. Norm addressees

2 Art. 32 DA addresses **providers of data processing services** within the meaning of Art. 2 no. 8 DA (→ Ch. 6 mn. 8). According to Art. 1(3)(f) DA, only those providers are covered who – regardless of their place of establishment – offer their services to customers in the EU. These are obliged in the DA primarily by the provisions of Chapter VI (→ Ch. 6 mn. 1 et seqq.). Providers of data processing services must now also comply with the obligations under Art. 32 DA.

3 Art. 31 DGA is directed, on the one hand, at **parties subject to obligations under other Chapters of the DGA**. These include providers of data intermediary services under Chapter III[2] and data altruism organisations recognised under Chapter

[1] Further details on the requirements laid down in the DGA in Schreiber/Pommerening/Schoel, New Data Governance Act. A Practitioner's Guide, Baden-Baden 2023.

[2] See Schreiber/Pommerening/Schoel New DGA Ch. 3.

IV of the DGA[3]. In addition to the provisions set out in the corresponding Chapters, these organisations are also subject to the provisions of Art. 31 DGA. Transfers of data to third countries by public bodies, as defined in Chapter II (→ mn. 7 et seqq.), are governed both by Art. 31 DGA and by Art. 5 DGA.[4] To understand the regulations on international data transfers in the DA, it is helpful to look at the corresponding regulations in the DGA. This is because both legal acts were enacted as part of the EU data strategy and complement each other. Interpretation difficulties can be better resolved by looking at both legal acts.

4 Secondly, Art. 31 DGA is also directed at **beneficiaries of the provisions of the DGA**. These are natural or legal persons granted the right to re-use data under Chapter II of the DGA.[5] These beneficiaries must comply with Art. 31 DGA, in addition to the conditions for third-country transfers of reused data laid down in Art. 5 DGA.

C. Third country transfer

5 The **transfer** of non-personal data to third countries and the state **access** to such data in third countries is regulated. However, Art. 32 DA and Art. 31 DGA do not cover every transfer and every access, but only the case of **unlawful** processes and aim to avoid these. A large number of international data transfers or accesses are conceivable that would conflict with Union or national law. This would also include, for example, hacker attacks by foreign governments on the norm addressees or the simple international data transfer of a recognised data altruistic organisation without the required permission of the data owner. The provisions therefore take a narrower regulatory approach than the **GDPR**, which in its Art. 44 covers any transfer of data to a third country or an international organisation. According to the GDPR, this also includes the lawful transfer to a third country. According to the prevailing view, the term 'transfer' under Art. 44 GDPR not only covers the transfer of the data itself to a third country, but also access to it from a third country by anyone, in practice regularly by support teams by means of remote access.[6] Art. 32 DA and Art. 31 DGA are narrower in three respects:

- first, the provisions apply exclusively to non-personal data;
- second, they are limited to unlawful conduct;
- third, in the case of access from a third country, only access by state authorities (under the DA) or governmental entities (under the DGA) is within scope.

6 What constitutes a **third country** within the meaning of Art. 32 DA and Art. 31 DGA is not defined. In the EU context, third countries are regularly distinguished from EU Member States. A third country is therefore any country that is not a member of the EU; in some cases, members of the European Economic Area are

---

[3] See Schreiber/Pommerening/Schoel New DGA Ch. 4.

[4] See Schreiber/Pommerening/Schoel New DGA Ch. 5.

[5] Schreiber/Pommerening/Schoel New DGA Ch. 5.

[6] For an understanding of the term under Art. 44 GDPR, see for example Schröder in Kühling/Buchner DS-GVO Art. 44 mn. 16 et seq.; on the relevance of access from third countries, EDPB, Recommendation 01/2020 on measures to supplement transfer tools to ensure the level of protection of personal data under Union law, adopted on 10.11.2020 (hereinafter: EDPB Recommendation 01/2020), mn. 13.

also excluded, at least if they have adapted the relevant legal act (EEA; Iceland, Liechtenstein and Norway).[7]

It is also notable that Art. 32(1) DA literally distinguishes between access and transfer **'international and third-country governmental'**. However, the DA does not clarify whether this distinction is intended to have any substantive meaning. On the one hand, both terms can also be found in other language versions, such as the German or French version. The EU legislator therefore seems to have considered it necessary to explicitly include data transfer or data access 'by third countries' in the text of the Regulation. On the other hand, the almost identical Art. 31 DGA merely refers to 'international transfers'. The title of Art. 32 DA also does not explicitly include third countries, but reads 'International governmental access and transfer'. In the further paragraphs of Art. 32 DA and in the appropriate recital (rec. 101 DA), only 'third countries' are mentioned. This suggests a synonymous understanding of 'international' and 'third countries'. In this respect, the wording of Art. 32(1) DA is misleading. 7

I. International transfer

The term 'transfer' is not legally defined in the DA. However, the same term is also used in relation to data and third countries in Art. 31 DGA and in particular in Art. 44 GDPR. There is much to be said for basically understanding the term in the same way in all three legal acts – also in terms of the objective of adequately protecting data despite third-country transfers.[8] In this respect, international transfer within the meaning of Art. 32 DA is also understood to mean any transfer of non-personal data to a location **outside the territory of the EU** and the EEA.[9] This includes the storage of data on servers located in a third country and the transfer there via communication lines or other technical means of transmission. 8

It is questionable whether the provision of data to recipients in a third country without them downloading the data and even the granting of access rights constitutes an international transfer. Under the GDPR, the majority of respondents were in favour of this.[10] In Art. 32 DA and Art. 31 DGA, however, the system argues for a different understanding: If this **access to data located in the EU from a third country** also constituted an international transfer, the second alternative, i.e. state access or access by government organisations, would not have been necessary. Even if the same terms are used in the English-language version in Art. 32 DA, Art. 31 DGA and Art. 44 GDPR, it can therefore be assumed that the **term transfer** under DA and DGA is to be understood **more narrowly** and only covers the change of location of data to a third country, but not access to data located in the EU from a third country.[11] 9

The **EDPB Guidelines** 05/2021 clarify the criteria for categorising a processing operation as a transfer. A transfer is deemed to have taken place if (i) the controller 10

---

[7] Cf. Beck in BeckOK DatenschutzR DS-GVO Art. 44 mn. 23 et seq.

[8] The same for DA and DGA Wienroeder in Hennemann/Ebner/Karsten/Lienemann/Wienroeder Data Act, p. 230.

[9] Schröder in Kühling/Buchner DS-GVO Art. 44 mn. 16.

[10] Instead of many Beck in BeckOK DatenschutzR DS-GVO Art. 44 mn. 15; Paal in Paal/Pauly DS-GVO Art. 44 mn. 5.

[11] Cf. Hennemann in HK-DGA Art. 31 mn. 32.

or processor ('exporter') is subject to the GDPR for the processing in question, (ii) personal data that is the subject of this processing is disclosed to the 'data importer' by transfer or other means and (iii) the importer is located in a third country, regardless of whether it is subject to Art. 3 GDPR for the processing in question or whether it is an international organisation.[12] Disclosure within the meaning of the second criterion also includes the granting of access rights. Even if data is only displayed via remote access and remains located in the EU, all criteria are otherwise fulfilled.[13]

II. State access

11 **Governmental access** to non-personal data stored in the Union in contravention of Union law or the national law of the Member State concerned is also a factual matter within the meaning of Art. 32 DA. From the systematic position and the context of Art. 32 DA, it can be concluded that this only concerns unlawful access by **third-country** governmental organisations; this follows from the title and the requirement of access contrary to EU and national law. Governmental organisations are **sovereign bodies** of third countries, first and foremost the national security authorities, but also all other state bodies.

12 The offence of Art. 31 DGA covers as well such **governmental access** to non-personal data stored in the Union that is contrary to Union law or the national law of the Member State concerned. Although the wording in some languages, especially the German version, differs between the DA and DGA, the English translation is the same and there is no reason why this term should be understood as different in the DA and DGA.

III. Permissible compliance with official and court decisions

13 **Judicial or administrative decisions issued by a third country** requiring the transfer of, or access to, non-personal data stored in the Union may only be complied with if certain conditions are met (Art. 32(2)–(4) DA). Only if these conditions are met is access not unlawful within the meaning of Art. 32(1) DA:

14 – Before the addressees comply with a judicial or official decision of a third country, they must **inform** the customer or the data owner of the existence of the third-country request (Art. 32(5) DA). This obligation to inform is only waived if the request serves law-enforcement purposes and would otherwise jeopardise the effectiveness of the law-enforcement measure.

15 – If there is an **international agreement** between the requesting third country and the Union or the Member State concerned, the judicial or administrative decisions of the third country can also be recognised or enforced in the Union (Art. 32(2) DA). As an example of such an international agreement under inter-

[12] EDPB, 'Guidelines 05/2021 on the interaction between the application of Article 3 and the provisions on international transfers under Chapter V GDPR, version 2.0, adopted on 14 February 2023' (hereinafter: EDPB Guidelines 05/2021), mn. 9.

[13] EDPB Guidelines 05/2021, mn. 16.

national law/international agreement, the text of a **mutual legal assistance agreement** is mentioned.

These regulations largely correspond to the provision in Art. 48 GDPR that applies to personal data. The prerequisite in both cases is a **sovereign request** by a third country. The purpose of the provisions is to limit access from third countries to non-personal data within the scope of the DA. Therefore, all judicial and administrative decisions of a third country are covered, regardless of their classification under procedural or administrative law.[14] Examples are: 16

- The Hague Convention on the Taking of Evidence Abroad in Civil or Commercial Matters of 18.3.1970 (Federal Law Gazette 1977 II 1472),
- the Convention on Cybercrime of the Council of Europe of 23.11.2001 (CETS No. 185),
- the agreements between the Union and the USA on extradition of 25.6.2003 (OJ 2003 L 181, 27) or
- the agreement between the Union and Japan on mutual legal assistance in criminal matters of 15.12.2009 (OJ 2010 L 39, 19).

– In the absence of an international agreement and if compliance with the third-country decision would place the addressee in conflict with Union law or the national law of the Member State concerned, the transfer or the granting of access is made subject to the following **cumulative conditions**, which are identical in the DA and the DGA (Art. 32(3) subpara. 1 DA; Art. 31(3) DGA): 17

- The legal system of the third country must stipulate that the judicial or administrative decision must be **justified, proportionate and specific** (point (a));
- a competent court of the third country must review the **addressee's** reasoned **objections** (point (b)); and
- the competent court of the third country issuing or reviewing the decision must be authorised to take into account the relevant **legal interests of the provider of** the data protected by Union or national law of the Member State concerned (point (c)).

In contrast to the DGA, Art. 32(3) subpara. 2 DA contains conditions under which the addressee of a judicial or official request to transfer or make data accessible may refuse this request. According to Art. 32(2) DA, the addressee is the provider of data processing services (→ Ch. 5 mn. 10). The latter may obtain the **opinion** of the competent national body or the authority responsible for international cooperation in legal matters on the decision or judgement in question. The purpose of this consultation procedure[15] is to determine whether the conditions of Art. 32(3) subpara. 1 DA are met. This option is particularly relevant if the addressee is of the opinion that the decision may concern business secrets, other sensitive content or content protected by intellectual property rights, or that the transfer of non-personal data may lead to re-identification. The competent body or authority may consult the European Commission on this opinion. An opinion may also be requested if the provider of data processing services considers that the decision or judgment affects the national security 18

[14] See Paal in Paal/Pauly DS-GVO Art. 48 mn. 5.
[15] Wiebe GRUR 2023, 1569 (1577).

or defence interests of the Union or its Member States. In this case, the relevant national bodies or authorities shall be asked for an opinion. The addressee shall be entitled to refuse the request to transmit data or grant access if it has not received a reply within one month or if the authority has concluded in its opinion that the conditions set out in subparagraph 1 are not met. In addition, the Commission shall issue guidelines to assess whether the conditions in subpara. 1 are met. The European Data Innovation Board should act in an advisory and supportive capacity.

19 – If there is no international agreement pursuant to Art. 32(2) DA and if the requirements pursuant to Art. 32(3) subpara. 1 DA cannot be met, the addressees may only transfer the minimum amount of data determined on the basis of a **reasonable interpretation** of the request (para. 4). The interpretation may be made by the addressee itself or by the body or authority that has issued an opinion pursuant to Art. 32(3) subpara. 2 DA. A data transfer based on a reasonable interpretation of the request only takes place if the conditions from para. 2 and 3 are fulfilled.[16] This also takes account of the fact that non-compliance with the request from a third country can have considerable legal consequences for the addressee. The addressees of the third-country request could otherwise find themselves in the awkward situation of having to break either Union law or the law of the third country.[17]

20 However, the required reasonable interpretation of the third-party request is rather **vague** and harbours corresponding **legal uncertainties**. The boundary to unlawful access by government organisations also remains unclear, especially as it falls within the sphere of risk of the norm addressee that it can also comply with the requirements of Art. 32 DA and that it is not itself obliged to comply with the decisions under foreign law. This has been discussed, for example, for access rights of the **US intelligence authorities** to data located in the EU under the Clarifying Lawful Overseas Use of Data Act (CLOUD Act) applicable in the USA if the data here in the EU is under the control of a company with a US branch or one of its subsidiaries.[18] Although the CLOUD Act provides that a company can take legal action against such an order, the scope of this right is limited.[19] In many cases, US companies are likely to be obliged under US law to provide US authorities with data stored on servers in the EU if the US company has possession, custody or control of this data. Whether this also applies if European subsidiaries exercise corresponding control over the data is an open question and has not yet been conclusively clarified.[20]

---

[16] Cf. Hennemann in HK-DGA Art. 31 mn. 57.

[17] See Pauly in Paal/Pauly DS-GVO Art. 48 mn. 4.

[18] See Gausling MMR 2018, 578 (579); Schröder in Kühling/Buchner DS-GVO Art. 48 mn. 25; Spies ZD-Aktuell 2018, 04291.

[19] Spies ZD-Aktuell 2018, 04291; see also Conrad/Licht/Strittmatter in Auer-Reinsdorff/Conrad IT- und DatenschutzR-HdB § 22 mn. 197; Gausling MMR 2018, 578 (580).

[20] Tending in favour EDPB-EDPS, 'Joint Response to the LIBE Committee on the impact of the US Cloud Act' (10.7.2019) <https://edpb.europa.eu/our-work-tools/our-documents/letters/edpb-edps-joint-response-libe-committee-impact-us-cloud-act_en> (last accessed: 7.1.2026); Schwartmann/Burkhardt ZD 2021, 235 (240); generally against Hessel NJW 2023, 2969 (2973); Moos/Rothkegel ZD 2020, 511 (525); for EU subsidiaries or data trustees, by contrast, Gausling MMR 2018, 578 (582); pointing to the lack of clarification DSK, 'Protokoll der 3. Zwischenkonferenz der unabhängigen Datenschutzaufsichtsbehörden

There is therefore much to suggest that a norm addressee who cannot rule out a violation of Art. 32 DA due to **specific references to a third country** may not become active within the scope of the respective regulation. 21

D. Protective measures

The norm addressees must take all appropriate **technical, legal and organisational measures** to prevent unlawful transfer and unlawful access (Art. 32(1) DA). Special protective measures in the context of third country transfers are intensively required for the protection of personal data under Art. 44 et seq. GDPR following the ECJ's **'Schrems II'** decision.[21] Due to the different structure of Art. 32 DA and Art. 31 DGA, the results of these discussions cannot be directly transferred, but they do contain important points of reference: 22

- **Technical protective measures** include securing the IT systems used in order to prevent unauthorised data transfers or access. Such technical measures include, for example, the use of firewalls, the encryption of non-personal data or the use of complex password protection.[22] 23
- **Legal protective measures** can consist of concluding agreements with contractual partners that ensure the protection of non-personal data against unlawful transfers or access. This may include the assumption of contractual guarantees, the obligation of contractual partners to use specific technical measures, the inclusion of contractual transparency requirements and information obligations.[23] 24
- **Organisational protective measures** complement the legal protective measures, but unlike these, they focus on internal processes and the establishment of structures that ensure security. This includes, for example, sensitising employees, establishing internal principles for data protection or involving IT security and legal advice.[24] 25

The protective measures that the addressee must take in individual cases depend on the specific circumstances. When assessing the **appropriateness**, the potential risk to the non-personal data is the first consideration. The storage of sensitive business secrets requires different protective measures than, for example, the storage of historical meteorological data. In the context of appropriateness, the state of the art and the available legal and organisational means, but also the costs of implementation and the probability (risk) of unlawful transmission or unlawful access must then be taken into account in accordance with Art. 32 GDPR. 26

Providers of data processing services are also obliged to provide a **general description** of these protective measures on their website and to keep this information up to date (Art. 28(1)(b) DGA). 27

---

des Bundes und der Länder am 22 September 2020' <https://www.datenschutzkonferenz-online.de/media/pr/20201030_protokoll_3_zwischenkonferenz.pdf> (last accessed: 7.1.2026), p. 12.

[21] ECJ 16.7.2020 – case C-311/18, ECLI:EU:C:2020:559 = NJW 2020, 2613 – Schrems II.

[22] See EDPB Recommendation 01/2020, mn. 79 et seq.

[23] See EDPB Recommendation 01/2020, mn. 97 et seq.

[24] See EDPB Recommendation 01/2020, mn. 122 et seq.

CHAPTER 10
THE EUROPEAN DATA INNOVATION BOARD

Bibliography: Pilniok, 'Struktur, Funktionen und Probleme der Expertengruppen der Europäischen Kommission: legitime Expertise oder unzulässige Einflussnahme?', EuR 2014, 62.

A. Introduction ... 1

B. Staffing ... 7
I. Task of the Commission ... 7
II. Members of the EDIB ... 8
III. Organisation ... 15

C. Tasks ... 18
I. Development of standardised practices ... 23
II. Development of standardised guidelines ... 27
III. Standardisation activities ... 29
1. Use and development of cross-sector standards ... 32
2. Data economy in the internal market ... 35
IV. Guidelines on 'Common European Data Spaces' ... 38
V. Facilitating cooperation ... 41
VI. Other tasks ... 47

A. Introduction

1 The DGA established the **European Data Innovation Board** (EDIB; Art. 1(1)(d) DGA). The relevant provisions can be found in Chapter VI DGA (Art. 29–30). The DA also includes the European Data Innovation Board – abbreviated as Data Innovation Board in the DA – in its regulations for specific cases. The European Data Innovation Board thus became a relevant institution in the EU Data Strategy as a whole, under the DGA in particular, but also under the DA.

2 The EDIB is an **expert group** that aims to support data-driven innovation, reduce transaction costs and prevent (further) sectoral fragmentation within the data economy.[1] The central task of the EDIB is to facilitate the **development of best practices by the authorities of the Member States**. The EDIB is set up by the Commission. In its proposal to establish such a body, the Commission focused in particular on processing applications for the re-use of data held by public sector bodies under Chapter II of the DGA and ensuring a harmonised approach to the notification framework for data intermediary services under Chapter III of the DGA and data altruism under Chapter IV of the DGA.[2] In addition, the EDIB is to advise and support the Commission in the management and development of strategic and cross-sectoral standardisation.[3] The exact composition of the EDIB is regulated in Art. 29 DGA, while Art. 30 DGA defines its tasks. Additional tasks can be found in the provisions of the DA (Art. 42), which are also concerned with standardising the application of the Regulation. According to rec. 110 DA, the EDIB should play a

[1] European Commission, 'Commission Staff Working Document: Impact assessment report accompanying the document Proposal for a Regulation of the European Parliament and of the Council on European data governance (Data Governance Act)' (25.11.2020), SWD(2020) 295 final, 28.

[2] Further details on the requirements laid down in the DGA in Schreiber/Pommerening/Schoel, New Data Governance Act. A Practitioner's Guide, Baden-Baden 2023.

[3] European Commission, 'Proposal for a Regulation of the European Parliament and of the Council on European data governance (Data Governance Act)' (25.11.2020), COM(2020) 767 final, 9.

'key role' in communication with the authorities and prevent 'fragmentation'. The EDIB was set up by the Commission Decision of 20.2.2023.[4]

3 Contrary to initial discussions, the EDIB is not organised as an independent European institution with legal personality. Instead, it is a **formal group of experts** with a secretariat provided by the Commission. The advantage of this solution lies in leaner structures with less regulatory intervention and greater flexibility.[5] However, it also harbours the risk of being less important, as the members of such an expert group only meet regularly on an ad hoc basis and perform other tasks outside of the EDIB. The **EU Ecolabelling Board** (EUEB) was a model for the chosen structure.[6] The EDIB is led by the Commission's DG Communications Networks, Content and Technologies (DG CONNECT).

4 Originally, it was considered giving the EDIB independent tasks or a supervisory function along the lines of the **European Data Protection Board** (EDPB) or the **European Union Agency for Cybersecurity** (ENISA).[7] According to the Commission's impact assessment, however, such an organisation of the EDIB would have led to considerable additional costs without any relevant benefits.[8]

5 It was also considered whether the tasks of the EDIB should be included in the remit of the **EDPB**. This consideration was ultimately rejected with reference to the areas of responsibility in relation to data sharing that go beyond the protection of personal data. This required expertise in the area of competition law and sector-specific data access and use regulations as well as technical knowledge of mechanisms and standards for data sharing.[9] A broader composition of the expert group is therefore to be welcomed.

6 With its organisation as a formal expert group in the final DGA, the EDIB will have an **advisory and support function**: It will accompany the Commission on issues relating to the shared use of data, with a focus on cross-sectoral issues.[10]

B. Staffing

I. Task of the Commission

7 The EDIB is formed and staffed by the Commission and should take the form of a permanent, formal group of experts. The members will be selected by the Commission in a public procedure. The EDIB was set up by a **decision** of the Commission.[11]

[4] C(2023) 1074 final.
[5] See SWD(2020) 295 final, 28 f.
[6] Art. 5 Regulation (EC) No 66/2010.
[7] SWD(2020) 295 final, 29.
[8] SWD(2020) 295 final, 52.
[9] SWD(2020) 295 final, 29.
[10] SWD(2020) 295 final, 29.
[11] European Commission, 'Commission Decision of 20 February 2023 setting up the European Data Innovation Board', C(2023) 1074 final; Art. 4 no. 1 of the 'Commission Decision of 30 May 2016 laying down horizontal provisions on the establishment and functioning of Commission expert groups', C(2016) 3301 final (hereinafter: Expert Group Decision); see also the standard template for the Establishment Decision in Annex 1 to the Expert Group Decision.

II. Members of the EDIB

8 The DGA determines the institutions and areas from which the members of the EDIB are drawn: Art. 29(1) DGA regulates the composition in detail.

9 The envisaged **categories of members** correspond to Types C, D and E of the Commission's horizontal rules on the creation and operation of expert groups (see Art. 7 no. 2 Expert Group Decision). These categories comprise **Member State authorities, EU institutions and agencies**, as well as **organisations in the broader sense** such as companies, trade unions, and NGOs (stakeholders). The latter are represented by the SME representatives and 'other representatives of relevant bodies in specific sectors and bodies with specific expertise'. This could include representatives of certain professional organisations. So far, these include the Deutsche Akademie der Technikwissenschaften, the European DIGITAL SME Alliance and Orgalim.[12] Stakeholders can only be appointed as members of the EDIB if they are registered in the EU **Transparency Register**[13] (Art. 8 no. 1 Expert Group Decision).

10 Specifically, the EDIB is to be composed of **representatives** of the following organisations in accordance with Art. 29(1) DGA:

- national authorities that fulfil tasks under the DGA:
  - authorities responsible for data intermediation services
  - authorities in charge of the registration of data altruistic organisations
- European Data Protection Board (EDPB)
- European Data Protection Supervisor (EDPS)
- European Union Agency for Cybersecurity (ENISA)
- EU Commission
- stakeholders:
  - EU SME representatives
  - other representatives of relevant bodies (sectors, specific expertise, for example from the development of sectoral data rooms).

Overall, the aim is to achieve a balanced representation of the various sectors and avoid overlaps with existing expert groups.[14]

11 Within the scope of these requirements, the Commission has a wide margin of discretion when appointing the experts. **Stakeholders** are to be selected via a public call for applications (Art. 10 no. 1 Expert Group Decision). According to rec. 53 DGA, the group of stakeholders is to be composed of **representatives from industry**, in particular from the fields of health, environment, agriculture, transport, energy, industrial manufacturing, media, cultural and creative industries, and statistics. Representatives from research, science, civil society and standardisation institutions or relevant European data spaces and bodies with specific expertise such as national statistical offices are to be included 'where appropriate'.

12 The discretion also relates to the exact **number of members** of the EDIB, which is not specified by the DGA. When determining the number of members, the Commission must take into account that all representatives listed in Art. 29(1) DGA are

---

[12] Previous members of the EDIB can be viewed at <https://ec.europa.eu/transparency/expert-groups-register/screen/expert-groups/consult?lang=en&groupID=3903> (last accessed: 7.1.2026).

[13] Available at <https://transparency-register.europa.eu/search-register-or-update/search-register_en> (last accessed: 7.1.2026).

[14] SWD(2020) 295 final, 28 et seq.

appointed, that there is no imbalance of opinion due to the appointment of more representatives in one category than in another and that not so many members are appointed overall that the EDIB becomes too large and therefore no longer able to work efficiently.

Overall, the Commission must ensure a high level of **expertise** and a **balanced representation** of relevant expertise and areas of interest when making its selection (Art. 10 no. 5 Expert Group Decision). When appointing individual experts, a balanced gender ratio and geographical balance among the members of the expert group should also be sought (Art. 29(1) sent. 2 DGA). 13

The EDIB will mainly consist of **civil servants or public sector employees**. 14 Involving the addressees of the DGA on the authority side and – via the stakeholders – also on the obligated party side can significantly increase the acceptance of the DGA and the acts of the EDIB. Particular care must be taken when selecting stakeholders to ensure that the enforcement of vested interests is counteracted.[15]

III. Organisation

The EDIB adopts its **rules of procedure** by a simple majority of its members, 15 based on a proposal agreed with the relevant Commission departments (Art. 17 no. 1 Expert Group Decision).[16] **Decisions** of the EDIB are taken by **simple majority** vote. Members who have voted against or abstained have the right to a document setting out the reasons for their position, which is attached to the opinions, recommendations or reports submitted (Art. 13 no. 8 Expert Group Decision).

The **Commission chairs** the meetings of the EDIB (Art. 29(3) DGA). It provides 16 a **secretariat** that supports the EDIB (Art. 29(4) DGA) and takes minutes (Art. 13 no. 7 Expert Group Decision). All relevant **documents** of the EDIB such as agendas, minutes of meetings or contributions by participants are published in an easily accessible manner in the register[17] of the expert groups (Art. 26 no. 1 Expert Group Decision). **EDIB meetings** are usually held on Commission premises. Officials from other Commission departments who are interested in the work of the EDIB may attend its meetings. By a simple majority vote, the members may decide to hold their deliberations in public (Art. 13 no. 2, 4 and 6 Expert Group Decision).

The internal organisation of the EDIB is set out in Art. 29(2) DGA. Its members 17 are divided into (at least) three subgroups:

- a subgroup consisting of the representatives of the competent **authorities of the Member States** (point (a)),
- a subgroup for **technical advice** on standardisation, transferability and interoperability (point (b)) and
- a subgroup for the **involvement of stakeholders** (point (c)).

The individual subgroups are each assigned a specific remit in Art. 29(2) DGA by reference to Art. 30 DGA.

---

[15] Cf. on this risk Pilniok EuR 2014, 62 (74).

[16] See also the standard template for the rules of procedure in accordance with Annex III of the Expert Group Decision.

[17] Available at <https://ec.europa.eu/transparency/expert-groups-register/screen/expert-groups?lang=en> (last accessed: 7.1.2026).

C. Tasks

18 The tasks of the EDIB are listed in a catalogue in Art. 30 DGA and Art. 42 DA. The tasks assigned to it primarily consist of **advising and supporting** the Commission in the implementation of the DGA. In some cases, this is further specified by the tasks of submitting guidelines and facilitating the cooperation of certain stakeholders. The catalogue of tasks is extended by Art. 42 DA, which describes the role of the EDIB in connection with the DA. Here, too, the EDIB has an advisory and supporting function with the aim of ensuring the standardised application of the Data Act.

19 The exact distinction between the EDIB's advisory and support function ('to advise and to assist the Commission') is not immediately clear from the text of the Regulation itself. From a purely linguistic understanding, it can be assumed that the **advisory function** has a more passive role, while the **support function** has a more active character. Where the EDIB has the task of simultaneously advising and supporting the Commission, this differentiation is, of course, invalid. In practice, it will rarely be relevant anyway. The decisive factor is that the EDIB has **no decision-making powers**.

20 In the task descriptions of existing Commission expert groups, the terms 'support' and 'advise' are sometimes used synonymously, so that no clear distinction can be made here either.[18] The tasks of advising the Commission mostly concern the **provision of expertise** in the development of implementation measures. Support tasks include, in particular, the **implementation of EU legislation, programmes and strategies**.[19] In view of the new provisions of the DGA and the DA, the latter is also likely to be the main component of the EDIB's advisory and support function.

21 The Commission's **Expert Group Decision**[20] states that expert groups do **not** make **binding decisions**, but issue opinions or recommendations and submit reports (Art. 3 Expert Group Decision). It is up to the Commission to decide how it takes into account the expertise and views of the experts.

22 In detail, the following **subject areas** are among the tasks of the EDIB:

I. Development of standardised practices

23 According to Art. 30(a)–(c) DGA, the EDIB advises and supports the Commission in the development of standardised practices. This is intended to ensure that the implementation of the DGA does not lead to inconsistent results due to different handling by the public authorities responsible for enforcement. The equivalent of these tasks in relation to the provisions of the DA can be found in Art. 42(a) DA. This states that the EDIB shall advise and assist the Commission with regard to the development of a consistent practice of the competent authorities in the enforcement of Chapters II, III, V and VII of the DA. Efficient enforcement of the DA can also only be ensured if the competent authorities do not pursue fundamentally different approaches.

[18] See, for example, the Gas Coordination Group, register number: X01096.

[19] See the allocation of tasks of the European Innovation Council (EIC) Committee, which should not be confused with the EDIB, register number: E03823.

[20] C(2016) 3300 final.

The Commission's advice and support in the **development of harmonised practices** relates to 24

- the processing of requests for the further use of data of the data categories from Art. 3(1) DGA (Art. 30(a) DGA),
- Union-wide data altruism (Art. 30(b) DGA) and
- the application of requirements of the respective competent authorities that apply to providers of data intermediation services and recognised data altruistic organisations (Art. 30(c) DGA).

Standardised practices are also to be developed for the following provisions in line with Art. 42(a) DA: 25

- data transfer from companies to consumers and between companies (Chapter II DA),
- obligations of data controllers who are obliged to provide data under Union law (Chapter III DA),
- provision of data to public sector bodies, the Commission, the European Central Bank and Union bodies on grounds of exceptional necessity (Chapter V DA); and
- unlawful government access to and unlawful government transfer of non-personal data in an international context (Chapter VII DA).

This area of responsibility is addressed in particular to the **subgroup** consisting of the authorities of the Member States. 26

II. Development of standardised guidelines

Art. 30(d) and (e) DGA assign the EDIB the task of advising and supporting the Commission in developing **standardised guidelines**. These standardised guidelines are aimed at 27

- ensuring the **protection** of non-personal data **against unauthorised access** (Art. 30(d) DGA) and
- defining **cybersecurity requirements** for the exchange and storage of data (Art. 30(e) DGA).

As far as the protection of non-personal data against unauthorised access is concerned, Art. 30(d) DGA mentions **sensitive business data** as well as non-personal data of content protected by **intellectual property rights**. These are to be optimally protected against theft of intellectual property or industrial espionage by the standardised guidelines. Consequently, this area of responsibility is also assigned to the **subgroup** consisting of the stakeholders who are to benefit from the protective measures. 28

III. Standardisation activities

Art. 30(f) and (g) DGA regulate the remit of the EDIB with regard to advising and supporting the Commission, **taking** particular **account of the contributions of standardisation bodies**. This concerns 29

- advising the Commission on the prioritisation of the use and development of **cross-sectoral standards** and the cross-sectoral comparison and exchange of best practices in relation to safety requirements and access procedures in specific sectors (Art. 30(f) DGA) and
- supporting the Commission in its efforts to counteract the fragmentation of the internal market and the **data economy in the internal market** (Art. 30(g) DGA).

30 The EDIB also provides advice and support in deciding whether the Commission should commission **standardisation organisations** to develop harmonised standards on the interoperability requirements introduced by the DA (Art. 42(c)(i) DA).

31 This assignment of tasks is aimed at the **subgroup** for technical advice on standardisation, portability and interoperability and the subgroup of the EDIB consisting of stakeholders. No further tasks have been assigned to the subgroup responsible for technical advice.

1. Use and development of cross-sector standards

32 Advising the Commission on prioritising the use and/or development of cross-sectoral standards relates to general data use and data sharing through new **common data spaces**. The EDIB is responsible for advising the Commission on standardisation activities with regard to their **suitability for cross-sectoral data use**.

33 Standardisation is intended to make data from different sectors easy **to use and exchange**. This involves the **technical and legal standards** for data transfer between two **processing environments**, which should enable the organisation of data spaces. To this end, the EDIB should follow the principles of the European Interoperability Framework[21] and use European and international standards and specifications (rec. 54 DGA). In doing so, it should also draw on the expert group[22] of the EU multi-stakeholder platform for ICT standardisation and on the services of the Connecting Europe Facility funding programme.

34 In this context, the EDIB has to differentiate between sector-specific and cross-sector standards and practices. **Sector-specific standardisation activities** relate to standards and practices that only cover data from a specific economic sector (e.g. the health sector) and cannot be used for other economic sectors. In contrast, **cross-sector standards and practices** should be suitable for data from different economic sectors and also enable the transferability of the relevant data between different sectors. Clarification of the question of which standards and practices are sector-specific and which are cross-sectoral must be given particular consideration in standardisation activities.

2. Data economy in the internal market

35 The EDIB also supports the Commission in its efforts to counteract the fragmentation of the internal market and the data economy in the internal market. This does not concern original standardisation.

[21] European Commission, 'Communication from the Commission to the European Parliament, the Council, the European Economic and Social Committee and the Committee of the Regions European Interoperability Framework – Implementation Strategy' (23.3.2017), COM(2017) 134 final.

[22] Registration number: E02758.

As part of this task, the EDIB should contribute to improving the cross-border and cross-sectoral **interoperability** of data and services for data sharing between different sectors, in particular to promote the creation of **common European data spaces**. Existing European, international or national standards should form the basis for the desired improvement in data sharing. The aim in this context is therefore not to develop new cross-sector standards, but to improve on the status quo. 36

One example of this support task of the EDIB is the **European Health Data Space** (EHDS), a Regulation which entered into force on 26.3.2025 (Regulation (EU) 2025/327). The EHDS is intended to create better access for individuals to their health data and an efficient environment for research, innovation, policy-making and regulatory activities through regulations, common standards and procedures, infrastructures and a governance framework. The Regulation stipulates, for example, cooperation between the EDIB and the newly created digital health authorities (Art. 92(8) Regulation (EU) 2025/327). 37

IV. Guidelines on 'Common European Data Spaces'

The EDIB should also submit **guidelines** on 'Common European Data Spaces'. This is concretised in Art. 30(h) DGA by naming guidelines on purpose- or sector-specific or cross-sectoral interoperable frameworks with common standards and practices for the joint use or processing of data. Among other things, this should favour the development of **new products and services**, scientific **research** or **civil society initiatives**. When adopting these guidelines, the EDIB should make proposals and thus also apply its expertise in this area in an advisory and supportive capacity (Art. 42(c)(iv) in conjunction with Art. 33(11) DA). The standards and practices developed with the help of the EDIB's guidelines should take account of applicable standards, comply with competition rules and ensure non-discriminatory access for all stakeholders in order to facilitate data sharing in the EU and realise the potential of existing and future data spaces. This task is assigned to the **sub-group consisting** of the respective **stakeholders**, as they should benefit from the guidelines created in this way, for example in the development of new products and services or in scientific research. 38

Art. 30(h) DGA expressly prescribes the treatment of the following areas: 39

- The use and development of cross-sectoral standards for cross-sectoral (shared) data use and the cross-sectoral comparison and exchange of best practices with regard to **sectoral security requirements and access procedures**. A distinction must be made here between cross-sectoral and sector-specific standards and practices. In contrast to the EDIB's task of advising the Commission on the prioritisation of the use and development of cross-sectoral standards and practices (Art. 30(f) DGA), the task of submitting guidelines in this regard takes a different perspective. This is less about the technical design of such cross-sectoral standards or the comparison and exchange of best practices than about the input of stakeholders.
- The requirements regarding the **elimination of market access restrictions** and the avoidance of **lock-in effects** in the interests of fair competition and interoperability.

- Adequate protection for **lawful data transfers to third countries**, including safeguards against data transfers prohibited under Union law.
- Adequate and non-discriminatory **representation of relevant stakeholders** in the management of common European data spaces.
- Compliance with applicable **cybersecurity requirements** under Union law.

40 The submission of corresponding guidelines serves to **involve various stakeholders**, in particular **business representatives**. The guidelines submitted in this way are intended to ensure that the specific interests of the addressees are taken into account when implementing the DGA.

V. Facilitating cooperation

41 According to Art. 30(i) and (j) DGA, the EDIB has the task of facilitating the **cooperation** of certain actors. This concerns cooperation

- of the **Member States** regarding the establishment of harmonised conditions for the authorisation to re-use categories of specially protected data held by public sector bodies throughout the internal market (Art. 30(i) DGA), and
- between the **authorities** responsible for data brokerage services and the **authorities** responsible for the registration of data altruistic organisations by means of capacity building and information exchange (Art. 30(j) DGA).

42 The DA also provides for a similar task: The EDIB shall facilitate cooperation between the authorities responsible for the application and enforcement of the DA through **capacity building** and **exchange of information** (Art. 42(b) DA).

43 The EDIB should thus work towards **standardising** the state conditions for the re-use of protected data held by public bodies. In contrast to the support of the Commission in accordance with Art. 30(a) DGA, the EDIB should contribute in this context to ensuring that standardised conditions (Art. 5 DGA) apply throughout the EU for the authorisation of re-use.

44 **Facilitating cooperation** between the authorities responsible for data brokerage services and the authorities responsible for the registration of data altruism organisations includes the definition of methods for an **efficient exchange of information** on the registration procedure for providers of data brokerage services (Art. 11 DGA) and the registration and monitoring of recognised data altruism organisations (Art. 19, 24 DGA). This aims to ensure consistent and standardised official action. This includes the coordination of fees and sanctions, and facilitating cooperation on cross-border data access and international data transfers.

45 With regard to the DA, the methods to be defined for the efficient exchange of information should relate to the **enforcement** of individual rights and obligations under the Data Regulation in **cross-border cases** (Art. 42(b) DA). This refers to the provisions on data sharing in the B2C and B2B sectors (Chapter II DA), the obligations of data holders (Chapter III DA) and the provision of data in cases of exceptional need (Chapter V DA). This also includes coordination with regard to the definition of sanctions for violations of the DA.

46 The facilitation of cooperation relates to an abstract level of capacity building and the exchange of information. The concrete application of the fees or sanctions determined with the help of the EDIB is the responsibility of the respective competent authorities. Consequently, this task falls to the **subgroup of** the EDIB consisting of representatives of the authorities.

VI. Other tasks

47 In Art. 30(k)–(m) DGA and in the DA, the EDIB is assigned further tasks for the implementation of the DGA. These include:

- advising and supporting the Commission in examining the question of whether **implementing acts** pursuant to Art. 5(11) and (12) DGA should be adopted (Art. 30(k) DGA),
- advising and supporting the Commission in the development of the European **consent form** for data altruism pursuant to Art. 25(1) DGA (Art. 30(l) DGA),
- advising the Commission on **improving the international regulatory environment** for non-personal data, including standardisation (Art. 30(m) DGA),
- advising and supporting the Commission with regard to the drafting of **implementing acts** pursuant to Art. 33(5), Art. 35(5), (8) and Art. 36(6) DA on interoperability requirements (Art. 42(c)(ii) DA) and
- advising and supporting in the preparation of **delegated acts** in accordance with Art. 29(7) and Art. 33(2) DA (Art. 42(c)(iii) DA).

48 The fact that the **recommendations** and advice of the EDIB must **be taken into account** is specified in other places in the DA, e.g. in the development of Commission guidelines on the calculation of an appropriate consideration for the provision of data (Art. 9(5) DA) or in the development of guidelines for the assessment of whether conditions for the transfer of data to third countries within the meaning of Art. 32(3) subpara. 1 DA are fulfilled (Art. 32(3) subpara. 2 DA). The recommendations of the EDIB must also be taken into account when imposing sanctions for violations of the DA. In addition, the Member States should ensure that the tasks of the competent authorities for the application and enforcement of the DA include cooperation with the EDIB (Art. 37(5)(f) DA). This is intended to ensure the harmonised and efficient application of the DA.

49 Of the tasks mentioned here, only advising and supporting the Commission with regard to the issue of adopting implementing acts is expressly assigned to a **subgroup** consisting of representatives of public authorities.

Annex: Data Act

REGULATION (EU) 2023/2854 OF THE EUROPEAN PARLIAMENT AND OF THE COUNCIL

of 13 December 2023

on harmonised rules on fair access to and use of data and amending Regulation (EU) 2017/2394 and Directive (EU) 2020/1828 (Data Act)

(Text with EEA relevance)

THE EUROPEAN PARLIAMENT AND THE COUNCIL OF THE EUROPEAN UNION,

Having regard to the Treaty on the Functioning of the European Union, and in particular Article 114 thereof,

Having regard to the proposal from the European Commission,

After transmission of the draft legislative act to the national parliaments,

Having regard to the opinion of the European Central Bank[1],

Having regard to the opinion of the European Economic and Social Committee[2],

Having regard to the opinion of the Committee of the Regions[3],

Acting in accordance with the ordinary legislative procedure[4],

Whereas:

(1) In recent years, data-driven technologies have had transformative effects on all sectors of the economy. The proliferation of products connected to the internet in particular has increased the volume and potential value of data for consumers, businesses and society. High-quality and interoperable data from different domains increase competitiveness and innovation and ensure sustainable economic growth. The same data may be used and reused for a variety of purposes and to an unlimited degree, without any loss of quality or quantity.

(2) Barriers to data sharing prevent an optimal allocation of data for the benefit of society. Those barriers include a lack of incentives for data holders to enter voluntarily into data sharing agreements, uncertainty about rights and obligations in relation to data, the costs of contracting and implementing technical interfaces, the high level of fragmentation of information in data silos, poor metadata management, the absence of standards for semantic and technical interoperability, bottlenecks impeding data access, a lack of common data sharing practices and the abuse of contractual imbalances with regard to data access and use.

---

[1] OJ C 402, 19.10.2022, p. 5.

[2] OJ C 365, 23.9.2022, p. 18.

[3] OJ C 375, 30.9.2022, p. 112.

[4] Position of the European Parliament of 9 November 2023 (not yet published in the Official Journal) and decision of the Council of 27 November 2023.

(3) In sectors characterised by the presence of microenterprises, small enterprises and medium-sized enterprises as defined in Article 2 of the Annex to Commission Recommendation 2003/361/EC[5] (SMEs), there is often a lack of digital capacities and skills to collect, analyse and use data, and access is frequently restricted where one actor holds them in the system or due to a lack of interoperability between data, between data services or across borders.

(4) In order to respond to the needs of the digital economy and to remove barriers to a well-functioning internal market for data, it is necessary to lay down a harmonised framework specifying who is entitled to use product data or related service data, under which conditions and on what basis. Accordingly, Member States should not adopt or maintain additional national requirements regarding matters falling within the scope of this Regulation, unless explicitly provided for herein, since this would affect its direct and uniform application. Moreover, action at Union level should be without prejudice to obligations and commitments in the international trade agreements concluded by the Union.

(5) This Regulation ensures that users of a connected product or related service in the Union can access, in a timely manner, the data generated by the use of that connected product or related service and that those users can use the data, including by sharing them with third parties of their choice. It imposes the obligation on data holders to make data available to users and third parties of the user's choice in certain circumstances. It also ensures that data holders make data available to data recipients in the Union under fair, reasonable and non-discriminatory terms and conditions and in a transparent manner. Private law rules are key in the overall framework for data sharing. Therefore, this Regulation adapts rules of contract law and prevents the exploitation of contractual imbalances that hinder fair access to and use of data. This Regulation also ensures that data holders make available to public sector bodies, the Commission, the European Central Bank or Union bodies, where there is an exceptional need, the data that are necessary for the performance of a specific task carried out in the public interest. In addition, this Regulation seeks to facilitate switching between data processing services and to enhance the interoperability of data and of data sharing mechanisms and services in the Union. This Regulation should not be interpreted as recognising or conferring any new right on data holders to use data generated by the use of a connected product or related service.

(6) Data generation is the result of the actions of at least two actors, in particular the designer or manufacturer of a connected product, who may in many cases also be a provider of related services, and the user of the connected product or related service. It gives rise to questions of fairness in the digital economy as the data recorded by connected products or related services are an important input for aftermarket, ancillary and other services. In order to realise the important economic benefits of data, including by way of data sharing on the basis of voluntary agreements and the development of data-driven value creation by Union enterprises, a general approach to assigning rights regard-

[5] Commission Recommendation 2003/361/EC of 6 May 2003 concerning the definition of micro, small and medium-sized enterprises (OJ L 124, 20.5.2003, p. 36).

ing access to and the use of data is preferable to awarding exclusive rights of access and use. This Regulation provides for horizontal rules which could be followed by Union or national law that addresses the specific situations of the relevant sectors.

(7) The fundamental right to the protection of personal data is safeguarded, in particular, by Regulations (EU) 2016/679[6] and (EU) 2018/1725[7] of the European Parliament and of the Council. Directive 2002/58/EC of the European Parliament and of the Council[8] additionally protects private life and the confidentiality of communications, including by way of conditions on any personal and non-personal data storing in, and access from, terminal equipment. Those Union legislative acts provide the basis for sustainable and responsible data processing, including where datasets include a mix of personal and non-personal data. This Regulation complements and is without prejudice to Union law on the protection of personal data and privacy, in particular Regulations (EU) 2016/679 and (EU) 2018/1725 and Directive 2002/58/EC. No provision of this Regulation should be applied or interpreted in such a way as to diminish or limit the right to the protection of personal data or the right to privacy and confidentiality of communications. Any processing of personal data pursuant to this Regulation should comply with Union data protection law, including the requirement of a valid legal basis for processing under Article 6 of Regulation (EU) 2016/679 and, where relevant, the conditions of Article 9 of that Regulation and of Article 5(3) of Directive 2002/58/EC. This Regulation does not constitute a legal basis for the collection or generation of personal data by the data holder. This Regulation imposes an obligation on data holders to make personal data available to users or third parties of a user's choice upon that user's request. Such access should be provided to personal data that are processed by the data holder on the basis of any of the legal bases referred to in Article 6 of Regulation (EU) 2016/679. Where the user is not the data subject, this Regulation does not create a legal basis for providing access to personal data or for making personal data available to a third party and should not be understood as conferring any new right on the data holder to use personal data generated by the use of a connected product or related service. In those cases, it could be in the interest of the user to facilitate meeting the requirements of Article 6 of Regulation (EU) 2016/679. As this Regulation should not adversely affect the data protection rights of data subjects, the data holder can comply with requests in those cases, inter alia, by anonymising personal data or, where the readily available data

---

[6] Regulation (EU) 2016/679 of the European Parliament and of the Council of 27 April 2016 on the protection of natural persons with regard to the processing of personal data and on the free movement of such data, and repealing Directive 95/46/EC (General Data Protection Regulation) (OJ L 119, 4.5.2016, p. 1).

[7] Regulation (EU) 2018/1725 of the European Parliament and of the Council of 23 October 2018 on the protection of natural persons with regard to the processing of personal data by the Union institutions, bodies, offices and agencies and on the free movement of such data, and repealing Regulation (EC) No 45/2001 and Decision No 1247/2002/EC (OJ L 295, 21.11.2018, p. 39).

[8] Directive 2002/58/EC of the European Parliament and of the Council of 12 July 2002 concerning the processing of personal data and the protection of privacy in the electronic communications sector (Directive on privacy and electronic communications) (OJ L 201, 31.7.2002, p. 37).

contains personal data of several data subjects, transmitting only personal data relating to the user.

(8) The principles of data minimisation and data protection by design and by default are essential when processing involves significant risks to the fundamental rights of individuals. Taking into account the state of the art, all parties to data sharing, including data sharing falling within scope of this Regulation, should implement technical and organisational measures to protect those rights. Such measures include not only pseudonymisation and encryption, but also the use of increasingly available technology that permits algorithms to be brought to the data and allow valuable insights to be derived without the transmission between parties or unnecessary copying of the raw or structured data themselves.

(9) Unless otherwise provided for in this Regulation, it does not affect national contract law, including rules on the formation, validity or effect of contracts, or the consequences of the termination of a contract. This Regulation complements and is without prejudice to Union law which aims to promote the interests of consumers and ensure a high level of consumer protection, and to protect their health, safety and economic interests, in particular Council Directive 93/13/EEC[9] and Directives 2005/29/EC[10] and 2011/83/EU[11] of the European Parliament and of the Council.

(10) This Regulation is without prejudice to Union and national legal acts providing for the sharing of, access to and the use of data for the purpose of the prevention, investigation, detection or prosecution of criminal offences or for the execution of criminal penalties, or for customs and taxation purposes, irrespective of the legal basis under the Treaty on the Functioning of the European Union (TFEU) on which such Union legal acts were adopted, as well as to international cooperation in that area, in particular on the basis of the Council of Europe Convention on Cybercrime, (ETS No 185), done at Budapest on 23 November 2001. Such acts include Regulations (EU) 2021/784[12], (EU) 2022/2065[13] and (EU) 2023/1543[14] of the European Parliament and of the Council and Directive (EU) 2023/1544 of the European Parliament

[9] Council Directive 93/13/EEC of 5 April 1993 on unfair terms in consumer contracts (OJ L 95, 21.4.1993, p. 29).

[10] Directive 2005/29/EC of the European Parliament and of the Council of 11 May 2005 concerning unfair business-to-consumer commercial practices in the internal market and amending Council Directive 84/450/EEC, Directives 97/7/EC, 98/27/EC and 2002/65/EC of the European Parliament and of the Council and Regulation (EC) No 2006/2004 of the European Parliament and of the Council ('Unfair Commercial Practices Directive') (OJ L 149, 11.6.2005, p. 22).

[11] Directive 2011/83/EU of the European Parliament and of the Council of 25 October 2011 on consumer rights, amending Council Directive 93/13/EEC and Directive 1999/44/EC of the European Parliament and of the Council and repealing Council Directive 85/577/EEC and Directive 97/7/EC of the European Parliament and of the Council (OJ L 304, 22.11.2011, p. 64).

[12] Regulation (EU) 2021/784 of the European Parliament and of the Council of 29 April 2021 on addressing the dissemination of terrorist content online (OJ L 172, 17.5.2021, p. 79).

[13] Regulation (EU) 2022/2065 of the European Parliament and of the Council of 19 October 2022 on a Single Market For Digital Services and amending Directive 2000/31/EC (Digital Services Act) (OJ L 277, 27.10.2022, p. 1).

[14] Regulation (EU) 2023/1543 of the European Parliament and of the Council of 12 July 2023 on European Production Orders and European Preservation Orders for electronic evidence in criminal proceedings and for the execution of custodial sentences following criminal proceedings (OJ L 191, 28.7.2023, p. 118).

and of the Council[15]. This Regulation does not apply to the collection or sharing of, access to or the use of data under Regulation (EU) 2015/847 of the European Parliament and of the Council[16] and Directive (EU) 2015/849 of the European Parliament and of the Council[17]. This Regulation does not apply to areas that fall outside the scope of Union law and in any event does not affect the competences of the Member States concerning public security, defence or national security, customs and tax administration or the health and safety of citizens, regardless of the type of entity entrusted by the Member States to carry out tasks in relation to those competences.

(11) Union law establishing physical design and data requirements for products to be placed on the Union market should not be affected unless specifically provided for by this Regulation.

(12) This Regulation complements and is without prejudice to Union law aiming to establish accessibility requirements on certain products and services, in particular Directive (EU) 2019/882 of the European Parliament and of the Council[18].

(13) This Regulation is without prejudice to Union and national legal acts providing for the protection of intellectual property rights, including Directives 2001/29/EC[19], 2004/48/EC[20] and (EU) 2019/790[21] of the European Parliament and of the Council.

(14) Connected products that obtain, generate or collect, by means of their components or operating systems, data concerning their performance, use or environment and that are able to communicate those data via an electronic communications service, a physical connection, or on-device access, often referred to as the Internet of Things, should fall within the scope of this Regulation, with the exception of prototypes. Examples of such electronic communications services include, in particular, land-based telephone networks, television cable networks, satellite-based networks and near-field communication networks. Connected products are found in all aspects of the economy and society, including in private, civil or commercial infrastructure,

---

[15] Directive (EU) 2023/1544 of the European Parliament and of the Council of 12 July 2023 laying down harmonised rules on the designation of designated establishments and the appointment of legal representatives for the purpose of gathering electronic evidence in criminal proceedings (OJ L 191, 28.7.2023, p. 181).

[16] Regulation (EU) 2015/847 of the European Parliament and of the Council of 20 May 2015 on information accompanying transfers of funds and repealing Regulation (EC) No 1781/2006 (OJ L 141, 5.6.2015, p. 1).

[17] Directive (EU) 2015/849 of the European Parliament and of the Council of 20 May 2015 on the prevention of the use of the financial system for the purposes of money laundering or terrorist financing, amending Regulation (EU) No 648/2012 of the European Parliament and of the Council, and repealing Directive 2005/60/EC of the European Parliament and of the Council and Commission Directive 2006/70/EC (OJ L 141, 5.6.2015, p. 73).

[18] Directive (EU) 2019/882 of the European Parliament and of the Council of 17 April 2019 on the accessibility requirements for products and services (OJ L 151, 7.6.2019, p. 70).

[19] Directive 2001/29/EC of the European Parliament and of the Council of 22 May 2001 on the harmonisation of certain aspects of copyright and related rights in the information society (OJ L 167, 22.6.2001, p. 10).

[20] Directive 2004/48/EC of the European Parliament and of the Council of 29 April 2004 on the enforcement of intellectual property rights (OJ L 157, 30.4.2004, p. 45).

[21] Directive (EU) 2019/790 of the European Parliament and of the Council of 17 April 2019 on copyright and related rights in the Digital Single Market and amending Directives 96/9/EC and 2001/29/EC (OJ L 130, 17.5.2019, p. 92).

vehicles, health and lifestyle equipment, ships, aircraft, home equipment and consumer goods, medical and health devices or agricultural and industrial machinery. Manufacturers' design choices, and, where relevant, Union or national law that addresses sector-specific needs and objectives or relevant decisions of competent authorities, should determine which data a connected product is capable of making available.

(15) The data represent the digitisation of user actions and events and should accordingly be accessible to the user. The rules for access to and the use of data from connected products and related services under this Regulation address both product data and related service data. Product data refers to data generated by the use of a connected product that the manufacturer designed to be retrievable from the connected product by a user, data holder or a third party, including, where relevant, the manufacturer. Related service data refers to data, which also represent the digitisation of user actions or events related to the connected product which are generated during the provision of a related service by the provider. Data generated by the use of a connected product or related service should be understood to cover data recorded intentionally or data which result indirectly from the user's action, such as data about the connected product's environment or interactions. This should include data on the use of a connected product generated by a user interface or via a related service, and should not be limited to the information that such use took place, but should include all data that the connected product generates as a result of such use, such as data generated automatically by sensors and data recorded by embedded applications, including applications indicating hardware status and malfunctions. This should also include data generated by the connected product or related service during times of inaction by the user, such as when the user chooses not to use a connected product for a given period of time and instead to keep it in stand-by mode or even switched off, as the status of a connected product or its components, for example its batteries, can vary when the connected product is in stand-by mode or switched off. Data which are not substantially modified, meaning data in raw form, also known as source or primary data which refer to data points that are automatically generated without any further form of processing, as well as data which have been pre-processed for the purpose of making them understandable and useable prior to subsequent processing and analysis fall within the scope of this Regulation. Such data includes data collected from a single sensor or a connected group of sensors for the purpose of making the collected data comprehensible for wider use-cases by determining a physical quantity or quality or the change in a physical quantity, such as temperature, pressure, flow rate, audio, pH value, liquid level, position, acceleration or speed. The term 'pre-processed data' should not be interpreted in such a manner as to impose an obligation on the data holder to make substantial investments in cleaning and transforming the data. The data to be made available should include the relevant metadata, including its basic context and timestamp, to make the data usable, combined with other data, such as data sorted and classified with other data points relating to them, or re-formatted into a commonly used format. Such data are potentially valuable to the user and support innovation and the development of digital and

other services to protect the environment, health and the circular economy, including through facilitating the maintenance and repair of the connected products in question. By contrast, information inferred or derived from such data, which is the outcome of additional investments into assigning values or insights from the data, in particular by means of proprietary, complex algorithms, including those that are a part of proprietary software, should not be considered to fall within the scope of this Regulation and consequently should not be subject to the obligation of a data holder to make it available to a user or a data recipient, unless otherwise agreed between the user and the data holder. Such data could include, in particular, information derived by means of sensor fusion, which infers or derives data from multiple sensors, collected in the connected product, using proprietary, complex algorithms and which could be subject to intellectual property rights.

(16) This Regulation enables users of connected products to benefit from after-market, ancillary and other services based on data collected by sensors embedded in such products, the collection of those data being of potential value in improving the performance of the connected products. It is important to delineate between, on the one hand, markets for the provision of such sensor-equipped connected products and related services and, on the other, markets for unrelated software and content such as textual, audio or audiovisual content often covered by intellectual property rights. As a result, data that such sensor-equipped connected products generate when the user records, transmits, displays or plays content, as well as the content itself, which is often covered by intellectual property rights, inter alia for use by an online service, should not be covered by this Regulation. This Regulation should also not cover data which was obtained, generated or accessed from the connected product, or which was transmitted to it, for the purpose of storage or other processing operations on behalf of other parties, who are not the user, such as may be the case with regard to servers or cloud infrastructure operated by their owners entirely on behalf of third parties, inter alia for use by an online service.

(17) It is necessary to lay down rules regarding products that are connected to a related service at the time of the purchase, rent or lease in such a way that its absence would prevent the connected product from performing one or more of its functions, or which is subsequently connected to the product by the manufacturer or a third party to add to or adapt the functionality of the connected product. Such related services involve the exchange of data between the connected product and the service provider and should be understood to be explicitly linked to the operation of the connected product's functions, such as services that, where applicable, transmit commands to the connected product that are able to have an impact on its action or behaviour. Services which do not have an impact on the operation of the connected product and which do not involve the transmitting of data or commands to the connected product by the service provider should not be considered to be related services. Such services could include, for example, auxiliary consulting, analytics or financial services, or regular repair and maintenance. Related services can be offered as part of the purchase, rent or lease contract. Related services could also be provided for products of the

same type and users could reasonably expect them to be provided taking into account the nature of the connected product and any public statement made by or on behalf of the seller, rentor, lessor or other persons in previous links of the chain of transactions, including the manufacturer. Those related services may themselves generate data of value to the user independently of the data collection capabilities of the connected product with which they are interconnected. This Regulation should also apply to a related service that is not supplied by the seller, rentor or lessor itself, but which is provided by a third party. In the event of doubt as to whether the service is provided as part of the purchase, rent or lease contract, this Regulation should apply. Neither the power supply, nor the supply of the connectivity are to be interpreted as related services under this Regulation.

(18) The user of a connected product should be understood to be a natural or legal person, such as a business, a consumer or a public sector body, that owns a connected product, has received certain temporary rights, for example by means of a rental or lease agreement, to access or use data obtained from the connected product, or receives related services for the connected product. Those access rights should in no way alter or interfere with the rights of data subjects who may be interacting with a connected product or a related service regarding personal data generated by the connected product or during the provision of the related service. The user bears the risks and enjoys the benefits of using the connected product and should also enjoy access to the data it generates. The user should therefore be entitled to derive benefit from data generated by that connected product and any related service. An owner, renter or lessee should also be considered to be a user, including where several entities can be considered to be users. In the context of multiple users, each user may contribute in a different manner to the data generation and have an interest in several forms of use, such as fleet management for a leasing enterprise, or mobility solutions for individuals using a car sharing service.

(19) Data literacy refers to the skills, knowledge and understanding that allows users, consumers and businesses, in particular SMEs falling within the scope of this Regulation, to gain awareness of the potential value of the data they generate, produce and share and that they are motivated to offer and provide access to in accordance with relevant legal rules. Data literacy should go beyond learning about tools and technologies and aim to equip and empower citizens and businesses with the ability to benefit from an inclusive and fair data market. The spread of data literacy measures and the introduction of appropriate follow-up actions could contribute to improving working conditions and ultimately sustain the consolidation, and innovation path of, the data economy in the Union. Competent authorities should promote tools and adopt measures to advance data literacy among users and entities falling within the scope of this Regulation and an awareness of their rights and obligations thereunder.

(20) In practice, not all data generated by connected products or related services are easily accessible to their users and there are often limited possibilities regarding the portability of data generated by products connected to the internet. Users are unable to obtain the data necessary to make use of

providers of repair and other services and businesses are unable to launch innovative, convenient and more efficient services. In many sectors, manufacturers are able to determine, through their control of the technical design of the connected products or related services, what data are generated and how they can be accessed, despite having no legal right to those data. It is therefore necessary to ensure that connected products are designed and manufactured, and related services are designed and provided, in such a manner that product data and related service data, including the relevant metadata necessary to interpret and use those data, including for the purpose of retrieving, using or sharing them, are always easily and securely accessible to a user, free of charge, in a comprehensive, structured, commonly used and machine-readable format. Product data and related service data that a data holder lawfully obtains or can lawfully obtain from the connected product or related service, such as by means of the connected product design, the data holder's contract with the user for the provision of related services, and its technical means of data access, without disproportionate effort, are referred to as 'readily available data'. Readily available data does not include data generated by the use of a connected product where the design of the connected product does not provide for such data being stored or transmitted outside the component in which they are generated or the connected product as a whole. This Regulation should therefore not be understood to impose an obligation to store data on the central computing unit of a connected product. The absence of such an obligation should not prevent the manufacturer or data holder from voluntarily agreeing with the user on the making of such adaptations. The design obligations in this Regulation are also without prejudice to the data minimisation principle laid down in Article 5(1), point (c), of Regulation (EU) 2016/679 and should not be understood as imposing an obligation to design connected products and related services in such a way that they store or otherwise process any personal data other than the personal data necessary in relation to the purposes for which they are processed. Union or national law could be introduced to outline further specificities, such as the product data that should be accessible from connected products or related services, given that such data may be essential for the efficient operation, repair or maintenance of those connected products or related services. Where subsequent updates or alterations to a connected product or a related service, by the manufacturer or another party, lead to additional accessible data or a restriction of initially accessible data, such changes should be communicated to the user in the context of the update or alteration.

(21) Where several persons or entities are considered to be users, for example in the case of co-ownership or where an owner, renter or lessee shares rights of data access or use, the design of the connected product or related service, or the relevant interface, should enable each user to have access to the data they generate. Use of connected products that generate data typically requires a user account to be set up. Such an account allows the user to be identified by the data holder, which may be the manufacturer. It can also be used as a means of communication and to submit and process data access requests. Where several manufacturers or related services providers have sold, rented or leased connected products or provided related services, integrated togeth-

er, to the same user, the user should turn to each of the parties with which it has a contract. Manufacturers or designers of a connected product that is typically used by several persons should put in place the necessary mechanisms to allow separate user accounts for individual persons, where relevant, or for the possibility of several persons using the same user account. Account solutions should allow users to delete their accounts and erase the data related to them and could allow users to terminate data access, use or sharing, or submit requests to terminate, in particular taking into account situations in which the ownership or usage of the connected product changes. Access should be granted to the user on the basis of simple request mechanism granting automatic execution and not requiring examination or clearance by the manufacturer or data holder. This means that the data should be made available only when the user actually wants access. Where automated execution of the data access request is not possible, for example via a user account or accompanying mobile application provided with the connected product or related service, the manufacturer should inform the user as to how the data may be accessed.

(22) Connected products may be designed to make certain data directly accessible from on-device data storage or from a remote server to which the data are communicated. Access to on-device data storage may be enabled via cable-based or wireless local area networks connected to a publicly available electronic communications service or mobile network. The server may be the manufacturer's own local server capacity or that of a third party or a cloud service provider. Processors as defined in Article 4, point (8), of Regulation (EU) 2016/679 are not considered to act as data holders. However, they can be specifically tasked with making data available by the controller as defined in Article 4, point (7), of Regulation (EU) 2016/679. Connected products may be designed to permit the user or a third party to process the data on the connected product, on a computing instance of the manufacturer or within an information and communications technology (ICT) environment chosen by the user or the third party.

(23) Virtual assistants play an increasing role in digitising consumer and professional environments and serve as an easy-to-use interface to play content, obtain information, or activate products connected to the internet. Virtual assistants can act as a single gateway in, for example, a smart home environment and record significant amounts of relevant data on how users interact with products connected to the internet, including those manufactured by other parties, and can replace the use of manufacturer-provided interfaces such as touch screens or smartphone apps. The user may wish to make available such data to third party manufacturers and enable novel smart services. Virtual assistants should be covered by the data access rights provided for in this Regulation. Data generated when a user interacts with a connected product via a virtual assistant provided by an entity other than the manufacturer of the connected product should also be covered by the data access rights provided for in this Regulation. However, only the data arising from the interaction between the user and a connected product or related service through the virtual assistant should be covered by this Regulation.

Data produced by the virtual assistant which are unrelated to the use of a connected product or related service are not covered by this Regulation.

(24) Before concluding a contract for the purchase, rent, or lease of a connected product, the seller, rentor or lessor, which may be the manufacturer, should provide to the user information regarding the product data which the connected product is capable of generating, including the type, format and the estimated volume of such data, in a clear and comprehensible manner. This could include information on data structures, data formats, vocabularies, classification schemes, taxonomies and code lists, where available, as well as clear and sufficient information relevant for the exercise of the user's rights on how the data may be stored, retrieved or accessed, including the terms of use and quality of service of application programming interfaces or, where applicable, the provision of software development kits. That obligation provides transparency over the product data generated and enhances easy access for the user. The information obligation could be fulfilled, for example by maintaining a stable uniform resource locator (URL) on the web, which can be distributed as a web link or QR code, pointing to the relevant information, which could be provided by the seller, rentor or lessor, which may be the manufacturer, to the user before concluding the contract for the purchase, rent or lease of a connected product. It is, in any case, necessary that the user is able to store the information in a way that is accessible for future reference and that allows the unchanged reproduction of the information stored. The data holder cannot be expected to store the data indefinitely in view of the needs of the user of the connected product, but should implement a reasonable data retention policy, where applicable, in line with storage limitation principle pursuant Article 5(1), point (e), of Regulation (EU) 2016/679, that allows for the effective application of the data access rights provided for in this Regulation. The obligation to provide information does not affect the obligation of the controller to provide information to the data subject pursuant to Articles 12, 13 and 14 of Regulation (EU) 2016/679. The obligation to provide information before concluding a contract for the provision of a related service should lie with the prospective data holder, independently of whether the data holder concludes a contract for the purchase, rent or lease of a connected product. Where information changes during the lifetime of the connected product or the contract period for the related service, including where the purpose for which those data are to be used changes from the originally specified purpose, it should also be provided to the user.

(25) This Regulation should not be understood to confer any new right on data holders to use product data or related service data. Where the manufacturer of a connected product is a data holder, the basis for the manufacturer to use non-personal data should be a contract between the manufacturer and the user. Such a contract could be part of an agreement for the provision of the related service, which could be concluded together with the purchase, rent or lease agreement relating to the connected product. Any contractual term stipulating that the data holder may use product data or related service data should be transparent to the user, including regarding the purposes for which the data holder intends to use the data. Such purposes could include improving the functioning of the connected product or related services,

developing new products or services, or aggregating data with the aim of making available the resulting derived data to third parties, provided that such derived data do not allow the identification of specific data transmitted to the data holder from the connected product, or allow a third party to derive those data from the dataset. Any change of the contract should depend on the informed agreement of the user. This Regulation does not prevent parties from agreeing on contractual terms the effect of which is to exclude or limit the use of non-personal data, or certain categories of non-personal data, by a data holder. Neither does it prevent parties from agreeing to make product data or related service data available to third parties, directly or indirectly, including, where applicable, via another data holder. Moreover, this Regulation does not prevent sector-specific regulatory requirements under Union law, or national law compatible with Union law, which would exclude or limit the use of certain such data by the data holder on well-defined public policy grounds. This Regulation does not prevent users, in the case of business-to-business relations, from making data available to third parties or data holders under any lawful contractual term, including by agreeing to limit or restrict further sharing of such data, or from being compensated proportionately, for example in exchange for waiving their right to use or share such data. While the notion of 'data holder' generally does not include public sector bodies, it may include public undertakings.

(26) To foster the emergence of liquid, fair and efficient markets for non-personal data, users of connected products should be able to share data with others, including for commercial purposes, with minimal legal and technical effort. It is currently often difficult for businesses to justify the personnel or computing costs that are necessary for preparing non-personal datasets or data products and to offer them to potential counterparties via data intermediation services, including data marketplaces. A substantial hurdle to the sharing of non-personal data by businesses therefore results from the lack of predictability of economic returns from investing in the curation and making available of datasets or data products. In order to allow for the emergence of liquid, fair and efficient markets for non-personal data in the Union, the party that has the right to offer such data on a market must be clarified. Users should therefore have the right to share non-personal data with data recipients for commercial and non-commercial purposes. Such data sharing could be performed directly by the user, upon the request of the user via a data holder, or through data intermediation services. Data intermediation services, as regulated by Regulation (EU) 2022/868 of the European Parliament and of the Council[22] could facilitate a data economy by establishing commercial relationships between users, data recipients and third parties and may support users in exercising their right to use data, such as ensuring the anonymisation of personal data or aggregation of access to data from multiple individual users. Where data are excluded from a data holder's obligation to make them available to users or third parties, the scope

[22] Regulation (EU) 2022/868 of the European Parliament and of the Council of 30 May 2022 on European data governance and amending Regulation (EU) 2018/1724 (Data Governance Act) (OJ L 152, 3.6.2022, p. 1).

of such data could be specified in the contract between the user and the data holder for the provision of a related service so that users can easily determine which data are available to them for sharing with data recipients or third parties. Data holders should not make available non-personal product data to third parties for commercial or non-commercial purposes other than the fulfilment of their contract with the user, without prejudice to legal requirements pursuant to Union or national law for a data holder to make data available. Where relevant, data holders should contractually bind third parties not to further share data received from them.

(27) In sectors characterised by the concentration of a small number of manufacturers supplying connected products to end users, there may only be limited options available to users for the access to and the use and sharing of data. In such circumstances, contracts may be insufficient to achieve the objective of user empowerment, making it difficult for users to obtain value from the data generated by the connected product they purchase, rent or lease. Consequently, there is limited potential for innovative smaller businesses to offer data-based solutions in a competitive manner and for a diverse data economy in the Union. This Regulation should therefore build on recent developments in specific sectors, such as the Code of Conduct on agricultural data sharing by contract. Union or national law may be adopted to address sector-specific needs and objectives. Furthermore, data holders should not use any readily available data that is non-personal data in order to derive insights about the economic situation of the user or its assets or production methods or about such use by the user in any other manner that could undermine the commercial position of that user on the markets in which it is active. This could include using knowledge about the overall performance of a business or a farm in contractual negotiations with the user on the potential acquisition of the user's products or agricultural produce to the user's detriment, or using such information to feed into larger databases on certain markets in the aggregate, for example databases on crop yields for the upcoming harvesting season, as such use could affect the user negatively in an indirect manner. The user should be given the necessary technical interface to manage permissions, preferably with granular permission options such as 'allow once' or 'allow while using this app or service', including the option to withdraw such permissions.

(28) In contracts between a data holder and a consumer as user of a connected product or related service generating data, Union consumer law, in particular Directives 93/13/EEC and 2005/29/EC, applies to ensure that a consumer is not subject to unfair contractual terms. For the purposes of this Regulation, unfair contractual terms unilaterally imposed on an enterprise should not be binding on that enterprise.

(29) Data holders may require appropriate user identification to verify a user's entitlement to access the data. In the case of personal data processed by a processor on behalf of the controller, data holders should ensure that the access request is received and handled by the processor.

(30) The user should be free to use the data for any lawful purpose. This includes providing the data the user has received while exercising its rights under this Regulation to a third party offering an aftermarket service that may

be in competition with a service provided by a data holder, or to instruct the data holder to do so. The request should be submitted by the user or by an authorised third party acting on a user's behalf, including a provider of a data intermediation service. Data holders should ensure that the data made available to the third party is as accurate, complete, reliable, relevant and up-to-date as the data the data holder itself may be able or entitled to access from the use of the connected product or related service. Any intellectual property rights should be respected in the handling of the data. It is important to preserve incentives to invest in products with functionalities based on the use of data from sensors built into those products.

(31) Directive (EU) 2016/943 of the European Parliament and of the Council[23] provides that the acquisition, use or disclosure of a trade secret shall be considered to be lawful, inter alia, where such acquisition, use or disclosure is required or allowed by Union or national law. While this Regulation requires data holders to disclose certain data to users, or third parties of a user's choice, even when such data qualify for protection as trade secrets, it should be interpreted in such a manner as to preserve the protection afforded to trade secrets under Directive (EU) 2016/943. In this context, data holders should be able to require users, or third parties of a user's choice, to preserve the confidentiality of data considered to be trade secrets. To that end, data holders should identify trade secrets prior to the disclosure, and should have the possibility to agree with users, or third parties of a user's choice, on necessary measures to preserve their confidentiality, including by the use of model contractual terms, confidentiality agreements, strict access protocols, technical standards and the application of codes of conduct. In addition to the use of model contractual terms to be developed and recommended by the Commission, the establishment of codes of conduct and technical standards related to the protection of trade secrets in handling the data could help achieve the aim of this Regulation and should be encouraged. Where there is no agreement on the necessary measures or where a user, or third parties of the user's choice, fail to implement agreed measures or undermine the confidentiality of the trade secrets, the data holder should be able to withhold or suspend the sharing of data identified as trade secrets. In such cases, the data holder should provide the decision in writing to the user or to the third party without undue delay and notify the competent authority of the Member State in which the data holder is established that it has withheld or suspended data sharing and identify which measures have not been agreed or implemented and, where relevant, which trade secrets have had their confidentiality undermined. Data holders cannot, in principle, refuse a data access request under this Regulation solely on the basis that certain data is considered to be a trade secret, as this would subvert the intended effects of this Regulation. However, in exceptional circumstances, a data holder who is a trade secret holder should be able, on a case-by-case basis, to refuse a request for the specific data in question if it is able to demonstrate to the user or to the third party

[23] Directive (EU) 2016/943 of the European Parliament and of the Council of 8 June 2016 on the protection of undisclosed know-how and business information (trade secrets) against their unlawful acquisition, use and disclosure (OJ L 157, 15.6.2016, p. 1).

that, despite the technical and organisational measures taken by the user or by the third party, serious economic damage is highly likely to result from the disclosure of that trade secret. Serious economic damage implies serious and irreparable economic loss. The data holder should duly substantiate its refusal in writing without undue delay to the user or to the third party and notify the competent authority. Such a substantiation should be based on objective elements, demonstrating the concrete risk of serious economic damage expected to result from a specific data disclosure and the reasons why the measures taken to safeguard the requested data are not considered to be sufficient. A possible negative impact on cybersecurity can be taken into account in that context. Without prejudice to the right to seek redress before a court or tribunal of a Member State, where the user or a third party wishes to challenge the data holder's decision to refuse or to withhold or suspend data sharing, the user or the third party can lodge a complaint with the competent authority, which should, without undue delay, decide whether and under which conditions data sharing should start or resume, or can agree with the data holder to refer the matter to a dispute settlement body. The exceptions to data access rights in this Regulation should not in any case limit the right of access and right to data portability of data subjects under Regulation (EU) 2016/679.

(32) The aim of this Regulation is not only to foster the development of new, innovative connected products or related services, stimulate innovation on aftermarkets, but also to stimulate the development of entirely novel services making use of the data concerned, including based on data from a variety of connected products or related services. At the same time, this Regulations aims to avoid undermining the investment incentives for the type of connected product from which the data are obtained, for instance, by the use of data to develop a competing connected product which is considered to be interchangeable or substitutable by users, in particular on the basis of the connected product's characteristics, its price and intended use. This Regulation provides for no prohibition on the development of a related service using data obtained under this Regulation as this would have an undesirable discouraging effect on innovation. Prohibiting the use of data accessed under this Regulation for developing a competing connected product protects data holders' innovation efforts. Whether a connected product competes with the connected product from which the data originates depends on whether the two connected products are in competition on the same product market. This is to be determined on the basis of the established principles of Union competition law for defining the relevant product market. However, lawful purposes for the use of the data could include reverse engineering, provided that it complies with the requirements laid down in this Regulation and in Union or national law. This may be the case for the purposes of repairing or prolonging the lifetime of a connected product or for the provision of aftermarket services to connected products.

(33) A third party to whom data is made available may be a natural or legal person, such as a consumer, an enterprise, a research organisation, a not-for-profit organisation or an entity acting in a professional capacity. In making the data available to the third party, a data holder should not abuse its

position to seek a competitive advantage in markets where the data holder and the third party may be in direct competition. The data holder should not therefore use any readily available data in order to derive insights about the economic situation, assets or production methods of, or the use by, the third party in any other manner that could undermine the commercial position of the third party on the markets in which the third party is active. The user should be able to share non-personal data with third parties for commercial purposes. Upon the agreement with the user, and subject to the provisions of this Regulation, third parties should be able to transfer the data access rights granted by the user to other third parties, including in exchange for compensation. Business-to-business data intermediaries and personal information management systems (PIMS), referred to as data intermediation services in Regulation (EU) 2022/868, may support users or third parties in establishing commercial relations with an undetermined number of potential counterparties for any lawful purpose falling within the scope of this Regulation. They could play an instrumental role in aggregating access to data so that big data analyses or machine learning can be facilitated, provided that users remain in full control of whether to provide their data to such aggregation and the commercial terms under which their data are to be used.

(34) The use of a connected product or related service may, in particular when the user is a natural person, generate data that relates to the data subject. Processing of such data is subject to the rules established under Regulation (EU) 2016/679, including where personal and non-personal data in a dataset are inextricably linked. The data subject may be the user or another natural person. Personal data may only be requested by a controller or a data subject. A user who is the data subject is, under certain circumstances, entitled under Regulation (EU) 2016/679 to access personal data concerning that user and such rights are unaffected by this Regulation. Under this Regulation, the user who is a natural person is further entitled to access all data generated by the use of a connected product, whether personal or non-personal. Where the user is not the data subject but an enterprise, including a sole trader, and not in cases of shared household use of the connected product, the user is considered to be a controller. Accordingly, such a user who as controller intends to request personal data generated by the use of a connected product or related service is required to have a legal basis for processing the data as required by Article 6(1) of Regulation (EU) 2016/679, such as the consent of the data subject or the performance of a contract to which the data subject is a party. Such user should ensure that the data subject is appropriately informed of the specified, explicit and legitimate purposes for processing those data, and of how the data subject may exercise their rights effectively. Where the data holder and the user are joint controllers within the meaning of Article 26 of Regulation (EU) 2016/679, they are required to determine, in a transparent manner by means of an arrangement between them, their respective responsibilities for compliance with that Regulation. It should be understood that such a user, once data has been made available, may in turn become a data holder if that user meets the criteria under this Regulation and thus becomes subject to the obligations to make data available under this Regulation.

(35) Product data or related service data should only be made available to a third party at the request of the user. This Regulation complements accordingly the right, provided for in Article 20 of Regulation (EU) 2016/679, of data subjects to receive personal data concerning them in a structured, commonly used and machine-readable format, as well as to port those data to another controller, where those data are processed by automated means on the basis of Article 6(1), point (a), or Article 9(2), point (a), or of a contract pursuant to Article 6(1), point (b) of that Regulation. Data subjects also have the right to have the personal data transmitted directly from one controller to another, but only where that is technically feasible. Article 20 of Regulation (EU) 2016/679 specifies that it pertains to data provided by the data subject but does not specify whether this necessitates active behaviour on the side of the data subject or whether it also applies to situations where a connected product or related service, by its design, observes the behaviour of a data subject or other information in relation to a data subject in a passive manner. The rights provided for under this Regulation complement the right to receive and port personal data under Article 20 of Regulation (EU) 2016/679 in a number of ways. This Regulation grants users the right to access and make available to a third party any product data or related service data, irrespective of their nature as personal data, of the distinction between actively provided or passively observed data, and irrespective of the legal basis of processing. Unlike Article 20 of Regulation (EU) 2016/679, this Regulation mandates and ensures the technical feasibility of third party access for all types of data falling within its scope, whether personal or non-personal, thereby ensuring that technical obstacles no longer hinder or prevent access to such data. It also allows data holders to set reasonable compensation to be met by third parties, but not by the user, for costs incurred in providing direct access to the data generated by the user's connected product. If a data holder and a third party are unable to agree on terms for such direct access, the data subject should in no way be prevented from exercising the rights laid down in Regulation (EU) 2016/679, including the right to data portability, by seeking remedies in accordance with that Regulation. It is to be understood in this context that, in accordance with Regulation (EU) 2016/679, a contract does not allow for the processing of special categories of personal data by the data holder or the third party.

(36) Access to any data stored in and accessed from terminal equipment is subject to Directive 2002/58/EC and requires the consent of the subscriber or user within the meaning of that Directive unless it is strictly necessary for the provision of an information society service explicitly requested by the user or by the subscriber or for the sole purpose of the transmission of a communication. Directive 2002/58/EC protects the integrity of a user's terminal equipment regarding the use of processing and storage capabilities and the collection of information. Internet of Things equipment is considered to be terminal equipment if it is directly or indirectly connected to a public communications network.

(37) In order to prevent the exploitation of users, third parties to whom data has been made available at the request of the user should process those data only

for the purposes agreed with the user and share them with another third party only with the agreement of the user to such data sharing.

(38) In line with the data minimisation principle, third parties should access only information that is necessary for the provision of the service requested by the user. Having received access to data, the third party should process it for the purposes agreed with the user without interference from the data holder. It should be as easy for the user to refuse or discontinue access by the third party to the data as it is for the user to authorise access. Neither third parties nor data holders should make the exercise of choices or rights by the user unduly difficult, including by offering choices to the user in a non-neutral manner, or by coercing, deceiving or manipulating the user, or by subverting or impairing the autonomy, decision-making or choices of the user, including by means of a user digital interface or a part thereof. In that context, third parties or data holders should not rely on so-called 'dark patterns' in designing their digital interfaces. Dark patterns are design techniques that push or deceive consumers into decisions that have negative consequences for them. Those manipulative techniques can be used to persuade users, in particular vulnerable consumers, to engage in unwanted behaviour, to deceive users by nudging them into decisions on data disclosure transactions or to unreasonably bias the decision-making of the users of the service in such a way as to subvert or impair their autonomy, decision-making and choice. Common and legitimate commercial practices that comply with Union law should not in themselves be regarded as constituting dark patterns. Third parties and data holders should comply with their obligations under relevant Union law, in particular the requirements laid down in Directives 98/6/EC[24] and 2000/31/EC[25] of the European Parliament and of the Council and in Directives 2005/29/EC and 2011/83/EU.

(39) Third parties should also refrain from using data falling within the scope of this Regulation to profile individuals unless such processing activities are strictly necessary to provide the service requested by the user, including in the context of automated decision-making. The requirement to erase data when no longer required for the purpose agreed with the user, unless otherwise agreed in relation to non-personal data, complements the data subject's right to erasure pursuant to Article 17 of Regulation (EU) 2016/679. Where a third party is a provider of a data intermediation service, the safeguards for the data subject provided for by Regulation (EU) 2022/868 apply. The third party may use the data to develop a new and innovative connected product or related service but not to develop a competing connected product.

(40) Start-ups, small enterprises, enterprises that qualify as a medium-sized enterprises under Article 2 of the Annex to Recommendation 2003/361/EC and enterprises from traditional sectors with less-developed digital capabilities struggle to obtain access to relevant data. This Regulation aims to facilitate access to data for those entities, while ensuring that the corresponding obli-

---

[24] Directive 98/6/EC of the European Parliament and of the Council of 16 February 1998 on consumer protection in the indication of the prices of products offered to consumers (OJ L 80, 18.3.1998, p. 27).

[25] Directive 2000/31/EC of the European Parliament and of the Council of 8 June 2000 on certain legal aspects of information society services, in particular electronic commerce, in the Internal Market ('Directive on electronic commerce') (OJ L 178, 17.7.2000, p. 1).

gations are as proportionate as possible to avoid overreach. At the same time, a small number of very large enterprises have emerged with considerable economic power in the digital economy through the accumulation and aggregation of vast volumes of data and the technological infrastructure for monetising them. Those very large enterprises include undertakings that provide core platform services controlling whole platform ecosystems in the digital economy and which existing or new market operators are unable to challenge or contest. Regulation (EU) 2022/1925 of the European Parliament and of the Council[26] aims to redress those inefficiencies and imbalances by allowing the Commission to designate an undertaking as a 'gatekeeper', and imposes a number of obligations on such gatekeepers, including a prohibition to combine certain data without consent and an obligation to ensure effective rights to data portability under Article 20 of Regulation (EU) 2016/679. In accordance with Regulation (EU) 2022/1925, and given the unrivalled ability of those undertakings to acquire data, it is not necessary to achieve the objective of this Regulation, and would therefore be disproportionate for data holders made subject to such obligations, to include gatekeeper as beneficiaries of the data access right. Such inclusion would also likely limit the benefits of this Regulation for SMEs, linked to the fairness of the distribution of data value across market actors. This means that an undertaking that provides core platform services that has been designated as a gatekeeper cannot request or be granted access to users' data generated by the use of a connected product or related service or by a virtual assistant pursuant to this Regulation. Furthermore, third parties to whom data are made available at the request of the user may not make the data available to a gatekeeper. For instance, the third party may not subcontract the service provision to a gatekeeper. However, this does not prevent third parties from using data processing services offered by a gatekeeper. Nor does it prevent those undertakings from obtaining and using the same data through other lawful means. The access rights provided for in this Regulation contribute to a wider choice of services for consumers. As voluntary agreements between gatekeepers and data holders remain unaffected, the limitation on granting access to gatekeepers would not exclude them from the market or prevent them from offering their services.

(41) Given the current state of technology, it would be overly burdensome on microenterprises and small enterprises to impose further design obligations in relation to connected products manufactured or designed, or the related services provided, by them. That is not the case, however, where a microenterprise or a small enterprise has a partner enterprise or a linked enterprise within the meaning of Article 3 of the Annex to Recommendation 2003/361/EC that does not qualify as a microenterprise or a small enterprise and where it is subcontracted to manufacture or design a connected product or to provide a related service. In such situations, the enterprise which has subcontracted the manufacturing or design to a microenterprise

[26] Regulation (EU) 2022/1925 of the European Parliament and of the Council of 14 September 2022 on contestable and fair markets in the digital sector and amending Directives (EU) 2019/1937 and (EU) 2020/1828 (Digital Markets Act) (OJ L 265, 12.10.2022, p. 1).

or a small enterprise is able to compensate the subcontractor appropriately. A microenterprise or a small enterprise may nevertheless be subject to the requirements laid down by this Regulation as data holder where it is not the manufacturer of the connected product or a provider of related services. A transitional period should apply to an enterprise that has qualified as a medium-sized enterprise for less than one year and to connected products for one year after the date on which they were placed on the market by a medium-sized enterprise. Such a one-year period allows such a medium-sized enterprise to adjust and prepare before facing competition in the market for services for the connected products that it manufactures on the basis of the access rights provided by this Regulation. Such a transitional period does not apply where such a medium-sized enterprise has a partner enterprise or a linked enterprise that does not qualify as a microenterprise or a small enterprise or where such a medium-sized enterprise was subcontracted to manufacture or design the connected product or to provide the related service.

(42) Taking into account the variety of connected products producing data of different nature, volume and frequency, presenting different levels of data and cybersecurity risks and providing economic opportunities of different value, and for the purpose of ensuring consistency of data sharing practices in the internal market, including across sectors, and to encourage and promote fair data sharing practices even in areas where no such right to data access is provided for, this Regulation provides for horizontal rules on the arrangements for access to data whenever a data holder is obliged by Union law or national legislation adopted in accordance with Union law to make data available to a data recipient. Such access should be based on fair, reasonable, non-discriminatory and transparent terms and conditions. Those general access rules do not apply to obligations to make data available under Regulation (EU) 2016/679. Voluntary data sharing remains unaffected by those rules. The non-binding model contractual terms for business-to-business data sharing to be developed and recommended by the Commission may help parties to conclude contracts which include fair, reasonable and non-discriminatory terms and conditions and which are to be implemented in a transparent way. The conclusion of contracts, which may include the non-binding model contractual terms, should not mean that the right to share data with third parties is in any way conditional upon the existence of such a contract. Should parties be unable to conclude a contract on data sharing, including with the support of dispute settlement bodies, the right to share data with third parties is enforceable in national courts or tribunals.

(43) On the basis of the principle of contractual freedom, parties should remain free to negotiate the precise conditions for making data available in their contracts within the framework for the general access rules for making data available. Terms of such contracts could include technical and organisational measures, including in relation to data security.

(44) In order to ensure that the conditions for mandatory data access are fair for both parties to a contract, the general rules on data access rights should refer to the rule on avoiding unfair contractual terms.

(45) Any agreement concluded in business-to-business relations for making data available should be non-discriminatory between comparable categories of data recipients, independently of whether the parties are large enterprises or SMEs. In order to compensate for the lack of information on the conditions contained in different contracts, which makes it difficult for the data recipient to assess whether the terms for making the data available are non-discriminatory, it should be the responsibility of data holders to demonstrate that a contractual term is not discriminatory. It is not unlawful discrimination where a data holder uses different contractual terms for making data available if those differences are justified by objective reasons. Those obligations are without prejudice to Regulation (EU) 2016/679.

(46) In order to promote continued investment in generating and making available valuable data, including investments in relevant technical tools, while at the same time avoiding excessive burdens on access to and the use of data which make data sharing no longer commercially viable, this Regulation contains the principle that in business-to-business relations data holders may request reasonable compensation when obliged pursuant to Union law or national legislation adopted in accordance with Union law to make data available to a data recipient. Such compensation should not be understood to constitute payment for the data itself. The Commission should adopt guidelines on the calculation of reasonable compensation in the data economy.

(47) First, reasonable compensation for meeting the obligation pursuant to Union law or national legislation adopted in accordance with Union law to comply with a request to make data available may include compensation for the costs incurred in making the data available. Those costs may be technical costs, such as the costs necessary for data reproduction, dissemination via electronic means and storage, but not for data collection or production. Such technical costs may also include the costs for processing, necessary to make data available, including costs associated with the formatting of data. Costs related to making the data available may also include the costs of facilitating concrete data sharing requests. They may also vary depending on the volume of the data as well as the arrangements taken for making the data available. Long-term arrangements between data holders and data recipients, for instance via a subscription model or the use of smart contracts, may reduce the costs in regular or repetitive transactions in a business relationship. Costs related to making data available are either specific to a particular request or shared with other requests. In the latter case, a single data recipient should not pay the full costs of making the data available. Second, reasonable compensation may also include a margin, except regarding SMEs and not-for-profit research organisations. A margin may vary depending on factors related to the data itself, such as volume, format or nature of the data. It may consider the costs for collecting the data. A margin may therefore decrease where the data holder has collected the data for its own business without significant investments or may increase where the investments in the data collection for the purposes of the data holder's business are high. It may be limited or even excluded in situations where the use of the data by the data recipient does not affect the data holder's own activities. The fact that the data is co-generated by a connected product owned, rented or leased by the user could also reduce

the amount of the compensation in comparison to other situations where the data are generated by the data holder for example during the provision of a related service.

(48) It is not necessary to intervene in the case of data sharing between large enterprises, or where the data holder is a small enterprise or a medium-sized enterprise and the data recipient is a large enterprise. In such cases, the enterprises are considered to be capable of negotiating the compensation within the limits of what is reasonable and non-discriminatory.

(49) To protect SMEs from excessive economic burdens which would make it commercially too difficult for them to develop and run innovative business models, the reasonable compensation for making data available to be paid by them should not exceed the costs directly related to making the data available. Directly related costs are those costs which are attributable to individual requests, taking into account that the necessary technical interfaces or related software and connectivity is to be established on a permanent basis by the data holder. The same regime should apply to not-for-profit research organisations.

(50) In duly justified cases, including where there is a need to safeguard consumer participation and competition or to promote innovation in certain markets, regulated compensation for making available specific data types may be provided for in Union law or national legislation adopted in accordance with Union law.

(51) Transparency is an important principle for ensuring that the compensation requested by a data holder is reasonable, or, if the data recipient is an SME or a not-for-profit research organisation, that the compensation does not exceed the costs directly related to making the data available to the data recipient and is attributable to the individual request concerned. In order to put data recipients in a position to assess and verify that the compensation complies with the requirements of this Regulation, the data holder should provide to the data recipient sufficiently detailed information for the calculation of the compensation.

(52) Ensuring access to alternative ways of resolving domestic and cross-border disputes that arise in connection with making data available should benefit data holders and data recipients and therefore strengthen trust in data sharing. Where parties cannot agree on fair, reasonable and non-discriminatory terms and conditions of making data available, dispute settlement bodies should offer a simple, fast and low-cost solution to the parties. While this Regulation only lays down the conditions that dispute settlement bodies need to fulfil to be certified, Member States are free to adopt any specific rules for the certification procedure, including the expiry or revocation of certification. The provisions of this Regulation on dispute settlement should not require Member States to establish dispute settlement bodies.

(53) The dispute settlement procedure under this Regulation is a voluntary procedure that enables users, data holders and data recipients to agree to bring their disputes before dispute settlement bodies. Therefore, the parties should be free to address a dispute settlement body of their choice, be it within or outside of the Member States in which those parties are established.

(54) To avoid cases in which two or more dispute settlement bodies are seized for the same dispute, in particular in a cross-border situation, a dispute settlement body should be able to refuse to deal with a request to resolve a dispute that has already been brought before another dispute settlement body or before a court or tribunal of a Member State.

(55) In order to ensure the uniform application of this Regulation, the dispute settlement bodies should take into account the non-binding model contractual terms to be developed and recommended by the Commission as well as Union or national law specifying data sharing obligations or guidelines issued by sectoral authorities for the application of such law.

(56) Parties to dispute settlement proceedings should not be prevented from exercising their fundamental rights to an effective remedy and a fair trial. Therefore, the decision to submit a dispute to a dispute settlement body should not deprive those parties of their right to seek redress before a court or tribunal of a Member State. Dispute settlement bodies should make annual activity reports publicly available.

(57) Data holders may apply appropriate technical protection measures to prevent the unlawful disclosure of or access to data. However, those measures should neither discriminate between data recipients, nor hinder access to or the use of data for users or data recipients. In the case of abusive practices on the part of a data recipient, such as misleading the data holder by providing false information with the intent to use the data for unlawful purposes, including developing a competing connected product on the basis of the data, the data holder and, where applicable and where they are not the same person, the trade secret holder or the user can request the third party or data recipient to implement corrective or remedial measures without undue delay. Any such requests, and in particular requests to end the production, offering or placing on the market of goods, derivative data or services, as well as those to end importation, export, storage of infringing goods or their destruction, should be assessed in the light of their proportionality in relation to the interests of the data holder, the trade secret holder or the user.

(58) Where one party is in a stronger bargaining position, there is a risk that that party could leverage such a position to the detriment of the other contracting party when negotiating access to data with the result that access to data is commercially less viable and sometimes economically prohibitive. Such contractual imbalances harm all enterprises without a meaningful ability to negotiate the conditions for access to data, and which may have no choice but to accept take-it-or-leave-it contractual terms. Therefore, unfair contractual terms regulating access to and the use of data, or liability and remedies for the breach or the termination of data related obligations, should not be binding on enterprises when those terms have been unilaterally imposed on those enterprises.

(59) Rules on contractual terms should take into account the principle of contractual freedom as an essential concept in business-to-business relationships. Therefore, not all contractual terms should be subject to an unfairness test, but only those terms that are unilaterally imposed. This concerns take-it-or-leave-it situations where one party supplies a certain contractual term and the other enterprise cannot influence the content of that term despite an

attempt to negotiate it. A contractual term that is simply provided by one party and accepted by the other enterprise or a term that is negotiated and subsequently agreed in an amended form between contracting parties should not be considered to have been unilaterally imposed.

(60) Furthermore, the rules on unfair contractual terms should apply only to those elements of a contract that are related to making data available, that is contractual terms concerning access to and use of the data as well as liability or remedies for breach and termination of data related obligations. Other parts of the same contract, unrelated to making data available, should not be subject to the unfairness test laid down in this Regulation.

(61) Criteria for identifying unfair contractual terms should be applied only to excessive contractual terms where a stronger bargaining position has been abused. The vast majority of contractual terms that are commercially more favourable to one party than to the other, including those that are normal in business-to-business contracts, are a normal expression of the principle of contractual freedom and continue to apply. For the purposes of this Regulation, grossly deviating from good commercial practice would include, inter alia, objectively impairing the ability of the party upon whom the term has been unilaterally imposed to protect its legitimate commercial interest in the data in question.

(62) In order to ensure legal certainty, this Regulation establishes a list of clauses that are always considered unfair and a list of clauses that are presumed to be unfair. In the latter case, the enterprise that imposes the contractual term should be able to rebut the presumption of unfairness by demonstrating that the contractual term listed in this Regulation is not unfair in the specific case in question. If a contractual term is not included in the list of terms that are always considered unfair or that are presumed to be unfair, the general unfairness provision applies. In that regard, the terms listed as unfair contractual terms in this Regulation should serve as a yardstick to interpret the general unfairness provision. Finally, non-binding model contractual terms for business-to-business data sharing contracts to be developed and recommended by the Commission may also be helpful to commercial parties when negotiating contracts. If a contractual term is declared to be unfair, the contract concerned should continue to apply without that term, unless the unfair contractual term is not severable from the other terms of the contract.

(63) In situations of exceptional need, it may be necessary for public sector bodies, the Commission, the European Central Bank or Union bodies to use in the performance of their statutory duties in the public interest existing data, including, where relevant, accompanying metadata, to respond to public emergencies or in other exceptional cases. Exceptional needs are circumstances which are unforeseeable and limited in time, in contrast to other circumstances which might be planned, scheduled, periodic or frequent. While the notion of 'data holder' does not, generally, include public sector bodies, it may include public undertakings. Research-performing organisations and research-funding organisations could also be organised as public sector bodies or bodies governed by public law. To limit the burden on businesses, microenterprises and small enterprises should only be under the obligation to provide data to public sector bodies, the Commission, the European Central

Bank or Union bodies in situations of exceptional need where such data is required to respond to a public emergency and the public sector body, the Commission, the European Central Bank or the Union body is unable to obtain such data by alternative means in a timely and effective manner under equivalent conditions.

(64) In the case of public emergencies, such as public health emergencies, emergencies resulting from natural disasters including those aggravated by climate change and environmental degradation, as well as human-induced major disasters, such as major cybersecurity incidents, the public interest resulting from the use of the data will outweigh the interests of the data holders to dispose freely of the data they hold. In such a case, data holders should be placed under an obligation to make the data available to public sector bodies, the Commission, the European Central Bank or Union bodies upon their request. The existence of a public emergency should be determined or declared in accordance with Union or national law and based on the relevant procedures, including those of the relevant international organisations. In such cases, the public sector body should demonstrate that the data in scope of the request could not otherwise be obtained in a timely and effective manner and under equivalent conditions, for instance by way of the voluntary provision of data by another enterprise or the consultation of a public database.

(65) An exceptional need may also arise from non-emergency situations. In such cases, a public sector body, the Commission, the European Central Bank or a Union body should be allowed to request only non-personal data. The public sector body should demonstrate that the data are necessary for the fulfilment of a specific task carried out in the public interest that has been explicitly provided for by law, such as the production of official statistics or the mitigation of or recovery from a public emergency. In addition, such a request can be made only when the public sector body, the Commission, the European Central Bank or a Union body has identified specific data that could not otherwise be obtained in a timely and effective manner and under equivalent conditions and only if it has exhausted all other means at its disposal to obtain such data, such as obtaining the data through voluntary agreements, including purchasing of non-personal data on the market by offering market rates, or by relying on existing obligations to make data available or the adoption of new legislative measures which could guarantee the timely availability of data. The conditions and principles governing requests, such as those related to purpose limitation, proportionality, transparency and time limitation, should also apply. In cases of requests for data necessary for the production of official statistics, the requesting public sector body should also demonstrate whether the national law allows it to purchase non-personal data on the market.

(66) This Regulation should not apply to, or pre-empt, voluntary arrangements for the exchange of data between private and public entities, including the provision of data by SMEs, and is without prejudice to Union legal acts providing for mandatory information requests by public entities to private entities. Obligations placed on data holders to provide data that are motivated by needs of a non-exceptional nature, in particular where the range of data

and of data holders is known or where data use can take place on a regular basis, as in the case of reporting obligations and internal market obligations, should not be affected by this Regulation. Requirements to access data to verify compliance with applicable rules, including where public sector bodies assign the task of the verification of compliance to entities other than public sector bodies, should also not be affected by this Regulation.

(67) This Regulation complements and is without prejudice to the Union and national law providing for access to and the use of data for statistical purposes, in particular Regulation (EC) No 223/2009 of the European Parliament and of the Council[27] as well as national legal acts related to official statistics.

(68) For the exercise of their tasks in the areas of prevention, investigation, detection or prosecution of criminal or administrative offences or the execution of criminal and administrative penalties, as well as the collection of data for taxation or customs purposes, public sector bodies, the Commission, the European Central Bank or Union bodies should rely on their powers under Union or national law. This Regulation accordingly does not affect legislative acts on the sharing, access to and use of data in those areas.

(69) In accordance with Article 6(1) and (3) of Regulation (EU) 2016/679, a proportionate, limited and predictable framework at Union level is necessary when providing for the legal basis for the making available of data by data holders, in cases of exceptional needs, to public sector bodies, the Commission, the European Central Bank or Union bodies, both to ensure legal certainty and to minimise the administrative burdens placed on businesses. To that end, data requests from public sector bodies, the Commission, the European Central Bank or Union bodies to data holders should be specific, transparent and proportionate in their scope of content and their granularity. The purpose of the request and the intended use of the data requested should be specific and clearly explained, while allowing appropriate flexibility for the requesting entity to carry out its specific tasks in the public interest. The request should also respect the legitimate interests of the data holder to whom the request is made. The burden on data holders should be minimised by obliging requesting entities to respect the once-only principle, which prevents the same data from being requested more than once by more than one public sector body or the Commission, the European Central Bank or Union bodies. To ensure transparency, data requests made by the Commission, the European Central Bank or Union bodies should be made public without undue delay by the entity requesting the data. The European Central Bank and Union bodies should inform the Commission of their requests. If the data request has been made by a public sector body, that body should also notify the data coordinator of the Member State where the public sector body is established. Online public availability of all requests should be ensured. Upon the receipt of a notification of a data request, the competent authority

[27] Regulation (EC) No 223/2009 of the European Parliament and of the Council of 11 March 2009 on European statistics and repealing Regulation (EC, Euratom) No 1101/2008 of the European Parliament and of the Council on the transmission of data subject to statistical confidentiality to the Statistical Office of the European Communities, Council Regulation (EC) No 322/97 on Community Statistics, and Council Decision 89/382/EEC, Euratom establishing a Committee on the Statistical Programmes of the European Communities (OJ L 87, 31.3.2009, p. 164).

can decide to assess the lawfulness of the request and exercise its functions in relation to the enforcement and application of this Regulation. Online public availability of all requests made by public sector bodies should be ensured by the data coordinator.

(70) The objective of the obligation to provide the data is to ensure that public sector bodies, the Commission, the European Central Bank or Union bodies have the necessary knowledge to respond to, prevent or recover from public emergencies or to maintain the capacity to fulfil specific tasks explicitly provided for by law. The data obtained by those entities may be commercially sensitive. Therefore, neither Regulation (EU) 2022/868 nor Directive (EU) 2019/1024 of the European Parliament and of the Council[28] should apply to data made available under this Regulation and should not be considered as open data available for reuse by third parties. This however should not affect the applicability of Directive (EU) 2019/1024 to the reuse of official statistics for the production of which data obtained pursuant to this Regulation was used, provided the reuse does not include the underlying data. In addition, provided the conditions laid down in this Regulation are met, the possibility of sharing the data for conducting research or for the development, production and dissemination of official statistics should not be affected. Public sector bodies should also be allowed to exchange data obtained pursuant to this Regulation with other public sector bodies, the Commission, the European Central Bank or Union bodies in order to address the exceptional needs for which the data has been requested.

(71) Data holders should have the possibility to either decline a request made by a public sector body, the Commission, the European Central Bank or a Union body or seek its modification without undue delay and, in any event, no later than within a period of five or 30 working days, depending on the nature of the exceptional need invoked in the request. Where relevant, the data holder should have this possibility where it does not have control over the data requested, namely where it does not have immediate access to the data and cannot determine its availability. A valid reason not to make the data available should exist if it can be shown that the request is similar to a previously submitted request for the same purpose by another public sector body or the Commission, the European Central Bank or a Union body and the data holder has not been notified of the erasure of the data pursuant to this Regulation. A data holder declining the request or seeking its modification should communicate the underlying justification to the public sector body, the Commission, the European Central Bank or a Union body requesting the data. Where the *sui generis* database rights under Directive 96/9/EC of the European Parliament and of the Council[29] apply in relation to the requested datasets, data holders should exercise their rights in such a way that does not prevent the public sector body, the Commission, the European Central Bank or Union body from obtaining the data, or from sharing it, in accordance with this Regulation.

---

[28] Directive (EU) 2019/1024 of the European Parliament and of the Council of 20 June 2019 on open data and the re-use of public sector information (OJ L 172, 26.6.2019, p. 56).

[29] Directive 96/9/EC of the European Parliament and of the Council of 11 March 1996 on the legal protection of databases (OJ L 77, 27.3.1996, p. 20).

(72) In the case of an exceptional need related to a public emergency response, public sector bodies should use non-personal data wherever possible. In the case of requests on the basis of an exceptional need not related to a public emergency, personal data cannot be requested. Where personal data fall within the scope of the request, the data holder should anonymise the data. Where it is strictly necessary to include personal data in the data to be made available to a public sector body, the Commission, the European Central Bank or a Union body or where anonymisation proves impossible, the entity requesting the data should demonstrate the strict necessity and the specific and limited purposes for processing. The applicable rules on personal data protection should be complied with. The making available of the data and their subsequent use should be accompanied by safeguards for the rights and interests of individuals concerned by those data.

(73) Data made available to public sector bodies, the Commission, the European Central Bank or Union bodies on the basis of an exceptional need should be used only for the purposes for which they were requested, unless the data holder that made the data available has expressly agreed for the data to be used for other purposes. The data should be erased once it is no longer necessary for the purposes stated in the request, unless agreed otherwise, and the data holder should be informed thereof. This Regulation builds on the existing access regimes in the Union and the Member States and does not change the national law on public access to documents in the context of transparency obligations. Data should be erased once it is no longer needed to comply with such transparency obligations.

(74) When reusing data provided by data holders, public sector bodies, the Commission, the European Central Bank or Union bodies should respect both existing applicable Union or national law and contractual obligations to which the data holder is subject. They should refrain from developing or enhancing a connected product or related service that compete with the connected product or related service of the data holder as well as from sharing the data with a third party for those purposes. They should likewise provide public acknowledgement to the data holders upon their request and should be responsible for maintaining the security of the data received. Where the disclosure of trade secrets of the data holder to public sector bodies, the Commission, the European Central Bank or Union bodies is strictly necessary to fulfil the purpose for which the data has been requested, confidentiality of such disclosure should be guaranteed prior to the disclosure of data.

(75) When the safeguarding of a significant public good is at stake, such as responding to public emergencies, the public sector body, the Commission, the European Central Bank or the Union body concerned should not be expected to compensate enterprises for the data obtained. Public emergencies are rare events and not all such emergencies require the use of data held by enterprises. At the same time, the obligation to provide data might constitute a considerable burden on microenterprises and small enterprises. They should therefore be allowed to claim compensation even in the context of a public emergency response. The business activities of the data holders are therefore not likely to be negatively affected as a consequence of the public sector bodies, the Commission, the European Central Bank or Union bodies having

recourse to this Regulation. However, as cases of an exceptional need, other than cases of responding to public emergencies, might be more frequent, data holders should in such cases be entitled to a reasonable compensation which should not exceed the technical and organisational costs incurred in complying with the request and the reasonable margin required for making the data available to the public sector body, the Commission, the European Central Bank or the Union body. The compensation should not be understood as constituting payment for the data itself or as being compulsory. Data holders should not be able to claim compensation where national law prevents national statistical institutes or other national authorities responsible for the production of statistics from compensating data holders for making data available. The public sector body, the Commission, the European Central Bank or the Union body concerned should be able to challenge the level of compensation requested by the data holder by bringing the matter to the competent authority of the Member State where the data holder is established.

(76) A public sector body, the Commission, the European Central Bank or a Union body should be entitled to share the data it has obtained pursuant to the request with other entities or persons when this is necessary to carry out scientific research activities or analytical activities it cannot perform itself, provided that those activities are compatible with the purpose for which the data was requested. It should inform the data holder of such sharing in a timely manner. Such data may also be shared under the same circumstances with the national statistical institutes and Eurostat for the development, production and dissemination of official statistics. Such research activities should, however, be compatible with the purpose for which the data was requested and the data holder should be informed about the further sharing of the data it has provided. Individuals conducting research or research organisations with whom those data may be shared should act either on a not-for-profit basis or in the context of a public-interest mission recognised by the State. Organisations upon which commercial undertakings have a significant influence, allowing such undertakings to exercise control due to structural situations which could result in preferential access to the results of the research, should not be considered to be research organisations for the purposes of this Regulation.

(77) In order to handle a cross-border public emergency or another exceptional need, data requests may be addressed to data holders in Member States other than that of the requesting public sector body. In such a case, the requesting public sector body should notify the competent authority of the Member State where the data holder is established in order to allow it to examine the request against the criteria established in this Regulation. The same should apply to requests made by the Commission, the European Central Bank or a Union body. Where personal data are requested, the public sector body should notify the supervisory authority responsible for monitoring the application of Regulation (EU) 2016/679 in the Member State where the public sector body is established. The competent authority concerned should be entitled to advise the public sector body, the Commission, the European Central Bank or the Union body to cooperate with the public sector bodies

of the Member State in which the data holder is established on the need to ensure a minimised administrative burden on the data holder. When the competent authority has substantiated objections as regards the compliance of the request with this Regulation, it should reject the request of the public sector body, the Commission, the European Central Bank or the Union body, which should take those objections into account before taking any further action, including resubmitting the request.

(78) The ability of customers of data processing services, including cloud and edge services, to switch from one data processing service to another while maintaining a minimum functionality of service and without downtime of services, or to use the services of several providers simultaneously without undue obstacles and data transfer costs, is a key condition for a more competitive market with lower entry barriers for new providers of data processing services, and for ensuring further resilience for the users of those services. Customers benefiting from free-tier offerings should also benefit from the provisions for switching that are laid down in this Regulation, so that those offerings do not result in a lock-in situation for customers.

(79) Regulation (EU) 2018/1807 of the European Parliament and of the Council[30] encourages providers of data processing services to develop and effectively implement self-regulatory codes of conduct covering best practices for, inter alia, facilitating the switching of providers of data processing services and the porting of data. Given the limited uptake of the self-regulatory frameworks developed in response, and the general unavailability of open standards and interfaces, it is necessary to adopt a set of minimum regulatory obligations for providers of data processing services to eliminate pre-commercial, commercial, technical, contractual and organisational obstacles, which are not limited to reduced speed of data transfer at the customer's exit, which hamper effective switching between data processing services.

(80) Data processing services should cover services that allow ubiquitous and on-demand network access to a configurable, scalable and elastic shared pool of distributed computing resources. Those computing resources include resources such as networks, servers or other virtual or physical infrastructure, software, including software development tools, storage, applications and services. The capability of the customer of the data processing service to unilaterally self-provision computing capabilities, such as server time or network storage, without any human interaction by the provider of data processing services could be described as requiring minimal management effort and as entailing minimal interaction between provider and customer. The term 'ubiquitous' is used to describe the computing capabilities provided over the network and accessed through mechanisms promoting the use of heterogeneous thin or thick client platforms (from web browsers to mobile devices and workstations). The term 'scalable' refers to computing resources that are flexibly allocated by the provider of data processing services, irrespective of the geographical location of the resources, in order to handle fluctuations in demand. The term 'elastic' is used to describe those computing resources

[30] Regulation (EU) 2018/1807 of the European Parliament and of the Council of 14 November 2018 on a framework for the free flow of non-personal data in the European Union (OJ L 303, 28.11.2018, p. 59).

that are provisioned and released according to demand in order to rapidly increase or decrease resources available depending on workload. The term 'shared pool' is used to describe those computing resources that are provided to multiple users who share a common access to the service, but where the processing is carried out separately for each user, although the service is provided from the same electronic equipment. The term 'distributed' is used to describe those computing resources that are located on different networked computers or devices and which communicate and coordinate among themselves by message passing. The term 'highly distributed' is used to describe data processing services that involve data processing closer to where data are being generated or collected, for instance in a connected data processing device. Edge computing, which is a form of such highly distributed data processing, is expected to generate new business models and cloud service delivery models, which should be open and interoperable from the outset.

(81) The generic concept 'data processing services' covers a substantial number of services with a very broad range of different purposes, functionalities and technical set-ups. As commonly understood by providers and users and in line with broadly used standards, data processing services fall into one or more of the following three data processing service delivery models, namely Infrastructure as a Service (IaaS), Platform as a service (PaaS) and Software as a Service (SaaS). Those service delivery models represent a specific, pre-packaged combination of ICT resources offered by a provider of data processing service. Those three fundamental data processing delivery models are further complemented by emerging variations, each comprised of a distinct combination of ICT resources, such as Storage as a Service and Database as a Service. Data processing services can be categorised in a more granular way and divided into a non-exhaustive list of sets of data processing services that share the same primary objective and main functionalities as well as the same type of data processing models, that are not related to the service's operational characteristics (same service type). Services falling under the same service type may share the same data processing service model, however, two databases might appear to share the same primary objective, but after considering their data processing model, distribution model and the use cases that they are targeted at, such databases could fall into a more granular subcategory of similar services. Services of the same service type may have different and competing characteristics such as performance, security, resilience, and quality of service.

(82) Undermining the extraction of the exportable data that belongs to the customer from the source provider of data processing services can impede the restoration of the service functionalities in the infrastructure of the destination provider of data processing services. In order to facilitate the customer's exit strategy, avoid unnecessary and burdensome tasks and to ensure that the customer does not lose any of their data as a consequence of the switching process, the source provider of data processing services should inform the customer in advance of the scope of the data that can be exported once that customer decides to switch to a different service provided by a different provider of data processing services or to move to an on-premises ICT

infrastructure. The scope of exportable data should include, at a minimum, input and output data, including metadata, directly or indirectly generated, or cogenerated, by the customer's use of the data processing service, excluding any assets or data of the provider of data processing services or a third party. The exportable data should exclude any assets or data of the provider of data processing services or of the third party that are protected by intellectual property rights or constituting trade secrets of that provider or of that third party, or data related to the integrity and security of the service, the export of which will expose the providers of data processing services to cybersecurity vulnerabilities. Those exemptions should not impede or delay the switching process.

(83) Digital assets refer to elements in digital form for which the customer has the right of use, including applications and metadata related to the configuration of settings, security, and access and control rights management, and other elements such as manifestations of virtualisation technologies, including virtual machines and containers. Digital assets can be transferred where the customer has the right of use independent of the contractual relationship with the data processing service it intends to switch from. Those other elements are essential for the effective use of the customer's data and applications in the environment of the destination provider of data processing services.

(84) This Regulation aims to facilitate switching between data processing services, which encompasses conditions and actions that are necessary for a customer to terminate a contract for a data processing service, to conclude one or more new contracts with different providers of data processing services, to port its exportable data and digital assets, and where applicable, benefit from functional equivalence.

(85) Switching is a customer-driven operation consisting of several steps, including data extraction, which refers to the downloading of data from the ecosystem of the source provider of data processing services; transformation, where the data is structured in a way that does not match the schema of the target location; and the uploading of the data in a new destination location. In a specific situation outlined in this Regulation, unbundling of a particular service from the contract and moving it to a different provider should also be considered to be switching. The switching process is sometimes managed on behalf of the customer by a third-party entity. Accordingly, all rights and obligations of the customer established by this Regulation, including the obligation to cooperate in good faith, should be understood to apply to such a third-party entity in those circumstances. Providers of data processing services and customers have different levels of responsibilities, depending on the steps of the process referred to. For instance, the source provider of data processing services is responsible for extracting the data to a machine-readable format, but it is the customer and the destination provider of data processing services who are to upload the data to the new environment, unless a specific professional transition service has been obtained. A customer who intends to exercise rights related to switching, which are provided for in this Regulation, should inform the source provider of data processing services of the decision to either switch to a different provider of data processing services, switch

to an on-premises ICT infrastructure or to delete that customer's assets and erase its exportable data.

(86) Functional equivalence means re-establishing, on the basis of the customer's exportable data and digital assets, a minimum level of functionality in the environment of a new data processing service of the same service type after switching, where the destination data processing service delivers a materially comparable outcome in response to the same input for shared features supplied to the customer under the contract. Providers of data processing services can only be expected to facilitate functional equivalence for the features that both the source and destination data processing services offer independently. This Regulation does not constitute an obligation to facilitate functional equivalence for providers of data processing services other than those offering services of the IaaS delivery model.

(87) Data processing services are used across sectors and vary in complexity and service type. This is an important consideration with regard to the porting process and timeframes. Nonetheless, an extension of the transitional period on the grounds of technical unfeasibility to allow the finalisation of the switching process in the given timeframe should be invoked only in duly justified cases. The burden of proof in that regard should fall fully on the provider of the data processing service concerned. This is without prejudice to the exclusive right of the customer to extend the transitional period once for a period that the customer considers to be more appropriate for its own purposes. The customer may evoke that right to an extension prior to or during the transitional period, taking into account that the contract remains applicable during the transitional period.

(88) Switching charges are charges imposed by providers of data processing services on the customers for the switching process. Typically, those charges are intended to pass on costs which the source provider of data processing services may incur because of the switching process to the customer who wishes to switch. Common examples of switching charges are costs related to the transit of data from one provider of data processing services to another or to an on-premises ICT infrastructure (data egress charges) or the costs incurred for specific support actions during the switching process. Unnecessarily high data egress charges and other unjustified charges unrelated to actual switching costs inhibit customers from switching, restrict the free flow of data, have the potential to limit competition and cause lock-in effects for the customers by reducing incentives to choose a different or additional service provider. Switching charges should therefore be abolished after three years from the date of entry into force of this Regulation. Providers of data processing services should be able to impose reduced switching charges up to that date.

(89) A source provider of data processing services should be able to outsource certain tasks and compensate third-party entities in order to comply with the obligations provided for in this Regulation. A customer should not bear the costs arising from the outsourcing of services concluded by the source provider of data processing services during the switching process and such costs should be considered to be unjustified unless they cover work undertaken by the provider of data processing services at the customer's

request for additional support in the switching process which goes beyond the switching obligations of the provider as expressly provided for in this Regulation. Nothing in this Regulation prevents a customer from compensating third-party entities for support in the migration process or parties from agreeing on contracts for data processing services of a fixed duration, including proportionate early termination penalties to cover the early termination of such contracts, in accordance with Union or national law. In order to foster competition, the gradual withdrawal of the charges associated with switching between different providers of data processing services should specifically include data egress charges imposed by a provider of data processing services on a customer. Standard service fees for the provision of the data processing services themselves are not switching charges. Those standard service fees are not subject to withdrawal and remain applicable until the contract for the provision of the relevant services ceases to apply. This Regulation allows the customer to request the provision of additional services that go beyond the provider's switching obligations under this Regulation. Those additional services, can be performed and charged for by the provider when they are performed at the customer's request and the customer agrees to the price of those services in advance.

(90) An ambitious and innovation-inspiring regulatory approach to interoperability is needed to overcome vendor lock-in, which undermines competition and the development of new services. Interoperability between data processing services involves multiple interfaces and layers of infrastructure and software and is rarely confined to a binary test of being achievable or not. Instead, the building of such interoperability is subject to a cost-benefit analysis which is necessary to establish whether it is worthwhile to pursue reasonably predictable results. The ISO/IEC 19941:2017 is an important international standard constituting a reference for the achievement of the objectives of this Regulation, as it contains technical considerations clarifying the complexity of such a process.

(91) Where providers of data processing services are in turn customers of data processing services provided by a third-party provider, they will benefit from more effective switching themselves while simultaneously remaining bound by this Regulation's obligations regarding their own service offerings.

(92) Providers of data processing services should be required to offer all the assistance and support within their capacity, proportionate to their respective obligations, that is required to make the switching process to a service of a different provider of data processing services successful, effective and secure. This Regulation does not require providers of data processing services to develop new categories of data processing services, including within, or on the basis of, the ICT infrastructure of different providers of data processing services in order to guarantee functional equivalence in an environment other than their own systems. A source provider of data processing services does not have access to or insights into the environment of the destination provider of data processing services. Functional equivalence should not be understood to oblige the source provider of data processing services to rebuild the service in question within the infrastructure of the destination provider of data processing services. Instead, the source provider of data

processing services should take all reasonable measures within its power to facilitate the process of achieving functional equivalence through the provision of capabilities, adequate information, documentation, technical support and, where appropriate, the necessary tools.

(93) Providers of data processing services should also be required to remove existing obstacles and not impose new ones, including for customers wishing to switch to an on-premises ICT infrastructure. Obstacles can, inter alia, be of a pre-commercial, commercial, technical, contractual or organisational nature. Providers of data processing services should also be required to remove obstacles to unbundling a specific individual service from other data processing services provided under a contract and make the relevant service available for switching, in the absence of major and demonstrated technical obstacles that prevent such unbundling.

(94) Throughout the switching process, a high level of security should be maintained. This means that the source provider of data processing services should extend the level of security to which it committed for the service to all technical arrangements for which such provider is responsible during the switching process, such as network connections or physical devices. Existing rights relating to the termination of contracts, including those introduced by Regulation (EU) 2016/679 and Directive (EU) 2019/770 of the European Parliament and of the Council[31] should not be affected. This Regulation should not be understood to prevent a provider of data processing services from providing to customers new and improved services, features and functionalities or from competing with other providers of data processing services on that basis.

(95) The information to be provided by providers of data processing services to the customer could support the customer's exit strategy. That information should include procedures for initiating switching from the data processing service; the machine-readable data formats to which the user's data can be exported; the tools intended to export data, including open interfaces as well as information on compatibility with harmonised standards or common specifications based on open interoperability specifications; information on known technical restrictions and limitations that could have an impact on the switching process; and the estimated time necessary to complete the switching process.

(96) To facilitate interoperability and switching between data processing services, users and providers of data processing services should consider the use of implementation and compliance tools, in particular those published by the Commission in the form of an EU Cloud Rulebook and a Guidance on public procurement of data processing services. In particular, standard contractual clauses are beneficial because they increase confidence in data processing services, create a more balanced relationship between users and providers of data processing services and improve legal certainty with regard to the conditions that apply for switching to other data processing services. In that

[31] Directive (EU) 2019/770 of the European Parliament and of the Council of 20 May 2019 on certain aspects concerning contracts for the supply of digital content and digital services (OJ L 136, 22.5.2019, p. 1).

context, users and providers of data processing services should consider the use of standard contractual clauses or other self-regulatory compliance tools provided that they fully comply with this Regulation, developed by relevant bodies or expert groups established under Union law.

(97) In order to facilitate switching between data processing services, all parties involved, including both source and destination providers of data processing services, should cooperate in good faith to make the switching process effective, enable the secure and timely transfer of necessary data in a commonly used, machine-readable format, and by means of open interfaces, while avoiding service disruptions and maintaining continuity of the service.

(98) Data processing services which concern services of which the majority of main features has been custom-built to respond to the specific demands of an individual customer or where all components have been developed for the purposes of an individual customer should be exempted from some of the obligations applicable to data processing service switching. This should not include services which the provider of data processing services offers at a broad commercial scale via its service catalogue. It is among the obligations of the provider of data processing services to duly inform prospective customers of such services, prior to the conclusion of a contract, of the obligations laid down in this Regulation that do not apply to the relevant services. Nothing prevents the provider of data processing services from eventually deploying such services at scale, in which case that provider would have to comply with all obligations for switching laid down in this Regulation.

(99) In line with the minimum requirement allowing switching between providers of data processing services, this Regulation also aims to improve interoperability for in-parallel use of multiple data processing services with complementary functionalities. This relates to situations in which customers do not terminate a contract to switch to a different provider of data processing services, but where multiple services of different providers are used in parallel, in an interoperable manner, to benefit from the complementary functionalities of the different services in the set-up of the customer's system. However, it is recognised that the egress of data from one provider of data processing services to another in order to facilitate the in-parallel use of services can be an ongoing activity, in contrast with the one-off egress required as part of the switching process. Providers of data processing services should therefore continue to be able to impose data egress charges, not exceeding the costs incurred, for the purposes of in-parallel use after three years from the date of entry into force of this Regulation. This is important, inter alia, for the successful deployment of multi-cloud strategies, which allow customers to implement future-proof ICT strategies and which decrease dependence on individual providers of data processing services. Facilitating a multi-cloud approach for customers of data processing services can also contribute to increasing their digital operational resilience, as recognised for financial service

institutions in Regulation (EU) 2022/2554 of the European Parliament and of the Council[32].

(100) Open interoperability specifications and standards developed in accordance with Annex II to Regulation (EU) No 1025/2012 of the European Parliament and of the Council[33] in the field of interoperability and portability are expected to enable a multi-vendor cloud environment, which is a key requirement for open innovation in the European data economy. As the market adoption of identified standards under the cloud standardisation coordination (CSC) initiative concluded in 2016 has been limited, it is also necessary that the Commission relies on parties in the market to develop relevant open interoperability specifications to keep up with the fast pace of technological development in this industry. Such open interoperability specifications can then be adopted by the Commission in the form of common specifications. In addition, where market-driven processes have not demonstrated a capacity to establish common specifications or standards that facilitate effective cloud interoperability at the PaaS and SaaS levels, the Commission should be able, on the basis of this Regulation and in accordance with Regulation (EU) No 1025/2012, to request European standardisation bodies to develop such standards for specific service types where such standards do not yet exist. In addition to this, the Commission will encourage parties in the market to develop relevant open interoperability specifications. After consulting stakeholders, the Commission, by means of implementing acts, should be able to mandate the use of harmonised standards for interoperability or common specifications for specific service types through a reference in a central Union standards repository for the interoperability of data processing services. Providers of data processing services should ensure compatibility with those harmonised standards and common specifications based on open interoperability specifications, which should not have an adverse impact on the security or integrity of data. Harmonised standards for the interoperability of data processing services and common specifications based on open interoperability specifications will be referenced only if they comply with the criteria specified in this Regulation, which have the same meaning as the requirements in Annex II to Regulation (EU) No 1025/2012 and the interoperability facets defined under the international standard ISO/IEC 19941:2017. In addition, standardisation should take into account the needs of SMEs.

(101) Third countries may adopt laws, regulations and other legal acts that aim to directly transfer or provide governmental access to non-personal data located outside their borders, including in the Union. Judgments of courts or tribunals or decisions of other judicial or administrative authorities, including law enforcement authorities in third countries requiring such transfer

[32] Regulation (EU) 2022/2554 of the European Parliament and of the Council of 14 December 2022 on digital operational resilience for the financial sector and amending Regulations (EC) No 1060/2009, (EU) No 648/2012, (EU) No 600/2014, (EU) No 909/2014 and (EU) 2016/1011 (OJ L 333, 27.12.2022, p. 1).

[33] Regulation (EU) No 1025/2012 of the European Parliament and of the Council of 25 October 2012 on European standardisation, amending Council Directives 89/686/EEC and 93/15/EEC and Directives 94/9/EC, 94/25/EC, 95/16/EC, 97/23/EC, 98/34/EC, 2004/22/EC, 2007/23/EC, 2009/23/EC and 2009/105/EC of the European Parliament and of the Council and repealing Council Decision 87/95/EEC and Decision No 1673/2006/EC of the European Parliament and of the Council (OJ L 316, 14.11.2012, p. 12).

or access to non-personal data should be enforceable when based on an international agreement, such as a mutual legal assistance treaty, in force between the requesting third country and the Union or a Member State. In other cases, situations may arise where a request to transfer or provide access to non-personal data arising from a third country law conflicts with an obligation to protect such data under Union law or under the national law of the relevant Member State, in particular regarding the protection of fundamental rights of the individual, such as the right to security and the right to an effective remedy, or the fundamental interests of a Member State related to national security or defence, as well as the protection of commercially sensitive data, including the protection of trade secrets, and the protection of intellectual property rights, including its contractual undertakings regarding confidentiality in accordance with such law. In the absence of international agreements regulating such matters, transfer of or access to non-personal data should be allowed only if it has been verified that the third country's legal system requires the reasons and proportionality of the decision to be set out, that the court order or the decision is specific in character, and that the reasoned objection of the addressee is subject to a review by a competent third-country court or tribunal which is empowered to take duly into account the relevant legal interests of the provider of such data. Wherever possible under the terms of the data access request of the third country's authority, the provider of data processing services should be able to inform the customer whose data are being requested before granting access to those data in order to verify the presence of a potential conflict of such access with Union or national law, such as that on the protection of commercially sensitive data, including the protection of trade secrets and intellectual property rights and the contractual undertakings regarding confidentiality.

(102) To foster further trust in data, it is important that safeguards to ensure control of their data by Union citizens, the public sector bodies and businesses are implemented to the extent possible. In addition, Union law, values and standards regarding, inter alia, security, data protection and privacy, and consumer protection should be upheld. In order to prevent unlawful governmental access to non-personal data by third-country authorities, providers of data processing services subject to this Regulation, such as cloud and edge services, should take all reasonable measures to prevent access to systems on which non-personal data are stored, including, where relevant, through the encryption of data, frequent submission to audits, verified adherence to relevant security reassurance certification schemes, and by the modification of corporate policies.

(103) Standardisation and semantic interoperability should play a key role to provide technical solutions to ensure interoperability within and among common European data spaces which are purpose or sector specific or cross-sectoral interoperable frameworks for common standards and practices to share or jointly process data for, inter alia, the development of new products and services, scientific research or civil society initiatives. This Regulation lays down certain essential requirements for interoperability. Participants in data spaces that offer data or data services to other participants, which are entities facilitating or engaging in data sharing within common European

data spaces, including data holders, should comply with those requirements insofar as elements under their control are concerned. Compliance with those rules can be ensured by adhering to the essential requirements laid down in this Regulation, or presumed by complying with harmonised standards or common specifications via a presumption of conformity. In order to facilitate conformity with the requirements for interoperability, it is necessary to provide for a presumption of conformity of interoperability solutions that meet harmonised standards or parts thereof in accordance with Regulation (EU) No 1025/2012, which represents the framework by default to elaborate standards that provide for such presumptions. The Commission should assess barriers to interoperability and prioritise standardisation needs, on the basis of which it may request one or more European standardisation organisations, pursuant to Regulation (EU) No 1025/2012, to draft harmonised standards which satisfy the essential requirements laid down in this Regulation. Where such requests do not result in harmonised standards or such harmonised standards are insufficient to ensure conformity with the essential requirements of this Regulation, the Commission should be able to adopt common specifications in those areas provided that in so doing it duly respects the role and functions of standardisation organisations. Common specification should be adopted only as an exceptional fall-back solution to facilitate compliance with the essential requirements of this Regulation, or when the standardisation process is blocked, or when there are delays in the establishment of appropriate harmonised standards. Where a delay is due to the technical complexity of the standard in question, this should be considered by the Commission before contemplating the establishment of common specifications. Common specifications should be developed in an open and inclusive manner and take into account, where relevant, the advice of the European Data Innovation Board (EDIB) established by Regulation (EU) 2022/868. Additionally, common specifications in different sectors could be adopted, in accordance with Union or national law, on the basis of specific needs of those sectors. Furthermore, the Commission should be enabled to mandate the development of harmonised standards for the interoperability of data processing services.

(104) To promote the interoperability of tools for the automated execution of data sharing agreements, it is necessary to lay down essential requirements for smart contracts which professionals create for others or integrate in applications that support the implementation of agreements for data sharing. In order to facilitate the conformity of such smart contracts with those essential requirements, it is necessary to provide for a presumption of conformity of smart contracts that meet harmonised standards or parts thereof in accordance with Regulation (EU) No 1025/2012. The notion of 'smart contract' in this Regulation is technologically neutral. Smart contracts can, for example, be connected to an electronic ledger. The essential requirements should apply only to the vendors of smart contracts, although not where they develop smart contracts in-house exclusively for internal use. The essential requirement to ensure that smart contracts can be interrupted and terminated implies mutual consent by the parties to the data sharing agreement. The applicability of the relevant rules of civil, contractual and consumer protec-

tion law to data sharing agreements remains or should remain unaffected by the use of smart contracts for the automated execution of such agreements.

(105) To demonstrate fulfilment of the essential requirements of this Regulation, the vendor of a smart contract, or in the absence thereof, the person whose trade, business or profession involves the deployment of smart contracts for others in the context of executing an agreement or part of it, to make data available in the context of this Regulation, should perform a conformity assessment and issue an EU declaration of conformity. Such a conformity assessment should be subject to the general principles set out in Regulation (EC) No 765/2008 of the European Parliament and of the Council[34] and Decision No 768/2008/EC of the European Parliament and of the Council[35].

(106) Besides the obligation on professional developers of smart contracts to comply with essential requirements, it is also important to encourage those participants within data spaces that offer data or data-based services to other participants within and across common European data spaces to support interoperability of tools for data sharing including smart contracts.

(107) In order to ensure the application and enforcement of this Regulation, Member States should designate one or more competent authorities. If a Member State designates more than one competent authority, it should also designate from among them a data coordinator. Competent authorities should cooperate with each other. Through the exercise of their powers of investigation in accordance with applicable national procedures, competent authorities should be able to search for and obtain information, in particular in relation to the activities of entities within their competence and, including in the context of joint investigations, with due regard to the fact that oversight and enforcement measures concerning an entity under the competence of another Member State should be adopted by the competent authority of that other Member State, where relevant, in accordance with the procedures relating to cross-border cooperation. Competent authorities should assist each other in a timely manner, in particular when a competent authority in a Member State holds relevant information for an investigation carried out by the competent authorities in other Member States, or is able to gather such information to which the competent authorities in the Member State where the entity is established do not have access. Competent authorities and data coordinators should be identified in a public register maintained by the Commission. The data coordinator could be an additional means for facilitating cooperation in cross-border situations, such as when a competent authority from a given Member State does not know which authority it should approach in the data coordinator's Member State, for example where the case is related to more than one competent authority or sector. The data coordinator should act, inter alia, as a single point of contact for all issues related to the application of this Regulation. Where no data coordinator has been designated, the compe-

[34] Regulation (EC) No 765/2008 of the European Parliament and of the Council of 9 July 2008 setting out the requirements for accreditation and repealing Regulation (EEC) No 339/93 (OJ L 218, 13.8.2008, p. 30).

[35] Decision No 768/2008/EC of the European Parliament and of the Council of 9 July 2008 on a common framework for the marketing of products, and repealing Council Decision 93/465/EEC (OJ L 218, 13.8.2008, p. 82).

tent authority should assume the tasks assigned to the data coordinator under this Regulation. The authorities responsible for the supervision of compliance with data protection law and competent authorities designated under Union or national law should be responsible for the application of this Regulation in their areas of competence. In order to avoid conflicts of interest, the competent authorities responsible for the application and enforcement of this Regulation in the area of making data available following a request on the basis of an exceptional need should not benefit from the right to submit such a request.

(108) In order to enforce their rights under this Regulation, natural and legal persons should be entitled to seek redress for infringements of their rights under this Regulation by lodging complaints. The data coordinator should, upon request, provide all the necessary information to natural and legal persons for the lodging of their complaints with the appropriate competent authority. Those authorities should be obliged to cooperate to ensure a complaint is appropriately handled and resolved effectively and in a timely manner. In order to make use of the consumer protection cooperation network mechanism and to enable representative actions, this Regulation amends the Annexes to Regulation (EU) 2017/2394 of the European Parliament and of the Council[36] and Directive (EU) 2020/1828 of the European Parliament and of the Council[37].

(109) Competent authorities should ensure that infringements of the obligations laid down in this Regulation are subject to penalties. Such penalties could include financial penalties, warnings, reprimands or orders to bring business practices into compliance with the obligations imposed by this Regulation. Penalties established by the Member States should be effective, proportionate and dissuasive, and should take into account the recommendations of the EDIB, thus contributing to achieving the greatest possible level of consistency in the establishment and application of penalties. Where appropriate, competent authorities should make use of interim measures to limit the effects of an alleged infringement while the investigation of that infringement is ongoing. In so doing, they should take into account, inter alia the nature, gravity, scale and duration of the infringement in view of the public interest at stake, the scope and kind of activities carried out, and the economic capacity of the infringing party. They should also take into account whether the infringing party systematically or recurrently fails to comply with its obligations under this Regulation. In order to ensure that the principle of *ne bis in idem* is respected, and in particular to avoid that the same infringement of the obligations laid down in this Regulation is penalised more than once, a Member State that intends to exercise its competence in relation to an infringing party that is not established and has not designated a legal representative in the

[36] Regulation (EU) 2017/2394 of the European Parliament and of the Council of 12 December 2017 on cooperation between national authorities responsible for the enforcement of consumer protection laws and repealing Regulation (EC) No 2006/2004 (OJ L 345, 27.12.2017, p. 1).

[37] Directive (EU) 2020/1828 of the European Parliament and of the Council of 25 November 2020 on representative actions for the protection of the collective interests of consumers and repealing Directive 2009/22/EC (OJ L 409, 4.12.2020, p. 1).

Union should, without undue delay, inform all data coordinators as well as the Commission.

(110) The EDIB should advise and assist the Commission in coordinating national practices and policies on the topics covered by this Regulation as well as in delivering on its objectives in relation to technical standardisation to enhance interoperability. It should also play a key role in facilitating comprehensive discussions between competent authorities concerning the application and enforcement of this Regulation. That exchange of information is designed to increase effective access to justice as well as enforcement and judicial cooperation across the Union. Among other functions, the competent authorities should make use of the EDIB as a platform to evaluate, coordinate and adopt recommendations on the setting of penalties for infringements of this Regulation. It should allow for competent authorities, with the assistance of the Commission, to coordinate the optimal approach to determining and imposing such penalties. That approach prevents fragmentation while allowing for Member State's flexibility and should lead to effective recommendations that support the consistent application of this Regulation. The EDIB should also have an advisory role in the standardisation processes and the adoption of common specifications by means of implementing acts, in the adoption of delegated acts to establish a monitoring mechanism for switching charges, imposed by providers of data processing services and to further specify the essential requirements for the interoperability of data, of data sharing mechanisms and services, as well as of the common European data spaces. It should also advise and assist the Commission in the adoption of the guidelines laying down interoperability specifications for the functioning of the common European data spaces.

(111) In order to help enterprises to draft and negotiate contracts, the Commission should develop and recommend non-binding model contractual terms for business-to-business data sharing contracts, where necessary taking into account the conditions in specific sectors and the existing practices with voluntary data sharing mechanisms. Those model contractual terms should be primarily a practical tool to help in particular SMEs to conclude a contract. When used widely and integrally, those model contractual terms should also have the beneficial effect of influencing the design of contracts regarding access to and the use of data and therefore lead more broadly towards fairer contractual relations when accessing and sharing data.

(112) In order to eliminate the risk that holders of data in databases obtained or generated by means of physical components, such as sensors, of a connected product and a related service or other machine-generated data, claim the *sui generis* right under Article 7 of Directive 96/9/EC, and in so doing hinder, in particular, the effective exercise of the right of users to access and use data and the right to share data with third parties under this Regulation, it should be clarified that the *sui generis* right does not apply to such databases. That does not affect the possible application of the *sui generis* right under Article 7 of Directive 96/9/EC to databases containing data falling outside the scope of this Regulation, provided that the requirements for protection pursuant to paragraph 1 of that Article are fulfilled.

(113) In order to take account of technical aspects of data processing services, the power to adopt acts in accordance with Article 290 TFEU should be delegated to the Commission in respect of supplementing this Regulation in order to establish a monitoring mechanism on switching charges imposed by providers of data processing services on the market, and to further specify the essential requirements in respect of interoperability for participants in data spaces that offer data or data services to other participants. It is of particular importance that the Commission carry out appropriate consultations during its preparatory work, including at expert level, and that those consultations be conducted in accordance with the principles laid down in the Interinstitutional Agreement of 13 April 2016 on Better Law-Making[38]. In particular, to ensure equal participation in the preparation of delegated acts, the European Parliament and the Council receive all documents at the same time as Member States' experts, and their experts systematically have access to meetings of Commission expert groups dealing with the preparation of delegated acts.

(114) In order to ensure uniform conditions for the implementation of this Regulation, implementing powers should be conferred on the Commission in respect of the adoption of common specifications to ensure the interoperability of data, of data sharing mechanisms and services, as well as of common European data spaces, common specifications on the interoperability of data processing services, and common specifications on the interoperability of smart contracts. Implementing powers should also be conferred on the Commission for the purpose of publishing the references of harmonised standards and common specifications for the interoperability of data processing services in a central Union standards repository for the interoperability of data processing services. Those powers should be exercised in accordance with Regulation (EU) No 182/2011 of the European Parliament and of the Council[39].

(115) This Regulation should be without prejudice to rules addressing needs specific to individual sectors or areas of public interest. Such rules may include additional requirements on the technical aspects of data access, such as interfaces for data access, or how data access could be provided, for example directly from the product or via data intermediation services. Such rules may also include limits on the rights of data holders to access or use user data, or other aspects beyond data access and use, such as governance aspects or security requirements, including cybersecurity requirements. This Regulation should also be without prejudice to more specific rules in the context of the development of common European data spaces or, subject to the exceptions provided for in this Regulation, to Union and national law providing for access to and authorising the use of data for scientific research purposes.

(116) This Regulation should not affect the application of the rules of competition, in particular Articles 101 and 102 TFEU. The measures provided for in this

---

[38] OJ L 123, 12.5.2016, p. 1.

[39] Regulation (EU) No 182/2011 of the European Parliament and of the Council of 16 February 2011 laying down the rules and general principles concerning mechanisms for control by the Member States of the Commission's exercise of implementing powers (OJ L 55, 28.2.2011, p. 13).

Regulation should not be used to restrict competition in a manner contrary to the TFEU.

(117) In order to allow actors within the scope of this Regulation to adapt to the new rules provided for herein, and to make the necessary technical arrangements, those rules should apply from 12 September 2025.

(118) The European Data Protection Supervisor and the European Data Protection Board were consulted in accordance with Article 42(1) and (2) of Regulation (EU) 2018/1725 and delivered their opinion on 4 May 2022.

(119) Since the objectives of this Regulation, namely ensuring fairness in the allocation of value from data among actors in the data economy and fostering fair access to and use of data in order to contribute to establishing a genuine internal market for data, cannot be sufficiently achieved by the Member States but can rather, by reason of the scale or effects of the action and cross-border use of data, be better achieved at Union level, the Union may adopt measures, in accordance with the principle of subsidiarity as set out in Article 5 of the Treaty on European Union. In accordance with the principle of proportionality as set out in that Article, this Regulation does not go beyond what is necessary in order to achieve those objectives,

HAVE ADOPTED THIS REGULATION:

CHAPTER I
GENERAL PROVISIONS

Article 1
Subject matter and scope

1. This Regulation lays down harmonised rules, inter alia, on:

(a) the making available of product data and related service data to the user of the connected product or related service;
(b) the making available of data by data holders to data recipients;
(c) the making available of data by data holders to public sector bodies, the Commission, the European Central Bank and Union bodies, where there is an exceptional need for those data for the performance of a specific task carried out in the public interest;
(d) facilitating switching between data processing services;
(e) introducing safeguards against unlawful third-party access to non-personal data; and
(f) the development of interoperability standards for data to be accessed, transferred and used.

2. This Regulation covers personal and non-personal data, including the following types of data, in the following contexts:

(a) Chapter II applies to data, with the exception of content, concerning the performance, use and environment of connected products and related services;
(b) Chapter III applies to any private sector data that is subject to statutory data sharing obligations;

(c) Chapter IV applies to any private sector data accessed and used on the basis of contract between enterprises;
(d) Chapter V applies to any private sector data with a focus on non-personal data;
(e) Chapter VI applies to any data and services processed by providers of data processing services;
(f) Chapter VII applies to any non-personal data held in the Union by providers of data processing services.

3. This Regulation applies to:

(a) manufacturers of connected products placed on the market in the Union and providers of related services, irrespective of the place of establishment of those manufacturers and providers;
(b) users in the Union of connected products or related services as referred to in point (a);
(c) data holders, irrespective of their place of establishment, that make data available to data recipients in the Union;
(d) data recipients in the Union to whom data are made available;
(e) public sector bodies, the Commission, the European Central Bank and Union bodies that request data holders to make data available where there is an exceptional need for those data for the performance of a specific task carried out in the public interest and to the data holders that provide those data in response to such request;
(f) providers of data processing services, irrespective of their place of establishment, providing such services to customers in the Union;
(g) participants in data spaces and vendors of applications using smart contracts and persons whose trade, business or profession involves the deployment of smart contracts for others in the context of executing an agreement.

4. Where this Regulation refers to connected products or related services, such references are also understood to include virtual assistants insofar as they interact with a connected product or related service.

5. This Regulation is without prejudice to Union and national law on the protection of personal data, privacy and confidentiality of communications and integrity of terminal equipment, which shall apply to personal data processed in connection with the rights and obligations laid down herein, in particular Regulations (EU) 2016/679 and (EU) 2018/1725 and Directive 2002/58/EC, including the powers and competences of supervisory authorities and the rights of data subjects. Insofar as users are data subjects, the rights laid down in Chapter II of this Regulation shall complement the rights of access by data subjects and rights to data portability under Articles 15 and 20 of Regulation (EU) 2016/679. In the event of a conflict between this Regulation and Union law on the protection of personal data or privacy, or national legislation adopted in accordance with such Union law, the relevant Union or national law on the protection of personal data or privacy shall prevail.

6. This Regulation does not apply to or pre-empt voluntary arrangements for the exchange of data between private and public entities, in particular voluntary arrangements for data sharing.

This Regulation does not affect Union or national legal acts providing for the sharing of, access to and the use of data for the purpose of the prevention, investigation, detection or prosecution of criminal offences or for the execution of criminal penalties, or for customs and taxation purposes, in particular Regulations (EU) 2021/784, (EU) 2022/2065 and (EU) 2023/1543 and Directive (EU) 2023/1544, or international cooperation in that area. This Regulation does not apply to the collection or sharing of, access to or the use of data under Regulation (EU) 2015/847 and Directive (EU) 2015/849. This Regulation does not apply to areas that fall outside the scope of Union law and in any event does not affect the competences of the Member States concerning public security, defence or national security, regardless of the type of entity entrusted by the Member States to carry out tasks in relation to those competences, or their power to safeguard other essential State functions, including ensuring the territorial integrity of the State and the maintenance of law and order. This Regulation does not affect the competences of the Member States concerning customs and tax administration or the health and safety of citizens.

7. This Regulation complements the self-regulatory approach of Regulation (EU) 2018/1807 by adding generally applicable obligations on cloud switching.

8. This Regulation is without prejudice to Union and national legal acts providing for the protection of intellectual property rights, in particular Directives 2001/29/EC, 2004/48/EC and (EU) 2019/790.

9. This Regulation complements and is without prejudice to Union law which aims to promote the interests of consumers and ensure a high level of consumer protection, and to protect their health, safety and economic interests, in particular Directives 93/13/EEC, 2005/29/EC and 2011/83/EU.

10. This Regulation does not preclude the conclusion of voluntary lawful data sharing contracts, including contracts concluded on a reciprocal basis, which comply with the requirements laid down in this Regulation.

Article 2
Definitions

For the purposes of this Regulation, the following definitions apply:

(1) 'data' means any digital representation of acts, facts or information and any compilation of such acts, facts or information, including in the form of sound, visual or audio-visual recording;
(2) 'metadata' means a structured description of the contents or the use of data facilitating the discovery or use of that data;
(3) 'personal data' means personal data as defined in Article 4, point (1), of Regulation (EU) 2016/679;
(4) 'non-personal data' means data other than personal data;
(5) 'connected product' means an item that obtains, generates or collects data concerning its use or environment and that is able to communicate product data via an electronic communications service, physical connection or on-device access, and whose primary function is not the storing, processing or transmission of data on behalf of any party other than the user;

(6) 'related service' means a digital service, other than an electronic communications service, including software, which is connected with the product at the time of the purchase, rent or lease in such a way that its absence would prevent the connected product from performing one or more of its functions, or which is subsequently connected to the product by the manufacturer or a third party to add to, update or adapt the functions of the connected product;

(7) 'processing' means any operation or set of operations which is performed on data or on sets of data, whether or not by automated means, such as collection, recording, organisation, structuring, storage, adaptation or alteration, retrieval, consultation, use, disclosure by transmission, dissemination, or other means of making them available, alignment or combination, restriction, erasure or destruction;

(8) 'data processing service' means a digital service that is provided to a customer and that enables ubiquitous and on-demand network access to a shared pool of configurable, scalable and elastic computing resources of a centralised, distributed or highly distributed nature that can be rapidly provisioned and released with minimal management effort or service provider interaction;

(9) 'same service type' means a set of data processing services that share the same primary objective, data processing service model and main functionalities;

(10) 'data intermediation service' means data intermediation service as defined in Article 2, point (11), of Regulation (EU) 2022/868;

(11) 'data subject' means data subject as referred to in Article 4, point (1), of Regulation (EU) 2016/679;

(12) 'user' means a natural or legal person that owns a connected product or to whom temporary rights to use that connected product have been contractually transferred, or that receives related services;

(13) 'data holder' means a natural or legal person that has the right or obligation, in accordance with this Regulation, applicable Union law or national legislation adopted in accordance with Union law, to use and make available data, including, where contractually agreed, product data or related service data which it has retrieved or generated during the provision of a related service;

(14) 'data recipient' means a natural or legal person, acting for purposes which are related to that person's trade, business, craft or profession, other than the user of a connected product or related service, to whom the data holder makes data available, including a third party following a request by the user to the data holder or in accordance with a legal obligation under Union law or national legislation adopted in accordance with Union law;

(15) 'product data' means data generated by the use of a connected product that the manufacturer designed to be retrievable, via an electronic communications service, physical connection or on-device access, by a user, data holder or a third party, including, where relevant, the manufacturer;

(16) 'related service data' means data representing the digitisation of user actions or of events related to the connected product, recorded intentionally by the user or generated as a by-product of the user's action during the provision of a related service by the provider;

(17) 'readily available data' means product data and related service data that a data holder lawfully obtains or can lawfully obtain from the connected product or

related service, without disproportionate effort going beyond a simple operation;

(18) 'trade secret' means trade secret as defined in Article 2, point (1), of Directive (EU) 2016/943;

(19) 'trade secret holder' means a trade secret holder as defined in Article 2, point (2), of Directive (EU) 2016/943;

(20) 'profiling' means profiling as defined in Article 4, point (4), of Regulation (EU) 2016/679;

(21) 'making available on the market' means any supply of a connected product for distribution, consumption or use on the Union market in the course of a commercial activity, whether in return for payment or free of charge;

(22) 'placing on the market' means the first making available of a connected product on the Union market;

(23) 'consumer' means any natural person who is acting for purposes which are outside that person's trade, business, craft or profession;

(24) 'enterprise' means a natural or legal person that, in relation to contracts and practices covered by this Regulation, is acting for purposes which are related to that person's trade, business, craft or profession;

(25) 'small enterprise' means a small enterprise as defined in Article 2(2) of the Annex to Recommendation 2003/361/EC;

(26) 'microenterprise' means a microenterprise as defined in Article 2(3) of the Annex to Recommendation 2003/361/EC;

(27) 'Union bodies' means the Union bodies, offices and agencies set up by or pursuant to acts adopted on the basis of the Treaty on European Union, the TFEU or the Treaty establishing the European Atomic Energy Community;

(28) 'public sector body' means national, regional or local authorities of the Member States and bodies governed by public law of the Member States, or associations formed by one or more such authorities or one or more such bodies;

(29) 'public emergency' means an exceptional situation, limited in time, such as a public health emergency, an emergency resulting from natural disasters, a human-induced major disaster, including a major cybersecurity incident, negatively affecting the population of the Union or the whole or part of a Member State, with a risk of serious and lasting repercussions for living conditions or economic stability, financial stability, or the substantial and immediate degradation of economic assets in the Union or the relevant Member State and which is determined or officially declared in accordance with the relevant procedures under Union or national law;

(30) 'customer' means a natural or legal person that has entered into a contractual relationship with a provider of data processing services with the objective of using one or more data processing services;

(31) 'virtual assistants' means software that can process demands, tasks or questions including those based on audio, written input, gestures or motions, and that, based on those demands, tasks or questions, provides access to other services or controls the functions of connected products;

(32) 'digital assets' means elements in digital form, including applications, for which the customer has the right of use, independently from the contractual relationship with the data processing service it intends to switch from;

(33) 'on-premises ICT infrastructure' means ICT infrastructure and computing resources owned, rented or leased by the customer, located in the data centre of the customer itself and operated by the customer or by a third-party;

(34) 'switching' means the process involving a source provider of data processing services, a customer of a data processing service and, where relevant, a destination provider of data processing services, whereby the customer of a data processing service changes from using one data processing service to using another data processing service of the same service type, or other service, offered by a different provider of data processing services, or to an on-premises ICT infrastructure, including through extracting, transforming and uploading the data;

(35) 'data egress charges' means data transfer fees charged to customers for extracting their data through the network from the ICT infrastructure of a provider of data processing services to the system of a different provider or to on-premises ICT infrastructure;

(36) 'switching charges' means charges, other than standard service fees or early termination penalties, imposed by a provider of data processing services on a customer for the actions mandated by this Regulation for switching to the system of a different provider or to on-premises ICT infrastructure, including data egress charges;

(37) 'functional equivalence' means re-establishing on the basis of the customer's exportable data and digital assets, a minimum level of functionality in the environment of a new data processing service of the same service type after the switching process, where the destination data processing service delivers a materially comparable outcome in response to the same input for shared features supplied to the customer under the contract;

(38) 'exportable data', for the purpose of Articles 23 to 31 and Article 35, means the input and output data, including metadata, directly or indirectly generated, or cogenerated, by the customer's use of the data processing service, excluding any assets or data protected by intellectual property rights, or constituting a trade secret, of providers of data processing services or third parties;

(39) 'smart contract' means a computer program used for the automated execution of an agreement or part thereof, using a sequence of electronic data records and ensuring their integrity and the accuracy of their chronological ordering;

(40) 'interoperability' means the ability of two or more data spaces or communication networks, systems, connected products, applications, data processing services or components to exchange and use data in order to perform their functions;

(41) open interoperability specification' means a technical specification in the field of information and communication technologies which is performance oriented towards achieving interoperability between data processing services;

(42) 'common specifications' means a document, other than a standard, containing technical solutions providing a means to comply with certain requirements and obligations established under this Regulation;

(43) 'harmonised standard' means a harmonised standard as defined in Article 2, point (1)(c), of Regulation (EU) No 1025/2012.

CHAPTER II
BUSINESS TO CONSUMER AND BUSINESS TO BUSINESS DATA SHARING

Article 3
Obligation to make product data and related service data accessible to the user

1. Connected products shall be designed and manufactured, and related services shall be designed and provided, in such a manner that product data and related service data, including the relevant metadata necessary to interpret and use those data, are, by default, easily, securely, free of charge, in a comprehensive, structured, commonly used and machine-readable format, and, where relevant and technically feasible, directly accessible to the user.

2. Before concluding a contract for the purchase, rent or lease of a connected product, the seller, rentor or lessor, which may be the manufacturer, shall provide at least the following information to the user, in a clear and comprehensible manner:

(a) the type, format and estimated volume of product data which the connected product is capable of generating;
(b) whether the connected product is capable of generating data continuously and in real-time;
(c) whether the connected product is capable of storing data on-device or on a remote server, including, where applicable, the intended duration of retention;
(d) how the user may access, retrieve or, where relevant, erase the data, including the technical means to do so, as well as their terms of use and quality of service.

3. Before concluding a contract for the provision of a related service, the provider of such related service shall provide at least the following information to the user, in a clear and comprehensible manner:

(a) the nature, estimated volume and collection frequency of product data that the prospective data holder is expected to obtain and, where relevant, the arrangements for the user to access or retrieve such data, including the prospective data holder's data storage arrangements and the duration of retention;
(b) the nature and estimated volume of related service data to be generated, as well as the arrangements for the user to access or retrieve such data, including the prospective data holder's data storage arrangements and the duration of retention;
(c) whether the prospective data holder expects to use readily available data itself and the purposes for which those data are to be used, and whether it intends to allow one or more third parties to use the data for purposes agreed upon with the user;
(d) the identity of the prospective data holder, such as its trading name and the geographical address at which it is established and, where applicable, of other data processing parties;
(e) the means of communication which make it possible to contact the prospective data holder quickly and communicate with that data holder efficiently;

(f) how the user can request that the data are shared with a third party and, where applicable, end the data sharing;
(g) the user's right to lodge a complaint alleging an infringement of any of the provisions of this Chapter with the competent authority designated pursuant to Article 37;
(h) whether a prospective data holder is the holder of trade secrets contained in the data that is accessible from the connected product or generated during the provision of a related service, and, where the prospective data holder is not the trade secret holder, the identity of the trade secret holder;
(i) the duration of the contract between the user and the prospective data holder, as well as the arrangements for terminating such a contract.

Article 4
The rights and obligations of users and data holders with regard to access, use and making available product data and related service data

1. Where data cannot be directly accessed by the user from the connected product or related service, data holders shall make readily available data, as well as the relevant metadata necessary to interpret and use those data, accessible to the user without undue delay, of the same quality as is available to the data holder, easily, securely, free of charge, in a comprehensive, structured, commonly used and machine-readable format and, where relevant and technically feasible, continuously and in real-time. This shall be done on the basis of a simple request through electronic means where technically feasible.

2. Users and data holders may contractually restrict or prohibit accessing, using or further sharing data, if such processing could undermine security requirements of the connected product, as laid down by Union or national law, resulting in a serious adverse effect on the health, safety or security of natural persons. Sectoral authorities may provide users and data holders with technical expertise in that context. Where the data holder refuses to share data pursuant to this Article, it shall notify the competent authority designated pursuant to Article 37.

3. Without prejudice to the user's right to seek redress at any stage before a court or tribunal of a Member State, the user may, in relation to any dispute with the data holder concerning the contractual restrictions or prohibitions referred to in paragraph 2:

(a) lodge, in accordance with Article 37(5), point (b), a complaint with the competent authority; or
(b) agree with the data holder to refer the matter to a dispute settlement body in accordance with Article 10(1).

4. Data holders shall not make the exercise of choices or rights under this Article by the user unduly difficult, including by offering choices to the user in a non-neutral manner or by subverting or impairing the autonomy, decision-making or choices of the user via the structure, design, function or manner of operation of a user digital interface or a part thereof.

5. For the purpose of verifying whether a natural or legal person qualifies as a user for the purposes of paragraph 1, a data holder shall not require that person to provide any information beyond what is necessary. Data holders shall not keep any information, in particular log data, on the user's access to the data requested beyond what is necessary for the sound execution of the user's access request and for the security and maintenance of the data infrastructure.

6. Trade secrets shall be preserved and shall be disclosed only where the data holder and the user take all necessary measures prior to the disclosure to preserve their confidentiality in particular regarding third parties. The data holder or, where they are not the same person, the trade secret holder shall identify the data which are protected as trade secrets, including in the relevant metadata, and shall agree with the user proportionate technical and organisational measures necessary to preserve the confidentiality of the shared data, in particular in relation to third parties, such as model contractual terms, confidentiality agreements, strict access protocols, technical standards and the application of codes of conduct.

7. Where there is no agreement on the necessary measures referred to in paragraph 6, or if the user fails to implement the measures agreed pursuant to paragraph 6 or undermines the confidentiality of the trade secrets, the data holder may withhold or, as the case may be, suspend the sharing of data identified as trade secrets. The decision of the data holder shall be duly substantiated and provided in writing to the user without undue delay. In such cases, the data holder shall notify the competent authority designated pursuant to Article 37 that it has withheld or suspended data sharing and identify which measures have not been agreed or implemented and, where relevant, which trade secrets have had their confidentiality undermined.

8. In exceptional circumstances, where the data holder who is a trade secret holder is able to demonstrate that it is highly likely to suffer serious economic damage from the disclosure of trade secrets, despite the technical and organisational measures taken by the user pursuant to paragraph 6 of this Article, that data holder may refuse on a case-by-case basis a request for access to the specific data in question. That demonstration shall be duly substantiated on the basis of objective elements, in particular the enforceability of trade secrets protection in third countries, the nature and level of confidentiality of the data requested, and the uniqueness and novelty of the connected product, and shall be provided in writing to the user without undue delay. Where the data holder refuses to share data pursuant to this paragraph, it shall notify the competent authority designated pursuant to Article 37.

9. Without prejudice to a user's right to seek redress at any stage before a court or tribunal of a Member State, a user wishing to challenge a data holder's decision to refuse or to withhold or suspend data sharing pursuant to paragraphs 7 and 8 may:

(a) lodge, in accordance with Article 37(5), point (b), a complaint with the competent authority, which shall, without undue delay, decide whether and under which conditions data sharing is to start or resume; or
(b) agree with the data holder to refer the matter to a dispute settlement body in accordance with Article 10(1).

10. The user shall not use the data obtained pursuant to a request referred to in paragraph 1 to develop a connected product that competes with the connected product from which the data originate, nor share the data with a third party with

that intent and shall not use such data to derive insights about the economic situation, assets and production methods of the manufacturer or, where applicable the data holder.

11. The user shall not use coercive means or abuse gaps in the technical infrastructure of a data holder which is designed to protect the data in order to obtain access to data.

12. Where the user is not the data subject whose personal data is requested, any personal data generated by the use of a connected product or related service shall be made available by the data holder to the user only where there is a valid legal basis for processing under Article 6 of Regulation (EU) 2016/679 and, where relevant, the conditions of Article 9 of that Regulation and of Article 5(3) of Directive 2002/58/EC are fulfilled.

13. A data holder shall only use any readily available data that is non-personal data on the basis of a contract with the user. A data holder shall not use such data to derive insights about the economic situation, assets and production methods of, or the use by, the user in any other manner that could undermine the commercial position of that user on the markets in which the user is active.

14. Data holders shall not make available non-personal product data to third parties for commercial or non-commercial purposes other than the fulfilment of their contract with the user. Where relevant, data holders shall contractually bind third parties not to further share data received from them.

Article 5
Right of the user to share data with third parties

1. Upon request by a user, or by a party acting on behalf of a user, the data holder shall make available readily available data, as well as the relevant metadata necessary to interpret and use those data, to a third party without undue delay, of the same quality as is available to the data holder, easily, securely, free of charge to the user, in a comprehensive, structured, commonly used and machine-readable format and, where relevant and technically feasible, continuously and in real-time. The data shall be made available by the data holder to the third party in accordance with Articles 8 and 9.

2. Paragraph 1 shall not apply to readily available data in the context of the testing of new connected products, substances or processes that are not yet placed on the market unless their use by a third party is contractually permitted.

3. Any undertaking designated as a gatekeeper, pursuant to Article 3 of Regulation (EU) 2022/1925, shall not be an eligible third party under this Article and therefore shall not:

(a) solicit or commercially incentivise a user in any manner, including by providing monetary or any other compensation, to make data available to one of its services that the user has obtained pursuant to a request under Article 4(1);

(b) solicit or commercially incentivise a user to request the data holder to make data available to one of its services pursuant to paragraph 1 of this Article;
(c) receive data from a user that the user has obtained pursuant to a request under Article 4(1).

4. For the purpose of verifying whether a natural or legal person qualifies as a user or as a third party for the purposes of paragraph 1, the user or the third party shall not be required to provide any information beyond what is necessary. Data holders shall not keep any information on the third party's access to the data requested beyond what is necessary for the sound execution of the third party's access request and for the security and maintenance of the data infrastructure.

5. The third party shall not use coercive means or abuse gaps in the technical infrastructure of a data holder which is designed to protect the data in order to obtain access to data.

6. A data holder shall not use any readily available data to derive insights about the economic situation, assets and production methods of, or the use by, the third party in any other manner that could undermine the commercial position of the third party on the markets in which the third party is active, unless the third party has given permission to such use and has the technical possibility to easily withdraw that permission at any time.

7. Where the user is not the data subject whose personal data is requested, any personal data generated by the use of a connected product or related service shall be made available by the data holder to the third party only where there is a valid legal basis for processing under Article 6 of Regulation (EU) 2016/679 and, where relevant, the conditions of Article 9 of that Regulation and of Article 5(3) of Directive 2002/58/EC are fulfilled.

8. Any failure on the part of the data holder and the third party to agree on arrangements for transmitting the data shall not hinder, prevent or interfere with the exercise of the rights of the data subject under Regulation (EU) 2016/679 and, in particular, with the right to data portability under Article 20 of that Regulation.

9. Trade secrets shall be preserved and shall be disclosed to third parties only to the extent that such disclosure is strictly necessary to fulfil the purpose agreed between the user and the third party. The data holder or, where they are not the same person, the trade secret holder shall identify the data which are protected as trade secrets, including in the relevant metadata, and shall agree with the third party all proportionate technical and organisational measures necessary to preserve the confidentiality of the shared data, such as model contractual terms, confidentiality agreements, strict access protocols, technical standards and the application of codes of conduct.

10. Where there is no agreement on the necessary measures referred to in paragraph 9 of this Article or if the third party fails to implement the measures agreed pursuant to paragraph 9 of this Article or undermines the confidentiality of the trade secrets, the data holder may withhold or, as the case may be, suspend the sharing of data identified as trade secrets. The decision of the data holder shall be duly substantiated and provided in writing to the third party without undue delay. In such cases, the data holder shall notify the competent authority designated pursuant to Article 37 that it has withheld or suspended data sharing and identify

which measures have not been agreed or implemented and, where relevant, which trade secrets have had their confidentiality undermined.

11. In exceptional circumstances, where the data holder who is a trade secret holder is able to demonstrate that it is highly likely to suffer serious economic damage from the disclosure of trade secrets, despite the technical and organisational measures taken by the third party pursuant to paragraph 9 of this Article, that data holder may refuse on a case-by-case basis a request for access to the specific data in question. That demonstration shall be duly substantiated on the basis of objective elements, in particular the enforceability of trade secrets protection in third countries, the nature and level of confidentiality of the data requested, and the uniqueness and novelty of the connected product, and shall be provided in writing to the third party without undue delay. Where the data holder refuses to share data pursuant to this paragraph, it shall notify the competent authority designated pursuant to Article 37.

12. Without prejudice to the third party's right to seek redress at any stage before a court or tribunal of a Member State, a third party wishing to challenge a data holder's decision to refuse or to withhold or suspend data sharing pursuant to paragraphs 10 and 11 may:

(a) lodge, in accordance with Article 37(5), point (b), a complaint with the competent authority, which shall, without undue delay, decide whether and under which conditions the data sharing is to start or resume; or
(b) agree with the data holder to refer the matter to a dispute settlement body in accordance with Article 10(1).

13. The right referred to in paragraph 1 shall not adversely affect the rights of data subjects pursuant to the applicable Union and national law on the protection of personal data.

Article 6
Obligations of third parties receiving data at the request of the user

1. A third party shall process the data made available to it pursuant to Article 5 only for the purposes and under the conditions agreed with the user and subject to Union and national law on the protection of personal data including the rights of the data subject insofar as personal data are concerned. The third party shall erase the data when they are no longer necessary for the agreed purpose, unless otherwise agreed with the user in relation to non-personal data.

2. The third party shall not:

(a) make the exercise of choices or rights under Article 5 and this Article by the user unduly difficult, including by offering choices to the user in a non-neutral manner, or by coercing, deceiving or manipulating the user, or by subverting or impairing the autonomy, decision-making or choices of the user, including by means of a user digital interface or a part thereof;
(b) notwithstanding Article 22(2), points (a) and (c), of Regulation (EU) 2016/679, use the data it receives for the profiling, unless it is necessary to provide the service requested by the user;

(c) make the data it receives available to another third party, unless the data is made available on the basis of a contract with the user, and provided that the other third party takes all necessary measures agreed between the data holder and the third party to preserve the confidentiality of trade secrets;
(d) make the data it receives available to an undertaking designated as a gatekeeper pursuant to Article 3 of Regulation (EU) 2022/1925;
(e) use the data it receives to develop a product that competes with the connected product from which the accessed data originate or share the data with another third party for that purpose; third parties shall also not use any non-personal product data or related service data made available to them to derive insights about the economic situation, assets and production methods of, or use by, the data holder;
(f) use the data it receives in a manner that has an adverse impact on the security of the connected product or related service;
(g) disregard the specific measures agreed with a data holder or with the trade secrets holder pursuant to Article 5(9) and undermine the confidentiality of trade secrets;
(h) prevent the user that is a consumer, including on the basis of a contract, from making the data it receives available to other parties.

Article 7
Scope of business-to-consumer and business-to-business data sharing obligations

1. The obligations of this Chapter shall not apply to data generated through the use of connected products manufactured or designed or related services provided by a microenterprise or a small enterprise, provided that that enterprise does not have a partner enterprise or a linked enterprise within the meaning of Article 3 of the Annex to Recommendation 2003/361/EC that does not qualify as a microenterprise or a small enterprise and where the microenterprise and small enterprise is not subcontracted to manufacture or design a connected product or to provide a related service.

The same shall apply to data generated through the use of connected products manufactured by or related services provided by an enterprise that has qualified as a medium-sized enterprise under Article 2 of the Annex to Recommendation 2003/361/EC for less than one year and to connected products for one year after the date on which they were placed on the market by a medium-sized enterprise.

2. Any contractual term which, to the detriment of the user, excludes the application of, derogates from or varies the effect of the user's rights under this Chapter shall not be binding on the user.

CHAPTER III
OBLIGATIONS FOR DATA HOLDERS OBLIGED TO MAKE DATA AVAILABLE PURSUANT TO UNION LAW

Article 8
Conditions under which data holders make data available to data recipients

1. Where, in business-to-business relations, a data holder is obliged to make data available to a data recipient under Article 5 or under other applicable Union law or national legislation adopted in accordance with Union law, it shall agree with a data recipient the arrangements for making the data available and shall do so under fair, reasonable and non-discriminatory terms and conditions and in a transparent manner in accordance with this Chapter and Chapter IV.

2. A contractual term concerning access to and the use of data, or liability and remedies for the breach or termination of data-related obligations, shall not be binding if it constitutes an unfair contractual term within the meaning of Article 13 or if, to the detriment of the user, it excludes the application of, derogates from or varies the effect of the user's rights under Chapter II.

3. A data holder shall not discriminate regarding the arrangements for making data available between comparable categories of data recipients, including partner enterprises or linked enterprises of the data holder when making data available. Where a data recipient considers that the conditions under which data has been made available to it are discriminatory, the data holder shall without undue delay provide the data recipient, upon its reasoned request, with information showing that there has been no discrimination.

4. A data holder shall not make data available to a data recipient, including on an exclusive basis, unless requested to do so by the user under Chapter II.

5. Data holders and data recipients shall not be required to provide any information beyond what is necessary to verify compliance with the contractual terms agreed for making data available or with their obligations under this Regulation or other applicable Union law or national legislation adopted in accordance with Union law.

6. Unless otherwise provided for in Union law, including Article 4(6) and Article 5(9) of this Regulation, or by national legislation adopted in accordance with Union law, an obligation to make data available to a data recipient shall not oblige the disclosure of trade secrets.

Article 9
Compensation for making data available

1. Any compensation agreed upon between a data holder and a data recipient for making data available in business-to-business relations shall be non- discriminatory and reasonable and may include a margin.

2. When agreeing on any compensation, the data holder and the data recipient shall take into account in particular:

(a) costs incurred in making the data available, including, in particular, the costs necessary for the formatting of data, dissemination via electronic means and storage;
(b) investments in the collection and production of data, where applicable, taking into account whether other parties contributed to obtaining, generating or collecting the data in question.

3. The compensation referred to in paragraph 1 may also depend on the volume, format and nature of the data.

4. Where the data recipient is an SME or a not-for-profit research organisation and where such a data recipient does not have partner enterprises or linked enterprises that do not qualify as SMEs, any compensation agreed shall not exceed the costs referred to in paragraph 2, point (a).

5. The Commission shall adopt guidelines on the calculation of reasonable compensation, taking into account the advice of the European Data Innovation Board (EDIB) referred to in Article 42.

6. This Article shall not preclude other Union law or national legislation adopted in accordance with Union law from excluding compensation for making data available or providing for lower compensation.

7. The data holder shall provide the data recipient with information setting out the basis for the calculation of the compensation in sufficient detail so that the data recipient can assess whether the requirements of paragraphs 1 to 4 are met.

Article 10
Dispute settlement

1. Users, data holders and data recipients shall have access to a dispute settlement body, certified in accordance with paragraph 5 of this Article, to settle disputes pursuant to Article 4(3) and (9) and Article 5(12) as well as disputes relating to the fair, reasonable and non-discriminatory terms and conditions for, and transparent manner of, making data available in accordance with this Chapter and Chapter IV.

2. Dispute settlement bodies shall make the fees, or the mechanisms used to determine the fees, known to the parties concerned before those parties request a decision.

3. For disputes referred to a dispute settlement body pursuant to Article 4(3) and (9) and Article 5(12), where the dispute settlement body decides a dispute in favour of the user or of the data recipient, the data holder shall bear all the fees charged by the dispute settlement body and shall reimburse that user or that data recipient for any other reasonable expenses that it has incurred in relation to the dispute settlement. If the dispute settlement body decides a dispute in favour of the data holder, the user or the data recipient shall not be required to reimburse any fees or other expenses that the data holder paid or is to pay in relation to the dispute settlement, unless the dispute settlement body finds that the user or the data recipient manifestly acted in bad faith.

4. Customers and providers of data processing services shall have access to a dispute settlement body, certified in accordance with paragraph 5 of this Article, to settle disputes relating to breaches of the rights of customers and the obligations of providers of data processing services, in accordance with Articles 23 to 31.

5. The Member State where the dispute settlement body is established shall, at the request of that body, certify that body where it has demonstrated that it meets all of the following conditions:

(a) it is impartial and independent, and it is to issue its decisions in accordance with clear, non-discriminatory and fair rules of procedure;
(b) it has the necessary expertise, in particular in relation to fair, reasonable and non-discriminatory terms and conditions, including compensation, and on making data available in a transparent manner, allowing the body to effectively determine those terms and conditions;
(c) it is easily accessible through electronic communication technology;
(d) it is capable of adopting its decisions in a swift, efficient and cost-effective manner in at least one official language of the Union.

6. Member States shall notify to the Commission the dispute settlement bodies certified in accordance with paragraph 5. The Commission shall publish a list of those bodies on a dedicated website and keep it updated.

7. A dispute settlement body shall refuse to deal with a request to resolve a dispute that has already been brought before another dispute settlement body or before a court or tribunal of a Member State.

8. A dispute settlement body shall grant parties the possibility, within a reasonable period of time, to express their points of view on the matters those parties have brought before that body. In that context, each party to a dispute shall be provided with the submissions of the other party to their dispute and any statements made by experts. The parties shall be given the possibility to comment on those submissions and statements.

9. A dispute settlement body shall adopt its decision on a matter referred to it within 90 days of receipt of a request pursuant to paragraphs 1 and 4. That decision shall be in writing or on a durable medium and shall be supported by a statement of reasons.

10. Dispute settlement bodies shall draw up and make publicly available annual activity reports. Such annual reports shall include, in particular, the following general information:

(a) an aggregation of the outcomes of disputes;
(b) the average time taken to resolve disputes;
(c) the most common reasons for disputes.

11. In order to facilitate the exchange of information and best practices, a dispute settlement body may decide to include recommendations in the report referred to in paragraph 10 as to how problems can be avoided or resolved.

12. The decision of a dispute settlement body shall be binding on the parties only if the parties have explicitly consented to its binding nature prior to the start of the dispute settlement proceedings.

13. This Article does not affect the right of parties to seek an effective remedy before a court or tribunal of a Member State.

Article 11
Technical protection measures on the unauthorised use or disclosure of data

1. A data holder may apply appropriate technical protection measures, including smart contracts and encryption, to prevent unauthorised access to data, including metadata, and to ensure compliance with Articles 4, 5, 6, 8 and 9, as well as with the agreed contractual terms for making data available. Such technical protection measures shall not discriminate between data recipients or hinder a user's right to obtain a copy of, retrieve, use or access data, to provide data to third parties pursuant to Article 5 or any right of a third party under Union law or national legislation adopted in accordance with Union law. Users, third parties and data recipients shall not alter or remove such technical protection measures unless agreed by the data holder.

2. In the circumstances referred to in paragraph 3, the third party or data recipient shall comply, without undue delay, with the requests of the data holder and, where applicable and where they are not the same person, the trade secret holder or the user:

(a) to erase the data made available by the data holder and any copies thereof;
(b) to end the production, offering or placing on the market or use of goods, derivative data or services produced on the basis of knowledge obtained through such data, or the importation, export or storage of infringing goods for those purposes, and destroy any infringing goods, where there is a serious risk that the unlawful use of those data will cause significant harm to the data holder, the trade secret holder or the user or where such a measure would not be disproportionate in light of the interests of the data holder, the trade secret holder or the user;
(c) to inform the user of the unauthorised use or disclosure of the data and of the measures taken to put an end to the unauthorised use or disclosure of the data;
(d) to compensate the party suffering from the misuse or disclosure of such unlawfully accessed or used data.

3. Paragraph 2 shall apply where a third party or a data recipient has:

(a) for the purposes of obtaining data, provided false information to a data holder, deployed deceptive or coercive means or abused gaps in the technical infrastructure of the data holder designed to protect the data;
(b) used the data made available for unauthorised purposes, including the development of a competing connected product within the meaning of Article 6(2), point (e);
(c) unlawfully disclosed data to another party;
(d) not maintained the technical and organisational measures agreed pursuant to Article 5(9); or

(e) altered or removed technical protection measures applied by the data holder pursuant to paragraph 1 of this Article without the agreement of the data holder.

4. Paragraph 2 shall also apply where a user alters or removes technical protection measures applied by the data holder or does not maintain the technical and organisational measures taken by the user in agreement with the data holder or, where they are not the same person, the trade secrets holder, in order to preserve trade secrets, as well as in respect of any other party that receives the data from the user by means of an infringement of this Regulation.

5. Where the data recipient infringes Article 6(2), point (a) or (b), users shall have the same rights as data holders under paragraph 2 of this Article.

Article 12
Scope of obligations for data holders obliged pursuant to Union law to make data available

1. This Chapter shall apply where, in business-to-business relations, a data holder is obliged under Article 5 or under applicable Union law or national legislation adopted in accordance with Union law, to make data available to a data recipient.

2. A contractual term in a data sharing agreement which, to the detriment of one party, or, where applicable, to the detriment of the user, excludes the application of this Chapter, derogates from it, or varies its effect, shall not be binding on that party.

CHAPTER IV
UNFAIR CONTRACTUAL TERMS RELATED TO DATA ACCESS AND USE BETWEEN ENTERPRISES

Article 13
Unfair contractual terms unilaterally imposed on another enterprise

1. A contractual term concerning access to and the use of data or liability and remedies for the breach or the termination of data related obligations, which has been unilaterally imposed by an enterprise on another enterprise, shall not be binding on the latter enterprise if it is unfair.

2. A contractual term which reflects mandatory provisions of Union law, or provisions of Union law which would apply if the contractual terms did not regulate the matter, shall not be considered to be unfair.

3. A contractual term is unfair if it is of such a nature that its use grossly deviates from good commercial practice in data access and use, contrary to good faith and fair dealing.

4. In particular, a contractual term shall be unfair for the purposes of paragraph 3, if its object or effect is to:

(a) exclude or limit the liability of the party that unilaterally imposed the term for intentional acts or gross negligence;

(b) exclude the remedies available to the party upon whom the term has been unilaterally imposed in the case of non-performance of contractual obligations, or the liability of the party that unilaterally imposed the term in the case of a breach of those obligations;
(c) give the party that unilaterally imposed the term the exclusive right to determine whether the data supplied are in conformity with the contract or to interpret any contractual term.

5. A contractual term shall be presumed to be unfair for the purposes of paragraph 3 if its object or effect is to:

(a) inappropriately limit remedies in the case of non-performance of contractual obligations or liability in the case of a breach of those obligations, or extend the liability of the enterprise upon whom the term has been unilaterally imposed;
(b) allow the party that unilaterally imposed the term to access and use the data of the other contracting party in a manner that is significantly detrimental to the legitimate interests of the other contracting party, in particular when such data contain commercially sensitive data or are protected by trade secrets or by intellectual property rights;
(c) prevent the party upon whom the term has been unilaterally imposed from using the data provided or generated by that party during the period of the contract, or to limit the use of such data to the extent that that party is not entitled to use, capture, access or control such data or exploit the value of such data in an adequate manner;
(d) prevent the party upon whom the term has been unilaterally imposed from terminating the agreement within a reasonable period;
(e) prevent the party upon whom the term has been unilaterally imposed from obtaining a copy of the data provided or generated by that party during the period of the contract or within a reasonable period after the termination thereof;
(f) enable the party that unilaterally imposed the term to terminate the contract at unreasonably short notice, taking into consideration any reasonable possibility of the other contracting party to switch to an alternative and comparable service and the financial detriment caused by such termination, except where there are serious grounds for so doing;
(g) enable the party that unilaterally imposed the term to substantially change the price specified in the contract or any other substantive condition related to the nature, format, quality or quantity of the data to be shared, where no valid reason and no right of the other party to terminate the contract in the case of such a change is specified in the contract.

Point (g) of the first subparagraph shall not affect terms by which the party that unilaterally imposed the term reserves the right to unilaterally change the terms of a contract of an indeterminate duration, provided that the contract specified a valid reason for such unilateral changes, that the party that unilaterally imposed the term is required to provide the other contracting party with reasonable notice of any such intended change, and that the other contracting party is free to terminate the contract at no cost in the case of a change.

6. A contractual term shall be considered to be unilaterally imposed within the meaning of this Article if it has been supplied by one contracting party and the other contracting party has not been able to influence its content despite an attempt to negotiate it. The contracting party that supplied the contractual term bears the burden of proving that that term has not been unilaterally imposed. The contracting party that supplied the contested contractual term may not argue that the term is an unfair contractual term.

7. Where the unfair contractual term is severable from the remaining terms of the contract, those remaining terms shall be binding.

8. This Article does not apply to contractual terms defining the main subject matter of the contract or to the adequacy of the price, as against the data supplied in exchange.

9. The parties to a contract covered by paragraph 1 shall not exclude the application of this Article, derogate from it, or vary its effects.

CHAPTER V
MAKING DATA AVAILABLE TO PUBLIC SECTOR BODIES, THE COMMISSION, THE EUROPEAN CENTRAL BANK AND UNION BODIES ON THE BASIS OF AN EXCEPTIONAL NEED

Article 14
Obligation to make data available on the basis of an exceptional need

Where a public sector body, the Commission, the European Central Bank or a Union body demonstrates an exceptional need, as set out in Article 15, to use certain data, including the relevant metadata necessary to interpret and use those data, to carry out its statutory duties in the public interest, data holders that are legal persons, other than public sectors bodies, which hold those data shall make them available upon a duly reasoned request.

Article 15
Exceptional need to use data

1. An exceptional need to use certain data within the meaning of this Chapter shall be limited in time and scope and shall be considered to exist only in any of the following circumstances:

(a) where the data requested is necessary to respond to a public emergency and the public sector body, the Commission, the European Central Bank or the Union body is unable to obtain such data by alternative means in a timely and effective manner under equivalent conditions;

(b) in circumstances not covered by point (a) and only insofar as non-personal data is concerned, where:

  (i) a public sector body, the Commission, the European Central Bank or a Union body is acting on the basis of Union or national law and has identified specific data, the lack of which prevents it from fulfilling a specific task carried out in the public interest, that has been explicitly provided for by law, such as the production of official statistics or the mitigation of or recovery from a public emergency; and

(ii) the public sector body, the Commission, the European Central Bank or the Union body has exhausted all other means at its disposal to obtain such data, including purchase of non-personal data on the market by offering market rates, or by relying on existing obligations to make data available or the adoption of new legislative measures which could guarantee the timely availability of the data.

2. Paragraph 1, point (b), shall not apply to microenterprises and small enterprises.

3. The obligation to demonstrate that the public sector body was unable to obtain non-personal data by purchasing them on the market shall not apply where the specific task carried out in the public interest is the production of official statistics and where the purchase of such data is not allowed by national law.

Article 16
Relationship with other obligations to make data available to public sector bodies, the Commission, the European Central Bank and Union bodies

1. This Chapter shall not affect the obligations laid down in Union or national law for the purposes of reporting, complying with requests for access to information or demonstrating or verifying compliance with legal obligations.

2. This Chapter shall not apply to public sector bodies, the Commission, the European Central Bank or Union bodies carrying out activities for the prevention, investigation, detection or prosecution of criminal or administrative offences or the execution of criminal penalties, or to customs or taxation administration. This Chapter does not affect applicable Union and national law on the prevention, investigation, detection or prosecution of criminal or administrative offences or the execution of criminal or administrative penalties, or for customs or taxation administration.

Article 17
Requests for data to be made available

1. When requesting data pursuant to Article 14, a public sector body, the Commission, the European Central Bank or a Union body shall:

(a) specify the data required, including the relevant metadata necessary to interpret and use those data;

(b) demonstrate that the conditions necessary for the existence of an exceptional need as referred to in Article 15 for the purpose of which the data are requested are met;

(c) explain the purpose of the request, the intended use of the data requested, including, where applicable, by a third party in accordance with paragraph 4 of this Article, the duration of that use, and, where relevant, how the processing of personal data is to address the exceptional need;

(d) specify, if possible, when the data are expected to be erased by all parties that have access to them;
(e) justify the choice of data holder to which the request is addressed;
(f) specify any other public sector bodies or the Commission, European Central Bank or Union bodies and the third parties with which the data requested is expected to be shared with;
(g) where personal data are requested, specify any technical and organisational measures necessary and proportionate to implement data protection principles and necessary safeguards, such as pseudonymisation, and whether anonymisation can be applied by the data holder before making the data available;
(h) state the legal provision allocating to the requesting public sector body, the Commission, the European Central Bank or the Union body the specific task carried out in the public interest relevant for requesting the data;
(i) specify the deadline by which the data are to be made available and the deadline referred to in Article 18(2) by which the data holder may decline or seek modification of the request;
(j) make its best efforts to avoid compliance with the data request resulting in the data holders' liability for infringement of Union or national law.

2. A request for data made pursuant to paragraph 1 of this Article shall:

(a) be made in writing and expressed in clear, concise and plain language understandable to the data holder;
(b) be specific regarding the type of data requested and correspond to data which the data holder has control over at the time of the request;
(c) be proportionate to the exceptional need and duly justified, regarding the granularity and volume of the data requested and frequency of access of the data requested;
(d) respect the legitimate aims of the data holder, committing to ensuring the protection of trade secrets in accordance with Article 19(3), and the cost and effort required to make the data available;
(e) concern non-personal data, and only if this is demonstrated to be insufficient to respond to the exceptional need to use data, in accordance with Article 15(1), point (a), request personal data in pseudonymised form and establish the technical and organisational measures that are to be taken to protect the data;
(f) inform the data holder of the penalties that are to be imposed pursuant to Article 40 by the competent authority designated pursuant to Article 37 in the event of non-compliance with the request;
(g) where the request is made by a public sector body, be transmitted to the data coordinator referred to in Article 37 of the Member State where the requesting public sector body is established, who shall make the request publicly available online without undue delay unless the data coordinator considers that such publication would create a risk for public security;
(h) where the request is made by the Commission, the European Central Bank or a Union body, be made available online without undue delay;
(i) where personal data are requested, be notified without undue delay to the supervisory authority responsible for monitoring the application of Regulation (EU) 2016/679 in the Member State where the public sector body is established.

The European Central Bank and Union bodies shall inform the Commission of their requests.

3. A public sector body, the Commission, the European Central Bank or a Union body shall not make data obtained pursuant to this Chapter available for reuse as defined in Article 2, point (2), of Regulation (EU) 2022/868 or Article 2, point (11), of Directive (EU) 2019/1024. Regulation (EU) 2022/868 and Directive (EU) 2019/1024 shall not apply to the data held by public sector bodies obtained pursuant to this Chapter.

4. Paragraph 3 of this Article does not preclude a public sector body, the Commission, the European Central Bank or a Union body to exchange data obtained pursuant to this Chapter with another public sector body or the Commission, the European Central Bank or a Union body in view of completing the tasks referred to in Article 15, as specified in the request in accordance with paragraph 1, point (f), of this Article or to make the data available to a third party where it has delegated, by means of a publicly available agreement, technical inspections or other functions to that third party. The obligations on public sector bodies pursuant to Article 19, in particular safeguards to preserve the confidentiality of trade secrets, shall apply also to such third parties. Where a public sector body, the Commission, the European Central Bank or a Union body transmits or makes data available under this paragraph, it shall notify the data holder from whom the data was received without undue delay.

5. Where the data holder considers that its rights under this Chapter have been infringed by the transmission or making available of data, it may lodge a complaint with the competent authority designated pursuant to Article 37 of the Member State where the data holder is established.

6. The Commission shall develop a model template for requests pursuant to this Article.

Article 18
Compliance with requests for data

1. A data holder receiving a request to make data available under this Chapter shall make the data available to the requesting public sector body, the Commission, the European Central Bank or a Union body without undue delay, taking into account necessary technical, organisational and legal measures.

2. Without prejudice to specific needs regarding the availability of data defined in Union or national law, a data holder may decline or seek the modification of a request to make data available under this Chapter without undue delay and, in any event, no later than five working days after the receipt of a request for the data necessary to respond to a public emergency and without undue delay and, in any event, no later than 30 working days after the receipt of such a request in other cases of an exceptional need, on any of the following grounds:

(a) the data holder does not have control over the data requested;
(b) a similar request for the same purpose has been previously submitted by another public sector body or the Commission, the European Central Bank or a

Union body and the data holder has not been notified of the erasure of the data pursuant to Article 19(1), point (c);

(c) the request does not meet the conditions laid down in Article 17(1) and (2).

3. If the data holder decides to decline the request or to seek its modification in accordance with paragraph 2, point (b), it shall indicate the identity of the public sector body or the Commission, the European Central Bank or the Union body that previously submitted a request for the same purpose.

4. Where the data requested includes personal data, the data holder shall properly anonymise the data, unless the compliance with the request to make data available to a public sector body, the Commission, the European Central Bank or a Union body requires the disclosure of personal data. In such cases, the data holder shall pseudonymise the data.

5. Where the public sector body, the Commission, the European Central Bank or the Union body wishes to challenge a data holder's refusal to provide the data requested, or where the data holder wishes to challenge the request and the matter cannot be resolved by an appropriate modification of the request, the matter shall be referred to the competent authority designated pursuant to Article 37 of the Member State where the data holder is established.

Article 19
Obligations of public sector bodies, the Commission, the European Central Bank and Union bodies

1. A public sector body, the Commission, the European Central Bank or a Union body receiving data pursuant to a request made under Article 14 shall:

(a) not use the data in a manner incompatible with the purpose for which they were requested;

(b) have implemented technical and organisational measures that preserve the confidentiality and integrity of the requested data and the security of the data transfers, in particular personal data, and safeguard the rights and freedoms of data subjects;

(c) erase the data as soon as they are no longer necessary for the stated purpose and inform the data holder and individuals or organisations that received the data pursuant to Article 21(1) without undue delay that the data have been erased, unless archiving of the data is required in accordance with Union or national law on public access to documents in the context of transparency obligations.

2. A public sector body, the Commission, the European Central Bank, a Union body or a third party receiving data under this Chapter shall not:

(a) use the data or insights about the economic situation, assets and production or operation methods of the data holder to develop or enhance a connected product or related service that competes with the connected product or related service of the data holder;

(b) share the data with another third party for any of the purposes referred to in point (a).

3. Disclosure of trade secrets to a public sector body, the Commission, the European Central Bank or a Union body shall be required only to the extent that it is strictly necessary to achieve the purpose of a request under Article 15. In such a case, the data holder or, where they are not the same person, the trade secret holder shall identify the data which are protected as trade secrets, including in the relevant metadata. The public sector body, the Commission, the European Central Bank or the Union body shall, prior to the disclosure of trade secrets, take all necessary and appropriate technical and organisational measures to preserve the confidentiality of the trade secrets, including, as appropriate, the use of model contractual terms, technical standards and the application of codes of conduct.

4. A public sector body, the Commission, the European Central Bank or a Union body shall be responsible for the security of the data it receives.

Article 20
Compensation in cases of an exceptional need

1. Data holders other than microenterprises and small enterprises shall make available data necessary to respond to a public emergency pursuant to Article 15(1), point (a), free of charge. The public sector body, the Commission, the European Central Bank or the Union body that has received data shall provide public acknowledgement to the data holder if requested by the data holder.

2. The data holder shall be entitled to fair compensation for making data available in compliance with a request made pursuant to Article 15(1), point (b). Such compensation shall cover the technical and organisational costs incurred to comply with the request including, where applicable, the costs of anonymisation, pseudonymisation, aggregation and of technical adaptation, and a reasonable margin. Upon request of the public sector body, the Commission, the European Central Bank or the Union body, the data holder shall provide information on the basis for the calculation of the costs and the reasonable margin.

3. Paragraph 2 shall also apply where a microenterprise and small enterprise claims compensation for making data available.

4. Data holders shall not be entitled to compensation for making data available in compliance with a request made pursuant to Article 15(1), point (b), where the specific task carried out in the public interest is the production of official statistics and where the purchase of data is not allowed by national law. Member States shall notify the Commission where the purchase of data for the production of official statistics is not allowed by national law.

5. Where the public sector body, the Commission, the European Central Bank or the Union body disagrees with the level of compensation requested by the data holder, they may lodge a complaint with the competent authority designated pursuant to Article 37 of the Member State where the data holder is established.

Article 21
Sharing of data obtained in the context of an exceptional need with research organisations or statistical bodies

1. A public sector body, the Commission, the European Central Bank or a Union body shall be entitled to share data received under this Chapter:

(a) with individuals or organisations in view of carrying out scientific research or analytics compatible with the purpose for which the data was requested; or
(b) with national statistical institutes and Eurostat for the production of official statistics.

2. Individuals or organisations receiving the data pursuant to paragraph 1 shall act on a not-for-profit basis or in the context of a public-interest mission recognised in Union or national law. They shall not include organisations upon which commercial undertakings have a significant influence which is likely to result in preferential access to the results of the research.

3. Individuals or organisations receiving the data pursuant to paragraph 1 of this Article shall comply with the same obligations that are applicable to the public sector bodies, the Commission, the European Central Bank or Union bodies pursuant to Article 17(3) and Article 19.

4. Notwithstanding Article 19(1), point (c), individuals or organisations receiving the data pursuant to paragraph 1 of this Article may keep the data received for the purpose for which the data was requested for up to six months following erasure of the data by the public sector bodies, the Commission, the European Central Bank and Union bodies.

5. Where a public sector body, the Commission, the European Central Bank or a Union body intends to transmit or make data available under paragraph 1 of this Article, it shall notify without undue delay the data holder from whom the data was received, stating the identity and contact details of the organisation or the individual receiving the data, the purpose of the transmission or making available of the data, the period for which the data is to be used and the technical protection and organisational measures taken, including where personal data or trade secrets are involved. Where the data holder disagrees with the transmission or making available of data, it may lodge a complaint with the competent authority designated pursuant to Article 37 of the Member State where the data holder is established.

Article 22
Mutual assistance and cross-border cooperation

1. Public sector bodies, the Commission, the European Central Bank and Union bodies shall cooperate and assist one another, to implement this Chapter in a consistent manner.

2. Any data exchanged in the context of assistance requested and provided pursuant to paragraph 1 shall not be used in a manner incompatible with the purpose for which they were requested.

3. Where a public sector body intends to request data from a data holder established in another Member State, it shall first notify the competent authority designated pursuant to Article 37 in that Member State of that intention. This requirement shall also apply to requests by the Commission, the European Central Bank and Union bodies. The request shall be examined by the competent authority of the Member State where the data holder is established.

4. After having examined the request in light of the requirements laid down in Article 17, the relevant competent authority shall, without undue delay, take one of the following actions:

(a) transmit the request to the data holder and, if applicable, advise the requesting public sector body, the Commission, the European Central Bank or the Union body of the need, if any, to cooperate with public sector bodies of the Member State in which the data holder is established with the aim of reducing the administrative burden on the data holder in complying with the request;
(b) reject the request on duly substantiated grounds in accordance with this Chapter.

The requesting public sector body, the Commission, the European Central Bank and the Union body shall take into account the advice of and the grounds provided by the relevant competent authority pursuant to the first subparagraph before taking any further action such as resubmitting the request, if applicable.

CHAPTER VI
SWITCHING BETWEEN DATA PROCESSING SERVICES

Article 23
Removing obstacles to effective switching

Providers of data processing services shall take the measures provided for in Articles 25, 26, 27, 29 and 30 to enable customers to switch to a data processing service, covering the same service type, which is provided by a different provider of data processing services, or to on-premises ICT infrastructure, or, where relevant, to use several providers of data processing services at the same time. In particular, providers of data processing services shall not impose and shall remove pre-commercial, commercial, technical, contractual and organisational obstacles, which inhibit customers from:

(a) terminating, after the maximum notice period and the successful completion of the switching process, in accordance with Article 25, the contract of the data processing service;
(b) concluding new contracts with a different provider of data processing services covering the same service type;
(c) porting the customer's exportable data and digital assets, to a different provider of data processing services or to an on-premises ICT infrastructure, including after having benefited from a free-tier offering;
(d) in accordance with Article 24, achieving functional equivalence in the use of the new data processing service in the ICT environment of a different provider of data processing services covering the same service type;

(e) unbundling, where technically feasible, data processing services referred to in Article 30(1) from other data processing services provided by the provider of data processing services.

Article 24
Scope of the technical obligations

The responsibilities of providers of data processing services laid down in Articles 23, 25, 29, 30 and 34 shall apply only to the services, contracts or commercial practices provided by the source provider of data processing services.

Article 25
Contractual terms concerning switching

1. The rights of the customer and the obligations of the provider of data processing services in relation to switching between providers of such services or, where applicable, to an on-premises ICT infrastructure shall be clearly set out in a written contract. The provider of data processing services shall make that contract available to the customer prior to signing the contract in a way that allows the customer to store and reproduce the contract.

2. Without prejudice to Directive (EU) 2019/770, the contract referred to in paragraph 1 of this Article shall include at least the following:

(a) clauses allowing the customer, upon request, to switch to a data processing service offered by a different provider of data processing services or to port all exportable data and digital assets to an on-premises ICT infrastructure, without undue delay and in any event not after the mandatory maximum transitional period of 30 calendar days, to be initiated after the maximum notice period referred to in point (d), during which the service contract remains applicable and during which the provider of data processing services shall:
   (i) provide reasonable assistance to the customer and third parties authorised by the customer in the switching process;
   (ii) act with due care to maintain business continuity, and continue the provision of the functions or services under the contract;
   (iii) provide clear information concerning known risks to continuity in the provision of the functions or services on the part of the source provider of data processing services;
   (iv) ensure that a high level of security is maintained throughout the switching process, in particular the security of the data during their transfer and the continued security of the data during the retrieval period specified in point (g), in accordance with applicable Union or national law;

(b) an obligation of the provider of data processing services to support the customer's exit strategy relevant to the contracted services, including by providing all relevant information;

(c) a clause specifying that the contract shall be considered to be terminated and the customer shall be notified of the termination, in one of the following cases:

(i) where applicable, upon the successful completion of the switching process;
(ii) at the end of the maximum notice period referred to in paragraph (d), where the customer does not wish to switch but to erase its exportable data and digital assets upon service termination;

(d) a maximum notice period for initiation of the switching process, which shall not exceed two months;
(e) an exhaustive specification of all categories of data and digital assets that can be ported during the switching process, including, at a minimum, all exportable data;
(f) an exhaustive specification of categories of data specific to the internal functioning of the provider's data processing service that are to be exempted from the exportable data under point (e) of this paragraph where a risk of breach of trade secrets of the provider exists, provided that such exemptions do not impede or delay the switching process provided for in Article 23;
(g) a minimum period for data retrieval of at least 30 calendar days, starting after the termination of the transitional period that was agreed between the customer and the provider of data processing services, in accordance with point (a) of this paragraph and paragraph 4;
(h) a clause guaranteeing full erasure of all exportable data and digital assets generated directly by the customer, or relating to the customer directly, after the expiry of the retrieval period referred to in point (g) or after the expiry of an alternative agreed period at a date later than the date of expiry of the retrieval period referred to in point (g), provided that the switching process has been completed successfully;
(i) switching charges, that may be imposed by providers of data processing services in accordance with Article 29.

3. The contract referred to in paragraph 1 shall include clauses providing that the customer may notify the provider of data processing services of its decision to perform one or more of the following actions upon termination of the maximum notice period referred to in paragraph 2, point (d):

(a) switch to a different provider of data processing services, in which case the customer shall provide the necessary details of that provider;
(b) switch to an on-premises ICT infrastructure;
(c) erase its exportable data and digital assets.

4. Where the mandatory maximum transitional period as provided for in paragraph 2, point (a) is technically unfeasible, the provider of data processing services shall notify the customer within 14 working days of the making of the switching request, and shall duly justify the technical unfeasibility and indicate an alternative transitional period, which shall not exceed seven months. In accordance with paragraph 1, service continuity shall be ensured throughout the alternative transitional period.

5. Without prejudice to paragraph 4, the contract referred to in paragraph 1 shall include clauses providing the customer with the right to extend the transitional period once for a period that the customer considers more appropriate for its own purposes.

Article 26
Information obligation of providers of data processing services

The provider of data processing services shall provide the customer with:

(a) information on available procedures for switching and porting to the data processing service, including information on available switching and porting methods and formats as well as restrictions and technical limitations which are known to the provider of data processing services;

(b) a reference to an up-to-date online register hosted by the provider of data processing services, with details of all the data structures and data formats as well as the relevant standards and open interoperability specifications, in which the exportable data referred to in Article 25(2), point (e), are available.

Article 27
Obligation of good faith

All parties involved, including destination providers of data processing services, shall cooperate in good faith to make the switching process effective, enable the timely transfer of data and maintain the continuity of the data processing service.

Article 28
Contractual transparency obligations on international access and transfer

1. Providers of data processing services shall make the following information available on their websites, and keep that information up to date:

(a) the jurisdiction to which the ICT infrastructure deployed for data processing of their individual services is subject;

(b) a general description of the technical, organisational and contractual measures adopted by the provider of data processing services in order to prevent international governmental access to or transfer of non-personal data held in the Union where such access or transfer would create a conflict with Union law or the national law of the relevant Member State.

2. The websites referred to in paragraph 1 shall be listed in contracts for all data processing services offered by providers of data processing services.

Article 29
Gradual withdrawal of switching charges

1. From 12 January 2027, providers of data processing services shall not impose any switching charges on the customer for the switching process.

2. From 11 January 2024 to 12 January 2027, providers of data processing services may impose reduced switching charges on the customer for the switching process.

3. The reduced switching charges referred to in paragraph 2 shall not exceed the costs incurred by the provider of data processing services that are directly linked to the switching process concerned.

4. Before entering into a contract with a customer, providers of data processing services shall provide the prospective customer with clear information on the standard service fees and early termination penalties that might be imposed, as well as on the reduced switching charges that might be imposed during the timeframe referred to in paragraph 2.

5. Where relevant, providers of data processing services shall provide information to a customer on data processing services that involve highly complex or costly switching or for which it is impossible to switch without significant interference in the data, digital assets or service architecture.

6. Where applicable, providers of data processing services shall make the information referred to in paragraphs 4 and 5 publicly available to customers via a dedicated section of their website or in any other easily accessible way.

7. The Commission is empowered to adopt delegated acts in accordance with Article 45 to supplement this Regulation by establishing a monitoring mechanism for the Commission to monitor switching charges, imposed by providers of data processing services on the market to ensure that the withdrawal and reduction of switching charges, pursuant to paragraphs 1 and 2 of this Article are to be attained in accordance with the deadlines laid down in those paragraphs.

Article 30
Technical aspects of switching

1. Providers of data processing services that concern scalable and elastic computing resources limited to infrastructural elements such as servers, networks and the virtual resources necessary for operating the infrastructure, but that do not provide access to the operating services, software and applications that are stored, otherwise processed, or deployed on those infrastructural elements, shall, in accordance with Article 27, take all reasonable measures in their power to facilitate that the customer, after switching to a service covering the same service type, achieves functional equivalence in the use of the destination data processing service. The source provider of data processing services shall facilitate the switching process by providing capabilities, adequate information, documentation, technical support and, where appropriate, the necessary tools.

2. Providers of data processing services, other than those referred to in paragraph 1, shall make open interfaces available to an equal extent to all their customers and the concerned destination providers of data processing services free of charge to facilitate the switching process. Those interfaces shall include sufficient information on the service concerned to enable the development of software to communicate with the services, for the purposes of data portability and interoperability.

3. For data processing services other than those referred to in paragraph 1 of this Article, providers of data processing services shall ensure compatibility with common specifications based on open interoperability specifications or harmonised standards for interoperability at least 12 months after the references to those com-

mon specifications or harmonised standards for interoperability of data processing services were published in the central Union standards repository for the interoperability of data processing services following the publication of the underlying implementing acts in the *Official Journal of the European Union* in accordance with Article 35(8).

4. Providers of data processing services other than those referred to in paragraph 1 of this Article shall update the online register referred to in Article 26, point (b) in accordance with their obligations under paragraph 3 of this Article.

5. In the case of switching between services of the same service type, for which common specifications or the harmonised standards for interoperability referred to in paragraph 3 of this Article have not been published in the central Union standards repository for the interoperability of data processing services in accordance with Article 35(8), the provider of data processing services shall, at the request of the customer, export all exportable data in a structured, commonly used and machine-readable format.

6. Providers of data processing services shall not be required to develop new technologies or services, or disclose or transfer digital assets that are protected by intellectual property rights or that constitute a trade secret, to a customer or to a different provider of data processing services or compromise the customer's or provider's security and integrity of service.

Article 31
Specific regime for certain data processing services

1. The obligations laid down in Article 23, point (d), Article 29 and Article 30(1) and (3) shall not apply to data processing services of which the majority of main features has been custom-built to accommodate the specific needs of an individual customer or where all components have been developed for the purposes of an individual customer, and where those data processing services are not offered at broad commercial scale via the service catalogue of the provider of data processing services.

2. The obligations laid down in this Chapter shall not apply to data processing services provided as a non-production version for testing and evaluation purposes and for a limited period of time.

3. Prior to the conclusion of a contract on the provision of the data processing services referred to in this Article, the provider of data processing services shall inform the prospective customer of the obligations of this Chapter that do not apply.

CHAPTER VII
UNLAWFUL INTERNATIONAL GOVERNMENTAL ACCESS AND TRANSFER OF NON-PERSONAL DATA

Article 32
International governmental access and transfer

1. Providers of data processing services shall take all adequate technical, organisational and legal measures, including contracts, in order to prevent international and third-country governmental access and transfer of non-personal data held in the Union where such transfer or access would create a conflict with Union law or with the national law of the relevant Member State, without prejudice to paragraph 2 or 3.

2. Any decision or judgment of a third-country court or tribunal and any decision of a third-country administrative authority requiring a provider of data processing services to transfer or give access to non-personal data falling within the scope of this Regulation held in the Union shall be recognised or enforceable in any manner only if based on an international agreement, such as a mutual legal assistance treaty, in force between the requesting third country and the Union, or any such agreement between the requesting third country and a Member State.

3. In the absence of an international agreement as referred to in paragraph 2, where a provider of data processing services is the addressee of a decision or judgment of a third-country court or tribunal or a decision of a third-country administrative authority to transfer or give access to non-personal data falling within the scope of this Regulation held in the Union and compliance with such a decision would risk putting the addressee in conflict with Union law or with the national law of the relevant Member State, transfer to or access to such data by that third-country authority shall take place only where:

(a) the third-country system requires the reasons and proportionality of such a decision or judgment to be set out and requires such a decision or judgment to be specific in character, for instance by establishing a sufficient link to certain suspected persons or infringements;

(b) the reasoned objection of the addressee is subject to a review by a competent third-country court or tribunal; and

(c) the competent third-country court or tribunal issuing the decision or judgment or reviewing the decision of an administrative authority is empowered under the law of that third country to take duly into account the relevant legal interests of the provider of the data protected by Union law or by the national law of the relevant Member State.

The addressee of the decision or judgment may ask the opinion of the relevant national body or authority competent for international cooperation in legal matters, in order to determine whether the conditions laid down in the first subparagraph are met, in particular when it considers that the decision may relate to trade secrets and other commercially sensitive data as well as to content protected by intellectual property rights or the transfer may lead to re-identification. The relevant national body or authority may consult the Commission. If the addressee considers that the decision or judgment may impinge on the national security or defence interests of the Union or its Member States, it shall ask the opinion of the relevant national body or authority in order to determine whether the data requested concerns national security or defence interests of the Union or its Member States. If the addressee has not received a reply within one month, or if the opinion of such body or authority concludes that the conditions laid down in the first subparagraph are not met, the addressee may reject the request for transfer or access, to non-personal data, on those grounds.

The EDIB referred to in Article 42 shall advise and assist the Commission in developing guidelines on the assessment of whether the conditions laid down in the first subparagraph of this paragraph are met.

4. If the conditions laid down in paragraph 2 or 3 are met, the provider of data processing services shall provide the minimum amount of data permissible in response to a request, on the basis of the reasonable interpretation of that request by the provider or relevant national body or authority referred to in paragraph 3, second subparagraph.

5. The provider of data processing services shall inform the customer about the existence of a request of a third-country authority to access its data before complying with that request, except where the request serves law enforcement purposes and for as long as this is necessary to preserve the effectiveness of the law enforcement activity.

CHAPTER VIII
INTEROPERABILITY

Article 33
Essential requirements regarding interoperability of data, of data sharing mechanisms and services, as well as of common European data spaces

1. Participants in data spaces that offer data or data services to other participants shall comply with the following essential requirements to facilitate the interoperability of data, of data sharing mechanisms and services, as well as of common European data spaces which are purpose- or sector-specific or cross-sectoral interoperable frameworks for common standards and practices to share or jointly process data for, inter alia, the development of new products and services, scientific research or civil society initiatives:

(a) the dataset content, use restrictions, licences, data collection methodology, data quality and uncertainty shall be sufficiently described, where applicable, in a machine-readable format, to allow the recipient to find, access and use the data;
(b) the data structures, data formats, vocabularies, classification schemes, taxonomies and code lists, where available, shall be described in a publicly available and consistent manner;
(c) the technical means to access the data, such as application programming interfaces, and their terms of use and quality of service shall be sufficiently described to enable automatic access and transmission of data between parties, including continuously, in bulk download or in real-time in a machine-readable

format where that is technically feasible and does not hamper the good functioning of the connected product;

(d) where applicable, the means to enable the interoperability of tools for automating the execution of data sharing agreements, such as smart contracts shall be provided.

The requirements can have a generic nature or concern specific sectors, while taking fully into account the interrelation with requirements arising from other Union or national law.

2. The Commission is empowered to adopt delegated acts, in accordance with Article 45 of this Regulation to supplement this Regulation by further specifying the essential requirements laid down in paragraph 1 of this Article, in relation to those requirements that, by their nature, cannot produce the intended effect unless they are further specified in binding Union legal acts and in order to properly reflect technological and market developments.

The Commission shall when adopting delegated acts take into account the advice of the EDIB in accordance with Article 42, point (c)(iii).

3. The participants in data spaces that offer data or data services to other participants in data spaces which meet the harmonised standards or parts thereof, the references of which are published in the *Official Journal of the European Union*, shall be presumed to be in conformity with the essential requirements laid down in paragraph 1 to the extent that those requirements are covered by such harmonised standards or parts thereof.

4. The Commission shall, pursuant to Article 10 of Regulation (EU) No 1025/2012, request one or more European standardisation organisations to draft harmonised standards that satisfy the essential requirements laid down in paragraph 1 of this Article.

5. The Commission may, by means of implementing acts, adopt common specifications covering any or all of the essential requirements laid down in paragraph 1 where the following conditions have been fulfilled:

(a) the Commission has requested, pursuant to Article 10(1) of Regulation (EU) No 1025/2012, one or more European standardisation organisations to draft a harmonised standard that satisfies the essential requirements laid down in paragraph 1 of this Article and:
  (i) the request has not been accepted;
  (ii) the harmonised standards addressing that request are not delivered within the deadline set in accordance with Article 10(1) of Regulation (EU) No 1025/2012; or
  (iii) the harmonised standards do not comply with the request; and

(b) no reference to harmonised standards covering the relevant essential requirements laid down in paragraph 1 of this Article is published in the *Official Journal of the European Union* in accordance with Regulation (EU) No 1025/2012 and no such reference is expected to be published within a reasonable period.

Those implementing acts shall be adopted in accordance with the examination procedure referred to in Article 46(2).

6. Before preparing a draft implementing act referred to in paragraph 5 of this Article, the Commission shall inform the committee referred to in Article 22 of Regulation (EU) No 1025/2012 that it considers that the conditions in paragraph 5 of this Article have been fulfilled.

7. When preparing the draft implementing act referred to in paragraph 5, the Commission shall take into account the advice of the EDIB and views of other relevant bodies or expert groups and shall duly consult all relevant stakeholders.

8. The participants in data spaces that offer data or data services to other participants in data spaces that meet the common specifications established by implementing acts referred to in paragraph 5 or parts thereof shall be presumed to be in conformity with the essential requirements laid down in paragraph 1 to the extent that those requirements are covered by such common specifications or parts thereof.

9. Where a harmonised standard is adopted by a European standardisation organisation and proposed to the Commission for the purpose of publishing its reference in the *Official Journal of the European Union*, the Commission shall assess the harmonised standard in accordance with Regulation (EU) No 1025/2012. Where the reference of a harmonised standard is published in the *Official Journal of the European Union*, the Commission shall repeal the implementing acts referred to in paragraph 5 of this Article, or parts thereof which cover the same essential requirements as those covered by that harmonised standard.

10. When a Member State considers that a common specification does not entirely satisfy the essential requirements laid down in paragraph 1, it shall inform the Commission thereof by submitting a detailed explanation. The Commission shall assess that detailed explanation and may, if appropriate, amend the implementing act establishing the common specification in question.

11. The Commission may adopt guidelines taking into account the proposal of the EDIB in accordance with Article 30, point (h), of Regulation (EU) 2022/868 laying down interoperable frameworks for common standards and practices for the functioning of common European data spaces.

Article 34
Interoperability for the purposes of in-parallel use of data processing services

1. The requirements laid down in Article 23, Article 24, Article 25(2), points (a)(ii), (a)(iv), (e) and (f) and Article 30(2) to (5) shall also apply *mutatis mutandis* to providers of data processing services to facilitate interoperability for the purposes of in-parallel use of data processing services.

2. Where a data processing service is being used in parallel with another data processing service, the providers of data processing services may impose data egress charges, but only for the purpose of passing on egress costs incurred, without exceeding such costs.

Article 35
Interoperability of data processing services

1. Open interoperability specifications and harmonised standards for the interoperability of data processing services shall:

(a) achieve, where technically feasible, interoperability between different data processing services that cover the same service type;
(b) enhance portability of digital assets between different data processing services that cover the same service type;
(c) facilitate, where technically feasible, functional equivalence between different data processing services referred to in Article 30(1) that cover the same service type;
(d) not have an adverse impact on the security and integrity of data processing services and data;
(e) be designed in such a way so as to allow for technical advances and the inclusion of new functions and innovation in data processing services.

2. Open interoperability specifications and harmonised standards for the interoperability of data processing services shall adequately address:

(a) the cloud interoperability aspects of transport interoperability, syntactic interoperability, semantic data interoperability, behavioural interoperability and policy interoperability;
(b) the cloud data portability aspects of data syntactic portability, data semantic portability and data policy portability;
(c) the cloud application aspects of application syntactic portability, application instruction portability, application metadata portability, application behaviour portability and application policy portability.

3. Open interoperability specifications shall comply with Annex II to Regulation (EU) No 1025/2012.

4. After taking into account relevant international and European standards and self-regulatory initiatives, the Commission may, in accordance with Article 10(1) of Regulation (EU) No 1025/2012, request one or more European standardisation organisations to draft harmonised standards that satisfy the essential requirements laid down in paragraphs 1 and 2 of this Article.

5. The Commission may, by means of implementing acts, adopt common specifications based on open interoperability specifications covering all of the essential requirements laid down in paragraphs 1 and 2.

6. When preparing the draft implementing act referred to in paragraph 5 of this Article, the Commission shall take into account the views of the relevant competent authorities referred to in Article 37(5), point (h) and other relevant bodies or expert groups and shall duly consult all relevant stakeholders.

7. When a Member State considers that a common specification does not entirely satisfy the essential requirements laid down in paragraphs 1 and 2, it shall inform the Commission thereof by submitting a detailed explanation. The Commission shall assess that detailed explanation and may, if appropriate, amend the implementing act establishing the common specification in question.

8. For the purpose of Article 30(3), the Commission shall, by means of implementing acts, publish the references of harmonised standards and common specifications for the interoperability of data processing services in a central Union standards repository for the interoperability of data processing services.

9. The implementing acts referred to in this Article shall be adopted in accordance with the examination procedure referred to in Article 46(2).

Article 36
Essential requirements regarding smart contracts for executing data sharing agreements

1. The vendor of an application using smart contracts or, in the absence thereof, the person whose trade, business or profession involves the deployment of smart contracts for others in the context of executing an agreement or part of it, to make data available shall ensure that those smart contracts comply with the following essential requirements of:

(a) robustness and access control, to ensure that the smart contract has been designed to offer access control mechanisms and a very high degree of robustness to avoid functional errors and to withstand manipulation by third parties;
(b) safe termination and interruption, to ensure that a mechanism exists to terminate the continued execution of transactions and that the smart contract includes internal functions which can reset or instruct the contract to stop or interrupt the operation, in particular to avoid future accidental executions;
(c) data archiving and continuity, to ensure, in circumstances in which a smart contract must be terminated or deactivated, there is a possibility to archive the transactional data, smart contract logic and code in order to keep the record of operations performed on the data in the past (auditability);
(d) access control, to ensure that a smart contract is protected through rigorous access control mechanisms at the governance and smart contract layers; and
(e) consistency, to ensure consistency with the terms of the data sharing agreement that the smart contract executes.

2. The vendor of a smart contract or, in the absence thereof, the person whose trade, business or profession involves the deployment of smart contracts for others in the context of executing an agreement or part of it, to make data available shall perform a conformity assessment with a view to fulfilling the essential requirements laid down in paragraph 1 and, on the fulfilment of those requirements, issue an EU declaration of conformity.

3. By drawing up the EU declaration of conformity, the vendor of an application using smart contracts or, in the absence thereof, the person whose trade, business or profession involves the deployment of smart contracts for others in the context of executing an agreement or part of it, to make data available shall be responsible for compliance with the essential requirements laid down in paragraph 1.

4. A smart contract that meets the harmonised standards or the relevant parts thereof, the references of which are published in the *Official Journal of the European Union*, shall be presumed to be in conformity with the essential requirements laid

down in paragraph 1 to the extent that those requirements are covered by such harmonised standards or parts thereof.

5. The Commission shall, pursuant to Article 10 of Regulation (EU) No 1025/2012, request one or more European standardisation organisations to draft harmonised standards that satisfy the essential requirements laid down in paragraph 1 of this Article.

6. The Commission may, by means of implementing acts, adopt common specifications covering any or all of the essential requirements laid down in paragraph 1 where the following conditions have been fulfilled:

(a) the Commission has requested, pursuant to Article 10(1) of Regulation (EU) No 1025/2012, one or more European standardisation organisations to draft a harmonised standard that satisfies the essential requirements laid down in paragraph 1 of this Article and:
  (i) the request has not been accepted;
  (ii) the harmonised standards addressing that request are not delivered within the deadline set in accordance with Article 10(1) of Regulation (EU) No 1025/2012; or
  (iii) the harmonised standards do not comply with the request; and

(b) no reference to harmonised standards covering the relevant essential requirements laid down in paragraph 1 of this Article is published in the *Official Journal of the European Union* in accordance with Regulation (EU) No 1025/2012 and no such reference is expected to be published within a reasonable period.

Those implementing acts shall be adopted in accordance with the examination procedure referred to in Article 46(2).

7. Before preparing a draft implementing act referred to in paragraph 6 of this Article, the Commission shall inform the committee referred to in Article 22 of Regulation (EU) No 1025/2012 that it considers that the conditions in paragraph 6 of this Article have been fulfilled.

8. When preparing the draft implementing act referred to in paragraph 6, the Commission shall take into account the advice of the EDIB and views of other relevant bodies or expert groups and shall duly consult all relevant stakeholders.

9. The vendor of a smart contract or, in the absence thereof, the person whose trade, business or profession involves the deployment of smart contracts for others in the context of executing an agreement or part of it, to make data available that meet the common specifications established by implementing acts referred to in paragraph 6 or parts thereof shall be presumed to be in conformity with the essential requirements laid down in paragraph 1 to the extent that those requirements are covered by such common specifications or parts thereof.

10. Where a harmonised standard is adopted by a European standardisation organisation and proposed to the Commission for the purpose of publishing its reference in the *Official Journal of the European Union*, the Commission shall assess the harmonised standard in accordance with Regulation (EU) No 1025/2012. Where the reference of a harmonised standard is published in the *Official Journal of the European Union*, the Commission shall repeal the implementing acts referred to

in paragraph 6 of this Article, or parts thereof which cover the same essential requirements as those covered by that harmonised standard.

11. When a Member State considers that a common specification does not entirely satisfy the essential requirements laid down in paragraph 1, it shall inform the Commission thereof by submitting a detailed explanation. The Commission shall assess that detailed explanation and may, if appropriate, amend the implementing act establishing the common specification in question.

CHAPTER IX
IMPLEMENTATION AND ENFORCEMENT

Article 37
Competent authorities and data coordinators

1. Each Member State shall designate one or more competent authorities to be responsible for the application and enforcement of this Regulation (competent authorities). Member States may establish one or more new authorities or rely on existing authorities.

2. Where a Member State designates more than one competent authority, it shall designate a data coordinator from among them to facilitate cooperation between the competent authorities and to assist entities within the scope of this Regulation on all matters related to its application and enforcement. Competent authorities shall, in the exercise of the tasks and powers assigned to them under paragraph 5, cooperate with each other.

3. The supervisory authorities responsible for monitoring the application of Regulation (EU) 2016/679 shall be responsible for monitoring the application of this Regulation insofar as the protection of personal data is concerned. Chapters VI and VII of Regulation (EU) 2016/679 shall apply *mutatis mutandis*.

The European Data Protection Supervisor shall be responsible for monitoring the application of this Regulation insofar as it concerns the Commission, the European Central Bank or Union bodies. Where relevant, Article 62 of Regulation (EU) 2018/1725 shall apply *mutatis mutandis*.

The tasks and powers of the supervisory authorities referred to in this paragraph shall be exercised with regard to the processing of personal data.

4. Without prejudice to paragraph 1 of this Article:

(a) for specific sectoral data access and use issues related to the application of this Regulation, the competence of sectoral authorities shall be respected;
(b) the competent authority responsible for the application and enforcement of Articles 23 to 31 and Articles 34 and 35 shall have experience in the field of data and electronic communications services.

5. Member States shall ensure that the tasks and powers of the competent authorities are clearly defined and include:

(a) promoting data literacy and awareness among users and entities falling within the scope of this Regulation of the rights and obligations under this Regulation;

(b) handling complaints arising from alleged infringements of this Regulation, including in relation to trade secrets, and investigating, to the extent appropriate, the subject matter of complaints and regularly informing complainants, where relevant in accordance with national law, of the progress and the outcome of the investigation within a reasonable period, in particular if further investigation or coordination with another competent authority is necessary;
(c) conducting investigations into matters that concern the application of this Regulation, including on the basis of information received from another competent authority or other public authority;
(d) imposing effective, proportionate and dissuasive financial penalties which may include periodic penalties and penalties with retroactive effect, or initiating legal proceedings for the imposition of fines;
(e) monitoring technological and relevant commercial developments of relevance for the making available and use of data;
(f) cooperating with competent authorities of other Member States and, where relevant, with the Commission or the EDIB, to ensure the consistent and efficient application of this Regulation, including the exchange of all relevant information by electronic means, without undue delay, including regarding paragraph 10 of this Article;
(g) cooperating with the relevant competent authorities responsible for the implementation of other Union or national legal acts, including with authorities competent in the field of data and electronic communication services, with the supervisory authority responsible for monitoring the application of Regulation (EU) 2016/679 or with sectoral authorities to ensure that this Regulation is enforced consistently with other Union and national law;
(h) cooperating with the relevant competent authorities to ensure that Articles 23 to 31 and Articles 34 and 35 are enforced consistently with other Union law and self-regulation applicable to providers of data processing services;
(i) ensuring that switching charges are withdrawn in accordance with Article 29;
(j) examining the requests for data made pursuant to Chapter V.

Where designated, the data coordinator shall facilitate the cooperation referred to in points (f), (g) and (h) of the first subparagraph and shall assist the competent authorities upon their request.

6. The data coordinator, where such competent authority has been designated, shall:

(a) act as the single point of contact for all issues related to the application of this Regulation;
(b) ensure the online public availability of requests to make data available made by public sector bodies in the case of exceptional need under Chapter V and promote voluntary data sharing agreements between public sector bodies and data holders;
(c) inform the Commission, on an annual basis, of the refusals notified under Article 4(2) and (8) and Article 5(11).

7. Member States shall notify the Commission of the names of the competent authorities and of their tasks and powers and, where applicable, the name of the data coordinator. The Commission shall maintain a public register of those authorities.

8. When carrying out their tasks and exercising their powers in accordance with this Regulation, competent authorities shall remain impartial and free from any external influence, whether direct or indirect, and shall neither seek nor take instructions for individual cases from any other public authority or any private party.

9. Member States shall ensure that the competent authorities are provided with sufficient human and technical resources and relevant expertise to effectively carry out their tasks in accordance with this Regulation.

10. Entities falling within the scope of this Regulation shall be subject to the competence of the Member State where the entity is established. Where the entity is established in more than one Member State, it shall be considered to be under the competence of the Member State in which it has its main establishment, that is, where the entity has its head office or registered office from which the principal financial functions and operational control are exercised.

11. Any entity falling within the scope of this Regulation that makes connected products available or offers services in the Union, and which is not established in the Union, shall designate a legal representative in one of the Member States.

12. For the purpose of ensuring compliance with this Regulation, a legal representative shall be mandated by an entity falling within the scope of this Regulation that makes connected products available or offers services in the Union to be addressed in addition to or instead of it by competent authorities with regard to all issues related to that entity. That legal representative shall cooperate with and comprehensively demonstrate to the competent authorities, upon request, the actions taken and provisions put in place by the entity falling within the scope of this Regulation that makes connected products available or offers services in the Union to ensure compliance with this Regulation.

13. An entity falling within the scope of this Regulation that makes connected products available or offers services in the Union, shall be considered to be under the competence of the Member State in which its legal representative is located. The designation of a legal representative by such an entity shall be without prejudice to the liability of, and any legal action that could be initiated against, such an entity. Until such time as an entity designates a legal representative in accordance with this Article, it shall be under the competence of all Member States, where applicable, for the purposes of ensuring the application and enforcement of this Regulation. Any competent authority may exercise its competence, including by imposing effective, proportionate and dissuasive penalties, provided that the entity is not subject to enforcement proceedings under this Regulation regarding the same facts by another competent authority.

14. Competent authorities shall have the power to request from users, data holders, or data recipients, or their legal representatives, falling under the competence of their Member State all information necessary to verify compliance with this Regulation. Any request for information shall be proportionate to the performance of the underlying task and shall be reasoned.

15. Where a competent authority in one Member State requests assistance or enforcement measures from a competent authority in another Member State, it shall submit a reasoned request. A competent authority shall, upon receiving such a

request, provide a response, detailing the actions that have been taken or which are intended to be taken, without undue delay.

16. Competent authorities shall respect the principles of confidentiality and of professional and commercial secrecy and shall protect personal data in accordance with Union or national law. Any information exchanged in the context of a request for assistance and provided pursuant to this Article shall be used only in respect of the matter for which it was requested.

Article 38
Right to lodge a complaint

1. Without prejudice to any other administrative or judicial remedy, natural and legal persons shall have the right to lodge a complaint, individually or, where relevant, collectively, with the relevant competent authority in the Member State of their habitual residence, place of work or establishment if they consider that their rights under this Regulation have been infringed. The data coordinator shall, upon request, provide all the necessary information to natural and legal persons for the lodging of their complaints with the appropriate competent authority.

2. The competent authority with which the complaint has been lodged shall inform the complainant, in accordance with national law, of the progress of the proceedings and of the decision taken.

3. Competent authorities shall cooperate to handle and resolve complaints effectively and in a timely manner, including by exchanging all relevant information by electronic means, without undue delay. This cooperation shall not affect the cooperation mechanisms provided for by Chapters VI and VII of Regulation (EU) 2016/679 and by Regulation (EU) 2017/2394.

Article 39
Right to an effective judicial remedy

1. Notwithstanding any administrative or other non-judicial remedy, any affected natural and legal person shall have the right to an effective judicial remedy with regard to legally binding decisions taken by competent authorities.

2. Where a competent authority fails to act on a complaint, any affected natural and legal person shall, in accordance with national law, either have the right to an effective judicial remedy or access to review by an impartial body with the appropriate expertise.

3. Proceedings pursuant to this Article shall be brought before the courts or tribunals of the Member State of the competent authority against which the judicial remedy is sought individually or, where relevant, collectively by the representatives of one or more natural or legal persons.

Article 40
Penalties

1. Member States shall lay down the rules on penalties applicable to infringements of this Regulation and shall take all measures necessary to ensure that they are implemented. The penalties provided for shall be effective, proportionate and dissuasive.

2. Member States shall by 12 September 2025 notify the Commission of those rules and measures and shall notify it without delay of any subsequent amendment affecting them. The Commission shall regularly update and maintain an easily accessible public register of those measures.

3. Member States shall take into account the recommendations of the EDIB and the following non-exhaustive criteria for the imposition of penalties for infringements of this Regulation:

(a) the nature, gravity, scale and duration of the infringement;
(b) any action taken by the infringing party to mitigate or remedy the damage caused by the infringement;
(c) any previous infringements by the infringing party;
(d) the financial benefits gained or losses avoided by the infringing party due to the infringement, insofar as such benefits or losses can be reliably established;
(e) any other aggravating or mitigating factor applicable to the circumstances of the case;
(f) infringing party's annual turnover in the preceding financial year in the Union.

4. For infringements of the obligations laid down in Chapter II, III and V of this Regulation, the supervisory authorities responsible for monitoring the application of Regulation (EU) 2016/679 may within their scope of competence impose administrative fines in accordance with Article 83 of Regulation (EU) 2016/679 and up to the amount referred to in Article 83(5) of that Regulation.

5. For infringements of the obligations laid down in Chapter V of this Regulation, the European Data Protection Supervisor may impose within its scope of competence administrative fines in accordance with Article 66 of Regulation (EU) 2018/1725 up to the amount referred to in Article 66(3) of that Regulation.

Article 41 Model contractual terms and standard contractual clauses

The Commission, before 12 September 2025, shall develop and recommend non-binding model contractual terms on data access and use, including terms on reasonable compensation and the protection of trade secrets, and non-binding standard contractual clauses for cloud computing contracts to assist parties in drafting and negotiating contracts with fair, reasonable and non-discriminatory contractual rights and obligations.

Article 42
Role of the EDIB

The EDIB established by the Commission as an expert group pursuant to Article 29 of Regulation (EU) 2022/868, in which competent authorities shall be represented, shall support the consistent application of this Regulation by:

(a) advising and assisting the Commission with regard to developing consistent practice of competent authorities in the enforcement of Chapters II, III, V and VII;
(b) facilitating cooperation between competent authorities through capacity-building and the exchange of information, in particular by establishing methods for the efficient exchange of information relating to the enforcement of the rights and obligations under Chapters II, III and V in cross-border cases, including coordination with regard to the setting of penalties;
(c) advising and assisting the Commission with regard to:
  (i) whether to request the drafting of harmonised standards referred to in Article 33(4), Article 35(4) and Article 36(5);
  (ii) the preparation of the implementing acts referred to in Article 33(5), Article 35(5) and (8) and Article 36(6);
  (iii) the preparation of the delegated acts referred to in Article 29(7) and Article 33(2); and
  (iv) the adoption of the guidelines laying down interoperable frameworks for common standards and practices for the functioning of common European data spaces referred to in Article 33(11).

CHAPTER X
SUI GENERIS RIGHT UNDER DIRECTIVE 96/9/EC

Article 43
Databases containing certain data

The *sui generis* right provided for in Article 7 of Directive 96/9/EC shall not apply when data is obtained from or generated by a connected product or related service falling within the scope of this Regulation, in particular in relation to Articles 4 and 5 thereof.

CHAPTER XI
FINAL PROVISIONS

Article 44
Other Union legal acts governing rights and obligations on data access and use

1. The specific obligations for the making available of data between businesses, between businesses and consumers, and on exceptional basis between businesses and public bodies, in Union legal acts that entered into force on or before 11 January 2024, and delegated or implementing acts pursuant thereto, shall remain unaffected.

2. This Regulation is without prejudice to Union law specifying, in light of the needs of a sector, a common European data space, or an area of public interest, further requirements, in particular in relation to:

(a) technical aspects of data access;
(b) limits on the rights of data holders to access or use certain data provided by users;
(c) aspects going beyond data access and use.

3. This Regulation, with the exception of Chapter V, is without prejudice to Union and national law providing for access to and authorising the use of data for scientific research purposes.

Article 45
Exercise of the delegation

1. The power to adopt delegated acts is conferred on the Commission subject to the conditions laid down in this Article.

2. The power to adopt delegated acts referred to in Article 29(7) and Article 33(2) shall be conferred on the Commission for an indeterminate period of time from 11 January 2024.

3. The delegation of power referred to in Article 29(7) and Article 33(2) may be revoked at any time by the European Parliament or by the Council. A decision to revoke shall put an end to the delegation of the power specified in that decision. It shall take effect the day following the publication of the decision in the *Official Journal of the European Union* or at a later date specified therein. It shall not affect the validity of any delegated acts already in force.

4. Before adopting a delegated act, the Commission shall consult experts designated by each Member State in accordance with the principles laid down in the Interinstitutional Agreement of 13 April 2016 on Better Law-Making.

5. As soon as it adopts a delegated act, the Commission shall notify it simultaneously to the European Parliament and to the Council.

6. A delegated act adopted pursuant to Article 29(7) or Article 33(2) shall enter into force only if no objection has been expressed either by the European Parliament or by the Council within a period of three months of notification of that act to the European Parliament and to the Council or if, before the expiry of that period, the European Parliament and the Council have both informed the Commission that they will not object. That period shall be extended by three months at the initiative of the European Parliament or of the Council.

Article 46
Committee procedure

1. The Commission shall be assisted by the Committee established by Regulation (EU) 2022/868. That committee shall be a committee within the meaning of Regulation (EU) No 182/2011.

2. Where reference is made to this paragraph, Article 5 of Regulation (EU) No 182/2011 shall apply.

Article 47
Amendment to Regulation (EU) 2017/2394

In the Annex to Regulation (EU) 2017/2394 the following point is added:

'29. Regulation (EU) 2023/2854 of the European Parliament and of the Council of 13 December 2023 on harmonised rules on fair access to and use of data and amending Regulation (EU) 2017/2394 and Directive (EU) 2020/1828 (Data Act) (OJ L, 2023/2854, 22.12.2023, ELI: http://data.europa.eu/eli/reg/2023/2854/oj).'

Article 48
Amendment to Directive (EU) 2020/1828

In Annex I to Directive (EU) 2020/1828 the following point is added:

'(69) Regulation (EU) 2023/2854 of the European Parliament and of the Council of 13 December 2023 on harmonised rules on fair access to and use of data and amending Regulation (EU) 2017/2394 and Directive (EU) 2020/1828 (Data Act) (OJ L, 2023/2854, 22.12.2023, ELI: http://data.europa.eu/eli/reg/2023/2854/oj).'

Article 49
Evaluation and review

1. By 12 September 2028, the Commission shall carry out an evaluation of this Regulation and submit a report on its main findings to the European Parliament and to the Council, and to the European Economic and Social Committee. That evaluation shall assess, in particular:

(a) situations to be considered to be situations of exceptional need for the purpose of Article 15 of this Regulation and the application of Chapter V of this Regulation in practice, in particular the experience in the application of Chapter V of this Regulation by public sector bodies, the Commission, the European Central Bank and Union bodies; the number and outcome of the proceedings brought to the competent authority under Article 18(5) on the application of Chapter V of this Regulation, as reported by the competent authorities; the impact of other obligations laid down in Union or national law for the purposes of complying with requests for access to information; the impact of voluntary data-sharing mechanisms, such as those put in place by data altruism organisations recognised under Regulation (EU) 2022/868, on meeting the objectives of Chapter V of this Regulation, and the role of personal data in the context of Article 15 of this Regulation, including the evolution of privacy-enhancing technologies;

(b) the impact of this Regulation on the use of data in the economy, including on data innovation, data monetisation practices and data intermediation services, as well as on data sharing within the common European data spaces;
(c) the accessibility and use of different categories and types of data;
(d) the exclusion of certain categories of enterprises as beneficiaries under Article 5;
(e) the absence of any impact on intellectual property rights;
(f) the impact on trade secrets, including on the protection against their unlawful acquisition, use and disclosure, as well as the impact of the mechanism allowing the data holder to refuse the user's request under Article 4(8) and Article 5(11), taking into account, to the extent possible, any revision of Directive (EU) 2016/943;
(g) whether the list of unfair contractual terms referred to in Article 13 is up-to-date in light of new business practices and the rapid pace of market innovation;
(h) changes in the contractual practices of providers of data processing services and whether this results in sufficient compliance with Article 25;
(i) the diminution of charges imposed by providers of data processing services for the switching process, in line with the gradual withdrawal of switching charges pursuant to Article 29;
(j) the interplay of this Regulation with other Union legal acts of relevance to the data economy;
(k) the prevention of unlawful governmental access to non-personal data;
(l) the efficacy of the enforcement regime required under Article 37;
(m) the impact of this Regulation on SMEs with regard to their capacity to innovate and to the availability of data processing services for users in the Union and the burden of complying with new obligations.

2. By 12 September 2028, the Commission shall carry out an evaluation of this Regulation and submit a report on its main findings to the European Parliament and to the Council, and to the European Economic and Social Committee. That evaluation shall assess the impact of Articles 23 to 31 and Articles 34 and 35, in particular regarding pricing and the diversity of data processing services offered within the Union, with a special focus on SME providers.

3. Member States shall provide the Commission with the information necessary for the preparation of the reports referred to in paragraphs 1 and 2.

4. On the basis of the reports referred to in paragraphs 1 and 2, the Commission may, where appropriate, submit a legislative proposal to the European Parliament and to the Council to amend this Regulation.

Article 50
Entry into force and application

This Regulation shall enter into force on the twentieth day following that of its publication in the *Official Journal of the European Union*.

It shall apply from 12 September 2025.

The obligation resulting from Article 3(1) shall apply to connected products and the services related to them placed on the market after 12 September 2026.

Chapter III shall apply in relation to obligations to make data available under Union law or national legislation adopted in accordance with Union law, which enters into force after 12 September 2025.

Chapter IV shall apply to contracts concluded after 12 September 2025.

Chapter IV shall apply from 12 September 2027 to contracts concluded on or before 12 September 2025 provided that they are:

(a) of indefinite duration; or
(b) due to expire at least 10 years from 11 January 2024.

This Regulation shall be binding in its entirety and directly applicable in all Member States.

Done at Strasbourg, 13 December 2023.

For the European Parliament
The President
R. METSOLA

For the Council
The President
P. NAVARRO RÍOS

Index

Bold numbers refer to chapters, normal ones to margin numbers.

Access
- fair and non-discriminatory **1** 18
- international **9** 9

Access by design
- deviating agreements **3** 60
- generated data **3** 52
- material defect **3** 59
- non-compliance, legal consequences **3** 55 et seqq.
- obliged party **3** 47
- prerequisites **3** 46
- product design obligation **3** 3
- product design requirements **3** 48 et seqq.
- user account **3** 54

Access procedure **10** 39

Acquiring provider **5** 34 et seqq.

Action for failure to act **8** 39

Addressees **2** 13

Administrative act
- data request **7** 14
- legal remedy **8** 35

AI Regulation **1** 22

Application and enforcement **3** 58

Area of application **2** 8 et seqq.

Artificial intelligence, Digital Strategy **1** 22

Authority, responsible, EDIB **10** 10, 41

Automotive sector **2** 38

Big data analysis **3** 99

Black clause **4** 14 et seqq.

Burden of proof rule, fairness test **4** 12

Business data **10** 28

Business model, Data Strategy **1** 10

Business representative **10** 40

Business-to-Government (B2G) **7** 1

Cancellation, cloud switching **5** 51

Charges, data processing service **6** 10

Charter of Fundamental Rights, related service **3** 36

Civil court enforcement **8** 41 et seqq.
- action for performance **8** 42
- temporary injunction **8** 43

CLOUD Act **9** 20

Cloud computing service
- ENISA **5** 22
- NIST **5** 20
- term **5** 19 et seqq.

Cloud switching **5** 1 et seqq., **8** 41
- addressees **5** 9 et seqq., 34
- cancellation **5** 51
- charges **5** 65
- compatibility **5** 60
- competition promotion **5** 2
- constellations **5** 3
- contract **5** 69 et seqq.
- contract, minimum content **5** 77
- contract design **5** 76
- customer information **5** 72 et seqq.
- destination provider **5** 34 et seqq.
- duty of loyalty **5** 68
- duty to inform **5** 69
- formal requirements **5** 76
- functional equivalence **5** 57
- IaaS **5** 54 et seqq.
- infrastructure provider **5** 54 et seqq.
- lock-in effect **5** 5
- MCTs **5** 82
- online register **5** 75
- open interface **5** 59
- SCCs **5** 8, 76 et seqq., 82
- small and micro enterprise **5** 37 et seq.
- source provider **5** 34 et seqq.
- switch **5** 51
- switching charges **5** 64 et seqq.
- technical aspects **5** 53 et seqq.
- termination **5** 80
- transparency obligation **5** 70 et seq.

Companies, business-to-business relations **3** 137 et seqq.
Compatibility, cloud switching **5** 60
Compensation for making data available **3** 160, **7** 60 et seqq.
- amount **3** 163
Competitive product, non-competition clause **3** 92 et seqq.
Competitor, direct **3** 115
Complaint **3** 109, 113, **8** 26 et seqq.
- compensation for making data available **7** 67
- data access **8** 29
- data request **7** 73
- forfeiture **8** 32
- procedure **8** 27
- public sector body **8** 30
- shape **8** 32
Confidentiality, supervisory authority **8** 10
Confidentiality agreement **3** 105
- intended use **3** 106
Confidentiality measure **3** 102
Conflict clause **2** 17
Connected product **3** 3, 25 et seqq.
- smartphone **3** 28
- term **3** 26
- use cases **3** 27
Connecting Europe Facility **10** 33
Consent form, EDIB **10** 47
Consideration making data available, transparency **3** 165
Consumer
- EU consumer protection law **3** 141
- making data available **3** 139
Content data **3** 42
Contract design **2** 22, **8** 41
- duties, commencement **2** 26
Contractual partner, term **3** 20
Contractual term, unfair **3** 156 et seqq., **4** 1 et seqq.
Contractual term control, making data available **3** 135
Cooperation, cross-border
- data request **7** 68 et seqq.
- notification obligation **7** 69
Customer **5** 39 et seqq.
Customer information, cloud switching **5** 72 et seqq.
Customising **5** 43 et seqq.
Cybersecurity **10** 39
- Digital Strategy **1** 23
- EDIB **10** 27

Dark patterns **3** 155
Data
- accessibility, easy **3** 65
- aggregated **3** 125
- anonymisation, costs **7** 64
- as a trade secret **3** 98 et seq.
- categories **2** 11
- covered **2** 11
- further use **7** 48
- preparation **3** 41
- private sector **2** 12, **7** 10
- pseudonymisation, costs **7** 64
- raw data **3** 99
- sensor-generated **3** 123
- sharing **3** 154
- term **1** 25
Data access **3** 1 et seqq., **8** 41
- actors **3** 12 et seqq.
- ad hoc **7** 46
- claims **3** 45 et seqq.
- complaint **8** 29
- duty to inform **3** 75 et seqq.
- making data available by data holder **3** 61 et seqq.
- negotiations **4** 1
- regulation system **3** 2
- relationship to data protection law **3** 82 et seqq.
- request **3** 114
- restriction **3** 89 et seqq.
- sharing data with third parties **3** 68 et seqq.
- subject matter **3** 24 et seqq.
Data access officer **8** 16
Data acquisition **7** 30
Data altruism, EDIB **10** 24

Database **3** 122 et seqq.
– mixed **3** 124
Database maker right, barrier **3** 122
Data coordinator **8** 12 et seq., 26
Data economy **1** 6
– actors **2** 4
– domestic market **10** 29
– EDIB **10** 35 et seqq.
Data exchange **6** 1
Data expertise **1** 18
– Data Strategy **1** 13
Data extraction fee **6** 10
Data Governance Act (DGA) **1** 30
– third country transfer **9** 3
Data holder **3** 137, 140, **7** 10
– controller under data protection law **3** 19
– data use **3** 127
– right of defence **3** 119
– term **3** 16 et seqq.
use of data **3** 127
Data holdership **3** 127
Data portability **6** 12
Data processing service **5** 10 et seqq.
– administrative expenses **5** 13
– application exceptions **5** 42 et seqq.
– charges **6** 10
– cloud computing service **5** 19 et seqq.
– computing resources, elastic **5** 16
– computing resources, scalable **5** 16
– customer **5** 39 et seqq.
– distributed computing resources **5** 17
– edge computing service **5** 28
– hosting service **5** 27
– interaction **5** 13
– interoperability **6** 8
– more customised **5** 43 et seqq.
– network access **5** 12
– on-premise service **5** 33
– provider **5** 34 et seqq.
– requirements **5** 52 et seqq.
– shared pool **5** 15
– switching **5** 1 et seqq.
– term **5** 10
– test and evaluation purposes **5** 46
Data protection, EDIB **10** 27
Data protection law **3** 82 et seqq.
– applicability **3** 83
– basis for authorisation **3** 84
– conflict case **3** 83
– relationship to the DA **2** 19 et seq.
Data protection supervisory authority **8** 3
– personal data **8** 4
Data provision, EDIB **10** 25
Data quality, fairness test **4** 15
Data recipient **3** 68
– business **3** 140
– term **3** 23
Data relation, fairness test **4** 4, 19
Data request **7** 14 et seqq.
– administrative act **7** 14
– challenge **7** 74
– competent authority **7** 41
– complaint **7** 73
– cooperation, cross-border **7** 68 et seqq.
– data transfer, notification obligation **7** 59
– data transfer for research purposes **7** 56
– data transfer to public authorities **7** 53 et seqq.
– data transfer to third parties **7** 54
– GDPR **7** 76
– informal requirement **7** 15
– information request **7** 19
– legal protection **7** 72 et seqq.
– legal protection, third parties **7** 77
– making data available **7** 32
– model template **7** 21
– modification **7** 35
– personal data **7** 40
– rejection **7** 35, 39
– relationship to other data provision obligations **7** 42 et seqq.
– requirements, formal **7** 17 et seqq.
– requirements, material **7** 20 et seq.
– rescissory action **7** 75

- risks **7** 38
- scope of usage **7** 47 et seqq.
- trade secret, disclosure **7** 34
- trade secret, protection **7** 50

Data room **10** 33

Data sharing **3** 154
- agreement **3** 134, 156
- interoperability **6** 5 et seqq.
- user requirements **3** 71

Data sovereignty, user **3** 159

Data space
- Data Strategy **1** 14
- interoperability **6** 5 et seqq.

Data Strategy **1** 4 et seqq., **2** 3
- business models **1** 10
- data expertise **1** 13
- data space **1** 14
- data usage **1** 8

Data transfer
- data coordinator **8** 12 et seq.
- EDIB **10** 25
- international **9** 8 et seqq.

Data use
- cross-sectoral **10** 32 et seqq.
- data holder **3** 127
- Data Strategy **1** 8
- limited **3** 129
- non-personal data **3** 129, **7** 29
- personal data **3** 129

Destination provider **5** 34 et seqq.

Digital health authority **10** 37

Digital Markets Act (DMA) **1** 21

Digital Omnibus **1** 26 et seqq.
- trade secrets **1** 31

Digital Services Act (DSA) **1** 21

Digital Strategy **1** 15 et seqq.
- Artificial Intelligence **1** 22
- components **1** 19
- cybersecurity **1** 23
- gatekeeper **1** 21
- information security **1** 23
- key measures **1** 17
- objectives **1** 16

Disclosure, prohibition **3** 131

Dispute settlement **3** 109, 113
- making data available **3** 166
- subject matter of the dispute **3** 176

Dispute settlement body
- accessibility **3** 172
- certification **3** 171 et seqq.
- decision, effect **3** 177 et seq.
- determination of fees **3** 175
- efficient decision-making **3** 172
- expertise **3** 172
- impartiality **3** 172
- independence **3** 172
- list **3** 174
- making data available **3** 166, 170
- private organisation **3** 173

Dispute settlement procedure
- legal remedy **3** 178
- making data available **3** 170

Duty of loyalty, cloud switching **5** 68

Duty to inform
- cloud switching **5** 69
- data access **3** 75 et seqq.
- making data available **3** 4

Duty to inform, data access
- authorised person **3** 77
- content details **3** 79
- obliged party **3** 76
- provision **3** 77

Edge computing service **5** 28 et seqq.
- description **5** 29

Edge service **5** 28 et seqq.

Effects **2** 5

Entry into force **2** 24

ePrivacy Directive **2** 17, 19

EU Ecolabel **10** 3

European Central Bank (ECB) **7** 5

European Data Innovation Board (EDIB) **10** 1 et seqq., 25
- application **10** 11
- cast **10** 7
- chair **10** 16
- consent form **10** 47
- consultancy, technical **10** 31
- consultancy function **10** 19
- cooperation **10** 41 et seqq.

- cybersecurity **10** 27
- data altruism **10** 24
- data altruistic organisation **10** 44
- data protection **10** 27
- data switching service **10** 44
- EU Commission **10** 16
- exchange of information **10** 44
- expert **10** 13
- expertise **10** 13, 20
- further use **10** 24, 43
- implementation of EU legislation **10** 20
- implementing act **10** 47
- internal organisation **10** 17
- interoperability **10** 36
- meeting **10** 16
- members **10** 8 et seqq., 12
- members, categories **10** 9
- organisation **10** 15 et seqq.
- public body **10** 43
- recommendations **10** 18
- representatives of the authorities **10** 10, 14, 26, 49
- rules of procedure **10** 15
- shared data room **10** 32, 38
- stakeholders **10** 9, 28
- standardisation **10** 29 et seqq.
- standardised guidelines **10** 27 et seq.
- standardised practices **10** 23 et seqq.
- subgroups **10** 17
- subject areas **10** 22
- support function **10** 19
- tasks **10** 18 et seqq., 22
- transparency register **10** 9
- voting **10** 15

European Data Protection Board (EDPB) **10** 4, 10

European Data Protection Supervisor (EDPS) **10** 10
- penalties **8** 24

European Data Space **1** 5

European Health Data Space (EHDS) **1** 11 et seq., **2** 37, **6** 5, **10** 37

European interoperability framework **10** 33

European Union Agency for Cybersecurity (ENISA) **10** 4, 10

Exceptional need **7** 22 et seqq.
- making data available **7** 1 et seqq.
- obligation to provide evidence **7** 31
- public emergency **7** 24 et seqq.
- requirements **7** 13 et seqq.

Exchange of information **10** 44

Exclusion of application **2** 16

Expert group **10** 2
- formal **10** 7
- register **10** 16

Factual control **3** 119

Fairness control, data sharing agreement **3** 156

Fairness test **4** 1, 13 et seqq.
- B2C relationship **4** 9
- black clause **4** 14 et seqq.
- burden of proof rule **4** 12
- Clause Directive **4** 8
- content control, split **4** 5
- data relation **4** 4, 15, 19
- general clause **4** 20 et seqq.
- general clause, good faith **4** 23
  general term, good commercial practice **4** 22
- grey clause **4** 17 et seqq.
- reduction to preserve validity **4** 24
- scope, material **4** 4 et seqq.
- scope, personal **4** 3
- scope, temporal **4** 7
- unilateral imposition **4** 10 et seqq.

Federal Network Agency **8** 2

Financial equalisation
- for making data available **7** 60 et seqq.
- small and microenterprises **7** 61

FRAND conditions **2** 2
- fair **3** 147
- making data available **3** 134, 136 et seqq., 144 et seqq.
- non-discriminatory **3** 147
- patent law **3** 149 et seqq.
- procedure **3** 149 et seqq.
- reasonable **3** 147

Freedom from instructions, supervisory authority **8** 11
Freedom of contract **2** 22
Free Flow of Data Regulation **1** 30, 32
Fulfilment of statutory tasks **7** 28 et seqq.
Functional equivalence
- cloud switching **5** 57
- IaaS **5** 56
Further use
- EDIB **10** 24, 43
- from data **7** 48
Further users, third country transfer **9** 21

Gatekeeper **3** 70
- Digital Strategy **1** 21
General Data Protection Regulation (GDPR) **2** 17, 19, **7** 76
- demarcation **9** 5
- third country transfer **9** 1
General term, fairness test **4** 20 et seqq.
Generated data **3** 52 et seq.
Goals **2** 1 et seqq.
Goods with digital elements **3** 32
Government organisation **9** 11
Government-to-Government (G2G) **7** 10
Grey clause **4** 17 et seqq.
GTC law **4** 11
Guest access **3** 54

Harmonised rules **2** 9
Head office, competence, supervisory authority **8** 14
Health data **10** 37
History of origin **2** 7
Hosting service **5** 19, 27

ICT infrastructure **5** 49
ICT standardisation **10** 33
Implementation deadline **2** 24
Independence, supervisory authority **8** 11 et seqq.
Information security, Digital Strategy **1** 23
Infrastructure **1** 18
Infrastructure-as-a-Service (IaaS)
- cloud switching **5** 54 et seqq.
- functional equivalence **5** 56
Infrastructure provider, cloud switching **5** 54 et seqq.
Innovation, aftermarket **3** 94
Intellectual property **10** 28
International agreement **9** 15
- exceptions **9** 17
International data access, EDIB **10** 25
International transfer **9** 8 et seqq.
Internet of Things product **3** 26
Interoperability **6** 1 et seqq.
- data portability **6** 12
- data processing service **6** 8
- delegated legislation **6** 7, 13
- minimum requirements **6** 4
- smart contracts **6** 14 et seqq.
- specifications and standards **6** 11
- transparency **6** 6

Legal protection **7** 72 et seqq.
- complaint **7** 73
- data request **7** 72 et seqq.
- rescissory action **7** 75
- third party **7** 77
Legal remedy **8** 34 et seqq.
- action for failure to act **8** 39
- administrative act **8** 35
- enforcement action **8** 35
- jurisdiction **8** 40
- multipolar legal relationships **8** 36
- rescissory action **8** 35
- right of action **8** 36
Lock-in effect **10** 39
- cloud switching **5** 5

Making data available **3** 1 et seqq., 132 et seqq., 154
- appropriate consideration **3** 134
- by data holder **3** 61 et seqq.
- compensation **3** 160, **7** 60 et seqq.

– compensation, calculation **7** 63
– compensation, complaint **7** 67
– compensation, transparency **3** 165
– consideration, amount of **3** 152
– consumer **3** 139
– contractual term control **3** 135
– costs **3** 162
– dispute **3** 167
– dispute settlement, out-of-court **3** 166
– dispute settlement body **3** 166, 170
– dispute settlement procedure **3** 170
– duty to inform **3** 4
– entitled body **7** 5
– entitled entity **7** 4 et seqq.
– entitled entity, obligations **7** 49 et seqq.
– exceptional need **7** 1 et seqq.
– FRAND conditions **3** 134, 136 et seqq., 144 et seqq.
– G2G **7** 10
– in situ **7** 33
– investment **3** 162
– legal right of access **3** 63
– obligated party **7** 10 et seqq.
– prohibition of discrimination **3** 158
– real time **3** 64
– regulation system **3** 2
– requirements **3** 64
– sharing **3** 6
– small and microenterprises **7** 11
– time of application **3** 143
– transparency requirement **3** 153 et seqq.
– user requirement **3** 66

Manufacturer **3** 13
– term **3** 15

Marketplace principle **2** 14 et seq.

Material defect, access by design **3** 59

Metadata **3** 53

Mobility Data Space **2** 37

Model Contractual Terms (MCTs) **2** 23, **3** 102, 152, 160 et seq.
– cloud switching **5** 82

Multi-stakeholder platform **10** 33

Mutual legal assistance treaty **9** 15

Network access, location-independent **5** 12

Non-compete clause **7** 50

Non-personal data **3** 85
– use **3** 129

Non-profit research organisation **3** 164

Obligation to make data available **3** 5, 142
– area of application **3** 137
– implementation deadline **2** 25
– start **2** 25

One-stop shop **8** 14

Online register, cloud switching **5** 75

On-premise service **5** 33

Open Data Directive **1** 9, 30

Open interface, cloud switching **5** 59

Original provider **5** 34 et seqq.

Overclaiming **3** 100 et seqq.

Patent law
– compulsory licence **3** 144
– standard-essential patent **3** 144

Penalties
– criteria **8** 20
– EDPS **8** 24
– fine **8** 22, 24
– notification obligation of the Member States **8** 23
– OWiG **8** 20
– recommendations of the EDIB **8** 20

Penalty **8** 19 et seqq.

Personal data **3** 84
– data use **3** 129

Preparation, data **3** 41

Privacy by design **3** 83

Private autonomy **2** 18

Private sector data **2** 12

Product data **3** 37 et seqq.
– term **3** 38

Product design obligation **2** 27 et seqq.
- access by design **3** 3
- relevant date **2** 29 et seqq.

Product version **2** 33

Prohibition of cartels, barrier **3** 126

Prohibition of circumvention **3** 118

Prohibition of discrimination, making data available **3** 158

Prosecution **2** 18

Protection mechanism, data access request **3** 114 et seqq.

Protective letter **8** 33

Protective measure
- appropriateness **9** 26
- legal **9** 24
- organisational **9** 25
- technical **9** 23
- third country transfer **9** 22 et seqq.

Public emergency **7** 24 et seqq.
- determination **7** 27

Public interest **7** 28 et seqq.

Public recognition **7** 60

Public sector body **7** 2, 6
- complaint **8** 30

Purpose **2** 1

Purpose of the contract, determination **3** 115

Raw data, term **3** 40

Reasonable consideration, making data available **3** 134

Refusal of access
- complaint **3** 109, 113
- dispute settlement **3** 109, 113
- duty to substantiate **3** 108
- economic damage **3** 111
- lack of secrecy **3** 107
- notification obligation **3** 108

Regulatory focus **2** 6

Related service **3** 29 et seqq.
- Charter of Fundamental Rights **3** 36
- goods with digital element **3** 32
- term **3** 30
- use cases **3** 31

Related service data **3** 37 et seqq.
- term **3** 39

Relationship to data protection **2** 19 et seq.

Relationship to trade secret protection **2** 21

Relevant market concept, market definition under antitrust law **3** 93

Representative, supervisory authority **8** 15

Representative of the authority **10** 46, 49

Requirement of certainty **3** 116

Rescissory action, data request **7** 75

Research **3** 164

Restriction of competition, competitive product **3** 92 et seqq.

Reverse engineering **3** 94

Right of access to data
- competitor **3** 126
- third party **3** 114
- user-accessible **3** 114

Right of action **8** 36

Right of defence, data holder **3** 119

Right to refuse performance, notification obligation **3** 91

Schrems II **9** 22

Security, requirements **3** 90 et seq., **10** 39

Service data **3** 37 et seqq.

Service type **5** 48

Shared data room **10** 32, 36, 38

Sharing of data **3** 6

Sharing of data with third parties
- limitation **3** 73
- prerequisites **3** 70

Small and medium-sized enterprises (SME) **5** 37 et seq., **7** 11
- making data available, compensation **3** 164

Small and microenterprises
- exceptions **3** 9 et seqq.

– financial compensation **7** 61
– subcontractor **3** 10
Smart contract **3** 117, **6** 1 et seqq.
– interoperability **6** 14 et seqq.
Smartphone **3** 28
Sole source database **3** 123
Source provider **5** 34 et seqq.
Stakeholder **10** 38
– EDIB **10** 9
Standard Contractual Clauses (SCCs) **3** 102
– cloud switching **5** 8, 76 et seqq., 82
Standardisation **10** 29 et seqq.
– cross-sectoral **10** 29 et seqq., 34
– EDIB **10** 29 et seqq.
– interoperability **10** 38
– legal **10** 33
– sector-specific **10** 34
– technical **10** 33
Subcontractor, small and microenterprises **3** 10
Subject matter **2** 9 et seq.
Supervisory authority **8** 2 et seqq.
– competence **8** 14
– confidentiality **8** 10
– consultancy and monitoring **8** 8
– cooperation **8** 9
– data access officer **8** 16
– data protection supervisory authority **8** 3
– freedom from instructions **8** 11
– independence **8** 11 et seqq.
– national **8** 2 et seqq.
– representative **8** 15
– representative, accountability **8** 17
– sectoral **8** 5
– supervision and enforcement **8** 7
– tasks **8** 6
Switching charges, cloud switching **5** 64 et seqq.

Technical and Organisational Measures (TOM) **3** 102
Technical protective measures **3** 117
Termination, cloud switching **5** 80
Third country **9** 6
Third country reference **9** 21
Third country transfer **9** 1 et seqq., **10** 39
– area of application **9** 5
– data processing service **9** 2
– data provision **9** 9
– further users **9** 4
– judicial and official decisions **9** 13 et seqq.
– legal uncertainty **9** 20
– more unlawful **9** 5
– protective measures **9** 22 et seqq.
– US authority **9** 20
Trade secret **3** 96 et seqq., **7** 50
– confidentiality measure **3** 102
– explanation and justification **3** 120 et seq.
– risks **3** 114
– Trade Secrets Directive **3** 121
Trade secret protection, relationship to DA **2** 21, **3** 96 et seqq.
Transparency **6** 6
Transparency obligation, cloud switching **5** 70 et seq.
Transparency register, EDIB **10** 9
Transparency requirements **3** 153 et seqq.
Transport interoperability **6** 12

Unilateral imposition **4** 10 et seqq.
Union body **7** 7 et seq.
Unity of the legal system **2** 35
US authority **9** 20
Use of data
– data holder **3** 127
– further use **7** 48
– research purposes **7** 48
User **3** 13
– data subject under data protection law **3** 22
– term **3** 21
User account **3** 54
User requirements **3** 71

Virtual assistant **3** 43 et seq.